Planned Short-Term Psychotherapy

A Clinical Handbook

BERNARD L. BLOOM
University of Colorado

ALLYN AND BACON
Boston London Toronto Sydney Tokyo Singapore

ISBN 0-205-16155-3

Printed in the United States of America
10 9 8 7 6 5   96 95 94

Credits: Quotations and therapy dialogues in Chapter 2 are from Wolberg,
L. H., in *Handbook of Short-Term Psychology,* New York, 1980, Thieme
Medical Publishers, Inc. Reprinted by permission. Bellak's therapy recommendations in Chapter 3 are reprinted by permission of C.P.S., Inc., P.O. Box 83,
Larchmont, NY 10538. Dialogue from a Davanloo therapy session in Chapter 4
is reprinted with permission of Jason Aronson Inc. Therapy excerpts in Box 5-1
are reprinted by permission of the publishers from *Short-Term Psychotherapy
and Emotional Crisis* by Peter Sifneos, Cambridge, Mass.: Harvard University
Press, Copyright © 1971 by the President and Fellows of Harvard College. Ex-
cerpts in Box 5-2 are reprinted with permission of the publisher from P. E.
Sifneos, *Short-Term Dynamic Psychotherapy: Evaluation and Technique* (New
York: Plenum, 1979). Therapy dialogue in Box 6-2 is from J. Mann and R.
Goldman, *A Casebook in Time-Limited Psychotherapy* (New York: McGraw-
Hill, 1982) and is reprinted with permission from American Psychiatric Press,
Inc. Quotations and the case example in Chapter 7 are reprinted from K. K.
Lewin, *Brief Encounters: Brief Psychotherapy* (St. Louis, MO: Warren H.
Green, 1970) by permission of Warren H. Green. Quotations and therapy ex-
tracts in Chapter 9 are reprinted from *The Complex Secret of Brief*

(continued on page 348)

Contents

SECTION THREE: *Cognitive and Behavioral Planned Short-Term Therapy*   157

Preface

This book on planned short-term psychotherapy is written for the practicing clinician. As such, it concentrates on providing a comprehensive yet succinct analysis of different approaches to brief psychotherapy that are deliberate in their intent and take place in a wide variety of settings. As will be seen, there are a large number of planned short-term psychotherapy practitioners whose theories are not only well articulated but whose approaches to time-limited psychotherapy are unique in some significant aspects. If this book accomplishes its principal objective, it will provide a meaningful view of the cognitive and (sometimes) affective worlds within which each of these practitioners functions.

Although I have been directly involved in the field of planned short-term psychotherapy for over a decade, preparing this book has provided me with the opportunity to become better acquainted with the work of these practitioners; it has been an unforgettable experience. I know many, but not all, of the people whose work is discussed in these pages, and I admire them all. I admire their self-imposed discipline, their clinical wisdom, their obvious caring, their willingness to take risks, and their intellectual passion.

My objective in deciding what to include in these chapters has been to select whatever seems to be innovative in theory or practice in the writings of the growing number of clinicians who have concerned themselves specifically with planned short-term psychotherapy. I have tried to keep in mind the needs of practicing clinicians for new ways of thinking about their patients and their therapy. Thus, I have included analyses of writings that have the potential for affecting how the short-term psychotherapist thinks about a patient and decides what to do to be of help to the patient. To put it another way, this book is designed to increase the choices, the possibilities, open to the therapist in working with patients.

In addition to examining a number of specific approaches to more traditional one-on-one planned short-term psychotherapy, this book also analyzes the literature that has focused on settings rather than on theories—time-limited psychotherapy with groups and families; planned short-term psychotherapy in psychiatric inpatient units; planned short-term therapy with medical patients; and brief contact therapy, that is, time-limited psychotherapy based on very brief individual contacts. Each of these domains has an important literature and a dedicated cast of characters. The book concludes with a review of issues in the selection of patients for short-term psychotherapy and a general analysis of the current status and future prospects of planned short-term psychotherapy.

Because this book is written for the clinician, transcripts of actual clinical interviews have been included whenever possible. Minor liberties have been taken with the transcripts in order to put them all into the same typographical format. Otherwise, the transcripts are faithful to their original content and sources.

I want to express my gratitude to the Brooks/Cole Publishing Company for their willingness to let me draw on my chapter on planned short-term therapy that appeared in *Community Mental Health: A General Introduction,* and to the Guilford Press for allowing me to excerpt sections of my chapter on focused single-session therapy that appeared in *Forms of Brief Therapy* edited by Simon Budman.

At the more personal level, I am indebted to Mechelle Renée Spence and to Virginia Boucher and her staff at Norlin Library for their help in locating books and journal references. I don't know how I could have managed without them. I also want to thank Natalie Sachs-Ericsson, Daniel Minerva, Stephen W. White, David P. Isenberg, Kathryn Lund, David Miklowitz, Nicholas A. Cummings, and Lynne A. Kellner for their critical reading of the manuscript. They helped make it a better piece of work, and for that I am most grateful.

SECTION ONE

The History and Evaluation of Planned Short-Term Psychotherapy

The single chapter in this introductory section briefly reviews the history and ideology of planned short-term psychotherapy and then examines efforts to evaluate its effectiveness within the framework of dose-response methodology.

Planned short-term psychotherapy, as a systematic field of inquiry, has a three-decade history. It began as part of the community mental health movement that emerged in the early and mid-1960s, particularly under the administration of John F. Kennedy. Planned short-term psychotherapy was initially an uneasy compromise—promulgated as a strategy for providing help to larger numbers of patients, that is, as a way of coping with the mental health needs of the community, without undermining the position of time-unlimited psychotherapy. But what began as a fairly single-minded interest slowly expanded as it became increasingly clear that brief psychotherapy (sometimes as brief as a single interview) could be remarkably effective.

Developing an appreciation of the usefulness of planned short-term psychotherapy is not easy for therapists who have devoted years to the study, practice, and mastery of time-unlimited therapy. But initially critical attitudes toward planned short-term psychotherapy are undergoing a profound transformation as more and more clinicians are coming to the conclusion that short-term therapists are on to something; that somehow, perhaps as a consequence of our training, we clinicians systematically underestimate how helpful we can be to our patients in brief periods of time. As the literature clearly shows, if we need confirmation of this state of affairs, we have only to ask our patients.

1

This section is designed to give the reader a running start for the subsequent examination of clinical aspects of time-limited therapy. For what testifies most persuasively to the importance of planned short-term psychotherapy is the extraordinary number of dedicated clinical practitioners who have devoted themselves to furthering their and our understanding of this mode of psychotherapy.

CHAPTER ONE

Planned Short-Term Psychotherapy: An Introduction

Overview

The Essential Characteristics of Planned Short-Term Psychotherapy

Therapist Attitudes Toward Time-Limited Psychotherapy

What Makes Planned Short-Term Psychotherapy Compelling

The Evaluation of Planned Short-Term Psychotherapy

Concluding Comments

Starting in 1963, coincident with the formal beginning of the community mental health movement, a series of major volumes began appearing that described and evaluated some particular form of what has since come to be called planned short-term psychotherapy (for example, Bellak and Small, 1965; Malan, 1963; Phillips and Wiener, 1966; Wolberg, 1965a; see also Flegenheimer, 1985). The word *planned* is important; these works describe short-term treatment that is intended to accomplish a set of therapeutic objectives within a sharply limited time frame. It is no coincidence, of course, that interest in planned short-term psychotherapy grew rapidly at the time of the development of the community mental health movement. That movement, with its emphasis on making psychotherapeutic help available to everyone in need, put a premium on delivering such services efficiently, effectively, and promptly. Planned short-term psychotherapy is thus short-term by design, not by default (Gurman, 1981; Weiss and Jacobson, 1981), and should be distinguished from what might be called unplanned short-term therapy, that is, services that are brief because treatment is terminated unilaterally by the client.

The growing interest in short-term therapy can be seen as part of the constantly developing history of psychotherapy. Most clinicians who write about brief psychotherapy come out of a psychoanalytic or psychodynamic orientation — an orientation that started out as relatively short-term but that is now the longest of the psychotherapies. Marmor (1979) has noted that Freud's initial therapy cases were often very short in duration. Bruno Walter, the conductor, was successfully treated for a chronic cramp in his right arm by Freud in six sessions (Sterba, 1951). The composer Gustav Mahler was treated for an obsessional neurosis and severe marital difficulties in a single four-hour session that took place while strolling with Freud through the town of Leyden in Holland (Jones, 1955, vol. 2, p. 80; see also Strupp, 1980e, p. 379).

The current interest in short-term therapy can thus be seen in part as a response to growing dissatisfaction with the lengthening of traditional psychodynamic treatment. Writers in the field of time-limited psychotherapy are fully aware that psychotherapists do not ordinarily have the luxury of unlimited time with their patients. As a consequence many writers have begun to search within their own experiences for wisdom they can share with those mental health professionals who have no alternative other than to try to be helpful to their patients in limited periods of time. What is helping this process along is the growing realization that significant changes in patients can and do take place in time-limited, often remarkably brief, psychotherapy.

A similar development is currently in an earlier phase in the case of the behavior therapies. These therapies were once thought of as quite short in duration, but they are now increasing in length. Wilson (1981) has observed that the average length of treatment at the New York City Institute of Behavior Therapy is fifty weekly one-hour sessions. Behavior therapists may evidence a growing interest in planned short-term therapy if this increasing duration of treatment continues (see also Butcher and Koss, 1978, pp. 726–727).

The Essential Characteristics of Planned Short-Term Psychotherapy

Short-term psychotherapy ranges in length from a minimum of one interview to a maximum of around twenty interviews, with an average duration of about six sessions. Few people talk about therapies longer than twenty interviews as short-term, although the upper limit is not really agreed upon. Five fundamental components, other than actual duration, usually characterize planned short-term psychotherapy (Bauer and Kobos, 1984; Budman and Gurman, 1983; Koss, Butcher, and Strupp, 1986; Manaster, 1989; Marmor, 1979). These components are: (1) prompt intervention

(Budman and Springer, 1987), (2) a relatively high level of therapist activity, (3) establishment of specific but limited goals, (4) the identification and maintenance of a clear focus, and (5) the setting of a time limit. You will find repeated references to each of these components throughout this handbook, although there are considerable differences in how writers use the term *focus,* what they mean by therapist activity, and how they go about setting a time limit.

Therapist Attitudes Toward Time-Limited Psychotherapy

Advocacy for planned short-term therapy stands in contrast to a deeply ingrained mental health professional value system (Aldrich, 1968; Gelso and Johnson, 1983, ch. 10; Karasu, 1987; O'Hanlon and Weiner-Davis, 1989, ch. 2; Ursano and Dressler, 1977). In that value system brief treatment is thought of as superficial, longer is equated with better, and the most influential and prestigious practitioners tend to be those who undertake intensive long-term therapy with a very limited number of clients.

Social workers expressed some early interest in planned short-term therapy, but adopted the Freudian long-term model as they sought a rationale for their own professionalization (H. J. Parad and L. G. Parad, 1968; L. G. Parad and H. J. Parad, 1968). L. G. Parad (1971) has provided a compelling history of this value system and has shown that its origin can be seen early in the twentieth century. Parad concludes her historical overview by noting that "while demands for service and other exigencies made it clear that the overwhelming majority of cases were short-term, the long-term intensive case has persisted as a therapeutic desideratum" (p. 129).

Psychotherapists differ in the extent to which they are drawn to the basic ideas of planned short-term psychotherapy, in part because they have differences of opinion regarding human behavior, as well as differences of opinion about the psychotherapeutic enterprise itself. According to Budman and Gurman (1983), while long-term therapists generally seek to change basic character, short-term therapists seek more parsimonious, limited, and conservative interventions. While long-term therapists believe that significant psychological change rarely occurs simply on the basis of experiences in day-to-day living, short-term therapists believe that significant psychological change in everyday life is not only common, but is, in fact, inevitable.

In addition, long-term therapists tend to view presenting complaints as symptoms of deeper psychopathology, while short-term therapists tend to take these presenting complaints seriously and see their removal as a legitimate goal of therapy. Long-term therapists tend to view therapy as always benign and useful, and therefore they believe that there can hardly be too much therapy. In contrast, short-term therapists believe that therapy can under some circumstances be counterproductive, particularly if it goes on too long. Finally, long-term therapists tend to view being in therapy as the single most important aspect of a patient's life. In contrast, short-term therapists tend to view being in therapy as only one of many important activities in which patients are involved. In a recent empirical examination of these hypothesized attitudinal differences, Burlingame and Behrman (1987) found that differences in attitude toward brief psychotherapy clearly exist among a randomly selected sample of psychotherapists and that these attitudes tend to be significantly associated with self-reported levels of skill in either time-limited or time-unlimited psychotherapy.

Hoyt (1985) has identified a number of related beliefs and tensions that may account for some of the continuing hesitancy of psychotherapists regarding short-term dynamic psychotherapy. The first of these beliefs is the conviction that more is better, that time-limited psychotherapy is necessarily inferior to time-unlimited therapy, simply because there can be less of it. A second belief is that some therapeutic techniques are simply impossible to carry out when faced with time constraints and that these specific techniques, such as uncovering or the provocation of affect, are essential to effective therapy. Among the sources of tension generated by the prospect of planned short-term psychotherapy is the mismatch between some therapists' convictions of the clinical superiority of long-term therapy and many patients' interests in having their therapy be as brief as possible. A second source of tension is the fact that time-limited psychotherapy is increasingly recognized as more demanding and often more difficult for the therapist than time-unlimited therapy. A third difficulty identified by Hoyt is the fiscal complexity inherent in trying to derive an adequate income from one's professional activities while encouraging a high turnover in patients. Finally, Hoyt suggests that a short-term therapy practice inevitably results in repeated psychological losses to therapists, a state of affairs that can often result in considerable personal stress and discomfort (see also Carmona, 1988).

What Makes Planned Short-Term Psychotherapy Compelling

In spite of these ideological and clinical issues, interest in planned short-term therapy is accelerating. This expanding attention has come about as a consequence of three interrelated factors: first, concern with efficiency and economy; second, changing concepts and theories of psychotherapy; and third, an accumulation of evidence that the effectiveness of planned short-term therapy appears to be indistinguishable from that of long-term treatment.

Efficiency and Economy

The efficiency and economy rationale for planned short-term therapy is stressed most notably by persons in the public sector. With limitations in both financial and staff resources, a community mental health facility, they argue, must derive the greatest possible effect from each one of the scarce therapeutic hours available to the public. Treatment would then be more feasible for larger numbers of clients (Avnet, 1965a; Frances and Clarkin, 1981). In fact, Hoffman and Remmel (1975) have suggested that hourly fee assessments can be increased when the agency begins to assume that all applicants are potential short-term clients, since the total cost to the client for the episode of care can be reduced. These authors report a doubling of fee income over a three-year period of time in their family service agency after that assumption was adopted.

With the increasing demand for service, a planned short-term therapy orientation could result in the virtual elimination of waiting lists, a source of chronic tension for staff, clients, and the public. Finally, for many clients, whether because of economic or ideological considerations, planned short-term therapy is the only real alternative to no treatment at all (Avnet, 1965b, p. 22).

More recently the private sector has also become interested in the efficiency and economy of planned short-term therapy, but for a somewhat different set of reasons. First, third-party insurance reimbursement for outpatient psychotherapy is being reduced as part of the efforts to cope with the soaring cost of medical care and of medical insurance. Second, new organizational forms of health care are being developed. These models, most notably health maintenance organizations, mental health maintenance organizations, and employee assistance programs, offer the promise of reducing the cost of medical care by reducing services that appear to be unnecessary. Third, primary care physicians, who until recently provided about two-thirds of all mental health services in the United States (Regier, Goldberg, and Taube, 1978), are continuing, if not expanding, their interest in providing mental health services. While surprisingly little is known about the nature of mental health services provided by primary care physicians, one thing is clear — those services are nearly always short-term in nature (see Chapter 20). Thus, the mental health professional is, in a real sense, in competition with the primary care physician.

Changing Concepts in Psychotherapy

Among the relatively recent changes in psychotherapeutic theory pertinent to the growing interest in planned short-term therapy, the following should be mentioned: (1) acceptance of limited therapeutic goals, (2) emphasis in ego psychology on strengths as well as weaknesses of the client, (3) impact of behavior modification techniques, (4) increasing centrality of crisis theory and crisis intervention in service delivery system planning, and (5) greater attention being paid to current precipitating circumstances in contrast to past predisposing circumstances.

These changes have resulted in making treatment more promptly available (Rosenbaum and Beebe, 1975, pp. 299–300), in the realization that when therapeutic time is limited both client and therapist work harder (Applebaum, 1975, pp. 427 ff.; Piper et al., 1984), and in exploring the possibility that planned short-term therapy would in some circumstances be the treatment of choice even if it were not less expensive (Ewing, 1978, p. 19; Hoch, 1965; pp. 53–54; Sifneos, 1967, p. 1069; Wolberg, 1965b).

The treatment-of-choice argument comes in part from the growing realization that most treatment (planned or unplanned) is short-term (Hoffman and Remmel, 1975, p. 259; Hoppe, 1977, p. 307; H. J. Parad and L. G. Parad, 1968, p. 346; L. G. Parad, 1971, pp. 126–129) and that there is some potential utility in making it advertently short-term. Hoffman and Remmel (1975) suggest that "long-term psychotherapy is indicated . . . only if the client both wants and needs it. Experience shows that the overwhelmingly majority of the clients do not want it" (p. 267; see also Cummings, 1977a, 1977b).

Mann (1973) states eloquently what a number of writers have noted: "There comes a point in the treatment of patients, whether in psychoanalysis or in psychotherapy, where time is no longer on the therapist's side insofar as the possibility of helping the patient to make further changes is involved, and where time serves far more the search by the patient for infantile gratification" (p. xi; see also Chapter 6).

The Evaluation of Planned Short-Term Psychotherapy

A large number of evaluation studies of planned short-term psychotherapy have been reported, enough so that there are now a number of published reviews and critical analyses of these evaluations (Bloom, 1984; Butcher and Koss, 1978; Casey and Berman, 1985; Cummings and Vandenbos, 1979; Johnson and Gelso, 1980; Keilson, Dworkin, and Gelso, 1979; Koss and Butcher, 1986; Koss, Butcher, and Strupp, 1986; Malan, 1963, pp. 15–36; Malan et al., 1968; Meltzoff and Kornreich, 1970; Parad, 1971; Phillips and

Wiener, 1966, pp. 27–58; Ryder, 1988; Sloane et al., 1975; Small, 1979, pp. 324–345; Smith, Glass, and Miller, 1980; Strupp, 1980e).

Virtually without exception, these empirical studies of short-term out-patient psychotherapy, or short-term inpatient psychiatric care (see, for example, Bloom, 1984, pp. 98–101; Gelso and Johnson, 1983; Kiesler, 1982; Mattes, Rosen, and Klein, 1977; Mattes et al., 1977; Miller and Hester, 1986; Riessman, Rabkin, and Struening, 1977; Rosen et al., 1976; Sifneos, 1968) have found that planned short-term psychotherapies are essentially equally effective and are, in general, as effective as time-unlimited psychotherapy, virtually regardless of diagnosis or duration of treatment (Koss and Butcher, 1986). Indeed, perhaps no other finding has been reported with greater regularity in the mental health literature than the equivalence of effect of time-limited and time-unlimited psychotherapy.

Some of this literature is nonquantitative in character, or based on very small samples (e.g., Barkham, 1989; Gottschalk, Mayerson, and Gottlieb, 1967; Grand et al., 1985; Kaffman, 1963; Lewin, 1970, pp. 245–261; H. J. Parad and L. G. Parad, 1968; L. G. Parad and H. J. Parad, 1968; Sifneos, 1972, pp. 124–143; Strupp, 1980a, 1980b, 1980c, 1980d; see also Schlesinger, 1984). But many reasonably large well-designed evaluations of planned short-term psychotherapy have been published (see, for example, Blowers, Cobb, and Mathews, 1987; Brockman et al., 1987; Brodaty and Andrews, 1983; Elkin, Weissberg, and Cowen, 1988; Gallagher and Thompson, 1983; Hawton et al., 1987; Husby et al., 1985; Meyer et al., 1981; Piper et al., 1984; Rosenthal and Levine, 1970, 1971; Stuhr, Meyer, and Bolz, 1981; Thompson, Gallagher, and Breckenridge, 1987; Waring et al., 1988).

Initially, these evaluation studies were primarily clinical in nature. In 1963, for example, Malan reported his first clinical outcome study. He contrasted the so-called conservative view of planned short-term therapy outcome, namely that results are palliative and consist only of symptom removal without dynamic longer-lasting changes, with the so-called radical view, namely that there is no essential difference between the results of brief and long-term methods. Malan concluded that "the result of this study was unequivocal support for every aspect of the radical view of brief psychotherapy" (1976, p. 20).

In 1976, Malan reported on the replication of his earlier study, concluding:

The previous finding is conclusively confirmed that with carefully selected patients the radical rather than the conservative view is correct on the three main aspects of brief psychotherapy: selection, technique, and outcome; that is, that relatively disturbed patients can be helped toward permanent major changes by a technique that contains all the essential elements of full-scale analysis. Moreover, with these patients, the more radical the technique the more favorable the out-

come. . . . The conservative view of brief psychotherapy — according to which only patients with the most mild and recent illnesses can be helped, the technique should be superficial and should not involve transference interpretations, and the results are only palliative — has been disproved, and should disappear from the literature, together with the view that the only patients suitable for brief psychotherapy are those in crisis. (pp. 54–55; see also Malan, 1980b).

More recently, evaluation studies have become increasingly empirical and sounder methodologically. Rosenthal and Levine (1970, 1971), for example, compared the outcomes of time-limited and time-unlimited psychotherapy with children. They randomly assigned sixty-six children to either brief therapy (a maximum of eight contact hours within a maximum of ten weeks) or long-term therapy (time and contact hours unlimited). A variety of therapists, with several therapeutic orientations and from several mental health professions, treated children under both time-limited and time-unlimited conditions. Evaluations of outcome were made three months, six months, and one year after treatment had begun. In addition to clinical evaluations, judgments of improvement were obtained from parents and teachers. In the long-term therapy group, 79 percent showed marked improvement at the end of one year, during which time the average length of therapy had been about forty weeks. In the brief therapy group, 76 percent showed marked improvement at the end of one year, during which time the average length of therapy had been only eight weeks. No difference in therapeutic effect had been found, even though one group received five times as much therapist time as the other.

Representative of the conclusions of the many reviews of the relationship of treatment duration to outcome is that of Koss and Butcher (1986), who recently commented: "Those studies that have directly compared brief and long-term methods have found equal effectiveness. Since brief therapy requires less time (both therapist and patient) and therefore less social cost, it has been suggested that brief methods are equally effective and more cost efficient than long-term psychotherapy" (p. 658).

These recent conclusions are virtually identical with those the same authors arrived at in an earlier review (Butcher and Koss, 1978). In addition, Koss, Butcher, and Strupp (1986) have suggested that these findings may actually underestimate the effectiveness of planned short-term therapy since so few of the therapists participating in the evaluation studies had received formal training in brief therapy techniques.

Luborsky, Singer, and Luborsky (1975) in their review of planned short-term therapy outcome studies noted: "Since Otto Rank, treatments that are structured at the outset as time-limited have been thought by some practitioners to be as good as the more usual time-unlimited treatment" (p. 1001).

Of the eight controlled comparative studies available at the time of their review, they found that time-limited psychotherapy was either superior to time-unlimited therapy (two studies) or equal to time-unlimited therapy (five studies). In only one study did time-unlimited therapy appear to be superior to time-limited treatment, and that superiority was in a very narrow cognitive domain.

In a general summary of psychotherapy evaluation studies, Strupp and Binder (1984), basing their conclusions on the earlier work of Smith, Glass, and Miller (1980), have observed that:

> *Psychotherapy is beneficial, consistently so and in many different ways. Its benefits are on a par with other expensive and ambitious interventions, such as schooling and medicine. . . . Different types of psychotherapy (verbal or behavioral; psychodynamic, client-centered, systematic desensitization) do not produce different types or degrees of benefit. Differences in how psychotherapy is conducted (whether in groups or individually, by experienced or novice therapists, for long or short periods of time, and the like) make very little difference in how beneficial it is. (p. 5)*

MacKenzie's (1988) even more recent summary statement regarding the effectiveness of time-limited psychotherapy is equally affirmative:

> *Considerable cumulative evidence suggests that brief therapeutic contact makes a significant clinical impact when compared with no treatment. In fact, the clinical effectiveness of brief psychotherapy may be underestimated in the literature. Most studies used therapists who were not trained in the specific techniques of brief psychotherapy, and many patients were arbitrarily assigned to the brief therapy category only because they terminated treatment prematurely. (p. 743; see also Garfield, 1989, pp. 146–147)*

It is important to view these positive evaluations in the context of the somewhat equivocal evaluation of psychotherapy in general. These evaluations suggest that while psychotherapy is usually, but not invariably, superior to no psychotherapy, psychotherapies are remarkably similar in their effects, there is no significant relationship between the duration of psychotherapy and its effects, and there is little evidence that professional training of the therapist improves therapeutic results (Barth et al., 1988; Berman and Norton, 1985; Hattie, Sharpley, and Rogers, 1984; Lambert, Shapiro, and Bergin, 1986; Landman and Dawes, 1982; Shapiro and Shapiro, 1982; Smith and Glass, 1977; Stiles, Shapiro, and Elliott, 1986; VandenBos and Pino, 1980;

Zilbergeld, 1983). We shall return to the interesting question of what factors seem to make a difference in therapeutic outcome in the final chapter of this book. What should already be clear from this discussion, however, is that planned short-term psychotherapy started out life thirty years ago as second-best, offered to patients apologetically. Today, however, planned short-term psychotherapy has become one of the most upbeat and professionally affirming developments in the field of clinical practice.

Another review of the planned short-term psychotherapy evaluation studies will not make a significant contribution to the literature or to this volume, but it is important to accomplish two more clinically relevant tasks in this chapter — to review what has been found about the length of therapy and client satisfaction and to put the existing evaluation literature in the larger context of *dose-response* studies.

Length of Therapy and Client Satisfaction

Mental health professionals undoubtedly tend to view early and unilateral termination by clients as a sign of therapeutic failure and client dissatisfaction. Professional attitudes toward unilateral termination of treatment by patients can be quickly discerned when it is noted that such clients are virtually always referred to as *dropouts*. The two modal responses on the part of clinicians faced by a patient's unilateral termination of therapy are either to conclude that the patient was unsuitable for psychotherapy or that they themselves made some fatal error in their therapeutic interactions with the patient. Thus, it may be reassuring to know that empirical studies of client satisfaction and length of treatment consistently fail to support this view.

Starting with Kogan's work more than thirty years ago, a number of investigations have examined patients who dropped out of therapy from the point of view of their level of satisfaction with the care they received. Kogan (1957a, 1957b, 1957c) examined the records of all new clients in the Division of Family Services of the New York Community Service Society for one month in late 1953. During that month 250 new cases had a first in-person interview. Of these 250 cases 141 (56 percent) were closed after one interview. Most of those closings were planned — that is, agreed upon in advance by client and therapist. But 30 percent were unplanned, in that the client failed to keep subsequent appointments.

Kogan was able to interview, either in person or by telephone, 80 percent of these 141 cases between three months and one year after the case was closed. He had similar success in contacting cases with planned and unplanned closings. In addition, therapist evaluations prepared at the time of case closings were analyzed. Kogan's results are illuminating. In the majority of cases, therapists had attributed unplanned closings to client resistance or lack of interest. Follow-up interviews with these single-session clients revealed, however, that reality-based factors prevented continuance and also that improvements in the problem situations may have accounted for a substantial proportion of these unplanned closings.

About two-thirds of all clients felt they had been helped. There was no difference in this proportion when clients with planned closings were compared to clients with unplanned closings. In contrast, therapists considered that clients were, in general, helped, but they believed that those with planned closings were helped significantly more than those with unplanned closings. Therapists consistently underestimated the help that clients with unplanned closings judged they had received, and they consistently overestimated how helpful they had been to clients with planned closings (see also Frings, 1951; Shyne, 1957).

More recently, Littlepage and associates (1976) assessed client satisfaction by contacting 130 former clients in a community mental health center out of the 349 who had terminated during 1974. These clients had had from one to twenty-four contacts with the center where they had been enrolled. General level of satisfaction was high and was unrelated to the number of treatment contacts. Clients whose treatment terminated after only limited center contact evaluated their experiences just as highly as clients who had had extended contact with the center. Clients who dropped out of therapy did not evaluate their experiences differently than clients who attended their final scheduled therapy session. These authors concluded that their findings "are not consistent with the implicit assumption that persons with limited contacts terminate therapy because of dissatisfaction with the services," and that one should not "automatically assume that early client terminations reflect treatment failures" (p. 167; see also Silverman and Beech, 1979).

In a particularly informative investigation, Fiester and Rudestam (1975) studied two different public-sector mental health programs and contrasted clients who unilaterally terminated after the first or second session with clients who remained for three or more sessions, regardless of final disposition. Demographic information (e.g., age, sex, education, socioeconomic status, and history of prior psychiatric care) and an array of pretherapy expectations and posttherapy reactions were collected prior to and following the first session from patients, and demographic and professional background information was collected from therapists. Results of these analyses were not the same in the two settings, a finding attributed by the authors to differences in therapist characteristics.

In the facility where the therapeutic staff was older, more experienced, more affluent, and psychodynamically oriented, the clients who dropped out early and unilaterally tended more often to be lower-class people who felt they had been attentive to the therapist, whom they found to be helpful and serious, but who found themselves angry during the interview without being able to talk about it. In this setting, clients who terminated early tended to be dissatisfied with the services they had received.

In the other setting, where the staff was younger, less experienced, less doctrinaire, and of lower social class, very few clients who terminated early were dissatisfied. Rather, most reported benefiting from their brief therapy. Clients described themselves as serious, in need of answers to questions, and desirous of an opportunity to express their emotions and resolve their problems. Furthermore, they tended to see the therapist as providing just what they needed. In this setting early termination was not usually equated with failure. Dropout rate was unusually high, however, in the case of seriously disturbed clients assigned to lower-status therapists, such as students, paraprofessionals, and mental health technicians.

The authors suggested that higher dropout rates among lower-class clients may take place primarily in settings where strict psychodynamic therapy is the treatment of choice; that is, the differential dropout rate is more closely related to therapist characteristics than to client characteristics. In the nondoctrinaire setting, "quite possibly, dropping out represents a problem primarily from the (rejected) therapist's perspective. This perspective is probably a corollary of clinical lore that asserts a direct relationship between length of treatment and patient improvement" (Fiester and Rudestam, 1975, p. 534; see also Hoppe, 1977; Lazare et al., 1972; Phillips, 1985b).

Finally, regarding the issue of length of treatment and patient improvement, with particular reference to patients who terminate psychotherapy unilaterally, Pekarik (1983) contrasted pretreatment and posttreatment scores on a brief symptom inventory in a group of forty-one dropouts and another group of twenty-three patients who were judged to have terminated treatment appropriately. Pekarik also examined these scores as a function of number of treatment sessions. Dropouts were defined as patients who were thought by their therapists to be in need of additional treatment beyond their last session. Initial scores on the symptom checklist did not differ substantially between dropouts and appropriate terminators, nor did the initial scores differ as a function of number of subsequent treatment sessions. The analysis, based on a follow-up assessment conducted about three months after the start of treatment, indicated that for those patients who had had only a single therapy session, those who were judged to be dropouts were functioning significantly more poorly than those patients judged to have terminated treatment appropriately. For all other patients—that is, for patients who had had two or more therapy sessions—no significant differences in symptom scores at the time of the follow-up assessment were found.

There thus appears to be no support for the clinical assumption that patients who unilaterally terminate treatment are dissatisfied with their care, and there is little support for the belief that they are functioning more poorly than patients whose terminations from therapy were mutually agreed upon ahead of time by therapist and patient.

Dose-Response Studies

A number of recent studies of psychotherapy effectiveness have drawn on *dose-response methodology* from the field of pharmacology. That methodology examines the relationship between the amount of exposure to a treatment and the degree of improvement (see, for example, Howard et al., 1986; Rush and Giles, 1982; Schlesinger et al., 1983). While invoking dose-response methodology in the evaluation of psychotherapy effectiveness raises a number of complex issues (Stiles and Shapiro, 1989), the growing interest in dose-response relationships is understandable since if it can be shown that there is a significant relationship between the amount of exposure to a treatment and the degree of improvement, the likelihood that the relationship is a causal one is increased (MacMahon and Pugh, 1970).

Dose-response studies seek to determine the relationship between the dose of a drug and characteristics of the resulting response. Response to psychotherapy has been studied as if psychotherapy were a drug, using number of sessions as a measure of dose. The linking of a well-established methodology from another field to the study of psychotherapy effectiveness is an important potential contribution of this line of inquiry.

Dose-response concepts from the field of pharmacology clearly provide a promising framework for enriching the continuing evaluation of psychotherapeutic effectiveness, and suggestions for a planned short-term therapy research agenda that can be related to these concepts have already appeared (Koss and Butcher, 1986; Koss, Butcher, and Strupp, 1986).

Dose-Response Methodology

A number of standard pharmacology texts describe the fundamental importance of dose-response studies (Bochner et al., 1978; Gerald, 1981; Gilman et al., 1980; Shepherd, Lader, and Rodnight, 1968; Tedeschi and Tedeschi, 1968). Such studies plot the size of the dose against some measure of effect. Dose-response curves need not be linear, however, and are often found to be concave upward or downward, or sigmoidal and not necessarily monotonic. A drug may produce a positive effect up to a certain dose and then begin producing a negative effect.

Dose-response studies assume that drugs have some measurable effects on the body if they are administered in sufficient dose; they seek to determine the characteristics of those effects. Efficacy is only one of those characteristics, however. In addition to efficacy, per se, dose-response studies examine treatment threshold, latency, potency, response variability and duration, treatment side effects, and margin of safety.

Regarding factors that may be associated with variability in drug effects, dose-response studies have most commonly examined such variables as route and time of administration, rate of inactivation and excretion, interaction with other drugs taken at the same time, and such demographic factors as age, body weight, gender, drug tolerance, pathological state, genetic factors, set or milieu, and other psychosocial factors (Gilman et al., 1980).

Most of these parameters have their parallels, at least theoretically, in the study of the effectiveness of psychotherapy. It thus seems clearly appropriate to examine psychotherapy effectiveness studies as if one were conducting dose-response investigations, assuming, of course, that the studies being examined meet minimal dose-response methodology requirements.

As for these requirements, the following quotations from a standard text on drug-evaluation principles (Tedeschi and Tedeschi, 1968) provide an adequate description.

> Perhaps the most important single principle in experimental design is randomization. Randomization is assumed in most data analyses, and can be omitted from a design only at the risk of biases in the conclusions. . . . The simplest experimental design is a one-way classification in which the subjects or test animals, supposedly equivalent, are assigned at random to as many different groups as there are treatments to be tested. . . . (p. 4)

> Especially in clinical experiments, a subject may react as much to the taking of a drug as to its pharmacological action. A standard correction for this effect is to include a placebo among the test preparations. For an unbiased response, the identity of each treatment must be unknown to both the subject and to those administering the drug or evaluating its effect, in a so-called double-blind test. . . . (p. 11)

> An all-or-none reaction provides less information than a response that varies quantitatively. Several designs have been proposed for increasing the precision of such experiments. One is to score the degree of response, such as nausea in a study of seasick remedies, as none, mild, [or] severe . . . in subjects known to be susceptible to motion sickness. The response is then multinomial rather than binomial. (p. 14)

Examination of these excerpts reveals that from the point of view of experimental methodology, dose-response studies have the same set of minimum requirements as are generally proposed for well-designed studies of psychotherapy effectiveness (Ciarlo et al., 1986; Cook and Ware, 1983;

Frank, 1968; Hazelrigg, Cooper, and Borduin, 1987; Wortman, 1983). These requirements include: (1) random assignment of clients into at least two treatments of differing levels of intensity, one of which could be an attention placebo group; (2) development of evaluation measures that have adequate psychometric robustness and employ appropriate levels of discrimination and an appropriate number of data collection points; and (3) evaluation of therapeutic outcome by judges who are not aware of the experimental study group to which any given client is assigned.

Special considerations in the evaluation of psychotherapy outcome should be noted regarding outcome judgments made by the treating therapist. Reports in the literature suggest, first, that the likelihood of finding long-term therapeutic interventions superior to short-term interventions declines dramatically as one moves from outcome judgments made by therapists to judgments based on objectively measured psychological symptoms or characteristics (Bloch et al., 1977; Gelso and Johnson, 1983; Johnson and Gelso, 1980). Second, even though a substantial minority of patients are reported by their therapists as showing improvement after a relatively small number of sessions, it has frequently been suggested that therapists tend to be biased toward long-term therapy (Budman and Gurman, 1983; Burlingame and Behrman, 1987). Without adequate controls that bias can fully account for the positive relationship often found in early studies of therapy duration and judged effectiveness (Avnet, 1965b; Fago, 1980; Howard et al., 1986; Kogan, 1957a, 1957b, 1957c; Robinson, Redlich, and Myers, 1954; Rosenthal and Frank, 1958; Shapiro and Shapiro, 1983).

Koss and Butcher (1986), in their critique of short-term therapy evaluation studies, specifically note that "many studies that purport to correlate therapy duration to outcome have methodological problems (e.g., confounding of time with time in treatment, biased raters or criteria, failure to utilize planned brief-therapy techniques) that render them irrelevant to the efficacy of brief methods" (p. 658).

Most early psychotherapy evaluation studies failed to meet dose-response methodological criteria. Untreated control or attention placebo groups were rarely created. Patients were rarely randomly assigned to treatment conditions of varying durations. Assessments of outcome were nearly always made either by the treating therapists, by judges (based on data provided by the treating therapists), or by the treated patients themselves, and only at the time of discharge. Finally, judgments of therapeutic outcome were generally made using procedures and measures of undemonstrated reliability and validity.

Early psychotherapy evaluation studies served primarily as psychotherapy process descriptions rather than as evaluations, and where data were available on therapy outcome and therapy duration, most authors were aware of the dangers of asserting any causal relationship between the two phenomena. For example, Rosenthal and Frank (1958) explicitly recognized the long-term therapy bias of most psychotherapists. Cappon (1964), Garfield and Affleck (1959), and Strassberg and colleagues (1977) commented on the limited validity of the outcome judgments made by the treating psychotherapists. In this connection Phillips (1985b) has recently reported that therapist and client evaluations of psychotherapy are essentially uncorrelated. Cappon (1964), Cole, Branch, and Allison (1962), and Jones (1980) expressed cautions about their dependent measures of therapy outcome. Brown and Kosterlitz (1964), as well as Cappon (1964), recognized the limitations of their conclusions because of the absence of control groups in their studies.

Not all psychotherapy evaluation studies have these methodological limitations, of course, and more recent studies are usually more sophisticated than studies conducted decades ago. Indeed, with the growing number of individuals seeking mental health services, there is no longer any reason why all dose-response methodological principles should not be fully implemented in psychotherapy outcome evaluation studies.

The Scope of Dose-Response Concepts

As has already been suggested, the study of the relationship of therapeutic dose and therapeutic outcome does not exhaust the potential contribution of the dose-response model to the understanding of psychotherapeutic effectiveness. The conclusions regarding the relationship of individual therapy outcome to treatment characteristics, based on scores of reasonably well-conducted evaluation studies (see Butcher and Koss, 1978; Koss and Butcher, 1986 for an extensive review of these studies), can now be reframed by returning to the variables that have been given special consideration in dose-response investigations.

Efficacy   Efficacy is defined as the maximum effect of a treatment employing its optimal dosage. Psychotherapy is unquestionably efficacious, but every psychotherapist would wish for its level of efficacy to be improved. About 75 percent of treated patients score above the mean of untreated control group patients on a variety of outcome measures (Casey and Berman, 1985; Landman and Dawes, 1982; Shapiro and Shapiro, 1982; Smith and Glass, 1977; Smith, Glass, and Miller, 1980). Inexorably, however, 25 percent of treated patients score below the mean of untreated control groups on these same outcome measures. Another way of describing the general magnitude of psychotherapy efficacy is to note that while about two-thirds of treated patients are judged to have improved at the time of follow-up, one-third of untreated patients are also judged to have improved (Lambert, Shapiro, and Bergin, 1986). Thus, while psychotherapy appears to increase improvement rate, from about 33 percent to 67 percent, a finding that is certainly impressive, one-third of treated patients are unimproved or worse following treatment. The treatment–no treatment dimension accounts for only 10 percent of the variance in outcome. Research findings have not yet made it possible to predict with any certainty which patients will benefit from psychotherapy and which will not. The search for ways to increase the efficacy of psychotherapy — that is, to increase its effect size — is underway (see Lambert, Shapiro, and Bergin, 1986, pp. 178 ff.).

Threshold Threshold is defined as the lowest dose capable of producing a discernible effect. Psychotherapy appears to have an extremely low threshold. As few as two or three sessions of psychotherapy have repeatedly been shown to have a significant effect in a large minority of cases, and there are numerous empirical as well as anecdotal reports of a single interview having a remarkable positive impact on some clients (Bloom, 1981; Cummings and Follette, 1976; Follette and Cummings, 1967; Talmon, 1989).

Latency Latency is defined as the speed with which discernable effects are produced. Psychotherapy appears to have a remarkably low latency, and its initial positive effects are commonly reported during or immediately after the first interview.

Potency Potency is defined as the absolute amount of the treatment that is required to produce a specified effect. Psychotherapy has relatively high potency. Its maximum effects appear to be reached with small doses, and beyond that point additional treatment appears to produce very little additional benefit (Bowers and Clum, 1988).

Duration of Effect Duration of effect is defined as the amount of time that a given treatment outcome is sustained. Regardless of the duration of the treatment, psychotherapy has a relatively long-lasting effect, and there is evidence that improvement continues for at least one year after the conclusion of an episode of brief psychotherapy (Cross, Sheehan, and Khan, 1982; Gelso and Johnson, 1983).

Variability of Effect The effectiveness of psychotherapy in general, and short-term psychotherapy in particular, appears to vary relatively little as a function of either therapist or therapy characteristics (Berman and Norton, 1985; Cross, Sheehan, and Khan, 1982; Durlak, 1979; Hattie, Sharpley, and Rogers, 1984; Parloff, 1982; Shiffman, 1987; Wolberg, 1965b). This is not to suggest that therapists will have the same results regardless of whom they treat or what therapeutic approach they use. But determining the most appropriate treatment for a given patient in the hands of a given therapist is a task of considerable complexity, one that cannot be expected to yield significant results unless it is approached with care and dedication.

Side Effects and Margin of Safety   While there is a literature describing the harmful side effects of psychotherapy (see, for example, Gross, 1978; Hadley and Strupp, 1976; Rush and Giles, 1982; Sachs, 1983; Strupp, 1989; Tennov, 1975; Zilbergeld, 1983), these reports consist mainly of the description of negative consequences associated with scandalously unethical therapeutic practices. Psychotherapy in the hands of an ethical psychotherapist, however, appears to produce few, if any, untoward side effects.

Concluding Comments

With the current concern about the high cost of medical care and with the growth of health maintenance organizations, mental health maintenance organizations, and other alternatives to fee-for-service health care, there is increasing interest in avoiding overtreatment, that is, in providing only those health-related services that are needed. The planned short-term therapy literature strongly suggests that the effectiveness of short-term psychotherapy is indistinguishable from that of long-term psychotherapy and that long-term encounters may very likely provide more psychotherapy than is needed (Budman and Stone, 1983; Cummings, 1986; Klerman, 1983; McGuire and Frisman, 1983).

One set of clues that can help explain the effectiveness of planned short-term psychotherapy can be found in the recent work of Piper and associates (1984) who found that relatively short-term individual psychotherapy (average of twenty-two sessions within six-month maximum) was consistently superior to time-unlimited individual psychotherapy (average of seventy-six sessions within two-year maximum) on a variety of outcome measures collected from patients, therapists, and independent assessors blind to treatment assignment. They reported that short-term therapy patients and therapists "felt the need to work hard and relatively quickly. Attention was concentrated and focused. Affective involvement was high. . . . At completion most patients felt that they had received something valuable from the therapist" (p. 277). In contrast, long-term individual therapy patients and clinicians were less satisfied. "The length of time available coupled with the frequency of one session per week seemed to favor an increase in resistance and a decrease in working through. Thus, the patient tended to behave as if there was always plenty of time to work later" (p. 277).

At the same time it is important not to promise more than can be delivered. Donovan (1987) has warned that when the proponents of time-limited psychotherapy suggest that their intervention is incontrovertibly the only reason for change in their patients' lives, they are engaging in clear speculation. People are in a constant state of change, and they use a variety of situations and relationships to support that growth, including but certainly not limited to psychotherapy. In addition, Budman and Stone (1983) have reminded us that among the many development-promoting relationships are several courses of psychotherapy, not just one. Mental health professionals themselves seek an average of five therapies over their adult lives, even when one therapy has been a "full" psychoanalysis. These facts, according to Budman and Stone, throw into question the claims that one sequence of brief treatment should lead to definitive and permanent change. The question of how much psychotherapy is needed is not a trivial one, yet it has hardly been addressed in the theoretical or empirical literature.

In 1971 Parad concluded her review of the short-term treatment literature in the field of social welfare by noting that:

> *for a variety of interlocking reasons — manpower shortages, demands for massive community mental health services, dissatisfaction with waiting lists, studies in goal-limited therapy, research on coping behavior and crisis phenomena — we are now witnessing a dramatic resurgence of interest in short-term approaches. Ours claims to be a pragmatic profession. If the level of outcome effectiveness evidenced in the recent studies is further substantiated in future large-scale experimental research, it would be logical to infer that short-term treatment should be the basic therapeutic approach for all but a relatively small selected group of applicants for family agency and child guidance services. (p. 145)*

Research that has been reported since that paper was published has repeatedly affirmed the remarkable efficacy of planned short-term psychotherapy. Rather than reacting defensively to the continuing reports of this efficacy, mental health professionals would do well to accept with grace the affirmation of their effectiveness in brief periods of time (Cummings, 1986) and proceed to develop strategies for institutionalizing that effectiveness.

SECTION TWO

Psychodynamic Approaches to Planned Short-Term Psychotherapy

In the next two sections we shall examine a number of remarkably different approaches to planned short-term therapy. This section will consider psychodynamic theories of planned short-term psychotherapy; the next will consider what are generally called cognitive and behavioral approaches to planned short-term psychotherapy. As will be seen, there is fully as much variation in both the theory and practice of planned short-term therapy as in long-term therapy.

It is useful to examine these various approaches for at least two reasons. First, a certain approach might prove to be superior for certain problems, or certain types of clients, for certain clinicians, or under certain circumstances. In this case, referrals or assignments to clinicians could be made much more rationally than is typical in a mental health agency, and one could anticipate general increases in therapeutic effectiveness. Second, exposure to different approaches to planned short-term therapy allows for the possibility that an individual clinician could develop a broader array of skills than might otherwise be the case. Under this circumstance a specific clinician could be effective with a more varied array of clients or problems.

Categorizing Approaches to Planned Short-Term Psychotherapy

There are, of course, a number of ways of categorizing approaches to planned short-term psychotherapy. In this book they are sorted into two major *groupings*—psychodynamic *and* cognitive-behavioral. *Regarding this particular approach to grouping the therapies, Malan (1979) has written:*

> Any form of psychotherapy *must* be incomplete unless it incorporates the psychodynamic point of view. This applies particularly, of course, to learning theory and behaviour therapy. But the converse is also true: dynamic psychotherapy itself is incomplete unless it incorporates the theory and techniques of other forms of therapy, of which behaviour therapy is probably the most important. It seems to me incontrovertible, for instance, that the success of behaviour therapy in dealing with certain symptoms, without dealing with unconscious conflict, means that there is something missing in psychodynamic theory in this area; for instance, that some process such as self-reinforcement must be operating to maintain symptoms and give them autonomy. On the other hand, honest behaviour therapists will readily admit that their own explanation of the *origin* of symptoms—a question to which the psychodynamic approach has a fairly complete answer—is hopelessly insufficient. (p. 254; see also Phillips, 1985a)

Grouping theories of planned short-term psychotherapy into two large categories can be considered something of an oversimplification, however. Burke, White, and Havens (1979; see also White, Burke, and Havens, 1981) have suggested that short-term therapies can be divided into those that are interpretive, *in that they stress the role of insight;* existential, *in that they stress the salutary effects of a brief empathic encounter with a therapist; or* corrective, *in that they stress therapist-induced behavioral change.*

Butcher and Koss (1978) divide brief therapies into those that are psychodynamically oriented, crisis-oriented, *and* behavioral. *Bouchard and associates (1987) have found significant differences in verbal activity among psychodynamically oriented, gestalt, and behavior therapists, suggesting that this differentiation represents a meaningful way of sorting therapy types. Peake, Borduin, and Archer (1988) group short-term therapies into three categories—* psychodynamic approaches, cognitive approaches, *and* strategic-systemic approaches *(see also Burlingame and Fuhriman, 1987).*

The assumption in dividing time-limited approaches to psychotherapy into two large categories in this book is that this division will account for most of the variance in the theories that are described. As will be seen, the strategic-systemic approach shares enough with cognitive and behavioral theories so that including it in that section in this book will not do either of these two approaches a significant disservice (see also Bauer and Kobos, 1987; Budman and Gurman, 1988; Flegenheimer, 1982; Thorpe, 1987).

Characteristics of Psychodynamic Short-Term Psychotherapy

Focusing specifically on psychodynamic theories of planned short-term psychotherapy, Marmor has described the psychodynamic perspective very succinctly and with enormous sensitivity in terms of its five essential assumptions:

> the recognition that human behavior is motivated; that the nature of this motivation is often largely concealed from awareness; that our personalities are shaped not only by our biological potentials, but also by experiential vicissitudes; that functional disturbances in human cognition, affect, and behavior are the result of contradictory and conflictual inputs or feedbacks; and that early developmental experiences are of particular significance in shaping subsequent perceptions and reactions in adolescence and adulthood. (1968, p. 5)

These essential characteristics of psychodynamic psychotherapy—the fact that behavior is motivated, that people are not fully aware of the complexities of their intrapsychic lives, that experience is as important as biology in determining what we are like as human beings, that we are in conflict about many issues in our lives, and that our childhoods shape what we become as adults—hold true for all the approaches analyzed in this section of the book. Of these characteristics, Edelstein (1990) accords special importance to experience, particularly to those experiences that are traumatic.

Differences among Psychodynamic Approaches

The psychodynamic approaches of ten practitioners of time-limited psychotherapy are presented and illustrated in this section, and it may be difficult to keep each of them in sharp focus. Accordingly, some introductory comments and observations about how these approaches differ from one another are in order to provide an orientation to what lies ahead and to draw the reader's attention to specific approaches to planned short-term psychotherapy that might potentially seem particularly pertinent.

Since these approaches are all fundamentally psychodynamic, it should not be surprising that there is relatively little variability in some dimensions— the importance of attending to transference phenomena and other aspects of the therapeutic relationship, special attention to issues at termination, and the importance of the concept of the unconscious. But there is also a surprising amount of variability among the approaches. Some approaches are particularly important because of the ideas that lie behind the therapeutic techniques used. This is true for the work of Wolberg (Chapter 2), Bellak (Chapter 3), Mann (Chapter 6), Lewin (Chapter 7), Horowitz (Chapter 10), and Klerman (Chapter 11). Other approaches seem as remarkable because of the therapeutic techniques used as for their underlying ideas. This is particularly true for the work of Davanloo (Chapter 4), Sifneos (Chapter 5), and Gustafson (Chapter 9).

In general, theorists vary in their aspirations, perhaps their passion, for short-term therapy, ranging from those who see it as equal to time-unlimited therapy in terms of its potential effectiveness to those who see it as useful but likely limited in its effect. Theorists vary in their relative emphasis on the patient's history versus the present predicament as described by the patient. Theorists differ in terms of the transparency of their therapy, in the sense of how aware the patient is likely to be of the hypotheses motivating the therapist's behavior. Theorists also differ in their activity level and in the nature of their interventions—confrontation versus support, challenge versus patient exploration.

To be more specific, the theorists whose work is described in this section appear to differ in their fundamental attitudes toward planned short-term psychotherapy. Some, such as Bellak (Chapter 3) and Bloom (Chapter 8), assume that short-term therapy should be thought of as the treatment of choice, if not for every patient, certainly for almost every patient, and certainly at first before any longer treatments are undertaken. Others, such as Sifneos (Chapter 5) and Gustafson (Chapter 9), see it as suitable only for certain patients and spend considerable time thinking about the criteria for suitability for planned short-term psychotherapy.

In addition to attitudinal differences, the therapists whose approaches are presented in this section vary in the methods of their practice of planned short-term psychotherapy. Contrasts and comparisons in the following eight areas are of particular interest.

1. Duration of Treatment. While most short-term therapists have a flexible approach to treatment duration, some consistent differences in attitudes toward optimal length of treatment can be found. At the low end of the duration spectrum can be found the work of Bellak (Chapter 3) and Bloom (Chapter 8). Durations in the mid range (ten to fourteen hours) are espoused by Mann (Chapter 6), Horowitz (Chapter 10), and Klerman (Chapter 11). Clearly, a number of therapists do not have an explicit number or range of sessions in mind. In addition, Mann's views of planned short-term psychotherapy have uniquely led him to develop a course of treatment that is fixed at exactly twelve hours.

2. Therapeutic Contract. A number of theorists assign special importance to an initial diagnostic study and therapeutic contract regarding

the theme of the work to be done. This importance is particularly seen in the work of Sifneos (Chapter 5) and Mann (Chapter 6).

3. Interpersonal Approaches. Theories of psychopathology and psychotherapy have in recent years turned to interpersonal aspects of human behavior. Most contemporary views of psychopathology and its treatment, regardless of their similarities or differences on other dimensions, accord interpersonal factors more or less equal importance with intrapsychic factors in identifying pathology and in developing remediation programs. That is, most psychodynamic approaches to psychotherapy view psychopathology in an interpersonal context. The author whose theories stress the interpersonal aspect of behavior most clearly is Klerman (Chapter 11), and we shall deal most directly with interpersonal theory in that chapter. To a somewhat lesser extent, the writings of Wolberg (Chapter 2), Bellak (Chapter 3), Sifneos (Chapter 5), and Horowitz (Chapter 10) also make reference to interpersonal aspects of psychopathology and psychotherapy.

4. Attention to Negative Transference Phenomena. Examination of transference reactions, both positive and negative, is one of the hallmarks of psychodynamically oriented psychotherapy. The most common attitude toward transference phenomena expressed by short-term therapists is to use the positive transference in the service of therapy and to try to avoid the development of negative transference reactions. The single and quite remarkable exception to this practice can be found in the work of Lewin (Chapter 7), who has developed a planned short-term therapy that is based on allowing the development of the negative transference and then examining its significance as part of the therapeutic process.

5. Diagnosis-Specific Approaches. While some approaches to planned short-term therapy are broad, in that they are thought of as suitable for any type of patient, a number of writers have suggested that their orientation, in either unmodified or modified form, may be particularly helpful for patients in certain diagnostic categories or who are facing certain life problems. Bellak (Chapter 3) has developed a number of suggestions for enhancing his approach with certain specific diagnostic problems. Horowitz (Chapter 10) has developed a type of brief psychotherapy that is specifically designed for patients who are coping with stressful life events, and within this group he has certain suggestions for how to be particularly helpful with patients with hysterical, compulsive, narcissistic, or borderline personalities. Klerman (Chapter 11) has developed a form of brief psychotherapy particularly suitable for patients who are suffering from nonpsychotic depressions. Lewin (Chapter 7) suggests that his approach is useful for treating patients with character disorders. Davanloo (Chapter 4) and Sifneos (Chapter 5) believe that their approach to brief psychotherapy is especially suitable for patients with oedipal issues who do not show evidence of significant regression.

6. The Mid-Session Intermission. While most theorists conduct

traditional uninterrupted individual sessions, a relatively new approach to the organization of the initial therapeutic hour is well illustrated in the work of Gustafson (Chapter 9). This practice, which will reappear in later chapters of this book, includes a somewhat longer initial interview appointment and a team of observers who, known to the patient, see and listen to the interview through a one-way mirror. At some point midway through the initial session, a brief intermission is proposed during which time the therapist meets with the observers to share observations of the patient and to develop a consensus regarding the nature of the patient's problems and how best to be of help. The therapeutic session is then resumed, and the therapist discusses this assessment with the patient as part of the treatment planning process.

7. Planned Follow-up Interviews. A consensus is developing among short-term therapists that a follow-up interview (usually a single interview, often by phone or even by letter) can be a valuable part of the therapeutic encounter. This point of view, and its justification, can be found in the writings of Wolberg (Chapter 2), Bellak (Chapter 3), Mann (Chapter 6), Bloom (Chapter 8), and Klerman (Chapter 11).

8. Importance of Evaluation of Outcome. Finally, among the writers in this section are several who have described their efforts to examine the effectiveness of their work. This group includes Sifneos (Chapter 5), Lewin (Chapter 7), Bloom (Chapter 8), Horowitz (Chapter 10), and Klerman (Chapter 11). These efforts range from rather informal clinical follow-up assessments to quite sophisticated controlled outcome studies.

CHAPTER TWO

Wolberg's Flexible Short-Term Psychotherapy

Overview

Therapeutic Goals

Therapeutic Techniques

Concluding Comments

Lewis Wolberg, a psychiatrist and psychoanalyst, founded and remained affiliated with the Postgraduate Center for Mental Health, a treatment and training facility in New York City, from 1945 until his death in 1988. Reminding the reader that Freud practiced short-term therapy, Wolberg (1965b, 1965c, 1968, 1980), one of the earliest writers in the field, suggested that its virtues have not been fully appreciated. He argued that short-term therapy requires its own methodology and the development of its own theoretical concepts—it is not simply less of traditional long-term psychotherapy. In approaching these requirements, Wolberg discussed the essential compromises in short-term therapy in terms of therapeutic goals, techniques, attitudes, and selection of cases and then presented an impressive rationale and set of principles for what he called "a flexible system of short-term psychotherapy" (1965c, p. 142). In doing so Wolberg acknowledged the contribution of Karl Menninger, who in 1963 wrote, "The special merit of psychoanalysis is that from the painstaking long-continued treatment of some individuals so much has been learned that is helpful in the shorter treatment of other individuals" (quoted in Wolberg, 1965c, pp. 152–153; Menninger, 1963).

While Wolberg came from a traditional psychoanalytic background and clearly had not made peace with the issue of whether planned short-term psychotherapy can be as effective as time-unlimited psychotherapy, his views of planned short-term psychotherapy were remarkably catholic. His 1980 handbook of short-term psychotherapy, for example, includes chapters on crisis intervention, hypnosis, use of dreams, relaxation techniques, and homework assignments.

Therapeutic Goals

Wolberg believed that abbreviated therapeutic goals must be accepted in short-term therapy. He mentioned specifically: (1) symptom relief, (2) restoration of prior level of functioning, (3) some understanding in the client of the factors operative in producing the problem for which help is sought, (4) beginning recognition of character traits that prevent a more satisfying life adjustment, (5) increased awareness of how early childhood experiences played a role in establishing these character traits, (6) recognition of some of the relationships between character traits and the current conflict, and (7) identification of some workable steps toward remediation.

With regard to techniques that have special salience in short-term psychotherapy, Wolberg identified the placebo influence, that is, the role of faith in the agency providing help; the therapeutic value of the relationship itself; the virtue of unburdening and emotional catharsis; the helpfulness of suggestion and teaching; and, finally, the unpredictable spontaneous forces and changes that arise from time to time with or without psychotherapy.

Therapeutic Techniques

The most important changes in therapeutic technique that are needed when traditional psychotherapists begin doing brief psychotherapy include a higher activity level; open expressions of interest, sympathy, and encouragement; a willingness to try a variety of therapeutic strategies in a responsible manner rather than insisting on a single therapeutic approach; and a need on the part of the therapist to overcome (where it exists) the "prejudice of depth." According to Wolberg this prejudice is found in the belief that discussing the past is necessarily more therapeutic than discussing the present, that discussing material about which the client is unaware is necessarily more therapeutic than discussing experiences that are conscious, and that discussing attitudes toward the therapist is necessarily more therapeutic than discussing attitudes toward other important figures in the client's life.

When one examines Wolberg's system of short-term psychotherapy, its indebtedness to psychoanalytic concepts of personality development and of remediation is always clear. Wolberg made important use of such concepts as dream interpretation, transference, the psychodynamic hypothesis, and resistance. But he also made use of concepts that arise from learning theory, environmental analysis, and interpersonal psychology; in addition, he proposed that attention be directed to the establishment of life values and a life philosophy. That is, Wolberg's approach was itself an illustration of the responsible eclecticism that he suggested is needed by all therapists doing short-term psychotherapy.

The initial step in Wolberg's flexible approach to short-term psychotherapy is the rapid establishment of a working relationship through sympathetic listening, communicating understanding and self-confidence, reassuring clients who seem without hope, and taking an active role in structuring the therapeutic situation. At the same time as a relationship is being established, Wolberg attempted to develop a diagnostic and psychodynamic formulation. In this process Wolberg drew heavily on psychoanalytic theories of personality development and psychopathology.

At about the time that the formulation of the client's problem begins to seem useful, the therapist and client must identify a specific problem area on which to focus. Often the focus is on the precipitating stress situation. Sometimes it is on the most distressing symptom or symptoms. Less often the focus is on characteristics of the relationship between the client and the therapist. Therapeutic techniques that are of particular importance to Wolberg include those actions that help clarify and interpret the client's behavior.

In addition, Wolberg helped his clients learn how to increase their own self-understanding. He identified five particular strategies in working with his clients. First, he suggested that they relate their outbursts of tension, anxiety, and symptom increase to provocative incidents in the environment and to insecurities within the self. Second, he urged clients to become sensitive to the nature of circumstances that boost or lower feelings about themselves. Third, he encouraged clients to observe the vicissitudes in their relationships with other people. Fourth, he believed that clients should become more expert in understanding their own dreams and daydreams. Finally, he believed that clients can become sensitive to those occasions when they fail to put their insights into action.

Wolberg believed that annual follow-up interviews are important, either in person, by telephone, or by a letter from the client outlining feelings and progress. Plans for the follow-up are generally made as part of the termination phase of the therapy.

A General Guide for Short-Term Psychotherapy

Wolberg believed that a number of general principles of psychodynamic short-term therapy apply regardless of the therapist's specific theoretical point of view, personality, or level of skill (see Box 2-1). These principles can be adapted to individual situations, but failure to employ these principles, however they are adapted, invites therapeutic failure.

BOX 2-1 • *Wolberg's General Principles of Short-Term Psychotherapy*

1. *Establish a Positive Working Relationship.* Basic to achieving any significant therapeutic results is the establishment of a therapeutic alliance through the display of warmth, understanding, acceptance, and empathy.

Patient: I feel helpless about getting well. Do you think I can get over this trouble of mine?

Therapist: Do you really have a desire to get over this trouble? If you really do, this is nine-tenths of the battle. You will want to apply yourself to the job of getting well. I will point out some things that you can do, and if you work at them yourself, I see no reason why you can't get better. (1980, p. 36)

2. *Deal with Initial Resistances.* Among the causes of resistance that are commonly encountered (particularly early in the short-term therapy) are a mismatch between the patient's fantasies about an ideal therapist and the actual therapist, being referred to a mental health professional for a problem that is physical in its manifestations, and lack of motivation. Wolberg provides a number of illustrative examples of exchanges that deal with these resistances.

Patient: Dr. Jones sent me here. I have a problem with stomach aches a long time and have been seeing doctors for it for a long time.

Therapist: As you know, I am a psychiatrist. What makes you feel your problem is psychological?

P: I don't think it is, but Dr. Jones says it might be, and he sent me here.

T: Do you think it is?

P: No, I can't see how this pain comes from my head.

T: Well, it might be organic, but with someone who has suffered as long as you have the pain will cause a good deal of tension and upset. *[To insist on the idea that the problem is psychological would be a poor tactic. First, the therapist may be wrong, and the condition may be organic though undetectable by present-day tests and examinations. Second, the patient may need to retain his notion of the symptom's organicity and even to be able to experience attenuated pain from time to time as a defense against over-*

whelming anxiety or, in certain serious conditions, psychosis.]

P: It sure does.

T: And the tension and depression prevent the stomach from healing. Tension interferes with healing of even true physical problems. Now when you reduce tension, it helps the healing. It might help you even if your problem is organic.

P: I hope so.

T: So what we can do is try to figure out what problems you have that are causing tension, and also lift the tension. This should help your pain.

P: I would like that. I get tense in my job with the people I work. Some of them are crumbs. *[Patient goes on talking, opening up pockets of anxiety.]* (1980, p. 37)

3. *Gather Historical Material and Other Data.* Let patients tell their stories with as little interruption as possible. From the individual story the therapist should be able to develop a tentative diagnosis and psychodynamic formulation. Questions that could be kept in mind while listening to the history include: What is the most important problem to the patient? Why does the patient come to treatment at this time? What has the patient done about the problem so far? What theory does the patient have about the causes of the problem? What does the patient expect or want from the therapy?

4. *Select the Symptoms That are Most Amenable to Treatment.* A focal problem needs to be selected and agreed upon by the therapist and patient in order to help organize the therapy. The therapist can then summarize the focus to make sure that the patient agrees.

Therapist: What you are complaining most about is a sense of hopelessness and depression. If we focused on these and worked toward eliminating them, would you agree?

Patient: I should say so, but I would also like to see how I could improve my marriage. It's been going downhill fast. The last fight I had with my husband was the limit.

T: Well, suppose we take up the problems you are having with your husband and see how these are connected with your symptoms.

P: I would like that, doctor. (1980, p. 39)

5. *Define the Precipitating Events.* Identifying the precipitating factors that seemed to cause the present symptoms helps identify fruitful directions for exploration. It is not always easy to identify these events, but the therapist should try to do so even if the patient seems to be unwilling or unenthusiastic.

Continued

BOX 2-1   *Continued*

Therapist: It seems as if you were managing to get along without trouble until your daughter told you about the affair she is having with this married man. Do you believe this started you off on the downslide?

Patient: Doctor, I can't tell you the shock this was to me. Janie was such an ideal child and never was a bit of a problem. And then this thing happened. She's completely changed, and I can't understand it. (1980, p. 40)

6. *Present a Working Hypothesis to the Patient.* After the first session the therapist should have enough information to formulate a working hypothesis to account for the patient's presenting problem and to suggest this hypothesis to the patient in a nontechnical manner designed to maintain the patient's sense of confidence in the therapist.

Therapist: Is it possible that you are afraid your husband will do to you what your father did to your mother?

Patient: (breaking out in tears) Oh, it's so terrible. I sometimes think I can't stand it.

T: Stand his leaving you or the fact that he had an affair?

P: If it could end right now, I mean if he would stop it (pause).

T: You would forget what had happened?

P: (pause) Yes, yes.

T: How you handle yourself will determine what happens. You can see that your present upset is probably linked with what happened in your home when you were a child. Would you tell me about your love life with your husband? (1980, pp. 40–41)

7. *Make a Tentative Diagnosis.* Wolberg acknowledges that diagnostic categories are of limited usefulness and that sometimes the diagnosis is determined by the policies of reimbursement agencies. Nevertheless, he urges that a tentative diagnosis be made because it may be helpful in developing a treatment plan.

8. *Enlist the Patient as an Active Participant in the Therapy.* Many patients are unaccustomed to taking an active role in their therapy. In the case of primary medical care, for example, patients often have to do little more than to comply with directives regarding medication. In other cases, when the treatment is administered in the physician's office, the level of active participation by the patient is very low indeed. The situation is quite different in the case of psychotherapy, a matter of particular salience when the patient has not had a significant prior history of psychotherapy.

Therapist: There is no magic about getting well. The way we can best accomplish our goals is to work together as a partnership team. I want you to tell me all the important things that are going on with you and I will try to help you understand them. What we want to do is to develop new, healthier patterns. *My* job is to see what is blocking you from achieving this objective by pointing out some things that have and are still blocking you. *Your* job is to act to put into practice new patterns we decide are necessary, you telling me about your experiences and feelings. Psychotherapy is like learning a new language. (1980, pp. 41–42)

   9. *Make a Verbal Contract with the Patient.* There should be an agreement with the patient regarding whatever characteristics of the therapeutic encounter can be specified in advance — particularly, the frequency of appointments, the number of sessions, the fee, and the termination date.

Therapist: We are going to have a total of 12 sessions. In that time we should have made an impact on your anxiety and depression. Now, let's consult the calendar. We will terminate therapy on October 9, and I'll mark it down here. Can you also make a note of it?

Patient: Will 12 sessions be enough?

T: Yes. The least it could do is to get you on the road to really working out the problem.

P: What happens if I'm not better?

T: You are an intelligent person and there is no reason why you shouldn't be better in that time. (1980, p. 42)

   10. *Use the Most Effective Techniques to Help the Patient.* Keeping in mind the need for flexibility and an active stance, therapists should implement the most effective techniques or combination of techniques at their disposal.

Therapist: At the start, I believe it would be helpful to reduce your tension. This should be beneficial to you in many ways. One of the best ways of doing this is by teaching you some relaxing exercises. What I would like to do for you is to make a relaxing cassette tape. Do you have a cassette tape recorder?

Patient: No, I haven't.

T: You can buy one quite inexpensively. How do you feel about this?

P: It sounds great.

T: OK. Of course, there are other things we will do, but this should help us get off to a good start. (1980, p. 42)

Continued

BOX 2-1   *Continued*

11. *Study the Patient's Reactions and Defensive Patterns.* Once the therapeutic program has been instituted, the patient will react. Attention to these reactions, including the ways in which the patient defends against the efforts of the therapist, provides very useful information for the therapist and patient to examine together. In part the usefulness of this information is due to the fact that the reactions are in operation right in the office for both patient and therapist to see.

Therapist: I noticed that when I asked you to lean back in the chair and try relaxing to my suggestions, you were quite uneasy and kept on opening your eyes. What were you thinking about?

Patient: (emotionally) My heart started beating. I was afraid I couldn't do it. What you'd think of me. That I'd fail. I guess I'm afraid of doctors. My husband is trying to get me to see a gynecologist.

T: But you kept opening your eyes.

P: (pause) You know doctor, I'm afraid of losing control, of what might come out. I guess I don't trust anybody.

T: Afraid of what would happen here, of what I might do if you shut your eyes? (smiling)

P: (laughing) I guess so. Silly. But the thought came to me about something sexual. (1980, p. 43)

12. *Be Sensitive to How the Past Is Influencing the Present.* Every psychodynamic approach to psychotherapy makes use of the relationships between the past and the present, and Wolberg's approach is no exception. He does note, however, that it is important to avoid being trapped in a endless exploration of the past. Attempts are made to learn how established patterns of behavior have operated throughout the patient's lifetime, and interpretations are made at propitious moments when the patient seems to have some beginning awareness of connections between past experiences and present behavior.

13. *Watch for Transference Reactions.* Wolberg suggests that the therapist need not deal with positive transference, but that negative transference reactions should be dealt with rapidly and sympathetically, since such reactions can interfere with the therapeutic alliance and inadvertently lengthen the duration of treatment.

Therapist: (noting the patient's hesitant speech) You seem to be upset about something.

Patient: Why, *should* I be upset?

T: You might be if I did something you didn't like.

P: (pause) No — I'm afraid, just afraid I'm not doing what I should. I've been here six times and I still have that panicky feeling from time to time. Do other patients do better?

T: You seem to be comparing yourself to my other patients.

P: I — I — I guess so. The young man that came before me. He seems so self-confident and cheerful. I guess I felt inferior, that you would find fault with me.

T: Do you think I like him better than I do you?

P: Well, wouldn't you, if he was doing better than I was?

T: That's interesting. Tell me more.

P: I've been that way. My parents, I felt, preferred my older brother. He always came in on top. They were proud of his accomplishments in school.

T: So in a way you feel I should be acting like your parents.

P: I can't help feeling that way.

T: Don't you think this is a pattern that is really self-defeating? We ought to explore this more.

P: (emotionally) Well, I really thought today you were going to send me to another doctor because you were sick of me.

T: Actually, the thought never occurred to me to do that. But I'm glad you brought this matter out because we will be able to explore some of your innermost fears about how people feel about you. (1980, pp. 43–44)

14. *Examine Possible Countertransference Feelings.* Wolberg cautions therapists that persistent irritability, boredom and anger, on the one hand, or extraordinary interest in or attraction to any patient, on the other hand, may signal the presence of significant countertransference feelings that call for therapist self-examination (see also Binder, Strupp, and Schacht, 1983; Hoyt and Farrell, 1984–85). Some patients may remind therapists of important figures in their lives, and without an appropriate examination of these feelings, the therapy may fail. If self-examination does not cure the countertransference feelings, Wolberg suggests that the patient be transferred to another therapist.

15. *Constantly Look for Resistances That Threaten Progress.* Continuing resistances must be brought out openly in an empathic and nonblaming manner if they are not to jeopardize the success of the time-limited psychotherapy. The therapist may want to help the patient identify the value

Continued

BOX 2-1 *Continued*

that the resistance must have. Sometimes simply bringing the evidence of resistance to the attention of the patient may help dissipate it.

Patient: I didn't want to come here. Last time I had a terribly severe headache. I felt dizzy in the head. (pause)

Therapist: I wonder why. Did anything happen here that upset you; did I do anything to upset you?

P: No, it's funny but it's something I can't understand. I want to come here, and I don't. It's like I'm afraid.

T: Afraid?

P: (Pause; patient flushes) I can't understand it. People are always trying to change me. As far back as I can remember, at home, at school.

T: And you resent their trying to change you.

P: Yes, I feel they can't leave me alone.

T: Perhaps you feel I'm trying to change you.

P: (angrily) Aren't you?

T: Only if *you* want to change. In what way do you want to change, if at all?

P: I want to get rid of my headaches, and stomach aches, and all the rest of my aches.

T: But you don't want to change to do this.

P: Well, doctor, this isn't true. I want to change the way *I* want to.

T: Are you sure the way *you* want to change will help you get rid of your symptoms?

P: But that's why I'm coming here so you will tell me.

T: But you resent my making suggestions to you because somehow you put me in the class of everybody else who you believe wants to take your independence away. And then you show resistance to what I am trying to do.

P: (laughs) Isn't that silly. I really do trust you.

T: Then supposing when you begin to feel you are being dominated you tell me, so we can talk it out. I really want to help you and not dominate you.

P: Thank you, doctor, I do feel better. (1980, p. 45)

    16. *Give the Patient Homework.* Time-limited psychotherapy assumes

that much of the treatment takes place between sessions. The therapist plays a role in how some of this between-session time is used by suggesting activities for the patient — keeping a log or diary, establishing schedules of one sort or another, having a conversation with a specific person or persons, rewarding oneself for some positive action, thinking about a certain problem, reading a particular book or article, self-hypnosis, or writing to someone, for example.

Therapist: What may help you is understanding what triggers off your headaches and makes them worse. Supposing you keep a diary and jot down the frequency of your headaches. Every time you get a headache write down the day and time. Even more important, write down the events that immediately preceded the onset of the headache or the feelings or thought you had that brought it on. If a headache is stopped by anything that has happened, or by anything you think about or figure out, write that down, and bring your diary when you come here so we can talk about what has happened. (1980, p. 45)

17. *Keep Accenting Prearranged Termination.* Time-limited therapy ends — often sooner than the patient wishes. But if excessive dependency needs are not to be encouraged nor fears of autonomy reinforced, it is important to remind the patient of the agreed-upon date of termination. Manifestations of regression that may occur as a consequence of these reminders need to be dealt with just as any other issue in therapy — by interpretation or any other appropriate maneuver.

Therapist: We have five more sessions, as you know, and then we will terminate.

Patient: I realize it, but I always have trouble breaking away. My wife calls me a holder-oner.

T: Yes, that's exactly what we want to avoid, the dependency. You are likely to resent ending treatment for that reason. What do you think?

P: (laughing) I'll try not to.

T: Well, keep thinking about it, and if you have any bad reactions let's talk about it. It's important not to make treatment a way of life. By the end of the five sessions, you should be able to carry on.

P: But supposing I don't make it?

T: There you go, see, anticipating failure. This is a gesture to hold on.

P: Well, doctor, I know you are right. I'll keep working on it. (1980, p. 46)

18. *Terminate Therapy on the Agreed-upon Date.* Wolberg treats the

Continued

BOX 2-1   *Continued*

termination date very seriously and, except in the rarest of circumstances, terminates the therapy as scheduled. He does suggest, however, that patients write to him at some time in the future to let him know how things are going. They also know that if a problem arises they can call and arrange for an appointment.

Therapist: This is, as you know, our last session. I want you now to try things out on your own. Keep practicing the things I taught you — the relaxation exercises, the figuring out what brings on your symptoms and takes them away, and so forth. You should continue to get better. But setbacks may occur from time to time. Don't let that upset you. That's normal and you'll get over the setback. In fact, it may help you figure out better what your symptoms are all about. Now, if in the future you find you need a little more help, don't hesitate to call me and I'll try to arrange an appointment. (1980, p. 46)

19. *Stress the Need for Continuing Work on Oneself.* Therapy continues beyond its formal end, and the therapist must not allow the patient to underestimate how important continuing self-therapy is for maintaining and improving upon therapeutic gains already made. The therapist may want to encourage the patient to isolate the past from the present and future, to accept tension and anxiety as a normal part of life, to recognize what can and what cannot be changed, and to stop regretting actions and thoughts of the past and anticipating disaster in the future.

20. *Arrange for Further Treatment if Necessary.* If a patient exhibits very little improvement at the time of discharge from time-limited psychotherapy, continuing treatment may be necessary. The continuing contact does not need to be intensive or prolonged, and the patient's needs can often be met by infrequent and short visits, for example, a fifteen- or twenty-minute appointment every two or three weeks (see Chapter 20). Often it is only necessary that the patient know that a supportive person is available if needed. A social support group can be suggested, and occasionally a referral can be made to another therapist who may have some special skills, such as biofeedback, for example, that may be appropriate.

The Therapist as Educator

Wolberg also believed that clients can profit from knowing a few general principles that can assist in increasing life satisfactions. While values can change slowly in the course of long-term therapy, in short-term therapy

Wolberg wondered whether therapists can "expedite matters by acting in an educational capacity, pointing out faulty values and indicating healthy ones that the patient may advantageously adopt" (1965c, p. 183). Among these life principles that can be shared, Wolberg mentioned a dozen that seem particularly salient to him. They are presented in Box 2-2 in summary form as a series of aphorisms.

Wolberg summarized the stages that seem to occur in the resolution of an emotional problem in the process of short-term psychotherapy:

> *1. The patient becomes reassured that he is not hopeless and that there is nothing so drastically wrong with him to prevent a resolution of his suffering. . . . 2. He develops some understanding of reasons for his emotional break-down and he becomes aware of the fact that he has had problems within himself that have sensitized him to his current*

BOX 2-2 · *Wolberg's Educational Aphorisms*

1. What's past is past. Stop worrying about what happened long ago!
2. Learn to recognize when you are tense or anxious and try to identify the sources of these feelings!
3. A certain amount of tension and anxiety is normal in life!
4. All people have to live with a certain amount of anger and hostile feelings, and should learn to tolerate those feelings!
5. Expect to be frustrated from time to time in life, and learn to accept those experiences!
6. If you find something in your environment that needs changing, get started correcting it!
7. Some life circumstances are irremediable. When something can't be changed, learn to live with it!
8. When you see that you are being self-destructive, figure out what you're doing. Remember, you have the power to change your behavior!
9. Keep the demands you make on yourself within realistic and reasonable limits!
10. People are different. Just because there are some things other people can do that you can't, doesn't make you inferior!
11. Life is to be enjoyed. Get all the pleasure you can out of it!
12. Value the opportunities you have to build better relationships with people with whom you interact. Try to see the world through their eyes!

From Wolberg, 1965b, pp. 183–189.

---

upset. . . . 3. On the basis of his understanding, he recognizes that there are things he can do about his current environmental situation, as well as about his attitudes toward people and toward himself. . . . 4. He accepts the fact that there are and probably always will be limitations in his environment and in himself which he may be unable to change. . . . 5. He fulfills himself as completely as possible in spite of handicaps in his environment and in himself, at the same time that he promotes himself to as great degrees of maturity and responsibility as are within his potential. (1965c, pp. 192–193)

Concluding Comments

Wolberg was one of the earliest writers in the field of time-limited psychotherapy, and his work bears the unmistakable stamp of traditional psychoanalysis, to which a full measure of compassionate flexibility has been added.

His work as a therapist was very eclectic, and it is astonishing how non-doctrinaire he was about the kinds of therapeutic techniques he recommended. His list of such techniques included teaching, relaxation tapes, hypnosis, homilies, direct suggestion, psychoactive drugs, catharsis, faith, counting on good luck, dream interpretation, and crisis intervention — all in the service of accomplishing significant therapeutic objectives in as short a time as feasible. Yet, he did not stray too far from his psychodynamic base, and while his fingers seem crossed, his approach to time-limited psychotherapy was firmly rooted, but at the same time practical and broad.

CHAPTER THREE

Bellak's Intensive Brief and Emergency Psychotherapy

Overview

Goals of Therapy

Therapeutic Techniques

Continued Development of Brief and Emergency Psychotherapy

Diagnosis-Specific Brief Therapy Recommendations

Concluding Comments

From 1958 until 1964, Leopold Bellak and Leonard Small (1965, 1978; see also Bellak, 1984) established and were associated with the Trouble Shooting Clinic, a service of the Psychiatric Department of the City Hospital at Elmhurst, Queens, New York, that served as a twenty-four-hour emotional first-aid station. This clinic, during its six-year life, offered "immediate, walk-in care of emotional problems of minor or major degree, from advice to the lovelorn to care of acute psychoses" (1965, p. 141). Its rationale was both therapeutic and preventive, in the sense that minor problems could be prevented from becoming more severe and that helping a client deal with a problem might make it easier for that client to deal with a future problem without professional assistance.

Goals of Therapy

Bellak and Small came out of a conservative psychoanalytic tradition and have tried to show in their volumes how psychoanalytic theory and therapeutic concepts can be used in providing brief and emergency psychotherapy. Rather than developing a separate theory, they argue that properly understood psychodynamic formulations can be successfully applied in brief psychotherapy. Bellak and Small use the term *brief* to mean between one and five or six (depending on whether there is a follow-up contact) fifty-minute therapy sessions.

In their earliest publications Bellak and Small suggested that "the goal of brief psychotherapy is limited to the removal or amelioration of specific symptoms: it does not attempt the reconstitution of personality except that any dynamic intervention may secondarily and, to a certain extent, autonomously lead to some restructuration" (1965, p. 9).

Brief psychotherapy seeks to help a client continue to function, so that nature can continue its work of healing, and also, where indicated, help increase the ability of the client to earn enough money so that more extensive psychotherapy can be undertaken. Bellak and Small, while acknowledging that relatively brief psychotherapy may be sufficient to help some clients continue growing on their own, saw it initially as having the potential for decreasing the sense of personal difficulty and increasing strength and adequacy of functioning so that improved earning power and improved motivation could lead the way to more substantial treatment. When circumstances would permit more prolonged treatment, Bellak and Small saw few if any instances where brief psychotherapy would be preferable.

Therapeutic Techniques

Bellak and Small's most important contributions to the practice of brief psychotherapy are technical. They see the steps in brief psychotherapy as including: (1) identification of the presenting problem; (2) taking a detailed history; (3) establishing an understanding of the relationship between that history and the presenting problem; (4) selecting and applying appropriate interventions; (5) working through the problem from differing perspectives; and (6) termination. They believe that this process can take place most successfully in an atmosphere in which the therapist is seen in a positive light as likable, reliable, understanding, accepting, hopeful, benign, interested, and helpful.

Understanding the history and the details of the presenting problem is basic to the development of formulations and intervention plans, and Bellak and Small allocate virtually all of the first interview to that task. They conceive of the history as comprising two distinguishable parts — first, the history of the chief complaint and the life setting within which it arose and, second, a comprehensive developmental history of the client. If the history is skillfully obtained, it should be possible to understand the onset of the present problem in dynamic terms, that is, in relation to genetic, developmental, and cultural events.

The process of establishing hypotheses linking current difficulties with past circumstances and events is, for Bellak and Small, clearly within the psychoanalytic theoretical tradition, and "requires every bit of intellectual and emotional equipment the psychotherapist can muster. . . . No unconscious process, no defensive reaction, no primitive quality in the human being can be alien to him" (1965, p. 49).

Bellak and Small describe the various intervention possibilities open to the therapist undertaking brief psychotherapy. The central intervention is the imparting of insight through judicious interpretations. Other interventions, often just as important as the increase of understanding, include increasing self-esteem; providing the opportunity for catharsis, that is, for the discharge of built-up emotions and tensions; helping repress and restrain drives that are destructive to adjustment; assisting clients to distinguish between what is fantasy and what is real; helping clients become more sensitive to warning signals that originate both inside of and outside them; providing clients with increased intellectual appreciation and understanding of salient issues that they are facing; and providing reassurance and support.

The goal of brief psychotherapy is to strengthen the likelihood that more mature behavior will take place and that older neurotic modes of adjustment will be extinguished. In brief psychotherapy there is relatively little time for the application of therapeutic gains in the therapeutic setting — on the other hand, however, the client can continue to learn by applying the lessons of psychotherapy in real life.

Bellak and Small's comments about termination illustrate their own initial uncertainties about the definitive benefits of brief psychotherapy, in that they seem to suggest that these comments would not apply to long-term psychotherapy. They write:

In brief psychotherapy, the patient must be left with a carefully cultivated positive transference and a clear understanding that he is welcome to return. The maintenance of the positive transference avoids a sense of rejection in the terminating process and permits the patient to retain the therapist as a benign, introjected figure. (1965, p. 73; see also 1978, p. 106)

Bellak and Small stress that while clients should be urged to apply what they have learned from the brief psychotherapy, it should be made clear that the therapist is available for additional help. The client should feel free to contact the therapist before future problems get out of hand, and the client can be urged to provide periodic follow-up reports by letter or telephone.

Continued Development of Brief and Emergency Psychotherapy

Five years after the publication of the second edition of Bellak and Small's description of their brief psychotherapy, Bellak and Siegel (1983) extended the presentation of their ideas. In their new volume they included the adjective *intensive* in describing their approach; they described it as an approach that draws on learning theory and systems theory as well as on psychoanalytic theory; and they suggested that it could be effective in working with "any and all problems brought to a clinic, an office, or a sick room" (p. 2). Bellak and his colleagues seem to have become more committed to time-limited psychotherapy as a strategy that by itself may fully serve the needs of the patient without lengthening the duration of the therapy—still five or six weekly fifty-minute sessions with one additional follow-up session a month later.

Fundamental Aspects of Intensive Brief and Emergency Psychotherapy

Bellak and Siegel identify ten fundamental aspects of intensive brief and emergency psychotherapy: (1) to focus on the crucial features of the presenting disorder; (2) to understand precisely why the patient came at this time for treatment, when the immediate problem began, and how such problems existed in the past; (3) to identify causal factors in understanding the presenting problems, that is, to bridge the discontinuity between childhood and adulthood, between what is conscious and what is unconscious, and between symptoms and underlying personality conflicts; (4) to establish the fact that symptoms are attempts at problem solving and coping; (5) to focus on learning—on what has been poorly learned and on what needs to be unlearned and relearned; (6) to identify defensive mechanisms used by the patient; (7) to focus on the most disturbing symptoms within the broadest possible framework in order to provide the most precise conceptualization of the problem; (8) to undertake a systematic focused approach to the therapy; (9) to acknowledge that the benefits of therapy may extend beyond the immediate focus; and (10) to accept the suitability of intensive time-limited psychotherapy for a very wide variety of problems and disorders—Bellak and Siegel select the problem they will treat, rather than selecting the patient they will treat.

As for its principal tenets, Bellak and Siegel suggest that intensive brief and emergency psychotherapy relates to traditional long-term therapy the way a short story relates to a novel. They write: "Those of you who appreciate short stories know what a tremendous impact they can have and those who have actually tried to write a short story know what a terribly demanding task it is" (p. 8). The novel and the short story are not in competition; each has its own strengths, and the writing of each requires its own set of skills. The basic tenet of Bellak's therapy is that the therapist should try to understand everything, should know a great deal, and then should "do the one thing that will make the crucial difference" (p. 8). Careful conceptualization makes time-limited psychotherapy possible.

Bellak believes that all patients can be helped, at least theoretically, by time-limited psychotherapy. Thus, brief therapy should be the first method of choice in working with any patient, whether it is someone with acute anxiety, a severe character neurosis, or a chronic psychotic. In order for time-limited therapy to be helpful, it has to take place within an understanding of the patient's history, current life situation, and general predispositions. Brief intensive therapy requires a careful historical exploration and psychodynamic appraisal of the person. Yet persons with relatively limited knowledge of psychodynamic principles can be taught to provide brief psychotherapy. Indeed, Bellak and Siegel suggest that a person specifically trained in brief emergency psychotherapy "may be more effective than someone more broadly trained but without specific knowledge . . . of brief intensive therapy" (p. 9).

Bellak and Siegel believe that emergency psychotherapy, in which the goal is clearly defined by whatever presents itself as the emergency, need not necessarily be limited to the goal of symptom removal. They believe that, despite the limited time that is available for the therapeutic encounter, there is an opportunity for the patient to achieve a higher level of psychosocial adjustment and maturity than was the case prior to the emergency. Bellak and Siegel suggest that in addition to its role in early treatment and in rehabilitation, brief psychotherapy may play a useful role in primary prevention in helping people work through the impact of a trauma, for example, before the trauma has had its full effect.

In addition, Bellak and Siegel believe that brief intensive therapy should be the treatment of choice whether the patient is seen in a public facility or in private practice. Finally, they urge the reader to understand that the demands on the therapist are far greater in doing intensive brief psychotherapy than in doing time-unlimited therapy, and that it may be especially difficult for a therapist who has been trained and who has considerable experience in a long-term therapeutic model to move into brief therapy comfortably.

Intensive Brief Therapy Intervention Techniques

Bellak and Siegel identify ten specific intervention techniques that are generally appropriate in all psychotherapy but that seem to them unusually useful in their intensive brief therapy. This list of therapeutic techniques is an elaborated and very useful extension of the similar list developed by them in their earlier publications. These techniques include: (1) classical interpretation—one of the fundamental methods in dynamic psychotherapy; (2) empathic encouragement of emotional expression; (3) auxiliary reality testing in which the therapist can clarify patients' distortions of reality; (4) advice and action directives, when patients' proposed courses of action (or inaction) seem likely to be harmful to them; (5) increasing self-awareness in patients by sensitizing them to their own signals of conflict; (6) education, when patients appear to lack information; (7) helping patients develop an intellectual understanding of their problems; (8) support and reassurance; (9) involvement of the family network when that seems likely to be useful as a strategy for helping identified patients; and (10) prescription of psychoactive drugs as appropriate, particularly in order to control anxiety, disturbed thought processes, or depression.

Diagnosis-Specific Brief Therapy Recommendations

A special strength of the Bellak and Small volumes is the discussion of the role of brief psychotherapy in the case of specific psychiatric syndromes and life situations—including depression, panic, depersonalization, phobias, anxiety hysterias, feelings of unreality, suicidal danger, acute psychotic states, acting out, and in catastrophic life events. In each instance a variety of brief case histories is presented to illustrate the general therapeutic guiding principles (Bellak, 1984, pp. 19 ff.; Bellak and Siegel, 1983, pp. 50 ff.).

Depression

In the case of depression Bellak is insistent that where there is a depression, regardless of type, there is a precipitating factor. He identifies a number of major considerations in the management of depression. These considerations, as can be seen, are firmly embedded within a contemporary psychoanalytic framework (see Box 3-1).

Acting Out

In the case of acting out (the translation of inner conflicts into socially unacceptable or self-destructive direct behavior rather than into internalized symptoms), Bellak and Small (1965; see also Bellak and Siegel, 1983) sug-

---

BOX 3-1 • *Bellak's Brief Therapy Recommendations: Depression*

1. Enhance self-esteem.
2. Reduce the punitive quality of the superego.
3. Reduce the patient's tendency toward intropunitiveness and self-denigration.
4. Help patients cope with loss, disappointments, and the sense that they have been deceived.
5. Help patients resolve their unrequited oral and dependent needs.
6. Help patients cope with the interpersonal aspects of their depression, particularly those related to frustrated narcissistic needs.
7. Identify how denial is used in the service of defense, particularly in obscuring the precipitating events of the depression.
8. Help patients cope with their disturbed object relations.

---

gest a number of useful therapeutic techniques in brief psychotherapy (see Box 3-2).

Suicidal Threats or Attempts

While the danger of suicide is unusually common among patients who are depressed, suicidal attempts are also found in patients who are in a panic, who are delusional or hallucinating or otherwise psychotic, or who are suffering from central nervous system disorders. It is particularly important to assess family history of suicidal thoughts, threats, or attempts and to determine whether other instances of violent acting out have occurred in the past. When patients are unambivalent about suicide, there is often little one can do to prevent the suicide from taking place. But, fortunately, many suicidal patients are ambivalent about their impulses and there are opportunities to provide life-saving clinical help. As for undertaking time-limited psychotherapy with suicidal patients, Bellak makes a number of specific recommendations, in addition to suggesting that therapists keep in mind the recommendations for dealing with depressed and with acting-out patients previously enumerated (see Box 3-3).

Acute Psychotic States

When the conditions are right, it is possible to provide very effective brief psychotherapy to acutely ill psychotic patients on an ambulatory basis. Bellak and Siegel (1983) suggest that when the patient is reasonably coop-

---

BOX 3-2 • *Bellak's Brief Therapy Recommendations: Acting Out*

1. Prohibit certain relationships or behavior.
2. Remove the client from the setting that precipitates the undesirable behavior.
3. Interpret prudently the meanings of the behavior.
4. Attempt to make the behavior unacceptable to the client.
5. Discuss, from a cognitive point of view, the meaning of the patient's behavior.
6. Predict acting-out behavior through an understanding of the factors that cause it as a way of preventing the behavior from taking place.
7. Encourage delay in acting-out behavior when outright prohibition seems impossible.
8. Strengthen that aspect of the client's personality that wishes to control the behavior, that feels the behavior is undesirable.
9. Help the client think of today's behavioral temptations in the light of the immediate but easily forgotten past.
10. Use drugs appropriately to reduce anxiety.
11. Enlist the help of others to inhibit harmful acting out.
12. Provide constantly available support and reassurance.
13. Make temporary hospitalization available during the most critical phases of the condition.
14. Reduce the inhibitions that prevent the client from successfully engaging in socially desirable behavior.

---

erative and nonassaultive, when the patient can identify at least one stable current relationship and some socially supportive family nearby, when the therapist can establish a good working relationship with auxiliary therapists, emergency centers, and with an inpatient facility, and when the patient has at least a minimally satisfactory housing arrangement, brief ambulatory therapy can be undertaken.

Bellak proposes a number of principles to keep in mind when treating acutely ill psychotics in time-limited psychotherapy (see Box 3-4).

Catastrophic Life Events

Psychodynamic approaches play an important role in helping people who are attempting to cope with contemporary life crises. That is, reactions to stressful life events can be viewed in a historical context just as can any

---

BOX 3-3 • *Bellak's Brief Therapy Recommendations: Suicidal Patients*

1. Assess the precipitating factors and the current situation, particularly level of hostility, oral needs, level of ego strength, and the specific dynamics of the suicidal impulses.
2. Determine how specific, concrete, and realistic the suicidal plans appear to be, and assess the level of impulse control.
3. Evaluate previous suicidal behavior and family history of suicidality and depression.
4. Abandon therapeutic neutrality under conditions of high lethality.
5. Expand array of options apparently open to the patient.
6. Identify and involve members of the entire social support system as well as community resources in monitoring the patient and in providing ongoing support and reassurance.
7. Establish liaison with patient's primary care physician and turn to medication and brief hospitalization as needed to control the suicidal impulses.

BOX 3-4 • *Bellak's Brief Therapy Recommendations: Acute Psychotic States*

1. Try to establish therapeutic contact with the patient and the patient's psychotic thinking.
2. Provide a rational perspective on how the patient's past plays a role in understanding his or her present predicament.
3. Reassure the patient that you will do everything you can to make sure that the patient will not be overwhelmed by his or her psychosis.
4. Reintroduce careful structure into the patient's life, when such structure has been lost.
5. Be available to the patient, if only by telephone, whenever needed, and provide supplementary therapeutic resources, such as crisis and emergency service addresses and telephone numbers.
6. Involve family members in the therapeutic effort, providing help to family members as needed in how to be of help to the patient.
7. Arrange for concrete help for the patient in the form of homemaking assistance or social services.
8. Serve as an auxiliary ego, testing reality for the patient, helping the patient make decisions, and confirming and supporting, where appropriate, decisions that the patient has made.
9. When needed, provide access to skilled recommendations regarding pharmacological treatments and hospitalization.

other form of psychological disability. Since the precipitating events are known, however, special therapeutic considerations come into play (see Box 3-5).

Phobias and Hysterias

Phobias and hysterias often lend themselves to time-limited therapeutic approaches and have historically been viewed within a psychodynamic context. Bellak and Siegel (1983) have provided a number of suggestions to keep in mind when working with such neurotic patients in time-limited psychotherapy (see Box 3-6).

Panic

According to Bellak and Siegel (1983), panic, a kind of severe free-floating anxiety, can be exogenous (precipitated by some external traumatic event) or endogenous (an overwhelming feeling of dread whose cause is unknown). In addition, a special type of panic can be drug-induced, in which the patient reacts in his or her unique way to the loss of control and sense of estrangement triggered by the use of the drug. Regardless of what type of panic, a number of specific recommendations can be made (see Box 3-7).

BOX 3-5 • *Bellak's Brief Therapy Recommendations: Catastrophic Life Events*

1. Provide the opportunity for catharsis.
2. Help the patient develop an understanding of the specific psychological meaning of the event, that is, the place of the event in the patient's unique life situation.
3. Explore the sense of guilt or responsibility that often occurs when catastrophic life events take place.
4. Be alert for evidence of long-term negative consequences of the event.
5. Pay particular attention to specific traumatic life events that have repeatedly been identified as unusually stressful, e.g., to job loss, retirement, marital disruption, and bereavement. Each of these life events is often associated with characteristic reaction patterns.
6. Catastrophic life events that have a violent component, such as robberies, muggings, rape, and severe disasters or accidents, require special therapeutic sensitivity.

BOX 3-6 • *Bellak's Brief Therapy Recommendations: Phobias and Hysterias*

1. Phobias and hysterias often have specific psychodynamic backgrounds whose successful exploration commonly provides significant therapeutic relief.
2. Some phobias and hysterias seem to have a family context, in that they appear to be transmitted as if they are contagious. In these instances, sociocultural dimensions may be particularly important in understanding the symptoms and their origin.
3. Phobias and hysterias often have sudden onsets. Under these conditions, exploration of the origin of the event can yield information about its unique meaning to the patient and can have significant therapeutic effect.
4. After initial exploration of the problem, it is appropriate to ask the patient to face the phobic situation and report on the consequences of the experience to the therapist.
5. Insights obtained during the process of examining the phobia or hysteria and its origin need to be fully considered in order to have an optimal effect on behavior.
6. Encourage the use of counterphobic defenses and practices as a way of mastering phobic or hysterical symptoms.
7. In the case of unlimited or spreading phobias or hysterias, particularly those that have a somatic component, therapy will have to discover and help the patient cope with what is likely to be a primitive basic anxiety.

Feelings of Unreality

The sense of depersonalization—characterized by the feeling that one is observing his or her own behavior as if from the outside, that there may no longer be a real world, and even that the patient no longer has a body and is no longer alive—presents special therapeutic challenges. Bellak and Siegel (1983) provide specific suggestions for how the patient can be helped to cope with such feelings in time-limited psychotherapy (see Box 3-8).

General Principles of Diagnosis-Specific Recommendations

Inductive examination of these diagnosis-specific recommendations reveals an important set of general principles that Bellak espouses in under-

---

BOX 3-7 • *Bellak's Brief Therapy Recommendations: Panic*

1. Explore the unconscious psychodynamic causes of the panic reaction.
2. Help the patient view the panic in a historical context and as a reaction to some precipitating factors.
3. Reassure the patient by providing a rational, intellectual explanation of the panic reaction.
4. In the case of a known precipitating event, examine the special significance of that event for the patient. Underline the special significance of the event as a way of helping the patient think of the panic reaction as ego-alien and relatively unlikely to have happened to others facing the same event.
5. Be unconditionally available to the patient during the times of greatest panic, and urge others in the social support system to minimize the occasions when the patient is alone.
6. Provide a rational structure to the therapeutic relationship to help control the anxiety associated with the panic reaction.
7. Panic occurs most commonly when the patient engages in denial or repression. The therapist should be on the alert for evidence of these defenses and help the patient get in more useful touch with both the affective and cognitive aspects of the panic reaction.

BOX 3-8 • *Bellak's Brief Therapy Recommendations: Feelings of Unreality*

1. View the symptoms of depersonalization as one point on the perceptual distortion and self-awareness continuum rather than as a unique set of symptoms. Consider changes in self-perception as associated with changes in how the external world is perceived.
2. Feelings of depersonalization can often be triggered by physiological processes that may, in turn, be the consequence of the use of certain drugs. Similarly, such feelings can often be successfully treated with the use of muscle relaxants or sedatives.
3. The sense of unreality can be a hysterical symptom, as can occur in the case of multiple personality. In this condition, symptoms can often be relieved by psychodynamic exploration of feelings that are not fully conscious to the patient.
4. The sense of unreality can be successfully treated by providing greater intellectual understanding of the phenomenon.

---

taking time-limited psychotherapy. First, the therapist must find allies in the work to be done—and find them quickly. These allies can include family members, the broader social support system, and the primary medical care system. Furthermore, the work of the outpatient psychotherapist may need to be supplemented with the use of medication and even with periods of brief hospitalization. Second, the therapist must be available to the patient virtually unconditionally and not just one hour per week, if severe psychopathology is to be treated successfully in limited periods of time. Third, the therapist must be active rather than passive, providing confident reassurance and support and temporarily taking over responsibilities that formerly were and once again will be those of the patient. Finally, Bellak believes that symptoms can be understood as responses to traumatic precipitating events and as part of a unique psychodynamic history. The belief that symptoms are intelligible is part of the great psychodynamic tradition, and may provide the greatest reassurance of all to the patient whose symptoms can no longer be mastered without outside help.

Concluding Comments

In some ways the most interesting aspect of Bellak's writing is the illustration of how one's attitudes toward planned short-term psychotherapy can be modified over time. Initially, Bellak kept faith with psychoanalytic theory and psychoanalysis. For him, planned short-term psychotherapy was not equivalent to traditional psychoanalytic treatment; it was something to tide patients over until they could enter into a real psychoanalysis.

Yet, Bellak worked for years to push the limits of a very brief psychotherapy—never more than six interviews. That was at the time a tremendous departure from traditional practice, and it must surely have caused many a raised eyebrow among his psychoanalytic colleagues. He kept his credibility, though, by his scholarly approach to his work and by his remarkably conservative approach to brief psychotherapy—as, for example, by allocating the entire first session to a diagnostic and dynamic assessment. His great initial and continuing contribution to brief therapy was his attention to how time-limited psychotherapy could be used specifically in the case of a wide variety of differing diagnostic categories. Here Bellak was at his clinical best.

Five years later, as part of the overall growing interest and confidence in what could be accomplished with planned short-term psychotherapy, Bellak reappeared as a true convert. He asserted that brief psychotherapy was often all that was needed to be of significant help to a patient and, perhaps even more courageously, that doing brief psychotherapy was more difficult and demanding than traditional psychotherapy and that special training was a

necessity. In terms of time, all he added to the planned short-term psychotherapy that he had developed five years earlier was a single follow-up session a month after the therapy had been completed. Thus, Bellak is in some
ways the paradigm case of the radicalized psychoanalytically oriented long-
term therapist.

CHAPTER FOUR

CHAPTER FOUR

Davanloo's Broad-Focus Psychotherapy

Overview

Davanloo's Psychodynamic Theory

The Seminal Work of David Malan

Therapeutic Techniques

A Case Example

Concluding Comments

Habib Davanloo (1978a, 1978b, 1979, 1980a, 1980b, 1980c, 1980d, 1980e), founding editor of the *International Journal of Short-Term Psychotherapy,* is based at McGill University in Montreal and has been practicing short-term psychotherapy for more than twenty years. He describes his broad-focused short-term dynamic psychotherapy in the following sentences:

It is a specific kind of dynamic psychotherapy with the aim of replacing the patient's neurotic pattern of behavior. It is based on psychoanalytic principles, using a special kind of focus interview. One focuses on the exploration of genetic [past history] material with the technique of confrontation, clarification, and exploration into conscious, pre-conscious, and the derivative of unconscious material. Dream interpretation and the analysis of transference reaction are used in varying degrees with an active attempt to avoid the development of transference neurosis. (1978c, pp. 23, 25)

Davanloo's Psychodynamic Theory

Davanloo's (1980c) conceptualization of the therapeutic process draws on two sets of interrelated variables, earlier elaborated by Malan (1963, 1976, 1978b, 1979). Malan, in turn, was trained and influenced in Great Britain by Balint (1957; Balint, Ornstein, and Balint, 1972; Hildebrand, 1986), who between 1956 and 1961 was developing the initial ideas of what later came to be called focal therapy. Malan and Davanloo have been in close touch with each other over the years and have been much influenced by each other's clinical work. Malan's ideas have, in fact, had a marked impact on an entire generation of short-term psychotherapists — not only Davanloo, but also Wolberg (Chapter 2), Sifneos (Chapter 5), Mann (Chapter 6), and Gustafson (Chapter 9), among others (see also Gustafson, 1981, 1986). The distinctions that Malan made between the goals and techniques appropriate to time-limited psychotherapy and those appropriate to long-term psychotherapy now constitute part of the foundation of most thinking regarding time-limited psychotherapy.

The Seminal Work of David Malan

The clinical practice implications of Malan's and Davanloo's work are so similar (Migone, 1985) that a separate chapter on Malan will not appear in this volume. But as already noted in the comments about Davanloo's work, both Malan's and Balint's seminal thinking justifies special review. Malan's thinking will be examined here, while Balint's work will be reviewed in Chapter 20 in conjunction with the discussion of brief contact therapy.

Malan (1963, 1976; Keller, 1984) wanted to call his brief therapy *radical* but, warned away from that term by its unfortunate connotations in America, chose the word *intensive* to describe the kind of brief psychotherapy undertaken by his group at the Tavistock Clinic in London and the Cassel Hospital in Richmond. Malan's studies of brief psychotherapy have been based on clients generally seen for between ten to forty sessions — certainly longer than the average number of contacts implied in the term *brief,* and another reason for not devoting more space to his work.

Malan finds himself in strong disagreement with traditional Freudian psychoanalysis, as can be seen in the following pithy paragraph:

> *It needs to be stated categorically that in the early part of this century Freud unwittingly took a wrong turning which led to disastrous consequences for the future of psychotherapy. This was to react to increasing resistance with increased passivity — eventually adopting the technique of free association on the part of the patient, and the role of*

*"passive sounding board," free-floating attention, and infinite patience
on the part of the therapist. The consequences have been strenuously
ignored or denied by generations of analysts and dynamic psychotherapists, but are there for all to see. The most obvious effect has been
an enormous increase in the duration of treatment — from a few weeks
or months to many years. A less obvious development is that the method
has become, to say the least, of doubtful therapeutic effectiveness, a
matter which has received little attention or proper investigation. A further practical consequence is the inability of most psychotherapeutic
agencies to provide sufficient service; with most vacancies filled by long-
term patients, there is little available for new patients who come seeking relief from their suffering. There is, then a hidden disillusion with
this method of treatment, one consequence of which may be called the
"flight into training," a maneuver in which experienced staff give up
practicing therapy to concentrate on teaching others to practice it, entirely ignoring the fact that the methods taught have never been shown
to be effective. (1980a, pp. 13–14)*

Malan's first set of theoretically interrelated variables, which has proven
so useful to Davanloo, has been referred to by Davanloo as the *triangle of
conflict*. This triangle includes the three variables impulse, defense, and anxiety. This triangle represents the classical psychoanalytic formulation of all
symptom formation — an unacceptable impulse generates anxiety, which is,
in turn, defended against. That is, the presence of anxiety signals that there
is some unacceptable impulse that is being denied expression.

The second of Malan's sets of interrelated variables that has been
adopted by Davanloo is called the *triangle of person* and includes significant people in the past (most often parental figures), in the current social
environment (spouse or work colleagues, for example), and the therapist.
The triangle of person can be noted, for example, when the patient's emotions or modes of behavior toward the therapist are similar to those he has
had toward significant people in his past or has toward significant people
in his current life outside of the therapeutic setting.

In the case of each of these three-component sets, meaningful interpretations can link any two components. In the case of the triangle of conflict, connections can be made, as appropriate, between impulse and defense,
between impulse and anxiety, and between defense and anxiety. In the case
of the triangle of person, psychologically meaningful connections can be
drawn between the patient's real or imagined interactions with important people in the past (e.g., parents, siblings) and present, between the patient's past
and observed transference phenomena, and, finally, between the patient's
life in the present outside of the therapist's office and transference phenomena
noted in the office. It is important to clarify the nature of the client's

conflicts in all three settings, but this is somewhat simpler than it sounds because very often the same patterns of anxiety, defense, and impulse occur in more than one setting.

With regard to the clinical aspects of the two hypothesized psychodynamic triangles that have become an important component of Davanloo's formulations, Malan (1976) has suggested that: (1) The triangle of conflict should be explored before the triangle of person, and its major components should be developed in one area of the patient's life before being linked to another area; (2) Within the triangle of conflict, the defense — that is, the most manifest aspect of the triangle — should be interpreted first. The impulse and anxiety components of the triangle can be interpreted together later, with the ultimate goal of identifying the underlying impulses that ordinarily serve as the source of the psychopathology; and (3) Within the triangle of person, the most important aim is to develop useful connections between the patient's past and the observed transference phenomena in the present.

Malan's brief psychotherapy differed from traditional long-term therapy in three important respects. First, it had a limited aim — specifically, to work through a particular conflict or set of conflicts partially and then see what results follow; second, the client understood from the very beginning that the number of sessions was limited; and third, the technique was focal in a remarkably single-minded manner in terms of the agreed-upon therapeutic plan that guided the therapy as a whole. Malan's aim was ambitious — to "*resolve* either the patient's central problem or at least an important aspect of his psychopathology" (1976, p. 248).

The techniques of brief psychotherapy employed by Malan derive quite directly from psychoanalytic principles. That is, Malan sees the strategic aim of psychotherapy to bring into consciousness the emotional conflicts the client is struggling with and to help the client experience and clarify them. Such conflicts are thought of as the result of the anxiety brought about by the unsuccessful or uneconomical use of defenses to ward off an unacceptable impulse or intolerable feeling. Central to Malan's therapy is the therapeutic plan and the correct selection of clients (see Chapter 21). Malan says, "Put briefly, the best way of keeping interpretations focal is to select focal patients in the first place and then to formulate a correct therapeutic plan" (1976, p. 263; see also Courtenay, 1968).

From a tactical point of view, the therapist is constantly acting on the basis of a judgment regarding: (1) which of the components of the impulse-defense-anxiety triad to interpret; (2) in which of the three person settings would it be most therapeutic to examine any component of the conflict triad; and (3) how can the most useful linking interpretations be made between settings. With regard to this view of psychotherapy, Malan writes:

It is the ability to formulate the patient's problem in terms of this kind that gives the therapist the opportunity to exert very considerable control over the course of therapy. . . . Provided the initial formulation is correct, a good patient will follow these moves actively; that is, having received a partial interpretation, he will go on to complete it; and having received one interpretation in the sequence, he will spontaneously lead the therapist toward the next. This is part of what is meant by the "therapeutic alliance." It is the combination of a simple initial formulation, a responsive and well-motivated patient, and a therapist who intuitively understands these principles, that results in focal therapy. (1976, p. 262)

Therapeutic Techniques

To return now to the short-term psychotherapy of Davanloo, his therapeutic techniques are remarkably persistent and confrontive. He himself uses the term *relentless* to describe his approach (1978a), but others have used the terms *remorseless* and even *bullying* (Hildebrand, 1986). Davanloo interprets transference reactions, thus avoiding the development of a transference neurosis that would require additional time to resolve. He challenges defenses. One result of this approach is that most patients experience feelings of anger, along with the defenses that they characteristically invoke in dealing with anger, such as denial, depression, or reaction formation (Migone, 1985). Perhaps because of the confrontive style of therapy employed by Davanloo, patients who are most appropriate are those who have not regressed significantly and who maintain a relatively strong ego.

Davanloo suggests that his brief broad-focused therapy is ordinarily suitable for patients with a predominantly oedipal problem or in whom the focus is loss; patients suffering from long-standing obsessional and phobic neuroses; and, finally and perhaps most remarkably, patients with severe forms of psychopathology and more than one focal conflict. Indeed, Davanloo is very affirmative about the broad applicability of brief psychotherapy. He writes:

I have never been convinced that short-term dynamic psychotherapy has a limited application and is a psychotherapeutic technique useful only in the treatment of mild neurotic cases. Nor have I ever agreed with those who see short-term dynamic psychotherapy as a technique which offers help best to those patients who are unable to deal with their emotional crisis and develop circumscribed neurotic conditions. Such therapy is of great value for this group of patients, but it has always been my conviction that it can be the psychotherapy of choice for patients suffering more severe psychoneurotic disorders of many years' duration, which have paralyzed their lives. (1978a, unpaginated preface)

Flegenheimer (1982) suggests that Davanloo's technique in particular requires that therapists need to be comfortable with their anger and generally in complete control of their feelings. The therapist needs to maintain an emotional neutrality, regardless of what is being discussed, lest the patient "interpret the technique as either sadistic or seductive" (p. 162).

Davanloo's brief psychotherapy tends to average between ten to twenty sessions but has varied from five to forty sessions. He recommends five to fifteen sessions for patients with a circumscribed neurotic conflict, fifteen to twenty-five sessions for patients with multiple foci, and twenty to thirty sessions for patients with severe character pathology. Just as in the case of Malan, these upper limits are substantially above what is ordinarily thought of as time-limited psychotherapy. He has reported, however, that improvement (as assessed by measures of patient's self-concept) tends to increase with number of sessions up to a maximum of about twenty sessions or so. After twenty sessions, therapists may find themselves having lost the focal conflict that serves as the integrating rationale of the therapy and may thus compromise the outcome (Ursano and Hales, 1986).

Davanloo is clearly convinced, however, that shorter brief therapy can be quite effective. In his experience, in successful cases, significant progress occurs in about eight sessions and can be seen in shifts in the patient's interpersonal relationships and in reduction of presenting symptoms. When such progress has been found, it is time to terminate the therapeutic relationship—a process that seems to take place without difficulty.

A Case Example

Box 4-1 presents excerpts from an initial interview that illustrate the persistently confrontive character of Davanloo's approach. The patient is a 29-year-old teacher who complains of depression, chronic anxiety, work difficulties, and disturbed relationships with men that have recently culminated in a breakup with a man she had planned to marry.

Concluding Comments

Davanloo's special contribution to the work of the planned short-term psychotherapist is his resolute and uncompromising fidelity to some of the

---

BOX 4-1 • *Davanloo at Work: An Initial Interview Excerpt*

Therapist: How do you feel about talking to me about yourself?

Patient: I feel uncomfortable. I have never done this before, so I don't really, you know, I feel I don't really know how to answer some of your questions.

T: Um-hum. But have you noticed that in your relationship here with me you are passive, and I am the one who has to question you repeatedly?

P: I know. . . .

T: Is this the way it is with other people, or is it only here with me, this passivity, lack of spontaneity?

P: Yeah. To some extent. I mean. I'm, there are a lot of things hidden, you know. Somebody once described me "like a hidden flower" or something. There are a lot of things about me that I don't think I have ever really, uh, explored that much.

T: Then from what you say you are passive with others. But from what you have told me you indicated that your mother has been a passive person. . . . Going back to yourself, do you see yourself as a passive person?

P: Yeah.

T: You do?

P: In certain situations where I don't feel, when I get involved with a man, I find I tend to take a passive role, and I don't like that.

T: What specifically do you mean by not liking it?

P: I feel upset inside.

T: What is it that you experience? You say, "upset?"

P: Perhaps irritated, something like that.

T: But you say "perhaps." Is it that you experience irritation and anger, or isn't it?

P: Ummm. Yeah. Yeah. I do.

T: You say you take a passive role in relation to men. Are you doing that here with me?

P: I would say so.

T: You "would" say so, but still you are not committing yourself.

P: (long, awkward pause) Well, I don't, you see, I don't know how to, uh,

Continued

BOX 4-1 *Continued*

I don't know about the situation, you know. I don't understand this whole situation, you know, I don't understand this whole situation yet. So I, I am here, and I am a passive recipient or a passive participant. I am not passive, really. I am active. I am participating, but I am—

T: Are you participating?

P: Well, sure.

T: Um-huh. To what extent?

P: (Pause) I am answering your questions.

T: What comes to my mind is, if I don't question you, what do you think would happen here?

P: Well, I might, I might start to tell, I might start something which would indicate, would tell you where I am going. It might be very intellectual, though, because I don't really know, I don't really understand the source of my depression.

T: Um-hum. In relationship with me, then you are passive; and it is the same with all men. . . . How do you feel when I indicate to you that you are passive?

P: I don't like it (the patient is laughing, but it is quite evident that she is irritated).

T: But you are smiling.

P: I know. Well, maybe that is my way of expressing my irritation.

T: Then you are irritated?

P: A little bit, yeah.

P: A little bit?

P: Actually, quite a bit (the patient is laughing).

T: But somehow you smile frequently, don't you?

P: It is inappropriate.

T: Let's look at what happened here. I brought to your attention your passivity, your noninvolvement. You got irritated and angry with me, and the way you dealt with your irritation was by smiling.

P: That is right.

From Davanloo 1980c, pp. 48–50.

most fundamental aspects of psychoanalytic theory. Davanloo treats time-limited psychotherapy as an intellectual task of the first magnitude. His use of the two triangles of conflict and of person as templates for understanding and treating a patient is an impressive example of how to put theory to work, and his insistence on remaining within the great traditions of psychoanalytic theory and practice have served to demonstrate the utility of time-limited psychotherapy that does not compromise those principles.

Davanloo makes virtually unremitting demands on his patients to search within themselves, however difficult the task, and, as he would be the first to admit, his approach to time-limited psychotherapy cannot be tolerated by everyone. The therapeutic encounter must be taken on his terms, which emphasize the cognitive aspects of psychotherapy far more than the affective. But for those patients who can meet his terms, his approach provides an unparalleled opportunity to learn about themselves and to inaugurate significant change based on that learning.

CHAPTER FIVE

Sifneos' Anxiety-Provoking Short-Term Psychotherapy

Overview

Defining Anxiety-Provoking Psychotherapy

The Phases of Anxiety-Provoking Psychotherapy

Therapeutic Techniques

Evaluation of Anxiety-Provoking Psychotherapy

Concluding Comments

Peter Sifneos (1972, 1979, 1981a, 1984, 1985, 1987) distinguishes two general types of psychotherapy whose suitability is determined on the basis of an assessment of the current anxiety level of the client. There is, according to Sifneos, an optimal level of anxiety—if it is too high, it should be reduced in the therapeutic setting; if it is too low, it should be increased. Thus, Sifneos distinguishes between what he calls anxiety-suppressing and anxiety-provoking therapeutic styles. While Sifneos has written about anxiety-suppressing psychotherapy, most of his technical writings have dealt with short-term anxiety-provoking psychotherapy, a form of therapy with which he has been identified since the late 1950s. Sifneos practices at the Psychiatric Clinic of the Beth Israel Hospital in Boston.

Defining Anxiety-Provoking Psychotherapy

Therapy that is anxiety-suppressive seeks to "decrease or eliminate anxiety by use of supportive therapeutic techniques, such as reassurance, environmental manipulation, hospitalization, or appropriate medication" (Sifneos,

1972, p. 45). Therapy that is anxiety-provoking is designed to increase anxiety in order to accomplish its more dynamic goals of emotional reeducation and the enhancement of improved problem-solving skills.

Both forms of therapy may be of varying duration. Sifneos distinguishes between crisis support (anxiety-suppressive therapy generally lasting less than two months), brief anxiety-suppressive psychotherapy lasting between two months and one year, and long-term anxiety-suppressive psychotherapy that might last indefinitely and might most commonly be used to help seriously disturbed clients. Parallel distinctions are made in the case of anxiety-provoking therapy. Crisis intervention is conceived as anxiety-provoking therapy lasting less than two months; short-term anxiety-provoking therapy is conducted in weekly forty-five-minute sessions, and most treatments last between twelve and sixteen sessions (Ursano and Hales, 1986). Psychoanalysis, according to Sifneos, is "anxiety-provoking psychotherapy of long-term duration" (1972, p. 71). Sifneos is primarily identified with short-term anxiety-provoking psychotherapy, and the remainder of this chapter will be devoted to an examination of his ideas regarding this type of therapy.

The Phases of Anxiety-Provoking Psychotherapy

Sifneos divides his psychotherapy into five phases: (1) the patient-therapist encounter, (2) early treatment, (3) height of the treatment, (4) evidence of change, and (5) termination. The first phase involves the building of a therapeutic alliance and the establishment of rapport. Sifneos takes advantage of initial positive feelings in order to interpret, as vigorously as seems necessary, the patient's resistance to getting down to work. During the first phase Sifneos formulates a tentative psychodynamic diagnosis based on a careful developmental history and attention to the nature of the transference relationship as it develops. Sifneos and the patient come to a mutually agreed-upon definition of the problem to be solved, often by some form of negotiation that results in an acceptable compromise. Sifneos summarizes the first phase by preparing a statement outlining the mutually agreed-upon goals and making an assessment of the work that has to be done in order to resolve the core neurotic problem.

During the early treatment phase Sifneos continues to confront the patient as appropriate, particularly in the service of differentiating the adult, realistic aspects of the patient's personality from the magical infantile aspects of his or her personality. Sifneos is careful to limit the degree of regression by confronting the patient and interpreting the positive transference reactions. During the third phase, the height of the treatment, Sifneos focuses on the historical development of the patient's current difficulties, returning to examine the transference when it interferes with acceptable therapeutic progress. Anxiety-provoking questions are used to confront the patient, a process that often produces anger, a reaction that is mitigated by the existence of a continued strong therapeutic alliance.

Sifneos takes a role that is part therapist and part teacher, putting the patient into a role that is part patient and part student. While he discourages lecturing, as the example in Box 5-1 shows, he certainly sees teaching as integral with therapy. The excerpt is from a mid-treatment interview with a 23-year-old female graduate student whose symptoms included anxiety and difficulties in achieving intimacy with men.

BOX 5-1 • *Sifneos as Therapist-Teacher*

Patient: Well, this being or not being friends business—

Therapist: Yes.

P: Well, it is something else. You see, I don't need you as a friend. This is not what bothers me most. I come in here, and I have nothing to offer you.

T: There we are again "offer me something." We went a full circle and got nowhere. Let me recapitulate. There is this feeling of irritation with me for not responding to you for being a "nonstructured nothing." You say you offer me nothing; you cannot get excited if there is no response. Then there is the atmosphere in this room that reminds you of something.

P: (interrupting) Well, if we had something to do. If, let's say, we could eat a sandwich and talk about baseball or something.

T: You mean like going to your father's office and having lunch together? You "feel so important." You remember?

P: I *never* thought of it. I *never* did. Isn't it remarkable!!!

T: How did your father react those times?

P: Well, he was friendly. He complimented me on my clothes. He was very nice. It was then that he used to talk to me about his troubles with my mother. I used to get excited and I would give him advice and stuff like that.

T: And I don't react in the same way.

P: Well, no. You don't respond in the same way. You don't make me feel at ease.

T: This frustrates you. I can see that. But you see, my job is not to make you at ease. My job is to help you solve this problem.

P: I used to enjoy those visits so much! I felt that I could give something to my father, that he needed me, and this made me feel so good.

T: What intrigues me is your emphasis here on having nothing to offer me. What about that?

P: Yes, and this is why the whole thing is confusing, 'cause at these times with my father I felt I had a lot to offer him.

T: But there are other times with your father.

P: (blushes slightly)

T: I think I know what you are thinking.

P: You mean?

T: Yes — the times you were parading in front of your father with no clothes on, when you were exhibiting yourself to him.

P: (blushing crimson) I had nothing to offer him then. Nothing at all.

T: So you see how your feelings from two different times in your life are mixed up and expressed here in reference to me. The episodes with your father in his office occurred when you were fifteen?

P: Sixteen and later on.

T: Yes, of course. The time you were running around with no clothes on was at the age of five or so, at the time of your brother's birth.

P: Yes. And I remember that it happened after my brother was born.

T: So you can see that these feelings really have nothing to do with me personally. Only the situation has revived feelings that have existed a long time ago.

From Sifneos, 1972, pp. 264–266.

During the fourth phase, evidence of change, the therapist tries to determine whether there has been sufficient diminution of the presenting emotional problem so that termination can be considered. Evidence of change comes from four sources — reduction of tension in the interview, reduction of symptoms, changes in interpersonal behavior related to the focal issue, and evidence that the patient can generalize that progress to new situations and new areas. Finally, when the patient and therapist are in agreement that the initial goals have been achieved, termination can take place. The date for termination is set, and the therapist deals with the anxieties associated with the impending ending of therapy. As long as the therapist accentuates the positive gains that have been made, encourages the patient to apply what has been learned to new situations, and resists the temptation to broaden the original focus, termination is generally uncomplicated.

Therapeutic Techniques

The therapeutic concept that sets Sifneos apart from other brief psychotherapists is that of anxiety provocation. Sifneos describes the concept in the following way:

> *Out of a variety of presenting complaints the patient is asked to assign top priority to the one emotional problem which he wants to overcome. The therapist . . . can obtain . . . enough information from the patient to . . . help him arrive at a formulation of the emotional conflicts underlying the patient's difficulty. Throughout the treatment he concentrates his attention especially on those conflicts in an effort to help the patient learn a new way to solve his emotional problem. To achieve these ends the therapist . . . must use anxiety-provoking questions in order to obtain the evidence he needs to substantiate or to modify his formulation. Also, by utilizing confrontations and clarifications, he must stimulate the patient to examine the areas of emotional difficulty which he tends to avoid in order to help him become aware of his feelings, experience the conflicts, and learn new ways of solving his problem. If the therapist is successful in his efforts, he achieves the stated goals of this kind of psychotherapy and is confident that the patient will use this novel experience and these newly developed problem-solving techniques to deal with the new critical situations in the future. (1972, pp. x–xi)*

It will be useful to provide an example of the anxiety-provoking character of Sifneos' psychotherapy. A 25-year-old social worker expressed concern because she claimed to have forgotten what the area of concentration for her therapy was going to be. The ensuing dialogue is excerpted in Box 5-2.

In this example in Box 5-2 the therapist's style is clear—a high level of activity, gentle yet unrelenting exploration, active confrontation, clarification, and interpretation. With regard to overall technique Sifneos characterizes therapist activity as concentrating on areas of unresolved emotional conflicts by the use of anxiety-provoking questions, while at the same time avoiding involvement with deep-seated character defects, such as excessive passivity, dependence, or narcissism. Sifneos focuses on oedipal

BOX 5-2 • *Sifneos at Work: Provoking Increased Anxiety*

Patient: I know that it may be significant, but the funny thing about it is that I cannot remember what we agreed to talk about last week.

Therapist: Why is it funny?

P: I meant it in the sense that it was peculiar.

T: But you used the word "funny." What's so amusing in forgetting what we decided to focus on during your therapy?

P: Well, it must have something to do with wanting some guidance of sorts. If I don't remember, then you will help me.

T: Yet, how can I help you when I don't know as yet why you have the problems that bring you to the clinic.

P: That's true.

T: So, there is a part of you which nevertheless wants me to do something which you know only too well I cannot do. Now, assuming that I tried to tell you what to talk about, how would you feel about it?

P: I'd like it.

T: Part of you would like it, but how would the other part feel? The part that knows that I cannot do it?

P: A little silly.

T: Meaning?

P: (hesitating) That you are a little silly, doing something like that when you really don't know.

T: Precisely! So, wouldn't it be funny then to see your therapist do something silly?

P: In a way, yes.

T: So the word "funny" was used appropriately.

P: I suppose so.

T: Now that we have clarified this point, let's return to your lapse of memory.

P: The funny thing is that I have just remembered what we have agreed to concentrate on during my treatment.

T: There are a lot of funny things going on today!

From Sifneos, 1979, pp. 63–64.

conflicts, and, while he deals with issues of loss, he does not believe that his psychotherapy is as suitable for such preoedipal issues.

Oedipal conflicts have a special place in psychoanalytic theory because their resolution is thought to be related to the consequent strengthening of the ego and the development of the superego, to gender identity, and to the management of feelings of competitiveness. Examples of therapeutic exchanges that maintain the oedipal focus have also appeared in the brief therapy literature. Horner (1985) has described the term *oedipal conflict* in perhaps its most traditional psychoanalytic context as:

> *. . . the wish to either have sexually the parent of the opposite sex or to be the preferred object by that parent. Although some patients may never acknowledge the sexual component of the wish, they can acknowledge the competitive wish to be special. They may also be aware of the specialness inherent in the sexual relationship and be angry that they were unable to compete because of the incest taboo. Along with the wish to be preferred by the parent of the opposite sex is the wish to defeat the rival, the parent of the same sex. In cases of extreme ambivalence, this competitive wish may have murderous overtones. (p. 26)*

In more general terms, Sifneos (1981a) has summarized what is required for short-term anxiety-provoking psychotherapy to be effective. These requirements are summarized in Box 5-3.

BOX 5-3 • *Requirements for Success in Short-Term Anxiety-Provoking Psychotherapy*

1. The delineation of a psychodynamic focus that both therapist and patient agree to investigate.
2. Presence of unresolved oedipal difficulties, problems relating to separation issues, or grief reactions.
3. The establishment of a functional working alliance between patient and therapist.
4. Active use of anxiety-provoking confrontation and clarification.
5. The transference is dealt with explicitly and early.
6. Avoidance of entanglements in pregenital characterological issues.
7. Interpretations based on adequate prior data collection from the patient, particularly linking preexisting relationships with parents and transferred attitudes toward the therapist.
8. Termination of therapy only after tangible evidence of change in neurotic behavior is found.

From Sifneos, 1981a, pp. 47–48.

Evaluation of Anxiety-Provoking Psychotherapy

Sifneos has taken the task of clinical evaluation of his work very seriously, primarily by means of follow-up studies of formerly treated patients. Initially, he reported that fifty patients had been treated by short-term anxiety-provoking psychotherapy and that twenty-one of them had been successfully located between one and one and a half years after the end of their brief therapy. All seemed to have benefited considerably from their treatment. Two additional evaluation studies were reported in 1964 and 1968 (Sifneos, 1968).

Sifneos (1981a) reports that in these follow-up interviews former patients indicate that: (1) they have a clear understanding of the conflicts underlying their difficulties; (2) they have a moderate degree of symptomatic relief; (3) there is a general improvement in their relationships with others; (4) there is a marked increase in their adaptive skills, problem-solving capacity, and self-esteem; (5) their feelings toward the therapist, who is viewed as an educator and friend, are predominantly positive; and (6) there is a feeling of achievement that is attributed primarily to the efforts of the patients themselves.

Concluding Comments

Sifneos believes, perhaps somewhat optimistically, that short-term dynamic psychotherapy "has eliminated, once and for all, several of the clichés or myths about psychotherapy in general" (1981a, p. 79). Among these myths Sifneos identifies the following: (1) Long-term dynamic psychotherapy is the treatment of choice for all neuroses; (2) research regarding psychotherapy, its processes and its evaluation, cannot be done; (3) the transference should not be examined unless it takes the form of resistance; and (4) the only way for the therapist to relate to the patient is by minimal activity.

Sifneos has concluded that by selecting patients who have a circumscribed chief complaint, reasonable ego strength, and high motivation to change (see Chapter 21), by employing active interventions, and by conscientious clinical examination of the therapeutic process and its consequences, short-term anxiety-provoking psychotherapy can be effective not only with patients who have mild neurotic disorders, but also with patients with much more severe problems. He furthermore believes that short-term psychotherapy should be employed with children, with couples and families, with groups, and in psychosomatic medicine. As this volume will attest, these applications are now being actively pursued.

CHAPTER SIX

Mann's Time-Limited Psychotherapy

Overview

Disadvantages of Long-Term Therapy

Theoretical Background

A Case Example

Concluding Comments

The critical word in James Mann's (1973, 1981, 1984, Mann and Goldman, 1982; see also Horowitz et al., 1984, pp. 17–22; Rasmussen and Messer, 1986; Ursano and Hales, 1986, pp. 1510–1511) time-limited psychotherapy is the word *time*. It is time with its many meanings that is not sufficiently understood, and it is the complex feelings toward the passage of time that help make the therapeutic relationship difficult for the client and therapist alike. Mann's work, primarily at the Division of Psychiatry at the Boston University School of Medicine, is based on an insistence that time be faced squarely and that it be used in the service of psychotherapeutic gain.

Mann and Goldman (1982) write eloquently about time:

> *Time is a source of confusion to us, and we express our ambivalence about it in many contradictory ways. Time is everything in our affective lives. Time is a great legalizer, a great teacher, a kind friend, a great leveler, a taskmaster, a liar, a sandpile, money. It is fleeting, out of joint, the only comforter. Father Time is portrayed as an old man with a beard and scythe, whereas immortality is portrayed as a woman. In the unconscious, one finds the origins of the fantasy of immortality in the return to the early mother—to child time. (p. 7)*

Disadvantages of Long-Term Therapy

With the duration of psychotherapy left open, Mann has found that a "well-intentioned sabotage" (1973, p. x) often takes place in clinical settings that are trying to see more clients by shortening the length of treatment. Long-term psychotherapy with insufficiently or inaccurately defined treatment goals, argues Mann:

> . . . *leads to a steady widening of and diffusion of content. This creates a growing sense of ambiguity in the mind of the therapist as to what he is about, and . . . it surely increases the patient's dependence on the therapist. The result is that patient and therapist come to need each other, so that bringing the case to a conclusion seems impossible. (1973, p. x)*

As a consequence, Mann argues that there comes a point in the treatment of patients when time is no longer on the therapist's side.

In an effort to counteract this nontherapeutic effect of time, Mann has experimented with a procedure that might make it possible to be of help to larger numbers of clients. He has established a short-term psychotherapy limited to exactly twelve treatment hours with a fixed ending date agreed to in advance by both therapist and client. It should be noted that not all planned short-term psychotherapists believe this is an appropriate strategy (see, for example, Binder, Henry, and Strupp, 1987). On the other hand, Gustafson (1981) has commented on how the fixed duration of therapy and termination date have influenced the field of planned short-term therapy: "We can get a little feeling for this in our own terms when we consider how psychotherapy has come to mean seeing the accepting doctor and talking endlessly. What a contrast when James Mann . . . tells his patient that 12 sessions will be all that he will need" (1981, p. 85)!

Mann and Goldman (1982) note that all forms of brief psychotherapy implicitly propose a time limit; the words *brief* and *short* have exactly that connotation. They write:

> *The uniqueness of time-limited psychotherapy, beyond the specific limitation of treatment to twelve sessions, lies in the fact that the time limit directly influences the progress and process of treatment, because of the unconscious meaning and experience of time in the course of personality development and because of its enduring role in giving meaning to the past, present, and future* affective *life of each person. (p. 2)*

Theoretical Background

Mann views attitudes toward time developmentally. In childhood, time seems infinite—the future seems forever beyond reach. In adolescence, we discover the limits of time—decisions have to be made, they cannot be put off. The older we get, the more real and inexorable becomes the passage of time. The special paradise of timelessness is the paradise of the child. With maturity comes a growing realization of the limits of time and of the ultimate separation of death that time brings. Mann argues that there is a sense of childlike timelessness within the unconscious of all human beings and that all short forms of psychotherapy revive these complex feelings about time both in the therapist and in the client.

Mann and Goldman distinguish between *categorical time,* the time of the clock and the calendar, and *existential time,* the time that is experienced or lived in. With development and the growth of the sense of reality comes a growing appreciation of categorical time and, later, a growing awareness that time is limited. Life as lived daily includes a fusion of eternal child time and categorical, finite adult time.

Thus, there is a child time and an adult time, and time-limited psychotherapy addresses them both. Mann writes, "The greater the ambiguity as to the duration of treatment, the greater the influence of child time on unconscious wishes and expectations. The greater the specificity of duration of treatment, the more rapidly and appropriately is child time confronted with reality and the work to be done" (1973, p. 11).

The Goals of Time-Limited Psychotherapy

Mann views life as (in part, to be sure) a series of separations from persons, such as parents, toward whom feelings are complex and often con-tradictory. Mann suggests that "it is as though each individual feels that he needed something more of the sustaining object when he was deprived of that object. If only he were able to go back in time to review negotiations with that object so that he could gain what he had not previously" (1973, p. 27). Mann's time-limited psychotherapy is designed to help reduce the negative self-image that arose as a consequence of these separations and losses.

Mann and Goldman (1982) summarize the clinical strengths of their time-limited psychotherapy by suggesting that it is the only brief therapy that aims at both a dynamic and a historical appreciation of (1) contemporary conflicts, (2) current attitudes toward the self, (3) residual childhood wishes toward important figures from the past, and (4) transference reactions toward contemporary figures that derive from this past history.

Selection of the Central Issue

In addition to the setting of a time limit, the other major objective during the start of therapy is identifying which of the patient's problems is to be at the center of the task. At the initial session the therapist attempts to identify the patient's chronic pain associated with his or her self-image and seeks agreement from the client that that theme will be the focal point of the treatment. The issue chosen for investigation is viewed both in terms of its historical as well as its current role in the client's personality. The central issue concerns itself with the patient's self-assessment; it has nothing to do with conflictual interpersonal relationships. The combination of the time limit and the identified central issue brings to the forefront, according to Mann and Goldman, the major private dilemma associated with the human condition — "the wish to merge with another but the absolute necessity of learning to tolerate separation and loss without undue damage to one's feelings about the self" (1982, p. 29).

Mann and Goldman describe the search for the central issue as a search for the patient's chronic pain. In this context they identify the goal of time-limited psychotherapy as to foster a resolution of this chronic pain and, in the process, to change the patient's negative self-image. In selecting the focal issue to work on, Mann draws heavily on psychoanalytic theory of personality and psychopathology. Mann believes that the number of such central unresolved issues is small, and he comments at some length on four such themes — independence versus dependence, activity versus passivity, adequate self-esteem versus diminished or loss of self-esteem, and unresolved or delayed grief.

Examples of such theme statements (Box 6-1) presented to patients by Mann for their consideration all recognize both the effort that the patient has made to effect change in the negative self-image, as well as the failure of that effort.

Phases in Time-Limited Psychotherapy

While not invariably so, Mann has found that the twelve treatment sessions often divide themselves into roughly equal thirds. During the first three or four meetings, there is often rapid symptomatic improvement. Two factors seem to account for this improvement — the patient's optimism, which helps create an unambivalent and positive relationship with the therapist, and a substantial relief of accumulated tension due to the abreaction that takes place when the patient begins to describe his or her troubling feelings and experiences. Mann suggests that this phenomenon can be understood as "consisting mostly in a surge of unconscious magical expectations that

---

BOX 6-1 • *Example of Central Themes as Conceptualized by Mann*

I gather from all that you have told me that the greatest problem facing you at this time is your very deep disappointment with yourself to find yourself as you are at this time in your life. (1973, p. 18)

Your major difficulty is that you feel inadequate and chronically depressed as a result of your need to challenge and to pacify men who are important to you. (1973, p. 20)

Because there have been a number of sudden and very painful events in your life, things always seem uncertain, and you are excessively nervous because you do not expect anything to go along well. (1973, p. 20)

You have always feared that despite your best efforts you will lose everything. (Mann and Goldman, 1982, p. 35)

You seem to be a decent man and you have always tried to please others, and yet you feel and you have always had the feeling that you are not wanted. (Mann and Goldman, 1982, p. 33)

You have devoted yourself so completely to your husband and children, and yet you never lose the feeling that you are inferior and inadequate. (Mann and Goldman, 1982, p. 33)

You have always given of yourself to so many others and yet you feel and have always felt both undeserving and unrewarded. (Mann and Goldman, 1982, p. 84)

---

long ago disappointments will now be undone and that all will be made forever well, as they should have been so long ago" (1973, p. 33).

During the middle phase of the therapy, the client's initial enthusiasm begins to wane. Symptoms can return, and a sense of pessimism about what will be achieved in treatment can be seen emerging. Old hurts are revived. Patients can begin feeling sorry for themselves. In addition, irrational feelings of antagonism, annoyance, and irritation begin to emerge as the specter of termination of therapy begins to loom. These feelings usually conceal strong dependency needs.

During the ending phase of the treatment, the client's reaction to termination becomes the focus of discussion; it is during this last phase that the definitive work of resolution will take place. Separation from the therapist stands in direct symbolic relationship with all previous losses and separations, and resolution of this separation is the key to the therapeutic effect. Because of the importance of helping the patient develop an enhanced sense of adult time, Mann cautions that "it is absolutely incumbent upon the therapist to deal directly with the reaction to termination in all its painful aspects and affects if he expects to help the patient come to some vividly affective understanding of the now inappropriate nature of his early unconscious conflict" (1973, p. 36).

The termination phase, however, continues the exploration and resolution of the central issue identified at the start of therapy and helps patients psychologically differentiate themselves from the therapist and from figures from the past. This process results in a stronger ego, a greater sense of self, and a less punishing superego that at last permits patients to increase their self-esteem, to reduce their sense of guilt, and to feel better about themselves.

Follow-up Contacts with Patients

While Mann and Goldman deliberately make no mention of it during the treatment, they generally conduct a single follow-up interview by phone or letter six months to a year after the termination of therapy in order to learn how the patient is getting along. They report that patients experience the follow-up interview very favorably and have a remarkably accurate recollection of the therapy and of the central issue as formulated by the therapist. Patients appear to be tolerating unpleasurable feelings, such as anxiety, anger, or shame, far better and seem to be more selective in how they deal with these feelings, in contrast with the virtually automatic way they invoked defenses at the start of therapy.

A Case Example

Excerpts from a case presented by Mann and Goldman (Box 6-2) give a sense of what transpires in Mann's time-limited psychotherapy. The case is that of a 32-year-old special education teacher who had taken leave of his job when his assignment to a classroom consisting of five disturbed children provoked extreme classical anxiety—physiological symptoms of perspiration, rapid heartbeat, and a sense of dread and a great "knot" in his stomach. The patient was now involved in a writing and research project that would come to an end in about two months. The patient was married and had two children and appeared to have a good marital and family relationship.

As a child the patient was big for his age and agreed to play football even though he was afraid of violent or uncontrolled behavior displayed by

---

BOX 6-2 • *Excerpts and Comments from a Case of Time-Limited Psychotherapy*

Session 2

Patient: I've been thinking about our meeting last week and I really don't think that the fear of being alone was very prominent in my life. *[I had touched on his fear of being alone and now he was objecting. On the basis of the data, I recognized that his statement was defensive and that inquiry into his objection would be necessary. Perhaps he had had experiences of being alone that should be explored.]*

Therapist: Let's look into that. Were you ever away from home prior to going off to college?

P: Oh, yes. I went to camp from age eight to seventeen—first as a camper and then as a counselor.

T: Tell me what you remember about camp.

P: That's funny, all I can remember is going to the railroad station and then getting off at the town nearest the camp. *[I regard this last statement as corroboration for him and for me that going to camp was indeed a struggle for him.]*

Session 3

[Structure and lack of structure, control and lack of control, are central in the patient's personality structure, and whenever he refers to these topics, directly or indirectly, it is imperative that attention be directed to them.]

T: Tell me what happens when one of the kids becomes uncontrollable.

P: Well, he must be removed physically into a quiet room.

T: What is the quiet room like?

P: It's a padded room, no furniture. There is a small screen in the door, his belt is taken off, and he is left alone.

T: And you know something about what it feels like to be left alone.

P: Do you think it's that that gets at me?

T: What did you do when you were left alone?

P: I would try to get them not to leave me. I would ask them, sometimes I would tell them that my tummy hurt.

T: Did you ever become angry at them?

P: No. I never raged at them or threw things or kicked or spit. *[This is the description, of course, of the uncontrollable children in the classroom.]*

T: The most you could do was to complain that your belly hurt?

P: Yes, but it didn't work.

T: It seems to me that the knot that you have described as coming on in your belly when you are in the classroom is the same knot that you felt when your mother left you in the morning.

P: You mean my body remembers?

Session 4

[And again the subject of control, the meaning of control or loss of control is to be scanned further. The central issue has now been enlarged and more clearly defined.]

T: You become so badly frightened not only when a child loses control in reality but even when you think it might happen. Obviously, the element of control, of self-control, is a very touchy one for you. Tell me about that.

P: You know, I have always been afraid that I might lose control and that I might never come out of it.

T: What do you mean, never come out of it?

P: Go crazy. Yet, something just hit me, there was a time when I deliberately challenged control. In my third year at college, I drove two friends to the big city, stopping at every bar en route. Another time I sky-dived when I was drunk.

T: Do you recall any such challenge even earlier?

P: When I was seventeen I raced a car at a track. I hit a tree and broke my neck.

T: Have you felt any more of this kind of challenge since college?

P: No, not at all. The only way I sometimes imagine myself losing control these days, well, I come home and find a man raping my wife and I kill him. *[The patient has now given a more graphic picture of his attempts to break through the restraints of control, risking his life in the process. It is important to note that these attempts took place in his adolescence, a time when renewed efforts are made to master earlier conflicts. That he tried desperately bespeaks a degree of ego strength and a capacity for change, since an easier solution for him would have been not to struggle but rather to remain passive and restricted.]*

Continued

BOX 6-2   *Continued*

Session 6

[I felt that more aggressive attention must now be turned to the question of the classroom and his return to it. We had now passed the midpoint of the treatment and soon heightened resistance to termination, another abandonment, would increase his anxiety and harden his resistance to returning to the classroom.]

T: Tell me more about your feelings for Mr. Z [a scholar with whom the patient was currently studying and working].

P: You remember that I said he was my guru. He is really a wonderful man.

T: How else do you feel about him?

P: I have a lot of respect for him. I really feel as though he is like a father to me.

T: Then, of course, he would be someone whose approval would be crucial to you?

P: Absolutely. You know I always felt that my father cared but he never showed it. We're closer now than we've ever been. I feel that closeness with Mr. Z and I can't afford to do anything to fail him.

T: Then the appointment to the panel [by Mr. Z] means once more that you dare not allow nine A's and one B.

P: It has to be straight A's.

T: So again, we see your need to be perfect as the only possible way for you to feel that you are approved, wanted, desirable — and since perfection of the kind you seek and need is impossible, there is a built-in guarantee of failure. In fact, your feeling about yourself is that you are a boy among the men. *[The phobic situation (return to the classroom) must be confronted regardless of the kind of treatment. In this interview a degree of pressure was exerted since I recognized that his need for my approval was important to him. Would he fail me and risk my disapproval?]*

Session 7

[The patient reported that he had gone back to the classroom the day before.]

T: Tell me what happened.

P: I felt that I handled the kids pretty well. The only time that I really felt tense was when we had to place an out-of-control kid in the seclusion room.

T: What was that like?

P: Another teacher and I took the kid and we literally had to stuff him into the room.

T: You stuffed him into the room, like in a box, you were very very aggressive.

P: I was, but I felt good about it. I stayed in the class for about three hours and when I left I got rid of it all by busying myself with my other work. As a matter of fact, I had no further thought about it until I was on my way here. . . . I think that I have made pretty good progress here. Do you think that I will need another five years of treatment back at my home base?

T: How many sessions do we have left?

P: I don't know — four?

T: No, five more and not five years. Do you recall the problem that I said you and I would work on?

P: Not at all, no recollection.

T: It was how you feel helpless when you're left alone, and now you are concerned as to how you will manage when I leave you.

P: Oh, yes, I remember it now. *[It was not surprising that the patient indirectly raised the shadow of termination after the sixth meeting. The seventh meeting is one distinct step beyond the midpoint. It is not unlike the experience of being on a two-week vacation: the first week is usually one of total anticipation of pleasure; the beginning of the second week forces the intrusion of the beginning of the end. In the case of the patient, his obsessional adherence to structure and to time would go along with a steady alertness to time. . . . In the treatment situation, his anxiety about the end of our time and his subsequent aloneness forced him into a defensive position of denial. Nevertheless, the pressure of his anxiety was not to be thwarted, so he found himself speaking of the progress he had made (and progress must lead to a conclusion) and then wondering whether he would need five more years of treatment back home. This latter statement clearly indicated his feeling that twelve sessions would not be enough, that he needs more.]*

Session 8

P: Whenever I go to a conference without my wife I will stay up most of the night to avoid going to bed alone.

T: You mean that you will keep busy with friends and colleagues until it is no longer possible to avoid going to bed?

P: That's right. Also, whenever I meet a new person and feel that I resonate with him, I feel that I must let the other person know all about me as quickly

Continued

BOX 6-2   *Continued*

as possible. Then I can read the signals and learn immediately about the future of our relationship.

T: You mean that you expose yourself in certain ways sufficient to be able to watch the reaction of the person and know right there whether he accepts you or not.

P: Yes. I didn't realize what I was really up to until now. It is so important to be accepted.

T: And to feel wanted.

P: I should tell you of a dream that I had. In it Mr. Z offers me a job with him and I grab it. I sell my house back home and I come here. And then Mr. Z takes a job elsewhere and leaves. *[This is a transparent, almost childlike dream. He has found the people he wants to be wanted by and who appear to want him, Mr. Z and the therapist, but his joy will soon turn to despair. I related the feelings in the dream to his childhood experiences as they continue for him even today. I added that we would keep an eye on his reactions now that the time for him to leave Mr. Z and his institution was only two weeks away. All the data relate to the impending termination of treatment as well.]*

Session 9

P: I'm going to ask you again. Will everything fall apart again when I go back home?

T: I don't think you will lose any of your gains. More than that, you are addressing a plea to me not to let you go.

P: I guess that's it. I think I'm ready to look at my feelings about leaving.

T: You and I have come to learn about the many different ways that you have been programmed to react to separation as a result of our work together, and we will have to deal with those feelings in the time that is left before we finish on Friday, July 12.

Session 10

[The patient asks the therapist for a prescription for sleeping pills, indicating that he has a painful back.]

T: Let's talk about it.

P: I slipped handling my boat on Sunday and fell on my coccyx. It hurt and I immediately remembered the pain that I had had when I had multiple surgery for a pilonidal cyst. The pain keeps me from sleeping.

T: A sleeping pill has no effect on pain.

P: From past experience I know that it works for me. I would like a ten-day supply. *[A ten-day supply would bring him precisely to the day of our final meeting.]*

T: Suppose I say no.

P: I'll be angry. Gee, I'm surprised I said that. It came right out. If you don't give me the prescription it will mean you don't give a damn. I could go to the infirmary and get it, but why should I pay twelve bucks for a prescription when you can give it to me.

T: You are asking me for succor. It is your indirect way of responding to my leaving you. If I say no, you become angry and it means I don't care. Yet you are asking me for a ten-day supply, exactly to the day that you leave me.

P: Last week, when I raised the question of transference and you said that I did have such feelings about you, when I was driving away from here I found myself saying that big shot is crazy. And then, maybe he knows what he is talking about.

T: What are your feelings about me?

P: Mixed and strange. I know I'm angry. I say to myself, what has this guy done for me? What have I gotten for the bucks I pay? I'll be glad to save the money. Then I think that I've learned a lot about myself that I never knew before.

T: Do you think that you will miss me?

P: Well, I know we have an agreement that said it would end on a certain date, but I did not at that time expect to feel this way.

Session 11

[The patient again wonders whether he might go back into therapy when he is home.]

T: We've heard this before. You've been telling me that things are in control, so this is your way of saying that you do not wish to separate, to be left, that you want more.

P: I see that. But will things fall apart when I am back home?

T: I know that you do not wish to leave but I believe that you will do very well.

P: I do feel together. I don't feel so tied to Mr. Z and I feel that I will leave him with his respect but without pats on the head, like the little boy looking

Continued

BOX 6-2   *Continued*

for approval. . . . I have thought again about winners and losers. I came to Boston with four goals to be met in seven months. I've done three of them. The other is uncertain and will have to wait for some months. It has never happened before that I could feel good about batting .750 and not 1.000.

T: You remember that nine A's were wiped out by one B. You have sought for perfection in order to be approved, admired, wanted, and that desire could never be met or satisfied because you would simply have to make ten A's every day.

P: I've never been able to settle for less. I marvel at my contented reaction. I've really come to feel very differently about myself over the few months here. I didn't realize when I started what kind of intensity would be created by the time limit and how strongly I would feel about the end. Well, now I have only to deal with leaving you at our last session.

Session 12

[The patient is feeling "high." His work is all done and he was able to sit at his desk and read two books this morning.]

[My suspicion is aroused. Is the "high" that he is feeling evidence of an inability to manage the separation? Is he moving into activity as a means of avoiding feelings that might merge into pathological overactivity?]

T: You read two books this morning?

P: I read that way. It was not a driven feeling. I felt relaxed and I was able to reflect on how many aspects of my professional work have come together in a way that I've never been able to do before.

T: How else have you been feeling?

P: Last night my wife and I had dinner with Mr. Z. Then we went home and I watched TV—something I rarely do. I slept "like a rock" all night and that's not too usual for me either.

T: More?

P: I'm aware that maybe I'm warding off other feelings but I do feel that rather than this being only a termination—for me it is a beginning—a new world of options has been opened to me that I never knew before.

T: I agree with you. Nevertheless, you might be avoiding other feelings. You may feel depressed or angry in the next days and if you do it will have to do with feelings about me.

P: I realize that your approval of me has become important. *[I used this remark to tell him that he has always sought approval, but since I am not in any position to promote him, give him references, or otherwise help his career, his feeling must be based on an old state of affairs. His wish for my approval is really the old wish for parental approval.]*

T: Do you like me?

P: I really do.

T: Then you may feel that since you worked so hard for me, why do I send you away, why do I leave you?

P: I know that I have made great gains and I know, too, about the gap between my head and my gut. Of course, you may have had better patients.

T: Shall I give you an A or A plus?

P: I'm really satisfied with .750.

T: But you see that there is the hint again of your wish for my approval.

P: You know, I've had the feeling of instant cure. I'm suspicious of that.

T: You are not cured. You will run up against these problems again but you will know what they are about and be able to handle them.

P: The compression of time is strange. What seemed so far in the future when we started is now about over.

T: I warn you again that you may feel depressed, or angry, or both, and it will have to do with feelings about me.

P: I think I'm in control. I feel that way, and I'll handle it.

[And we say good-bye.]

From Mann and Goldman, 1982, pp. 63–77.

---

others. He loved a verbal fight, however, and did well in school. To make nine A's and one B in school meant that he was a "loser." His parents were business people and left for work early each morning. He remembered always being afraid of being left alone, and he dealt with his fear by engaging in some kind of activity, often losing himself in reading.

He appeared to be quite obsessional, and any kind of unstructured situation aroused pathological levels of anxiety. The disturbed children in the classroom were uncontrollable, unpredictable, and very aggressive; their behavior precipitated in him the sense that he had been abandoned, he would be rendered helpless, subject to his own uncontrollable rage, and that he would soon be out of control. Mann formulated the central issue in the following words: "Although you are a big man physically and although you are successful in your work, you have long been plagued by the fear of helplessness if you are left alone" (Mann and Goldman, 1982, p. 65). Comments about the therapy (in italics) are those of Dr. Mann.

Concluding Comments

No theorist in the field of planned short-term psychotherapy has thought more about the word *time* than has Mann. In fact, except in a very specific and limited sense, no other theorist seems to have thought much about the term at all. Yet, time is central to the concept of *time-limited* psychotherapy, and its thoughtful consideration has had a significant impact on most short-term psychotherapists. The importance of the concept of time may, in fact, be felt most powerfully by older writers who sense their own time coming to an end. Indeed, the early writing in the field of planned short-term psychotherapy was undertaken by established therapists who were considerably older than the average therapist who would be reading what they wrote.

But the literature contains a good deal of controversy about the wisdom of establishing a specified number of sessions and termination date in advance. Many therapists would like more flexibility regarding those two decisions than Mann's approach provides. Yet, if one is to take Mann's views about both conscious and unconscious aspects of time seriously, then the notion of setting that ending date unequivocally seems quite logical.

Mann's work is an excellent example of what is commonly called clinical research—the careful, often quite detailed, examination of clinical material with an eye toward inductively identifying common phenomena across patients. In this connection Mann's systematic use of follow-up interviews as a way of collecting information on the vicissitudes of the therapeutic process after its formal conclusion is exemplary. The follow-up contact, in Mann's case conducted without prior indication of his intent to do so, provides an excellent way of accomplishing two objectives at the same time—enhancing the effects of the therapy while at the same time enhancing one's understanding of the therapeutic process.

CHAPTER SEVEN

Lewin's Brief Confrontive Therapy

Overview

Theoretical Background

Therapeutic Techniques

A Case Example

Concluding Comments

Karl Lewin's (1970) brief psychotherapy represents the application of a somewhat unorthodox view of the psychoanalytic theory of psychopathology to the process of helping clients quickly understand themselves better. Because the theory and the therapeutic strategy that Lewin subscribes to are inseparable, a review of those aspects of psychoanalytic theory that are most important to Lewin in understanding what takes place in the therapeutic process is necessary.

Theoretical Background

Lewin's therapeutic strategy deliberately concentrates on superego issues — that is, issues of guilt, shame, and conscience, or what has been called psychic masochism (Bergler, 1949). This emphasis is based on the importance to Lewin of the process of introjection, the "process of incorporation of another person, usually a parent, into the child's self, the assimilation of another's personality" (1970, p. 13). Lewin believes that that process begins within the first year of life and that it can continue throughout adulthood. A previous introject can be extruded and replaced, although with increasing age the process becomes more difficult.

How the process of introjection takes place is not well understood. Why some children incorporate a loving, tender, accepting mother, while other children incorporate the cold, disapproving, rejecting aspect of that same mother, remains a mystery. The choice of introject does not necessarily follow the real, objective attitude of that mother. Lewin notes that position in the family can dictate the choice; if the role of the good child has already been filled by a sibling, another child might well become the bad child by introjecting less giving aspects of the mother. Most often the child introjects that view of his mother that he feels he deserves. Lewin suggests that if children are ashamed or feel guilty about aspects of themselves, they are more likely to introject a disapproving, punitive mother.

The importance of the nature of the introject to psychological well-being cannot be overemphasized. Lewin writes:

The presence of a good introject sustains us in times of privation. A good introject constantly replenishes our capacity to give love, to think well of ourselves and of others, and to have an optimistic view of life. It allows us to be alone without the oppression of loneliness. Conversely, the child who does not incorporate, or who ejects that which he previously incorporated without replacement, very likely is schizophrenic, and his loneliness is a terrifying void, regardless of life circumstances. While the child with a good introject is happy within the limits of his actual life situation, experiencing the pleasures of living, the child with a bad introject is in constant psychic pain, suffering in the midst of plenty. (1970, p. 15)

Based on the nature of the introject, shame and guilt can play vastly differing roles in a person's psychological functioning. Shame and guilt can serve constructive purposes for the child with a good introject. Shame, by producing anxiety when children have not measured up to their ego ideal, spurs them to useful action. Guilt, by producing anxiety when children have hurt others, encourages them to do better by them in the future. For the child with a bad introject, shame and guilt serve no constructive purposes and become weapons for self-punishment. Shame nags them with the humiliation of their failure to achieve their ego ideal, and guilt serves as punishment for their wrong-doing. Neither shame nor guilt improves their future actions. Rather, they merely convince them that they are hopelessly bad.

As the reader might anticipate, Lewin sees the principal goal of psychotherapy as countering the client's psychic masochism, the internalized guilt and shame; as exposing and replacing the client's bad introject and disabling sense of right and wrong. The therapist sides with the client's ego, as it were, against the common enemy — a punishing and vindictive conscience. In this process the therapist is active, confrontive, and, if necessary, critical. "Confrontations in brief therapy must be made in such a way that the patient sees them as helpful though painful. The doctor should emerge as a strong figure of assistance who is not afraid of, or repelled by, those traits of the patient about which he comments. The therapist represents both ego and healthy conscience" (1970, p. 37).

Therapeutic Techniques

Perhaps most unusual from the point of view of therapeutic technique is Lewin's handling of negative feelings a client might have about the therapist — that is, toward what is commonly called the negative transference. This one characteristic sets Lewin's thinking apart from that of all other brief therapists (see, for example, Bauer and Kobos, 1987, pp. 176 ff.). Lewin (1970) writes:

> *This method of brief therapy depends precisely on the development of initial negative transference. After all, people get sick from unpleasant feelings — envy, jealousy, greed, and anger — and those will surface immediately, if given a chance. The exposure of the patient's negative feelings toward him enables the therapist to confront the patient with his masochistic response to anger. . . . Almost invariably, patients react to any confrontation with anger, evident to the therapist* [only in the manner in which the patient defends against expressing it openly to the doctor]. *This is the characteristic masochistic maneuver of turning anger inward upon the self. The patient may flush, fall silent, cry, fumble with fingers, clench his fist, or show suppressed rage in some other fashion. At that point, the therapist confronts the patient, not merely with his anger, but with the patient's reluctance to express the anger openly out of fear of antagonizing the therapist, the figure upon whom the patient depends for help in his illness. He is asked, if he has so much conflict about his expression of anger at his doctor, a relatively unimportant stranger in his life, how much worse are his conflicts about his family and loved ones? (pp. 35–36)*

The purposes of Lewin's brief psychotherapy are to restore the clients' functioning, help them understand how their conflicts have led to their self-destructive actions, and to suggest other ways of handling their conflicts. As much as possible, the therapy seeks to replace clients' punitive introjects with less pathological ones. Temporarily, the therapist's model of an introject is offered as a substitute. Success of the therapy depends in part on the ability of the client to accept the substitute. Lewin comments, in discussing the evaluation of his brief psychotherapy, that the results are good and are generally comparable with the results of long-term therapy.

Lewin's book is rich with powerful clinical illustrations. His examples are not verbatim interview transcripts, such as might be made from a tape recording, however, but rather reconstructed interactions based on shorthand note taking. Yet they illustrate very dramatically the ways in which the conduct of the clinical interview follows from the theoretical formulations just described.

A Case Example

In Box 7-1 is an example of Lewin's presentation of his clinical work. The context of this case illustration was the legal requirement, in effect at the

---

BOX 7-1 • *Case Example: Lewin's Brief Confrontive Therapy*

(Miss R.A., a 20-year-old high school graduate, was referred by a gynecologist for evaluation for therapeutic abortion. A very pale, distraught young girl, she barely acknowledged my greeting and slumped into the chair. Her eyelids were puffy, her eyes were blood shot, and her nose was red and swollen as though she had been crying recently and copiously. Her breathing was rather shallow and jerky, and her thin chest heaved spasmodically from what soon appeared to be vain efforts to control her sobbing.)

Therapist: What brought you to see me?

Patient: I don't want to have this baby—I'm going on three months. I can't sleep, I can't eat, I just cry all the time.

T: Tell me about the circumstances of your getting pregnant.

P: I don't care about the person from whom I'm pregnant. I had too much to drink at a party. Usually, we just dance at those parties. I never have more than one drink.

T: What made you behave differently this time?

P: (weeping uncontrollably) I found out the person I was in love with was getting married to someone else. I used to see him a couple of times a week. Tom is twenty-five—he's nice and understanding, a fiberglass laminator. I hadn't wanted to marry right away. I'm too young. I have a sister who married young and she missed out on life. But that isn't the reason he broke off with me. We argued over stupid things that I started. I was too demanding and bossy. Like I expected him to call me at certain times.

T: You recognize that you were driving him away. It sounds like a part of your personality is trying to see to it that you don't get what you want. (At this point she stops crying)

P: I couldn't seem to stop doing it. I knew that I was doing it, I told myself what would happen, but I kept doing it. Then one day he told me that he was marrying the girl he used to go with—that was one week before I got pregnant.

T: How did you feel when he told you?

P: I cried. At first I was angry and then I just didn't care any more.

T: Did you express any anger to him?

P: No. In fact I even forgot that I was angry until right now. All I thought was—just not caring about anything any more.

T: You were angry at him and took it out on yourself. He's not suffering from this pregnancy; you are—look at you! You have the kind of conscience that punishes you for angry feelings. And I suspect it was working on you even before, forcing you to drive him away from you in the first place.

P: Looking back on it, it does seem almost deliberate. I got myself drunk, which I never do, went out with a guy I don't even like after the dance, let him park and have intercourse with me, when I never did that before with anybody. And even drunk I knew he wasn't using any protection, but I didn't stop him. I thought of killing myself so as not to tell my parents. I always wanted to make my father proud of me. We're very close. He was disappointed in my sisters. My mother and father were divorced and both remarried. I'm living with my father and stepmother. I have two sisters, thirty and twenty-seven, two step-sisters, twenty-six and twenty-five, a step-brother twenty and half-brother, sixteen. My mother lives by herself now. She's very sick with a nervous condition. She can't work—she has pains in the head. I was a baby when they were divorced. I don't know anything about that. I lived with my mother and two sisters until I was six. During that time, I visited my father a lot. He had a big house and had lots of toys for me to play with. It was lots of fun. Whatever I wanted was given to me. I moved in with my father when I was six.

T: What made you leave then?

P: I don't know. It was my idea. My father had remarried about two years after the divorce. My mother remarried when I was five. My sisters didn't get along with her husband, but I did.

Continued

BOX 7-1 *Continued*

T: That sounds like more than a coincidence. You'd been mother's baby and then she remarried and a year later you move out for no reason. Is it possible you were jealous of her new husband and the attention he took from you for your mother?

P: I don't remember ever feeling jealous.

T: Have you had any feelings about your having left her?

P: I do feel guilty about her being sick. Maybe I could have helped her if I stayed. My mother's all alone. She divorced again about ten years ago. They didn't get along and my sisters didn't get along with him.

T: I don't know whether this is part of the guilt that makes your conscience punish you, but it could be. Your present predicament also followed someone's getting married, hurting you.

P: I think I'm an awfully nervous person. *[The adjective she used to describe her mother's illness].* I get impatient, like when I'm stuck in traffic. I feel like screaming. Maybe it's my spoiledness, getting what I wanted all the time as a child. Sometimes I'm afraid of ending up like my mother.

T: Your conscience would be pleased with that—it would feel that's your just reward for jilting your mother. You seem to feel disloyal, living a soft life with your father.

P: I was in no hurry to marry. If I found the right guy—I wouldn't settle for just anyone—I planned to marry for security reasons. *[From one foster mother to another.]*

T: You mean some day your father will die and you'll need someone else to take care of you.

P: (flushing) You know, I never considered how babyish and selfish I'm being until I heard you say that. That's exactly what I've been feeling. He's taken care of everything for me. He had to find out anyhow for me to have this pregnancy ended because I'm under twenty-one. He accepted it very well—both my sisters had to get married—but I know I let him down. He expected better of me. But he's paying for everything. I feel guilty about the expense I'm putting him to. *[Notice the double meaning of "he's paying for everything."]*

T: You were angry at what I said, but you're afraid of antagonizing me, because you need the letter. I intend to write it regardless of what you say, so go ahead.

P: I came here feeling sorry for myself. Maybe I needed a good spanking. All right, it did hurt, hearing you say it. I sound like a terrible person. But you didn't say anything that isn't true. I guess it's time I grew up. I'm twenty years old, I shouldn't be a baby any more. I have to do it on my own.

T: I'll write the doctor today. I wonder if you'd mind letting me know how things are with you after you get out of the hospital. You could call or drop me a note.

P: Mind? It's kind of you to care. You've opened my eyes to something I didn't want to see.

From Lewin, 1970, pp. 89–92.

---

time of the interview, for a woman who was pregnant and wanted a therapeutic abortion to obtain a written statement from two physicians that her continued pregnancy would be injurious to her physical or emotional well-being. Lewin believes that the physician who provides the written statement would do the patient a disservice if the request is treated simply as a formality rather than as a therapeutic encounter. Lewin believes that women who do not use or do not insist that their partners use contraceptives and who manage to get themselves pregnant against their conscious will are displaying clear evidence of masochism. He writes:

> *No matter what other neurotic conflicts are being enacted through pregnancy, the need to hurt themselves is paramount. . . . Very likely, their unwanted pregnancy will be only one of the first serious episodes in what will become a life-time of self-destructive acts. Since, characteristically, most of these patients are under thirty years of age, the psychiatrist could conceivably spare them that life-time of suffering were he to confront them with their need to punish themselves before they ruin their lives irreparably. (1970, pp. 88–89)*

In concluding his presentation Lewin returns to the issue of the negative transference. He suggests that the most common reason given by clinicians for avoiding the negative transference is that it makes the rapid resolution that should take place in time-limited psychotherapy far more difficult. Needless to say, Lewin disagrees with this assertion. Rather, Lewin suggests that the negative transference is more typically avoided because it is unpleasant both to therapist and to patient.

Lewin believes that patients can tolerate far more than most therapists think and can understand most therapeutic propositions if they are presented clearly and accurately. Thus, the therapeutic interpretation "You must be very upset that you want to injure your brother in a fit of jealousy," a proposition that recognizes the feeling of guilt as well as of conflict, is far more acceptable than "You hate your brother." Similarly, while the interpretation "You think I'm stupid" will probably lead nowhere, the alternative "You must feel very badly that the person you've come to for help seems so inept" can lead to a continuing productive therapeutic relationship. In that relationship, patients can come to grips with their conflicts as well as their guilt and can learn that it is possible to change their feelings about another person and that in the meantime it is possible to dislike someone and still work with him or her.

Concluding Comments

Lewin's work is absolutely unique in the writings about time-limited psychotherapy. His ideas about psychic masochism, about the role of the superego in making people ill, about the importance of the bad introject, and about brief psychotherapy that can help the patient come to grips with these issues are of paramount importance in enriching the clinician's alternative views of psychopathology and its brief treatment. It is hard to find another orientation to time-limited psychotherapy that draws so productively and so uncompromisingly on a specific and somewhat narrow theory of personality.

The psychoanalytic concept of the introject helps us understand enduring personality traits of optimism or pessimism, as well as many aspects of character structure. Lewin uses these concepts to identify the most important purposes of his time-limited psychotherapy—to counter psychic masochism, to extrude the bad introject, and to temper a vindictive and overly punitive conscience.

These more stable aspects of the person are the ones most therapists think of as unusually difficult to modify; yet Lewin deals directly with these character issues. Reading about his theoretical orientation and examining his case examples lead one to be impressed with the considerable effect his approach has with what might commonly be thought of as very demanding and difficult patients.

CHAPTER EIGHT

Bloom's Focused Single-Session Therapy

Overview

The Effectiveness of a Single Therapeutic Session

Focused Single-Session Therapy

Therapeutic Techniques

A Case Example

Concluding Comments

Single-session episodes of care are far more common than most mental health professionals realize. Phillips (1985a) has noted that about half of the patients who come to a clinic do not come back again at that time. They may come again months or years later or may go to another clinic, but a very large minority of clinical contacts take place in a single session. Similar findings have been reported in many different clinical settings (Bloom, 1975; Ewalt, 1973; Fiester and Rudestam, 1975; Hoffman and Remmel, 1975; Jacobson et al., 1965; Kogan, 1957a, 1957b, 1957c; Littlepage et al., 1976; Reed, Myers, and Scheidemandel, 1972; Spoerl, 1975; Sue, Allen, and Conaway, 1978; Talmon, 1990). Single-session episodes of care seem almost as common in university mental health facilities as in community agencies (Dorosin, Gibbs, and Kaplan, 1976; Glasscote and Fishman, 1973; Sarvis, Dewees, and Johnson, 1959; Speers, 1962).

Somewhat lower figures have been reported from Great Britain regarding the frequency with which single sessions of psychotherapy take place (Johnson, 1973a, 1973b). In the National Health Service, mental health care or consultation is provided upon referral from a primary care physician or other first-line health care worker (e.g., community psychiatric nurse or social worker). About 20 percent of patients referred to mental health professionals are seen only once and are then discharged back to their primary care physician or other referral source.

The Effectiveness of a Single Therapeutic Session

Not only is the frequency of single sessions of therapy underestimated, but, more importantly, their therapeutic impact appears to be underestimated as well. Such encounters appear to have positive consequences, whether their primary objective is therapy or evaluation, and as Rubin and Mitchell (1976) reported, interviews whose primary purpose is research may have substantial clinical impact on subjects as well. Should the apparent effectiveness of single therapeutic sessions be substantiated in additional empirical research, the policy implications of such findings would be quite profound.

Clinical assertions regarding the effectiveness of single-session therapy appear from time to time in the literature. Here are some examples:

> *There is a tendency to overlook the fact that a* single interview *can have beneficial therapeutic consequences. . . . Even when further interviews are available, they may not be needed. (Barten, 1971, p. 17)*

> *Even patients who have only one visit are under certain circumstances considered treated. Therapeutic intent is present from the start in a conscious and systematic way, with no formal separation of treatment and diagnosis, and each hour is considered as if it may be the last treatment opportunity. (Jacobson et al., 1965, p. 1179)*

> *Clearly, psychiatrists who undertake consultations should not automatically assign patients to long-term psychotherapy or even to brief psychotherapy, but should be aware of the possibility that a single dynamic interview may be all that is needed. (Malan et al., 1975, p. 126)*

> *If a patient is seen, even for a single interview, it should be a therapeutic experience. . . . Psychiatrists are accustomed to a passive therapy lasting many months, perhaps several years. But "brief psychotherapy" is brief only to the psychiatrist. Except for those sophisticated in the ways of psychoanalysis, most people have never had even a single personal, intensive, interrelated interview with a doctor. (Lewin, 1970, pp. 49, 69)*

> *Treatment begins in the first interview, and the majority of work, in fact, may often be accomplished at that time. There are occasions when the client feels better after one session, and if this happens, the therapist*

need not feel like a failure for not involving him in continued treatment. (Hoffman and Remmel, 1975, p. 262)

At times, however, the therapeutic impact of the evaluation or of the first interview is such that there is no need for further psychotherapy, because in reality the patient's problem is actually being solved. (Sifneos, 1979, p. 70)

An interview format has been described that structures and guides the physician in conducting a single-session family interview. Based on established principles of medical interviewing and family systems theory, this format is intended to be useful to both experienced physicians and those in training. In the author's experience, this format has been helpful in the resolution of family difficulties and in the enhancement of the family physician's repertoire of skills. (Erstling and Devlin, 1989, p. 560)

In addition to these assertions, a small number of successful single-session therapy case histories (sometimes including verbatim transcripts of portions of the interview) have appeared in the literature. In chronological order these case histories include Freud in the 1890s (Breuer and Freud, 1895/1957, pp. 125–134), Tannenbaum (1919), Groddeck in 1927 (Groddeck, 1951, pp. 90–95), Reider (1955, pp. 116–118), Kaffman (1963, pp. 223–225), Rosenbaum (1964, p. 511), Gillman (1965, pp. 603–604), Seagull (1966), Lewin (1970, pp. 88–93), Oremland (1976), Davanloo (1978b), Scrignar (1979), Sifneos (1979, pp. 70–73), Bloom (1981), Springmann (1982), Sifneos (1984), Shulman (1989), Powers and Griffith (1989), and Talmon (1990).

Such assertions and case histories do not, of course, substitute for more objectively conducted empirical research studies. A small number of such studies have been reported, however, and they uniformly support the conclusion that a single interview can have significant therapeutic impact.

For example, Talmon (1990) reported that more than three-quarters of 200 patients whom he had previously seen only once reported that they were improved or much improved. Based on this observation, Talmon, along with two colleagues, attempted to conduct single-session psychotherapy with sixty randomly assigned adults who appeared for noncrisis routine intake appointments. The three therapists differed substantially in their general approaches to psychotherapy, and the patients were a very heterogeneous group in terms of severity of presenting complaint, race, ethnic background, age, and education. Between three and twelve months later, fifty-eight of the sixty patients were reached by telephone for a follow-up interview conducted by someone other than the patient's therapist.

Of the fifty-eight patients who were contacted, thirty-four (58 percent) were, in fact, seen only once. That is, in these cases patient and therapist mutually agreed that no additional appointments were necessary. Of the thirty-four patients seen only once, 88 percent reported that they were either improved or much improved—a figure slightly and insignificantly greater than among the twenty-four patients seen more than once (see also Chick et al., 1988; Chapman and Huygens, 1988; Edwards et al., 1977; Getz, Fujita, and Allen, 1975; Malan et al., 1975; Zweben, Pearlman, and Li, 1988).

Focused Single-Session Therapy

Focused single-session therapy (Bloom, 1981) builds on this evidence by creating, examining, and evaluating encounters designed to provide a significant therapeutic impact in a single interview. The theoretical orientation of focused single-session therapy is psychodynamic. While in a sense the objective of focused single-session therapy may seem outrageous, it is not greatly different from the ways that more traditional time-limited psychotherapists describe their objectives. For example, Strupp and Binder (1984) write: "We propose that each session be viewed as a minitherapy, with palpable progress as its aim" (p. 304). Butcher, Stelmachers, and Maudal, in their overview of crisis intervention and emergency psychotherapy, write: "Every crisis psychotherapy session should be conducted as though it may be the last contact with the patient" (1983, p. 591).

Most of my experience in focused single-session therapy has occurred in our local community mental health center, where, for a few months at a time, I spent one-half day per week seeing patients who were referred to me. There have been two series of such patients. The most important difference between the two series was the length of the appointments. In the first series the appointments were scheduled for fifty minutes. In the second series I decided to make up to two hours available for each interview. This change was initiated because I was often unable to limit the intervention to one session in the first series. In fact, I saw about half of the patients in the first series for two separate interviews. In the second series all cases were terminated after a single session that usually lasted from between sixty and eighty minutes.

After introducing myself to the patient, getting the patient's permission to record the interview, and explaining my volunteer status at the mental health center, the contractual agreement I made with each patient was that I would try to be as helpful as possible during the interview. If, at the conclusion of the interview, we both felt that another appointment was necessary, we would schedule it for the following week. If not, I would give the patient my card and invite him or her to call me if there was a need to get in touch with me for any reason—with a problem or a progress report, for example. Finally, I said that if the patient did not contact me in three or four months, I would call to see how he or she was getting along. In this very primitive type of evaluation, I have learned that nearly all found the intervention helpful, are doing well, and have not sought additional professional help.

Therapeutic Techniques

The examination of focused single-session psychotherapy reveals that a number of recurring technical principles are particularly important in the therapeutic process. While many of these principles are not dramatically different from those that might be identified in time-unlimited dynamic psychotherapy, their importance in short-term psychotherapy seems unusually striking.

The principles divide themselves into two major categories: (1) those that play a role in helping patients uncover something significant about themselves and (2) those that play a role in starting a therapeutic process that can continue after the interview has ended.

Uncovering New Material

Identify a Focal Problem
I try to identify a piece of psychological reality that is pertinent to the patient's presenting problem, below the patient's initial level of usable awareness, and yet acceptable to the patient in the form of an interpretation or observation. In doing so I am careful not to focus too early or foreclose too quickly. The success of the session seems to depend on my ability to identify and focus on one salient and relevant issue. As has been observed elsewhere in this volume, the briefer the psychotherapy, the greater the need to focus on a limited number of issues (see, for example, Bauer and Kobos, 1987, pp. 157 ff.).

The focal problem is sometimes issue-oriented and sometimes process-oriented. Thus, a patient may present a problem that seems to be related to something more fundamental and less obvious. For example, a patient may come in complaining about his marriage and leave with some beginning realization that his own low self-esteem is making it hard for him to decide whether to try to save his marriage. Or a patient may come in complaining about her lack of progress in graduate school and end up being more aware of her anger toward her parents because of their lack of support for her professional aspirations. In these cases the goal of the therapeutic encounter is to help patients become more aware of some aspect of their cognitive or affective lives.

In contrast, other patients may never have had the opportunity to share their feelings about themselves with other people. These patients can profit from the opportunity to do so in the therapeutic hour, not only because of the positive effects of that experience, but also because the process can serve as a model for how to talk about themselves with others.

The concept of a salient issue is similar to French's notion of a focal conflict (see Balint, Ornstein, and Balint, 1972, pp. 10–11). French distinguished between what he termed a *nuclear* conflict, that is, a dormant and repressed conflict originating during crucial developmental periods in early life, and a *focal* conflict, by which he meant a preconscious derivative of these deeper and earlier nuclear conflicts, which is able to explain much of the clinical material in a therapeutic interview.

A related concept can be found in the work of Balint (Balint, Ornstein, and Balint, 1972), who used the term *focal psychotherapy* to mean therapy with a focal aim (see Chapter 20). The aim, according to Balint, could be psychodynamic, that is, to interpret a specific conflict. But it could also be interpersonal, that is, to bring about a specific kind of interaction with the therapist that could lead to a new kind of mastery for the patient. Finally, the aim could be existential, that is, to help the patient confront and bear previously unbearable feelings (see Gustafson, 1981, p. 122).

I have no reason to believe that there is only one correct focal issue in working with a particular patient. There are many ways of being helpful to a patient during a therapeutic interview. What is important is to develop a sense of how the patient is in the world and what processes can be started that can make a difference (see also Grand et al., 1985, pp. 131 ff.).

Do Not Be Overambitious

I try not to do too much. If I can find just one issue, just one idea, that is useful to the patient, the intervention can be a successful one. My experience, from listening to both my own interviews and those of others, is that it is hard for patients to make real use of more than two or three ideas in a single interview. Consequently, the choice of which ideas to elaborate on when exploring an issue is very important. But, in addition, it is important to keep the ideas simple. My personal rule of thumb is to try to formulate any comments I make in ten words or less.

What seems absolutely counterproductive in focused single-session psychotherapy is to leave the patient reeling from fifteen or so different interpretations, however accurate the interpretations might be. In contrast, to leave the patient sobered by the power and salience of a single observation is quite a different matter. A patient can chew on that observation for weeks and continue to make use of it long after the interview is over. But the more interpretations one offers, the greater the likelihood that the patient will dismiss the entire interview as useless, even though the patient may have a nagging feeling that there might have been something to these interpretations if only he or she remembered and understood them.

Be Prudently Active

Most people who write about planned short-term therapy seem to agree that it requires a higher level of activity on the part of the therapist than is typically reported in time-unlimited psychodynamic therapy (see, for example, Bauer and Kobos, 1988, pp. 149 ff.). I too have found it useful to be more active than I have been accustomed, but active in specific ways, and primarily during the latter half of the interview. I am not more active, certainly not early in the interview, if activity level is measured by how many words I utter. I generally ask questions rather than make statements. I do not make speeches or lecture. I do virtually no self-disclosure. When I do ask questions, I avoid those that have yes or no answers. When appropriate, I give information, but in the context of the patient's presenting problem, and I keep it simple. I use the patient's language but try to make sure that I understand what is meant by the key words and phrases he or she uses. Helping patients understand themselves requires that we learn their language, that is, what they mean by the words they use. Balint (Balint, Ornstein, and Balint, 1972) once described being supervised by Max Eitington; he remembered Eitington saying to him, "Every new patient must be treated as if he had come directly from Mars; and as no one has met a Martian, everything about each patient must be considered as utterly unknown" (p. 126). During the first half or so of the interview, the real risk is that the therapist can talk too much, can be too active. Even during the last part of the interview, it is important to be economical with the words you use, in order to leave the primary responsibility for communication with the patient.

To the extent that activity is an internal cognitive process, it is certainly important to be active. I begin the interview knowing nothing about the patient and have relatively little time to try to figure out a way to be helpful. That challenge requires a good deal of effort and is what can make time-limited psychotherapy very hard work. Thus, the higher level of activity is measured by internal intellectual and strategic thought rather than by who holds center stage for the longest period of time. Migone (1985) makes a similar point when he notes that "what is important in dynamic psychotherapy is not to establish whether a technique is active or passive, but to observe, on the one hand, which interventions are done and which are avoided, and, on the other, what meaning they have for the patient" (p. 622).

Explore, Then Present Interpretations Tentatively

In my interpretations I try to do all the necessary exploration first and then tentatively present an idea in such a way that it is persuasive yet may be disagreed with without jeopardizing my potential effectiveness. I say something like "Do you think it is possible that —"; or "Have you ever wondered why —"; or "I wonder if —".

It is easy to move too quickly in time-limited psychotherapy. I have become increasingly aware that it is not necessary to rush, even when there is very limited time available in the therapeutic encounter. There are many steps in getting an idea from my head into the patient's head, if the idea is to be a useful one. For example, before dealing with why an obviously depressed patient may be depressed, it is necessary to establish that the patient is aware of being depressed. In turn, that may mean helping the patient discover that he or she is sad, blue, down in the dumps, or whatever label the person is willing to tolerate. And sometimes, before patients can consider the possibility that they feel sad, they have to come to accept the more elementary possibility that they have feelings of any kind.

Encourage the Expression of Affect

I encourage and explicitly recognize the expression of affect and use its expression as a way of pointing to important life events or figures — "It's okay to cry"; "That really upsets you, doesn't it"; and so forth. Similarly, when it seems timely, I point out incongruities in affect: "You're laughing, but there doesn't seem to be anything to laugh about." In my experience with focused single-session therapy, I haven't found any more effective technique than the explicit and accurate recognition of the feelings that the patient is carrying around.

These feeling states — whether of sadness, anger, frustration, disappointment, loneliness, or desperation — are usually easy to recognize and label, and in my experience identifying them often has very salutary consequences. In these instances the ability to be empathic has an enormous payoff. I have learned by listening to the tapes of my own interviews and those of colleagues to expect the appearance of new and important material immediately after an accurate, sincere, and timely empathic statement on the part of the therapist (see also Havens, 1986).

Keep Track of Time

There is a tempo, a pacing, to an interview. When two hours are available, there is enough time so I do not feel rushed. Yet, I have to be aware of the passing time and keep planning how to use it. Sometimes I make a few notes to myself, jotting down topics I want to make sure to talk about. More often, I don't need to keep notes, but either way it is important to estimate how much time will be needed to discuss a particular topic and to make sure that there is a reasonably good match between the time that is needed and the time that is available.

In addition to the question of making sure of the availability of time, there is also the issue of the phases through which the interview passes. I have begun to think about the introductory material, the middle identification and development of important themes, the planning period, and the gradual closing of the interview. It is something of an exaggeration, to be sure, but in a way I think about minutes the way I used to think about hours.

Similarly, I tend to judge how much or how little anxiety patients bring with them to the interview and how much seems to be generated by the interview. I act accordingly, now exploring in a way I know will raise anxiety, now modulating the anxiety, now introducing humor, now being very serious, all this in an effort to keep the interaction at its optimal level — enough anxiety to ensure progress but not so much as to be disabling.

Keep Factual Questions to a Minimum

I avoid collecting demographic information or doing a traditional mental status examination. It is my experience that the answers will nearly always be forthcoming without my having to ask the questions. I rarely ask a patient's age or number of siblings or information about parents or children. Asking such questions can be intrusive, and the most important information will emerge in the normal course of the interview. Sometimes, however, it is useful to ask for identifying information as a way of reducing a momentarily excessive level of anxiety or in order to change the subject deliberately.

Except for these occasions, the quest for demographic information about the patient and significant people in the patient's life seems a poor use of time. I am nearly always sorry when I ask for such information, since it seems to produce so little useful data.

Do Not Be Overly Concerned about the Precipitating Event

Focused single-session therapy is not crisis intervention, so I feel no necessity to identify a crisis or event that precipitated a patient's coming to the mental health agency. In many cases, patients seem not to know exactly whey they came in. So I simply begin an interview by asking, "What can I do to be helpful?" The patient has come in because something is wrong for which help is needed, not because he or she has a regular appointment at that time every week. Since the patient has inaugurated the therapeutic encounter, the therapist has every right to expect the patient to get to work, to describe the problem, and to begin moving toward its resolution. No interview has more leverage in this regard than the first interview, and that leverage is further enhanced by the fact that both patient and therapist know that it is likely to be the only interview.

Avoid Detours

I have had to learn to avoid attractive detours and to remain single-minded about what I am trying to accomplish. There are numerous occasions in every intervention when I find myself wishing I could explore some little phrase for just a few minutes, but such diversions have nearly always turned out to be errors. Initially, of course, I have no idea where I am heading, so I keep all my options open. I try to narrow the domain of inquiry in proportion to what I am learning about the patient, and I do not single out a particular issue or conflict to concentrate on until I have every reason to believe that it is an appropriate target for investigation and clarification. All this means that not only is there no time to explore side issues, but that such exploration detracts from the potential effectiveness of the therapy.

Do Not Overestimate a Patient's Self-Awareness

Finally, I am continuing to learn not to overestimate how much patients know about themselves. Patients may be totally oblivious of something about themselves that seems perfectly obvious to me and would, I believe, be perfectly obvious to everyone who knows them. I have had patients scream at me that they are not angry and tearfully tell me that they are not sad. While patients in one sense are experts on what is going on inside them, they are often unable to label, acknowledge, or use that knowledge effectively. Increasing a patient's useful self-awareness, even in only one critical area, can have an important impact on the adequacy of his or her functioning. In working toward that objective an accurate appraisal of what patients do or do not know about themselves is critically important.

Starting a Therapeutic Process

Use the Interview to Start a Problem-Solving Process

I try to identify important unresolved issues and the figures in the patient's life pertinent to those issues and to start or encourage a process of getting some of that unfinished business taken care of. "Have you ever told your mother that when you were a little girl you used to be so frightened of her?"; "Have you ever talked with your sister about that?"; "Do you think your father could shed some light on why you used to do that?"; "Does your mother know how upset you are about her divorce?" In a way this effort gives the single session some increased longevity by attempting to internalize a process that can continue for a period of time.

It is important to identify the types of unfinished business that can be finished. Two judgments have to be made. First, what myths or false beliefs do patients carry around regarding themselves and important figures in their lives? Second, can additional experiences with these important figures convert those myths or beliefs into a less distorted appreciation of reality? In a way this strategy is a kind of behavior modification. The repertoire—talking, sharing, questioning—exists. It need only be explored with appropriate targets.

Do Not Underestimate Patients' Strengths

I think of the therapy session as having the potential for breaking through an impasse in the patient's psychological life, so that the patient can resume the normal process of growth and development. I count on patients' abilities to work on an identified issue on their own, particularly if I can be helpful in identifying what that issue might be. I count on patients' ego strengths and on their abilities to mobilize those strengths.

Trying to identify an impasse in the patient's life is an intellectually and technically challenging task and is what makes focused single-session psychotherapy so exciting. It is as if I am trying to answer the question "What have these patients failed to understand about their lives that could make a difference in how they are conducting themselves now and how they might manage their lives in the future?"

Patients find their way to the mental health center all by themselves, most of them are holding down jobs, and they are generally able to manage a major part of their lives without help from others. The purpose of the psychotherapeutic encounter is to provide significant help in a useful way at a crucial time, and to do it as quickly as seems appropriate.

Help Mobilize Social Supports

Some of the important people in the patient's life may play supportive roles. Others may not currently but could do so if asked. The research literature on the positive effects of a strong social support system in minimizing the negative consequences of stressful life events or chronic stressful life circumstances is so persuasive that it seems critically important to encourage the patient to mobilize available social supports wherever that is possible.

Some family members or friends may potentially play a sounding board role. Others may have information that the patient may not have, and they may willingly provide that information if asked.

Educate When Patients Appear to Lack Information

Therapists can easily assume that patients know more than they really do about psychopathology, psychotherapy, or factors related to their own particular disorder. If therapists remain alert for evidence that a patient lacks pertinent factual information, they can be helpful by providing that missing information in a sentence or two. Lectures or extended comments are rarely helpful, but a pithy brief pertinent statement can often be just what is needed. Some patients, for example, may not understand that some disorders are genetic, or how stress can affect the body, or how different varieties of child rearing have consequences for children's development. A strategically placed factual comment or suggestion about something the patient might profitably read can often serve as a useful supplement to the therapeutic process.

Build in a Follow-up Plan

The development of a plan for problem solving ties in with the follow-up procedure I have developed (see Malan, 1980b). If the patient does not call me following the interview, I call the patient. The plans we made or talked about for dealing with unfinished business can be one of the matters discussed in the brief follow-up conversation. The conversation is not a request for a recital of accomplishments, nor does it attempt to instill a sense of obligation in undertaking a process that the patient may not be ready for. But it can be couched in terms of, "Did it make sense to you to try to do what we talked about?" If the patient indicates that it did, we can talk about what that experience was like and what the patient learned. If not, the patient can be reminded that finishing that unfinished business can be something the patient can keep in mind for the future, whenever the time seems right.

A Case Example

In order to provide an example of the clinical process that takes place in focused single-session psychotherapy, the annotated transcript of the beginning eleven minutes and the final twelve minutes of an eighty-minute interview is presented in Box 8-1, along with a transcript of portions of the telephone follow-up conversation conducted four months after this interview

---

BOX 8-1 • *Excerpts of a Single-Session Psychotherapy*

Therapist: Tell me what I can do to be helpful.

Patient: Well, I don't know. I didn't want to come here, but my girl friend told me I should come here and do something. But I'm not sure what to say now. I had it all planned out. (pause) I don't know what to say now. *[The patient has rehearsed what he wants to say—that seems a positive sign to me because it indicates that the patient thought that the appointment was important enough to prepare for it. But he has forgotten what he rehearsed. So he is likely quite ambivalent about being in the mental health center. I will have to be careful.]*

T: Take a sip of coffee.

P: (after taking a sip) Um, let's see. I guess I have a lot of stuff built up inside of me and I don't have anybody to talk to. I get tired of talking to some people, unless they're strangers. I don't know if that's normal or not. And, I've been under a lot of pressure lately, both at work and with, with her and another girl. I'm real indecisive. I don't know what the hell to do with myself here, and, I don't know what else to say. *[We are off to a very shaky start. This patient is clearly reluctant and uneasy about coming to the mental health center and talking about his difficulties even though he knows he needs to. I have to get him engaged in the process of talking about himself and my potential virtue is that I am that "stranger" he needs to talk to—his word that I file away to be used later when and if it is needed.]*

T: Why don't you tell me a little bit about yourself.

P: You mean what do I do? (therapist nods) I work in a gun shop as a gunsmith downtown. I live by myself in a house. A three-bedroom house for two hundred bucks a month in Boulder is pretty good.

T: It certainly is.

P: (pause) I've been going out with this girl for quite a while, less than a year, but it's been quite a while. And, let's see. We've had a good relationship and stuff. *["Stuff" is a generic term that the patient uses as a shorthand for inner tension. I file that word away too.]* And, oh, about a month ago, this old high-school girl friend of mine stopped by for a week, or for five days. And I told my other girl friend, "Oh, there's nothing to worry about, you know. We're just old friends. We've always been friends." She's somebody I can talk to. And a much different kind of relationship developed than what I ever thought, whatever, either one of us had ever thought. I got in big trouble with my girl friend here in Boulder. And, she's going to break up with me and stuff. *[There's that word again.]* And I didn't want that, because this other girl lives in _____ and I didn't want that, yet I'd like to be able to see this other girl any time I want it. And, I don't know. I just don't know what to do as far as that, and then at work I feel like, well, this is our busy time of year, because it's hunting season. And I get lots of pressure to get stuff done. And, I don't know, for a while here, somehow I feel like the two guys I work for are going to get rid of me after hunting season for some reason, just by the way they act. One of the guys I've known for about ten years, and he just doesn't even hardly talk to me any more. I don't like that, because I like where I work a lot, because it's a real small shop, and it's friendly. Everybody's got time to shoot the shit, but, it doesn't seem like we have it any more. Like I say, maybe I shouldn't be here, because maybe I've just got to thrash things out in my head. But the only way my girl friend would stay with me is if I came to see someone. *[This is a fine opening statement from this man who is not sure he should be talking with me at all. In spite*

Continued

BOX 8-1 *Continued*

of the fact that he isn't sure he should have come to the interview, he does lay out his problems. But, for the moment, he is there only because his girl friend has insisted. I can't help noticing the parallels between his descriptions of his work situation and his home situation, even though there are two entirely different casts of characters. Thus it could be that it won't make any difference whether we talk about his home or work situation. Since the patient returns to the situation with his girl friend, I choose to return to that theme. Again, the patient seems to be saying that he can be helped if he can do during the interview what he ordinarily doesn't do — "thrash things out" in his head.]

T: What do you think she was thinking when she said to go to the mental health center? *[This can be a very difficult question for someone who is not psychologically minded, since it requires that this patient put himself inside the head of another person and try to figure out that other person's thought processes. The question, then, is somewhat risky, but provides a good test of this patient's psychological mindedness and willingness to take the position of another person.]*

P: Oh, she said, "At least talk to somebody." (pause) Well, she told me she, let's see, she told me that I didn't know what I really wanted, and I got to thinking about that and I guess I don't. And I think the thing that kicked it off was when this girl friend of mine from _____ was over, I knew my girl friend in Boulder was going to come over one night, and she caught us in bed, and I knew she was going to come over. It was like I wanted to get caught, but I didn't want to get caught, because it was a big thing. And then last week she found a letter I wrote to this girl in _____. And I had it in my daypack for over a week and a half. I never sent it, and I know she always goes in there. So maybe I want to, I don't know, maybe I do want to break up with my girl friend in Boulder. I don't know. I got a bunch of other pressures, too. I found out yesterday she's pregnant. I had known that, I guess, for a couple of weeks. (pause) So you see, maybe I shouldn't be here. Maybe I should just sit back and think stuff out, but, *[The patient does fine with my question, and continues to present new material. We learn two important additional pieces of information. First, the patient clearly wanted to precipitate the crisis he is in by virtually arranging to get caught; and second, his girl friend is pregnant. He certainly does have a lot to talk about and think about, and I see my task as helping him do that. I'm not sure yet how to go about that, however, or what to focus on in terms of content or process. So I continue trying to make it easier for him to talk about himself.]*

T: I think sometimes it helps to think things out out loud.

P: Yes.

T: And you said you think you don't have anybody to talk with.

P: That's right. I, like I say, we've been going together for a long time, but we just, we don't talk a lot about what goes on inside of my head. I think a lot. She's always asking me what's going on. And I just say, "It's nothing." And,

T: But there is stuff going on in your head. *[I deliberately use his word, "stuff."]*

P: Oh, yes.

T: But you just don't talk with her about it.

P: Yes. I don't talk with too many people unless I, like I said, they're strangers. *[That's the second time he has used this word. I will make a mistake not to use it myself in the proper context.]* Because, I don't know why. Because probably you don't know them, and they aren't involved or something.

T: Yeah.

P: (pause) Work's been bothering me a lot, though. *[The patient simply won't acknowledge that his problems with his girlfriend are more (or less) important than his problems at work. So I had better make sure to cover both areas during this interview.]*

T: Well, you've got some time right now — with a stranger. *[I think it is appropriate to label this use of the word "stranger" by describing myself that way quite overtly. While it might seem obvious that I am a stranger, the connection between that obvious fact and what the patient has said about it being easier to talk with a stranger may not be obvious to the patient. Thus, explicitly labeling myself as that stranger can help the patient see that there is psychological significance and coherence to what he says, and that he can learn more about his psychological self by using this opportunity to talk about himself as freely as he can.]*

P: Yes, I don't what what else to say though.

T: Sure. What's, when you say there's a lot of stuff going on in your head, what are you talking about mainly? *[Here I decide to continue my risk-taking with this patient by testing out the degree of access he has to his own thought processes. So I start exploring how he is able to talk about his inner life.]*

P: Oh, I'm always thinking about something but not a whole lot — if we're watching television or sitting around the house or something. I'm usually pretty quiet around her. (pause) I just think of stuff. Since that other girl came to visit, I've been thinking of her a lot. And, I think I fantasize a hell of a lot.

Continued

BOX 8-1 *Continued*

T: What's that mean?

P: Fantasize? Picture yourself doing something else, or being somebody else, or whatever.

T: What do you fantasize? When you say you fantasize a lot, what do you mean?

P: That's hard to explain. (pause) Characters in books, or whatever book I'm reading, or —

T: Can you give me an example?

P: Characters from Ray Bradbury books, something like that, or —

T: Do you remember the last time you fantasized being a character in a book? *[I'm not at all sure here that it was such a good idea to push him about his fantasies. Nothing much is happening.]*

P: Yes. I don't really get, you know, I don't get carried away where I just don't hear what anybody says. You know, you're just thinking about that stuff all the time.

T: Tell me what you think about when you think about that stuff. (pause) Just as an example. *[I am about ready to quit this line of inquiry. The patient is getting a trifle defensive and I think I have gone about as far as I can go.]*

P: I don't know, they just come and go all the time. Probably a good one is when there's a John Wayne movie on. Everybody likes John Wayne. That's a common one, I guess. I've always liked John Wayne. *[Bingo! John Wayne — the strong silent hero figure for this patient who is a gunsmith by profession. This movie figure is a fine symbolic representation of this patient, whose feelings run deep but who doesn't talk about them.]*

T: So you fantasize being him, or being that character.

P: Yes, I guess —

T: Is that what you mean?

P: Yes. Not John Wayne, but just being a character like that.

T: Right.

P: Or, jeez, I don't know.

T: *[I decide to review here, to make sure I've understood the situation thus far, to give the patient a chance to catch his breath, to let the patient know that if he talks, I'll listen, and to get a clue as to what direction to move toward.]* Okay. Well, you've got a _____ girl friend who's pregnant, and a _____ girl friend who's —

P: (interrupting) — who's not pregnant.

T: (continuing) — who's new and who is far more appealing to you than you ever thought would be the case.

P: Right. And, I think the grass looks greener on the other side, but maybe it's not. *[The patient is with me now in this reviewing process, and I think we are going to do just fine.]*

T: Yes. And you feel some pressure at work, and you're not sure just what your status really is on the job. *[I am deliberately even-handed about giving work-related problems the same importance as girl friend–related problems.]*

P: Yes. And I know I could go take off and work for somebody else. But I guess I lack the confidence to do it. I've always had a big confidence problem in myself. I have to be pushed into some things.

T: [Now I make a major decision to help the patient tell me the story of his life, particularly as it revolves around work and around heterosexual experiences. I have come to the tentative conclusion that he has probably never had an opportunity to be autobiographical in this kind of way and that among the therapeutic gains that could come from such an inquiry would be that he would become less of a stranger to himself, he would see the continuity between the past and the present, and he would see that talking and thinking about himself out loud might be more productive than living the life of the strong silent man who doesn't look inward — in a word, that if the decision is a good one, he might be able to talk with his girl friend the way he will, I hope, talk with me.] How long have you lived in Boulder?

[About fifty minutes elapse. He has told me the story of his life, and then we have returned to talking about the events leading up to his decision to come to the mental health center]

T: How is it that _____ got pregnant? *[Now it is time to look at the pregnancy in light of what we have learned about this patient's history and his characteristic ways of dealing with his thoughts and feelings — that is, his habitual pretending that if he doesn't think about something or talk about something, it isn't there.]*

P: It just happened. I don't know. She didn't use her diaphragm for a while there.

T: Why was that, do you know?

P: No.

Continued

BOX 8-1 *Continued*

T: Did she, did you know she wasn't using a diaphragm when you were making love?

P: Uh-hum. She would just love to have a baby, and to be with it too. — She loves little kids. So do I, but I'm not ready for it, I tell you that. I suppose nobody ever is, but I just don't —

T: I don't think that's true. *[I gently disagree with the patient.]*

P: No? Some people are ready?

T: Sure.

P: Well, I'm sure if you're married and plan it out. That's what I'd rather do. But I'm just not ready for this at all.

T: Well, you guys are, you and _____ both are doing some things very deliberately, *[I begin a kind of recapitulation of the main issue in this interview—the patient's habitual way of communicating by action instead of by words]*

P: (interrupting) Yeah, I know.

T: (continuing)—that, uh, I guess you're not really acknowledging. I think you're trying to get caught. I think you wanted, the only way to interpret it is that you wanted to get caught in bed, and you wanted _____ to read the letter. How else can you interpret it?

P: Yeah.

T: And it sounds like _____ wanted to get pregnant.

P: Yeah. That's what I think too, because she's said stuff like that to me before when we go over to her friend's house for supper. These friends of mine, they have a nice new baby and she just loves it. She gives you one of those looks that says, "Oh, let's have one of these." I really don't want to have a baby.

T: _____ knows that?

P: Yeah.

T: What's she thinking about doing in regards to the baby? *[I think we have to discuss the reality issues pertinent to this pregnancy.]*

P: She says she wants to keep it. And, it's hard for me because I think both ways on the subject. I was kind of neutral about abortion. I said it just depends on the circumstance. I don't want to have a baby, that's for sure. I would like to someday, but not now.

T: Well, I think you are doing a lot of communicating, instead of by talking, which is the way people usually communicate with each other, you're doing an awful lot of it by —

P: (interrupting) By other ways.

T: (continuing) — by what you do in life. And you have to, the trouble with that is that somebody then has to try to figure out then what you're trying to say.

P: Yeah.

T: It's like with _____ [a previous girl friend]. You don't really know what happened to her, or what's going on in her head, what went on with her. It's like the girl you lived with for two years in _____. You never knew what was going on in her head, and every time that happens it sets things up for people not to be very honest with each other.

P: Yeah. See, you know, I realize all these things. In the back of my head I know, I didn't want to get caught, but I did. You know, that's so dumb. I don't know why I just can't say stuff out.

T: It's not like you're not aware of what is going on inside your head. I think you, you know pretty well what you really do believe. It may be hard to admit it, but I think you know. It's not like you're a stranger to yourself.

P: Yeah.

T: I mean, you could really tell _____ about the girl who went to _____, about _____, and about _____ [previous girl friends]. You, you're aware, pretty aware of your feelings. Sounds like you've grown up in a way where you don't talk about things very much. *[We have not talked at all about the patient's early childhood, and this comment is meant to give the patient an opportunity to say a word or two about his early years and his family.]*

P: So that's, my family are big talkers.

T: They are?

P: Yeah. But I've never been that way. My dad's a real intellectual. He likes to have heavy discussions, and I don't. Doing a pretty good job today, though. *[This last comment is a nice confirmation that the interview is going well.]*

T: You feel like you are?

P: Yeah, I think I'm talking pretty good today. I don't do that. Um, my sister in _____ is a big talker. I just never have been, I just, do a lot of thinking inside my head.

T: Like John Wayne. Never said very much, carried a gun, the strong, silent man. *[The metaphor is repeated.]*

Continued

BOX 8-1 *Continued*

P: Yeah.

[This discussion continues for a couple of minutes.]

T: Do you think you could talk with, talk with ____ more like you are talking here today?

P: Yeah. I've been trying, this last week, to talk quite a bit. Talked last night, pretty good, and it's coming around.

T: It's even okay to say, "I'm mixed up. I don't know what I think. I don't know what I want. And I want to be a father and I don't want to be a father. I want to get married and—

P: (interrupting) and I don't want to get married.

T: And "I don't want to hurt anybody."

P: Yeah.

T: Those are all okay things to say. Whatever.

P: Yeah. Just some sort of communication. (pause) Yeah. If a guy would just pay attention, he could tell a lot more about himself by what's going on around him.

T: So what did, what did ____ have in mind when she said to come on in and talk to someone—"Go on in and talk to somebody." What did she have in mind? *[The recapitulation of the first moments of the interview serves as the beginning of the ending phase of this encounter.]*

P: Sitting down and talking to somebody, like this. I'm sure. And she said, I said if I go on in and talk to somebody, will you stay, will you not, will you see me some more? She said, "Yeah, only if you go see somebody." I said, "Okay, I'll do it." So, I called the next day.

T: And why, why do you think she wanted you to talk to somebody?

P: Because she knows I got a lot going on in my head, and I haven't been able to talk to her about it. I think I'll see this pregnancy through okay, whatever way it goes. I just feel a lot of pressure, if she felt, if she wants to keep the baby. (pause) And I don't want to.

T: So right now, if you had your wish, you'd kind of encourage her to have an abortion.

[The discussion continues for another minute or two]

T: Well, have you done enough talking for today?

P: Yeah.

T: Let me make a suggestion to you. Uh, call me up and let me know how you're doing. Call me up in about a month. I'll give you my phone number.

P: Okay.

T: And, I want to get your phone number, in case I don't hear from you, I'll call you up and see how you're doing.

P: Okay.

T: And I'd be happy to have you give me a call in a month or so and let me know how you're doing. Call me, feel free to call earlier if there's some reason you want to.

P: Will you remember who I am?

T: Yeah.

P: Okay. You must see a lot of people.

T: I do, but I think I'll remember. And if you have to remind me, it won't take long to remember you.

P: All right.

T: Just tell me you're John Wayne.

[Four months later, I contact the patient by telephone]

T: I was just listening to the tape recording of the interview we made together. Jeez, it was a long time ago. And I realized I hadn't gotten back to you as quickly as I intended to. So I thought if you had a few minutes, I'd like to ask you how you're doing.

P: Oh, I'm pretty good. (pause) Um, me and _____ are getting married.

T: Are you!

P: Yeah, in June.

T: Are you pleased about that?

P: Yeah.

T: Good, good. How's _____ feeling? *[I assume that _____ is considerably further along in her pregnancy.]*

P: She's fine.

T: Good. How did it work out that you decided to do that?

P: Um, oh, I don't know. We talked about it a couple of times, and I didn't

Continued

BOX 8-1 *Continued*

want to do it and I held off for a long time. And we broke up a few times, and then finally I just said, "The hell with it. Instead of messing around and changing my mind all the time, I should just go ahead and do it."

T: Well, it sounds like it wasn't awfully hard to decide that, but it wasn't easy either.

P: No. It wasn't very easy for me. I was kind of reluctant. But I figure, what the hell, I might as well do it.

T: Yeah. When's the baby due?

P: Um, _____ went ahead and had the abortion.

T: She did? *[I am genuinely surprised.]*

P: Yeah, she sure did.

T: Hmm. That's funny, when you said you were going to get married, I assumed that she was going to keep the baby.

P: No. We just decided to get married about four weeks ago.

T: So, in other words, the decision to have the abortion came earlier.

P: Yes.

T: How did that work out?

P: It was pretty rough.

T: I bet it was.

P: I held out again till the last minute, and, I don't know, like the day before the abortion date, I decided to go ahead and keep it, and then, that morning we woke up, _____ said that she'd just wanted to go ahead and have it. She wanted to have the baby real bad, and then she decided she wanted to have the abortion.

T: Yeah.

P: She thought that would be better.

T: So, even toward the end you weren't sure whether to go ahead and have the abortion or not. So why do you think _____ decided to have the abortion?

P: I'm not sure. I think she, she just decided that she didn't want to have the baby. *[I don't have a good understanding about how they decided to go ahead with the abortion, but I don't think any more questions about it will play a useful role.]*

T: And then you kept seeing each other, and you say you, you broke up a couple of times.

P: Well, yes. We just had a few hassles. She wanted to get married, and I didn't, and she said, "Well, okay, see you later." And then a week later we'd see each other. And we did it one more time, and finally I went back over to her house and I said, "I'm through holding out. I give in."

T: That's how you think of it? *[I hoped there was more to his decision to get married than simply giving in.]*

P: Well, no.

T: That's the words you used.

P: Yeah. I just figured the hell with it, I guess I really want to do this. —I just figured I wanted to do it because I don't want to, I don't want to move. I don't want her to be out of my life.

T: Yes. Well, that's a good reason to get married. —Things still going okay on the job?

P: Yes. Going real good.

T: Good. This time of year was the time that you said things slowed down a little bit.

P: Yes, but they haven't slowed down a bit.

T: No kidding.

P: Yes. We're still five weeks behind.

T: Is that right?

P: Work is going better than ever.

T: Is that right?

P: I'm making better money, getting along better with the people I work with.

T: You mentioned, when we saw each other, that you weren't sure how well you were getting along with the guys you were working with.

P: Right. Well, after I saw you, about a week after I saw you, um, just before we closed down to go hunting, it must have been right at the end of October, I sat down and talked with the guy I worked with downstairs. And I asked him what was bugging him, and he told me, and I told him what was bugging me. And, then we, this was like a day before we closed down to go hunting, he said, "Well, think about it when you're hunting." And, we came back and talked about it some more. I decided to stay, and they

Continued

BOX 8-1 *Continued*

decided to keep me, and things are going really good. I don't feel as much pressure, near as much pressure as I did before hunting season. And I'm keeping up with five weeks worth of work. We're just swamped.

T: Is that right?

P: Yes. And I, I don't feel any pressure at all. Very little. And I've been trying to get myself physically fit so that helps me too. Exercising. Running. Things are just going much better, much better.

T: Well, I'm really delighted to hear that. It sounds like the hour and a half we spent together was well worth it.

P: Yeah, I think so. Jeez, it only cost me fourteen bucks. It was worth it.

T: (laughs) Well, good. I'm glad you found it useful.

P: Yes. But things just seem to be falling in place, going much better. But after we had that talk at work, um, he told me that, see, back at that time I was getting some work back, and some complaints.

T: Oh, I see.

P: And, I told him what was going on, what was bugging me, like _____ being pregnant. And, that was a lot of pressure. And I guess he took that as a, you know, he gave me some time to think about it, like when I was hunting, and then when we came back, he said, "Well, let's just start with a clean sheet." And, I talked to him about some things that I didn't like, too, at work. So I guess we both got it out in the open. *[I'm very glad that I asked about his work situation. I think that the problems at work were every bit as important to this patient as were the problems with his girl friend.]*

T: Well, that's fine.

P: I thought the interview was real good. It laid a lot of, it showed me things that I already knew that I wanted to do. I thought about that quite a bit.

T: Oh, good.

P: Me and _____ are talking more. It's still hard to talk. We have to work on that.

---

occurred. The patient, a 27-year-old white male, was seen in the adult outpatient clinic of the Boulder County Community Mental Health Center. He came into the office carrying a cup of hot coffee that he had just obtained in the admitting office. Italic comments in brackets represent an effort to reconstruct my thoughts during the interview.

Concluding Comments

Focused single-session therapy tests the fundamental principles of planned short-term therapy by deliberately creating and examining the limiting case. As such, it attempts to accomplish enough therapeutic work in a single interview to start a therapeutic process that can continue without additional direct intervention of the therapist. The understanding of the therapist and the patient is that the patient can always return for another interview when whatever benefits have been derived from the previous session have been exhausted.

To be sure, many patients will require more than a single therapy session in order to attain significant relief. But what can be exciting to the therapist is to keep open the possibility throughout the initial contact with a patient that it may be the only contact that is necessary. Indeed, working on the assumption that one session can and perhaps should be sufficient may be an increasingly useful mode of functioning for today's clinician, given the evidence that so large a proportion of patients are, planfully or otherwise, seen only once.

This chapter has made reference to the special training that is thought to be necessary to achieve a high level of competence as a short-term psychotherapist. In all likelihood the best training for planned short-term therapy, certainly for single-session therapy, is the opportunity to undertake supervised psychotherapy where there are no time constraints. Beginning therapists are and should be expected to be inefficient. But with increasing experience, therapists ought to be able to accomplish their therapeutic objectives more quickly and more effectively than would have been required earlier in their training. That is, the best short-term therapists may be found among the most experienced long-term therapists.

Focused single-session therapy matches the general ways in which primary medical care is delivered. The therapist provides some form of remediation that is judged to be pertinent to the presenting problem, with the understanding that the patient should feel free to return if the remedy does not appear to be sufficiently effective. Thus, focused single-session therapy can be thought of as primary mental health care. As such, it can appropriately be followed by additional contact between the patient and the therapist, if and when that additional contact is needed.

CHAPTER NINE

Gustafson's Briefer Psychotherapy

Overview

The Brief Therapy Clinic Treatment Program

A Case Example

Concluding Comments

James Gustafson's (1981, 1986) clinical ideas come from two important sources: (1) his careful and remarkably eloquent analysis of psychoanalytic and psychodynamic writings pertinent to time-limited psychotherapy, and (2) his clinical experiences at the Brief Therapy Clinic at the University of Wisconsin.

Gustafson's book draws primarily on his experiences with patients who are mildly disturbed college students. He writes as if his ideas are not pertinent to patients who may be more seriously disturbed, but it may be useful to keep this possibility in mind when considering his ideas. In describing his orientation to time-limited psychotherapy, Gustafson writes:

> *Many of the cases in this book are taken from the teaching practice of the Brief Therapy Clinic at the University of Wisconsin, which routinely offers about a semester of once-a-week sessions to its individual patients. But since I see few major differences in principle between brief and long-term therapy, individual and family therapy, the reader will also find illustrations from all these domains. This book could rightly be described as being about* briefer *therapy. (1986, p. 4)*

Given the specificity with which Gustafson describes his approach to short-term psychotherapy, he is remarkably nondoctrinaire about his work.

He clearly believes that there is no universal method of time-limited psychotherapy and that every way of examining the process of therapy has its advantages. Indeed, in his major work on time-limited psychotherapy (Gustafson, 1986), he allocates more than half of the pages to a description of a variety of what he calls observing positions—ranging from Freud, Breuer, Ferenczi, Rank, and Reich to Alexander and French, Sullivan, Winnicott (1971, 1975), and Balint, and finally to Gedo (1981), Havens (1986), Malan, Sifneos, Davanloo, Bateson (1979), Palazzoli (Palazzoli et al., 1978), and Maturana (Maturana and Varela, 1980). Several of these names will not appear elsewhere in this volume. Gustafson's concluding comments in his book underline this catholic view of psychotherapeutic thinking:

> *The first principle is to take the entire tradition of psychotherapy as our province for learning. The point is not to amass knowledge. No, it is rather to become familiar with what is powerful and deep in the many different guises, genres, and schools which are possible in such a diverse tradition. (1986, p. 344)*

It is possible to view Gustafson's work as comprising two distinct components—a scholarly and compelling review and critique of psychodynamic writings pertinent to brief psychotherapy, and a description of his own method of undertaking such interventions. In this chapter we shall examine his particular approach to time-limited psychotherapy.

The Brief Therapy Clinic Treatment Program

Time-limited psychotherapy at the Brief Therapy Clinic takes place in three distinct phases. First there is a preliminary interview. If the prospective patient is deemed suitable to continue, there is a two- to three-hour trial therapy session, which is perhaps the most unusual aspect of his approach. If that session seems to be helpful, the patient is invited to complete a one-semester therapeutic program. Like many other psychotherapists, Gustafson spends a good deal of time thinking about who might and who might not be suitable for his time-limited psychotherapy (see Chapter 21).

The Preliminary Interview

Before the preliminary interview the clinician has an opportunity to examine the patient's medical chart and the responses to an open-ended questionnaire and to a symptom checklist that were completed just before the interview. The open-ended questionnaire includes such questions as "What specific reasons made you come to the clinic now?" and "Describe your major problem or difficulty in your own words."

Preliminary Questions

The therapist looks for answers to three questions during the preliminary interview, which lasts about thirty minutes. First, there is an effort to determine whether the patient is looking for the kind of help that is available at the clinic. If it appears that there is a good match between the patient's interests and the clinic's program, then two additional questions are posed — what Gustafson refers to as the "best news" and the "bad news" questions. The best news comes from the determination of how the patient has been able to allow others to be of help in the past. The bad news comes from the answers to the question of how patients feel, think, and act when they are at their worst.

Gustafson, who thinks of the program at the Brief Therapy Clinic as most suitable for relatively healthy students with some recurrent distress that they want to talk over, writes, "If the patient is after something we might give, if the patient has gotten help in a serious way from other people, if the patient at worst has been in no serious danger, then we are likely to offer a trial therapy" (1986, p. 281). Gustafson reports that about half of the patients referred to the Brief Therapy Clinic are accepted for treatment, a rate that seems just about right to him.

Preliminary Interview Errors

Gustafson describes a number of errors that can occur during the preliminary interview. The first is to pass a patient on to the trial therapy session who either has an unrealistic idea of how brief time-limited therapy might be, given the nature and history of the problem, or who is offended at the idea that a charge will be made for all subsequent therapeutic sessions. The second is to pass a patient on to the trial therapy session who has had past experiences in psychotherapy that are inconsistent with the Brief Therapy Clinic program, for example, someone who talks endlessly, as he or she did in previous psychotherapy, and is startled to discover that the clinician becomes somewhat impatient. The third is to ignore the parents' objections to the patient entering psychotherapy, since their ideas can frequently be at great variance with those of the prospective patient.

Another group of errors occurs because the clinician underestimates the severity of the problem as initially presented by the patient. Many initial presentations can be quite routine and can obscure profound psychopathology, such as described in the following excerpt.

A 29-year-old, single graduate student was referred to us for depression. He complained to us that his girlfriend had broken off with him, which was bothering him more than usual because the girlfriend would not allow him to see their one-year-old daughter. . . . When I asked [him] what went through his mind when he thought of missing his daughter, he told me he thought of shaving his head so he could place it in a noose. When I asked him what kept him from this proceeding, he cried and said his little daughter was the only person he loved in the world. When I asked when he would get to see her again, he cried again and told me that his girlfriend had just proposed to leave the state in a few months. (1986, p. 289)

At the other extreme are patients who give an unusually pathological or generally negative initial impression but who may, in fact, be far healthier than they admit. Often this occurs when the patient-therapist relationship is not positive, such as might occur when the patient doesn't like or is frightened by the therapist.

The Trial Therapy Session

The trial therapy session is divided into three components — an initial individual interview, a discussion between the interviewer and one or more members of the clinical team who have been observing the interview behind a one-way mirror, and a concluding individual interview. The entire trial therapy session may last as long as three hours. Its rationale is to determine whether some significant progress can be made in a brief period of time. If so, it is likely that additional significant progress can be made in additional brief periods of time; if not, it is unlikely that significant change will occur in brief psychotherapy.

The initial individual interview begins with the presenting problem and attempts to develop a history starting when the patient seemed to be functioning satisfactorily, then continuing to when things started to go wrong. In Gustafson's words the interview attempts to "reach what is worthwhile about the individual," attempts to "reach the illness," and at the same time tries to determine why the patient has had to be exactly as he or she has been (p. 296).

The team discussion, which can produce a good deal of anxiety and confusion in the therapist if it is not skillfully managed by all participants, is designed to give the therapist an opportunity to describe his or her impressions of the patient and the other observing team members to provide their impressions, optimally for the benefit of the therapist. Such team discussions usually last about twenty minutes.

The concluding individual interview, which usually lasts about an hour, is more future-oriented — for example, what if the patient entered psychotherapy, or didn't enter psychotherapy, or what if the presenting problem were to continue, or were to disappear. By the end of the trial therapy session, the therapist is in a position to offer or not to offer a continuing therapeutic experience, and the patient is in a position to accept or decline the offer, if made.

The Continuing Psychotherapy

Gustafson (1986) describes the continuing therapeutic sessions as "first sessions which are given over as often as they are needed by the patient" (p. 315). It is worth quoting him on this point, since it is important in understanding his rationale for continuing beyond the trial therapy session.

> *Only if you are ingenious about separations can you retain the thrill and scope of first meetings. . . . This is exactly what happens in many relations between patients and doctors. The relations become routine when the connection is assured. No longer standing back from one another, doctor and patient locate smaller points of interest. But what if the doctor has a method for meeting his patient many times as if their meeting were the first meeting? . . . You give a "therapeutic consultation" and then you repeat it several more times if necessary. . . . Single meetings could be repeated and still be singular if they could be far enough apart. (1986, pp. 316–317)*

What seems to distinguish the continuing psychotherapy from the initial interview and trial therapy session is its complexity. The patient and therapist need to examine several life variables at the same time, keeping in mind their multiple interactions and multiple contradictions. Gustafson tries to locate a current problem in every session; find a useful perspective for examining the problem; clarify and revise hypotheses that serve to organize how the problem is best understood; appreciate the complexity of the patient's life, identifying all of the significant players and their roles; and at the same time assess the patient's psychological status more or less continuously.

Termination Issues

Like nearly all psychodynamically oriented psychotherapists, Gustafson is drawn to examine the termination phase of the psychotherapy. According to him, the danger of an unskillful termination is that the gains will be lost, either through the patient's provocation of others to undo what has occurred in the therapy or through a kind of hopeless self-debasement. Hence, the final comments from the therapist have the goal of blocking that self-defeating behavior, by helping patients develop the capacity to enlarge the number of possibilities that might be open to them in the future.

A Case Example

An example of the work of Gustafson's group is given in Box 9-1. It is the beginning section of the initial individual interview that constitutes the first portion of the trial therapy session, along with a brief commentary about the mid-session discussion with the observer and the beginning of the resumed trial therapy session following the mid-session break. The patient is a 22-year-old woman who complained of feelings of insecurity and a low self-image and who was afraid that she might never be able to have a normal relationship with a man. She was chronically self-depreciating. During the preliminary interview she met all the criteria for eligibility for a trial therapy session. She was troubled but sound; she had a good support system; she had a problem she wanted to explore. It was also learned that a year earlier she had had two near disasters. She had been struck by an automobile and had nearly died of complications while being treated in the hospital. This excerpt provides an excellent illustration of Gustafson's thought processes during the initial interview. An offer of continuing psychotherapy was made and accepted by this patient, who subsequently entered into a complex and helpful course of time-limited therapy.

BOX 9-1 · *Beginning of Gustafson's Initial Trial Therapy Session*

Therapist: Where do you think we ought to start today?

Patient: I guess what I really want to know is—I was hoping you guys would give me some good ideas on how to improve my self-image.

T: OK, then we need to have some idea of what you think is wrong with that. So that's what you'd like to get out of us today—how to improve your self-image?

P: I guess that's my biggest problem. It's that I have a low opinion of myself.

T: You come across as a person with a certain amount of confidence, nevertheless, so I would imagine that at one time you felt pretty good about yourself.

Continued

BOX 9-1   *Continued*

P: Well, no. I mean I do like some things about myself. I think I'm intelligent, I guess that gives me some confidence. I feel OK about my looks. I guess it's my personality I think is wrong.

T: All right, should we see about that? We can hardly make any suggestions unless we understand what is wrong.

P: I don't know, like I said before I feel like I'm boring. I feel like what I have to say isn't worthwhile.

T: OK, so you feel you're boring and what you say isn't worthwhile? What do you mean?

P: You know, like it's stupid. Like it seems like a contradiction because on the one hand I say I feel intelligent but I say stupid things so it's like I'm good at learning. I'm good at taking tests. I'm good in school.

T: School intelligent?

P: Yeah.

T: But you don't feel smart outside?

P: Right. Like I'm good at regurgitating—that's why I'm good in school.

T: Well, that's no mean talent. So you're good at that but you don't feel—.

P: But it's like I'm not really original.

T: You don't feel original? Compared to whom?

P: I don't know.

T: Who's original?

P: I don't know, some people just are.

T: Well, whom do you admire?

P: I don't know. Nobody in particular.

T: Well, one is always comparing oneself to other people and you look like you're comparing yourself with someone who is original, compared to you.

P: Let's see. OK, like my friend Harry. It's like he is really funny. He just finds funny things to say. *[For me there are two crucial statements here which catch this woman by surprise. "You come across as a person with a certain amount of confidence." She may have jumped in her seat when I said that to her. I thought she did. Here she was saying she had a "low opinion of myself," and I was saying I didn't think she did. But I also say that I accept*

BOX 9-1 *Continued*

her "low opinion" and I am interested in how she arrives there: "You don't feel original. Compared to whom?" Here she may have jumped again. Again, I thought she did. The eye for her confidence and the eye for her comparing herself badly, together, give a double description which brings depth of field and then depth of feeling. We drop down fast into what is most painful to her, because we have a hold on what is right about her. We are "working the opposing currents."]

T: So Harry is funny?

P: Yeah.

T: So you admire that in a man?

P: Yeah, like at work it kind of bugs me because there's this man, but I feel really weird that it bothers me so much. [She begins to cry.]

T: Yeah, but it does. There's some Kleenex right here.

P: He's just so friendly, everyone likes him. I guess I compare myself to him because he's so comfortable with himself and it seems like he's just so friendly, he's just so like outgoing, just easygoing.

T: So this is painful to you by comparison to yourself. How would you describe yourself?

P: Just really afraid.

T: So you criticize yourself for being too fearful? What are you fearful about?

P: Like afraid of rejection.

T: Why shouldn't you be afraid of rejection?

P: Because I'm so afraid that I don't take risks so I don't gain anything either. I'm always protecting myself and by doing that I don't get what I really need.

T: Like what?

P: Like I'm afraid of people not liking me so I don't really try so they don't —

T: Sometimes a person learns to be a little cautious or protective and that's a good thing.

P: But why is it good?

T: You can get hurt.

P: Yeah, but I think it's better not to be afraid than to get hurt.

T: Really?

Continued

BOX 9-1 *Continued*

P: No pain, no gain. *[Now I'm leading into history. She proposes she "should not be fearful." I propose that she had to have had good reason. I propose we appreciate the necessity of her fearfulness. She tells me very clearly about her family.]*

T: It depends on what the experience has been. Some people have had an easy time of it or a pleasant time of it or a protective time of it. So you know, you've had some rough hits already. But you criticize yourself for your caution. I was quite impressed that you've already been through two terrible things.

P: But they don't seem terrible to me.

T: They're a lot harder than what most people go through. There must be some reason why you're cautious and you don't take risks. I mean this just didn't—this must have a history.

P: I don't think I ever have. Nobody in my family builds anybody else up; it's more like cutting down.

T: So your family doesn't give each other much appreciation.

P: No. It's kind of weird. I don't know if that's the way I take it because I'm the youngest and so I was always called the baby of the family. I was always told that I was spoiled, and like my sister and two of my brothers always called me a little brat, and my older brother, Sam, I liked him because he was my favorite. My brother, Jim, and I, he's the second oldest, we always used to fight and I used to get him in trouble, like I'd do something to him and he'd do something back and I would start crying and my dad would yell at him. But my dad was like the head of the family so I always got the better end of it and like my dad would be yelling at my brother and my mom would tell me what a brat I was. And like now, those are the things I remember. Sometimes she would say, "Oh, you're such a good kid," but the feeling that I got was that I wasn't and like now she says, "When people called you a brat nobody meant it," she's kidding but it's like—you just don't say things like that.

T: Did she think you were a brat?

P: If I was a bad person or how I interpret it?

T: What did she think was bad about you?

P: That I was getting my brother in trouble and acting that way.

T: Your view is that she was siding with Jim and seeing you as being a troublemaker?

BOX 9-1 *Continued*

P: I was, it was true, but I think a lot of kids are like that.

T: That's not unusual, the youngest fights back. But your mother was pretty harsh, you felt.

P: Yeah, she was. I don't think she realized. It was hard because I think she is very good at not remembering things that she doesn't want to. I'll tell her stuff she did and she'll say, "I said that to you and I did that? I don't remember that." On the one hand I feel like maybe I exaggerated it, but on the other hand I think that maybe she is just protecting herself because she really did do those things.

T: You certainly feel it very keenly from your demeanor. It sounds like we got into that because we were talking about this self-image of yours and you were saying to me why you might be afraid and might even be a devil.

P: Yeah.

T: I mean the fight with your brother and ordinary things like that. Maybe it dates back to taking a lot of criticism from your mom for fairly ordinary things.

P: I know she has a really low self-image too. I never thought she did but she has told me.

T: Maybe you got cautious somewhere back there. It sounds like you were actually taking some risks in the family there for a while, a fight with your brother and all that.

P: How is that taking a risk?

T: You could have been sweet and nice instead you were having fights with your older brother. Isn't that taking a risk? You could have been a nice little girl. *[She describes being run down by her mother, which allowed her to be close to her father. But she also describes her mother's disconfirming that she ran her down. I could see how she could have been quite confused, being disconfirmed about being a worthwhile kid, but also disconfirmed about being run down.]*

At the conclusion of the first hour of this trial therapy session, the therapist suggests taking a break that will allow him to discuss the session with the observer. Two technical problems were discussed with the observer during the break. One was the missing history of what had gone wrong lately that had resulted in her seeking therapy. The other was the risk that her family would run true to form—that is, would not want her to undertake therapy, even if she felt she were making progress. A compromise was chosen by the therapist. He would ask for information about the events that precipitated her coming to therapy, but would also discuss the family. The therapist

Continued

BOX 9-1   *Continued*

knew that if he did not establish the right relationship with the family in the therapy with the patient, she would not continue in therapy. After that discussion the interviewer summarizes the thinking and suggests how to proceed for the remaining 45 minutes of time available to them.

T: The picture we have so far is that you came here to ask us what we thought about your self-esteem, your self-image, and how it could be improved and so far we have this picture that there are two things that have put holes in your self-esteem. One is that there is this kind of reflex to think you have done something terribly wrong on minimum evidence. And then there have been times where people have really let you have it. Both of those things would tend to weaken your confidence—both letting people hit you and what you're regularly hitting yourself with. That's so far. We've got another 45 minutes right now, you and I, and hopefully we can understand some more about you. So then, the question is: There are so many things we could talk about, so we have to choose where to take a look in the next 45 minutes. I have several thoughts about that. One is to look at what's been going on this fall when you chose to come in. Maybe we should attend to that. I mean you were distressed about it enough this time, and I don't have clear enough sense of what was so painful this fall that made you come here. Can we start there?

Excerpted from Gustafson, 1986, pp. 300–308.

Concluding Comments

Without question, Gustafson is the most literary and probably the most literate of the contemporary writers in the field of planned short-term psychotherapy. His book is worth reading if only for its review of the thinking of earlier scholars. But Gustafson is clearly more than a chronicler. He has developed a unique, very sensitive, and thought-provoking approach to planned short-term psychotherapy that makes a substantial demand of time and energy on a team of therapists, but that seems organized to allow for a maximum effect on the patient. Indeed, one question that future clinical research might seek to answer is the issue of when to choose to offer continuing therapy to a patient who has demonstrated considerable gain during the trial therapy session—that is, under what conditions, if any, might a successful trial therapy session be therapy enough.

There is a strong commitment to training at the Brief Therapy Clinic that adds time to what would be required were Gustafson describing the same clinical activities in a context that did not involve an active training component. It is not clear how his specific form of clinical practice was developed and what aspects of the clinical work that is described would not be necessary were training not a significant part of the clinical setting.

Gustafson works in an academic setting, and his patients are mainly college students — one would assume most of them to be bright, in reasonably good psychological shape, and motivated to do more with their lives. It is not clear how his approach would need to be modified, if at all, to make it possible for him to work productively with patients who were far less bright and accomplished. On the university campus he apparently chooses to reject patients who do not meet his admission criteria. But that rejection may not be as necessary as seems indicated to him. Gustafson (1986) notes that he routinely refuses to treat people who have made suicidal attempts in the past, who are borderline in terms of their adjustment, or who have had extremely difficult childhoods (pp. 291–292) — potential patients whom other short-term therapists would certainly attempt to treat. It may well be that Gustafson's approach will be found to be useful for a far greater proportion of potential patients than it might seem at first.

CHAPTER TEN

Horowitz's Stress Response Psychotherapy

Overview

Goals of Stress Response Psychotherapy

The Stress Response

Therapeutic Techniques

Personality Styles and the Therapeutic Process

Therapeutic Outcome

Concluding Comments

Based on their review of the psychotherapy evaluation literature and on their own clinical experience, Mardi Horowitz and his colleagues (1976, Horowitz and Kaltreider, 1978; Horowitz, Marmar, Krupnick, et al., 1984a; Horowitz, Marmar, Weiss, et al., 1984b; Horowitz et al., 1986; Marmar et al., 1988; see also Kleber and Brom, 1987) at the Langley Porter Psychiatric Institute at the University of California Medical School believe that "brief therapy can be expected to ameliorate focal symptoms, to change delimited irrational beliefs, and, perhaps, to put the person back on the track of adaptive life development" (1984a, p. 31).

Because the most unequivocal focal symptoms arise in conjunction with stressful life events, Horowitz has chosen to study time-limited psychotherapy in the context of patients who entered treatment following one particular such event, namely, the death of a parent (Horowitz, Wilner, and Alvarez, 1979). This particular event, according to Horowitz and his colleagues, heightens issues related to self-concept and to interpersonal relationships. Thus, learning about the process of time-limited psychotherapy with this group of patients might likely be pertinent to more general psychodynamic issues as they relate to difficulties in current relationships.

Goals of Stress Response Psychotherapy

The goal of Horowitz's stress response psychotherapy is to help people work through their reactions to the stressful event, that is, to help them improve their current level of functioning while eliminating any symptoms associated with the event, in order to return to their previous level of functioning and, if possible, to resolve whatever impediments exist that inhibit further psychological and interpersonal development. There is some similarity between Horowitz's stress response psychotherapy and the work of people who are concerned with crisis intervention, whose therapy program has a focused intervention strategy that is based on a prompt case formulation designed to understand the personal meanings of the stressful life event and the inability of the patient to cope successfully with it. The premise governing the work of Horowitz and his colleagues is that a pathological reaction to a stressful life event indicates that the event stands in some meaningful relationship to current developmental issues facing the patient.

The case formulation is a fairly formal process (Horowitz, 1987) involving an analysis of the recurrent states of mind of the patient, of self-concepts and role relationships, and of cognitive and affective functioning and expression at three points in time — before therapy, during therapy, and at the conclusion of therapy.

The Stress Response

A stressful life event usually brings with it a psychological, if not literal, outcry, followed by intrusion and denial. Under normal circumstances these reactions lead to successful coping with the event, followed by a return to the preevent equilibrium. If the reaction to the event is excessively intense or prolonged, pathological stress reactions can occur. The initial event can result in a feeling of being overwhelmed. The outcry can manifest itself as panic, confusion, and exhaustion. Denial can result in maladaptive withdrawal, suicide, counterphobic frenzy, selective inattention, amnesia, or numbness.

Normal intrusions can become unmanageable states of sadness, fear, rage, or guilt or can result in sleep disturbances, inability to concentrate, confusion, anxiety, or intropunitiveness. Instead of productive coping, the person can become constricted or frozen or can develop psychosomatic reactions. Instead of the return to the preevent equilibrium, permanent character disturbances can occur that can result in an inability to act or to love.

Horowitz proposes that "inner psychological structures of meaning," otherwise called the "inner model," (1984a, p. 39) must be modified in the process of coping with a serious stressful life event, such as the death of a parent. Until this modification is completed the stressful life event and all associations with it reside in active memory, where they will remain and produce those strong emotional reactions that are collectively called the stress response syndrome. Until the event is incorporated within this inner model, unconscious decisions are made (in traditional psychoanalytic terminology, defenses are erected) to avoid pain. In Horowitz's brief therapy the therapist "aims to facilitate the patient's mastery of experience by bringing about a gradual, in-depth contemplation of the personal implications of the event" (1984a, p. 40). The therapist assists the patient in differentiating realistic appraisals of the event from fantasy-based appraisals. The therapist focuses both on the stressful life event and on the set of associations related to it. Horowitz and associates write:

> *After the death of a parent, various preexisting fantasies about the relationship with that parent, as well as actual memories of interactions, will be activated for review. This provides an occasion to do a kind of differentiation between reality and fantasy, now with an adult mind, that the individual may not have accomplished since the original fantasies were established during childhood. (1984a, p. 41)*

Horowitz notes that stressful life events often serve as a precipitant for people to enter into psychotherapy, even if the events are not catastrophic — events that might include separations, failed love affairs, being fired from a job, or inadequate role performance as a parent. If the therapeutic relationship is viewed by the patient as a safe one, a gradual modification of the defenses can take place that will allow the patient to reappraise the stressful life event and its associated meanings. With this reappraisal, patients will be able to revise their inner models of themselves and of their world and will be able to make new decisions and to engage in other adaptive actions. Among these adaptations, patients will have to cope with the loss of their therapists, a loss that can become a replay of the earlier loss.

Basing their therapeutic program on the prior work of Davanloo and Malan (see Chapter 4), Sifneos (see Chapter 5), and Mann (see Chapter 6), Horowitz and his colleagues have developed a brief psychotherapy program with a time limit of twelve sessions. The overview of the twelve-session stress response psychotherapy program can be found in Box 10-1.

BOX 10-1 • *Overview of Stress Response Psychotherapy Program*

Session	Relationship Issues	Patient Activity	Therapist Activity
1	Initial positive feeling for helper	Patient tells story of event	Preliminary focus discussed
2	Decreased pressure as sense of trust is established	Event related to life of patient	Takes psychiatric history
3	Patient tests therapist	Patient adds associations	Realignment of focus; interpretation of resistances with empathic recognitions of why they are currently reasonable based on past relationships
4	Therapeutic alliance deepened		Further interpretation of defenses and warded-off
5		Work on what has been avoided	contents with linking of the latter to stress event and responses
6			Time of termination discussed
7–11	Transference reactions interpreted as they occur and linked to other configurations	Continued working through of central conflicts and issues of termination as related to the life event and reactions to it	Clarification and interpretation related to central conflicts and termination; clarification of unfinished issues and recommendations
12	Saying goodbye	Realization of work to be continued on own	Acknowledgment of real gains and real future work involving continuation of mourning and experimentation with new relationship patterns

From Horowitz et al., 1984a, p. 43.

Therapeutic Techniques

Within the traditional context of the therapeutic relationship, Horowitz and his colleagues pay particular attention to what they call *transference potentials* (p. 42), by which they mean evidence that role-relationship models with important figures from the past, including the lost parent, are being repeated with people in the present, including the therapist. If there are inappropriate or maladaptive aspects of past role relationships that appear to characterize current relationships, those parallels become important subjects for therapeutic intervention.

In stress response psychotherapy it is important to identify and help modify defensive styles as observed in the transference relationship. Patients with hysterical personality characteristics often look for remediation of their entire history of psychic injuries. Patients with narcissistic personality characteristics often construe the therapeutic relationship as one of entitlement, in which the therapists must do whatever is asked of them. Under any of these circumstances, therapists have to be supportive without promising unlimited gratification. Patients with obsessive-compulsive character traits represent therapeutic challenges because of their tendencies to keep relationships at an unemotional, intellectual plane.

When one is working with patients who are coping with stressful life events, a number of themes appear with sufficient frequency so that they can be considered virtually universal. These themes include: (1) sadness over the loss; (2) fear of repetition; (3) fear of merger with the deceased; (4) shame and rage as a consequence of the realization of one's vulnerability; (5) rage at the source of the event; (6) rage at those who have not suffered the stressful life event; (7) guilt, shame, or fear of loss of control of aggressive impulses; (8) guilt because of survival; and (9) guilt stemming from an exaggerated sense of responsibility for the event. These themes interfere with a patient's sense of competence and require therapeutic intervention in the form of reconstructive interpretation designed to help patients place their memories and affects in an orderly sequence, make appropriate linkages, and differentiate reality from fantasy.

Finally, it is important for the therapist to help patients become more aware of their defensive patterns that can inhibit or distort both affective and cognitive functioning. Therapeutic techniques that appear to be helpful include gentle but detailed questioning, labeling of emotions, helping patients put imagery into words, staying with a theme to encourage conceptual mastery of it, tactful pointing out of reality distortions, and clarification designed to help reappraisal, all within the context of empathic support.

As the period of therapy comes to an end, termination is discussed in the context of yet another loss. The therapist can encourage the continuation of the process of therapy by focusing on the future work that patients will be able to undertake on their own in order to continue with the task of problem resolution.

Horowitz provides a simplified and idealized model case (Box 10-2) in order to outline what has to take place in stress response psychotherapy.

BOX 10-2 · *Prototypical Case: Stress Response Therapy*

Patient: I am angry with my father for dying before he apologized for declaring me a bad person, and before he declared me to be a good person.

Therapist: Why does that trouble you?

P: Because now I will go on feeling like a bad person forever.

T: Are you a bad person?

P: No.

T: Do you think your father died on purpose, in order to deprive you of his blessings?

P: Yes.

T: Is that rational?

P: No. He just died, not on purpose. So I will change my mind about the idea that he died on purpose.

T: Can you call yourself a good person on your father's behalf?

P: Yes. He actually would like me as I am. There are some bad things, but I'm pretty much okay.

T: Can you forgive your father?

P: Yes. He had problems of his own.

T: Can you accept yourself for being angry with him?

P: Yes. My anger was based on an irrational belief that he died on purpose, in order to deprive me of his blessing. But that is the way the mind works, and I know that it is not true. That cuts down the anger now. But my feeling angry did not hurt him. So I have changed my mind and do not feel that I am to blame for his death.

T: Then I think we can terminate therapy.

P: Yes. Thank you.

From Horowitz et al., 1984a, pp. 58–59.

Personality Styles and the Therapeutic Process

Horowitz and his colleagues (1984a) have made an effort to describe their approach to planned short-term psychotherapy in the case of patients who present differing personality and information-processing styles. They identify for particular emphasis the hysterical, compulsive, narcissistic, and borderline personalities. Personality style is defined as "a repertoire of states of mind, self-concepts and patterns of relationships, and ways of coping with stress and defending against threat . . . [including] characteristic patterns of regulating perceptions, thought, feelings, decisions, plans, and actions" (p. 68). All the cases they discuss presented symptoms of stress response syndromes following the death of a parent. In addition, however, many of these cases had quite discernable personality styles, which have significant implications for how time-limited psychotherapy should be conducted.

The Hysterical Personality

The *hysterical personality* (the term preferred by Horowitz and colleagues) is officially referred to as the *histrionic personality disorder* in the Diagnostic and Statistical Manual of the American Psychiatric Association (DSM-III-R). Such persons are:

> *overly dramatic, reactive, and intensely expressive . . . always drawing attention to themselves . . . prone to exaggeration . . . typically attractive and seductive . . . impressionable and easily influenced by others or by fads . . . overly trusting of others, suggestible, and show an initially positive response to any strong authority figure who they think can provide a magical solution for their problems. (American Psychiatric Association, 1980, pp. 313–314)*

Such character traits present a variety of problems for the time-limited psychotherapist, mainly in the form of special demands to be active and to be a liberator or redeemer. Horowitz and colleagues suggest that such patients tend to inhibit their verbal expression of key ideas and feelings. They write:

> *As the therapist tries to focus on a specific problem, the patient will avoid clarity, limit associational connections, and abruptly change mood. If the therapist persists with a specific focus, the patient is prone to feel neglected or misunderstood, forget what just happened, or simply comply without real efforts at understanding or changing. . . . If the*

therapist provides clarification and insight rather than solace, the patient will feel neglected and believe that the therapist is insensitive to his or her needs. If the therapist tries to give "more," the patient will feel that a special "beyond therapy" relationship has been established. When it turns out that this is not so, the patient may respond with shock, disbelief, sadness, or rage. (Horowitz et al., 1984a, p. 73)

In dealing with patients with a hysterical personality style, the therapist needs to counter the patient's tendencies to be diffuse, global, and inhibited by being focused, repetitive, concrete, and specific. The therapist needs to counter the patient's habitual tendencies to say "I don't know" by restating what the patient has just said, by requesting details about events and feelings, keeping topics open for further discussion, clarifying vague statements, providing labels for unclear terms, interpreting warded-off feelings when data for such interpretations are sufficient, and by being supportive and hopeful without accepting the role of caretaker.

Some hysterical personalities may be so disturbed that they become depressed, disorganized, erratic, jealous, possessive, confused, emotionally labile, and aggressive. In addition, they may suffer a significant drop in self-esteem and sense of self-efficacy. Under these circumstances the therapist can easily feel overwhelmed. But if the therapist slows down the pace, it can be possible to help the patient work through a limited set of problems. Techniques that can be particularly helpful under these circumstances include the request for details, and careful reconstruction of sequences of events and behaviors, again while being supportive. Rather than working toward exploring aspects of the patient's behavior that may be unconscious, with particularly disturbed hysterical personalities, stability can be restored by helping the patient forge links between conscious memories, fantasies, wishes, and fears.

The Compulsive Personality

The essential features of the *compulsive personality* are the restricted ability to express warm and tender emotions, excessive dominance, perfectionism, pathological devotion to work, and indecisiveness. Such people are often stingy with their possessions as well as with their emotions; are preoccupied with rules, procedures, and trivial details; are inordinately fearful of making mistakes; procrastinate; are generally unaware of their impact on others; and are often unable to experience or tolerate pleasure. They are characteristically unable to deal with their emotions, and make frequent use of the defenses of isolation of affect, doing and undoing, and reaction formation (American Psychiatric Association, 1980, pp. 326–328).

Patients with compulsive personalities often view psychotherapy as an intellectual exercise in which they present issues in excessive detail while at the same time displaying a pathological inability to be spontaneous. The relationship with the therapist can quickly become adversarial, and the patient, fearing the loss of control that is associated with any feeling of dependence upon the therapist or fearing hostile impulses, can precipitously bolt from therapy. Under these circumstances it is usually very difficult to develop a workable therapeutic alliance.

Therapists need to be active and somewhat directive while at the same time maintaining a relatively neutral stance, avoiding their own counter-transference feelings of frustration and hostility. Interpretations need to be presented carefully not as "elementary or obvious, but as interesting observations" (Horowitz et al., 1984a, p. 163) that the patient might want to think about.

The Narcissistic Personality

Patients with *narcissistic personality* styles have a grandiose sense of self-importance, are exhibitionistic and preoccupied with fantasies of their potential great successes, and have an insatiable need for constant attention and admiration. They exploit others, lack empathy, are extremely self-centered and self-absorbed, and may lie or fake feelings in order to impress the therapist (American Psychiatric Association, 1980, p. 315). Horowitz and colleagues (1984a) suggest, quite understandably, that there may be "less than the usual gratification for the therapist in treating this type of patient" (p. 208).

Narcissistic personalities have a kind of immature dependence, expecting the therapist to act as a parent and rescue them from whatever distress they may be experiencing. Faced with feelings of hostility toward their therapist and, at the same time, shame and sadness because of their attitudes toward the therapist, such patients often act as if their therapist can do them no good, while guarding against the expression of the very needs that brought them into therapy. In spite of these expressions of derision, narcissistic patients are very vulnerable and need therapists who can be unusually tactful while also being firm.

Tact is needed to avoid forcing the patient into a position where lying might be necessary and to ensure that confrontations are presented palatably. Narcissistic patients are, at one and the same time, frightened of the therapist because they expect criticism for what they have said and afraid that they will fool the therapist so easily that the therapist will not be capable of understanding them and thus will be unable to help them.

The Borderline Personality

The patient with a *borderline personality* is characterized by intense and unstable interpersonal relationships, marked shifts of attitude over time, impulsive and unpredictable behavior that may be physically self-damaging, and unstable moods. Such personalities are uncertain about their gender identity, self-image, long-term goals, and values. They have difficulty tolerating being alone and suffer from chronic feelings of emptiness and boredom (American Psychiatric Association, 1980, p. 321; see also American Psychiatric Association, 1987, pp. 346–347).

Patients with a borderline personality cannot usefully manage ambivalence. The world is either dangerous and chaotic or is all good. The threatened emergence of ambivalent feelings precipitates enormous anxiety. Accompanying that anxiety are massive confusion, temporal disorientation, and often a sense of depersonalization. Often supplementing this near psychotic behavior pattern are severe projection, isolation of affect, undoing, and other evidence of loss of cognitive control. As can be expected, the relationship of a borderline patient who has suffered parental loss with the therapist is intense and unstable. Such patients can neither engage in self-observation nor establish any sort of useful relationship with the therapist.

Undertaking time-limited psychotherapy with such a borderline patient is problematical and hardly to be recommended, except under special circumstances, such as to deal with a stress-related regression following successful long-term psychotherapy. The therapist needs to help the patient distinguish between reality and fantasy and modulate the extreme feelings of undervaluation or overidealization that such patients often ascribe to the therapist. Therapeutic work has to be carefully focused and has to remain in that limited focal area, ordinarily the stressful life event that led to the entrance into therapy. Brief therapy rarely provides enough time for the repetitive working through of the complex good and bad images of others that borderline patients hold, but it may provide a restorative relationship within which a stressful life event may start to be mastered.

Therapeutic Outcome

Horowitz and colleagues (1984a) have examined therapeutic outcome, both in terms of changes in presenting symptoms and in more general character structure in the same three topical areas that they use in case formulation — states of mind, self-concepts and role relationships, and cognitive functioning. Not surprisingly, changes in presenting symptoms are found more commonly than changes in character structure. In the case of states of mind, stress response psychotherapy has been noted to convert explosive rage into anger, panic into anxiety or dread, and self-tormenting despair into sadness and a sense of poignant loss. As for changes in character traits, Horowitz and his colleagues have found that some patients who formerly could not mourn are able to feel and express grief at the conclusion of therapy, and that other patients are able to enter into intimate relationships far more freely and successfully than was the case before the therapy began.

In the area of self-concepts and role relationships, Horowitz and colleagues have found that maladaptive views of the self and of others are often transformed into views that are more differentiated and more under the control of the person. Views of the self become more complex and modulated; affects are more accessible, coping with ambivalent feelings is more successful, and formerly unacceptable aspects of the self are integrated with the entire view of the self into a more realistic whole. Finally, symptom reduction is a common consequence of therapy, and changes in defensive patterns have been noted through increased awareness of how those patterns are invoked and function.

Horowitz and colleagues summarize their findings by noting that:

> *The principal aim of these brief therapies—to work through stress-related and personality-related problems of a focal nature—often could be accomplished within the specified time limit. Major revision of character style seemed to be a goal seldom accomplished . . . Some types of personality change were noted in patients who gained from new experiences with the therapist and then continued developmental progress after completing the brief therapy. . . . The more flexible the personality, the more the therapy process can focus on working through trains of thoughts to reduce strain. The more restrained, rigidly stereotyped, and limited the person's personality style, the more this style itself impedes the working-through process. (1984a, p. 329)*

Concluding Comments

Horowitz and his colleagues have created a psychodynamic time-limited psychotherapy that has two especially remarkable attributes. First, it is presented as particularly suitable for persons who are coping with parent loss, a specific stressful life event; and, second, it proposes that personality style variations among patients have clear implications for how time-limited psychotherapy should be conducted.

Thus, it is not yet clear how generalizable stress response psychotherapy may be—that is, whether it can be successfully employed with patients who have not had to come to grips with parent loss or perhaps, by extension, with any other major life stressor. The underlying theory that Horowitz proposes — namely, that pathological reactions to stressful life events occur because the events are psychologically related to chronic unresolved problems — would suggest, however, that stress response psychotherapy will be shown to be appropriate for a wide variety of issues that may not involve such events. Furthermore, the large research literature on stressful life events (see, for example, Bloom, 1984) indicates that such events are remarkably common and that they often precipitate psychiatric disorders in persons who are healthy but vulnerable.

As for personality style variations, Horowitz and his colleagues have performed an important intellectual task in considering how different character types can best be treated by psychotherapists or, in other words, how the diagnostic and statistical manual of the American Psychiatric Association can be more useful to mental health professionals. Few other time-limited psychotherapy theorists have yet given significant consideration to how their ideas about therapeutic technique should be modified by diagnostic considerations, and this work may be the harbinger of similar efforts in the future.

CHAPTER ELEVEN

Klerman's Interpersonal Psychotherapy

Overview

Basic Characteristics of Interpersonal Psychotherapy

Diagnostic and Strategic Principles in Interpersonal Therapy

Specific Therapeutic Techniques

Becoming and Being an Interpersonal Psychotherapist

Efficacy of Interpersonal Psychotherapy

Concluding Comments

Gerald Klerman and his colleagues (Klerman and Weissman, 1982; Klerman et al., 1984a, 1984b; Neu, Prusoff, and Klerman, 1978; Rounsaville and Chevron, 1982) have developed a psychodynamic time-limited psychotherapy designed specifically to meet the needs of nonpsychotic, nonbipolar depressed patients. Its central assumption is that the precipitation and perpetuation of many psychiatric disorders are closely related to disturbances in current interpersonal functioning (see Horowitz and Vitkus, 1986). Treatment duration averages about fourteen weekly one-hour sessions, and the therapy is designed to improve the quality of the patient's current interpersonal functioning.

Since its central belief is not necessarily specific to the diagnosis of depression, interpersonal psychotherapy is being modified, as appropriate, for use in treating other psychiatric conditions (see, for example, Rounsaville, Gawin, and Kleber, 1985). But the most common psychiatric diagnosis that has been of interest to planned short-term psychotherapists in general—and to interpersonal therapists in particular—has been depression (see, for example, Rush, 1982). Depressions are unusually common—perhaps as many as 15 percent of the total population will be significantly depressed at some time in their lives. In addition, depressions are the most lethal of all psychiatric disorders, putting patients at high risk for suicide (Yapko, 1988).

Klerman and colleagues originally described interpersonal psychotherapy of depression as a "psychological treatment designed specifically for the needs of depressed patients. It is a focused, short-term, time-limited therapy that emphasizes the current interpersonal relations of the depressed patient while recognizing the role of genetic, biochemical, developmental, and personality factors in causation of and vulnerability to depression" (1984, p. 5).

The crucial aspects of interpersonal psychotherapy that set it apart from other psychotherapies are its emphasis on brevity, its proactive rather than reactive therapeutic stance, and its single-minded focus on interpersonal relationships. Depression, as well as other forms of psychopathology, is seen as embedded in a social matrix, and Klerman and his colleagues believe that if therapists avoid that social matrix, their effectiveness will suffer.

Basic Characteristics of Interpersonal Psychotherapy

Klerman and his colleagues are convinced that clinical depression occurs in an interpersonal context and that therapeutic interventions directed at this interpersonal context will help the patient recover from the acute episode and possibly prevent relapse and recurrence.

In contrast with many other psychotherapies, interpersonal psychotherapy: (1) is time-limited, not long-term; (2) is focused, not open-ended—that is, it is directed toward one or two agreed-upon problem areas in the patient's current interpersonal functioning; (3) is interpersonal, not intrapsychic—that is, the patient's predicament is explored in terms of interpersonal relations rather than as a manifestation of internal conflict; (4) deals with current, not past, interpersonal relationships; and (5) tries to change the ways the patient reacts in interpersonal relationships rather than other behaviors, such as distorted thoughts, excessive guilt, or negative cognitions that may be troublesome to the patient in their own right and in settings that do not involve other people.

Interpersonal psychotherapy does not aspire to have a significant impact on personality or character structure. Accordingly, while recognizing the personality of the patient, the therapy does not focus on personality. The personality of the patient may have an effect on the patient-therapist relationship and may be a determinant of the interpersonal difficulties that are the focus of the psychotherapy. But personality factors have not been found to be significantly related to short-term outcome of interpersonal psychotherapy and are treated as quite secondary in importance.

Klerman and his colleagues contrast interpersonal psychotherapy with noninterpersonal psychotherapies with the use of the summary statements in Box 11-1.

While interpersonal psychotherapy differs from traditional psychodynamic therapies in certain important ways, it has many similarities as well, since the nature of social relationships has become increasingly important in the thinking of most psychotherapists. While traditional psychodynamic therapy concentrates on unconscious mental processes, interpersonal psychotherapy concentrates on social roles and interactions in the patient's past and current life experiences. Yet both interpersonal and psychodynamic therapies have a life-span orientation, attend to transference issues when they appear to be interfering with therapeutic progress, and respect the importance of early experience. Klerman and his colleagues write:

BOX 11-1 · *Comparison of Interpersonal Psychotherapy with Other Psychotherapies*

Interpersonal Therapy	*Other Psychotherapies*
What has contributed to this patient's depression right now?	Why did the patient become what he/she is and/or where is the patient going?
What are the current stresses?	What was the patient's childhood like?
Who are the key persons involved in the current stress: What are the current disputes and disappointments?	What is the patient's character?
Is the patient learning how to cope with the problem?	Is the patient cured?
What are the patient's assets?	Who are the patient's defenses?
How can I help the patient ventilate painful emotions—talk about situations that evoke guilt, shame, resentment?	How can I find out why this patient feels guilty, ashamed, or resentful?
How can I help the patient clarify his or her wishes and have more satisfying relationships with others?	How can I understand the patient's fantasy life and help him/her get insight into the origins of present behavior?
How can I correct misinformation and suggest alternatives?	How can I help the patient discover false or incorrect ideas?

From Klerman et al., 1984, p. 17.

"The psychodynamic therapist is concerned with object relations while the interpersonal therapist focuses on interpersonal relations. The psychodynamic therapist listens for the patient's intrapsychic wishes and conflicts; the interpersonal therapist listens for the patient's role expectations and disputes" (1984, p. 18).

Diagnostic and Strategic Principles in Interpersonal Therapy

Four specific interpersonal difficulties have been identified as being of particular importance in the treatment of depression—grief, interpersonal role disputes, role transitions, and interpersonal deficits (Rounsaville and Chevron, 1982). Each of these problem areas presents its own diagnostic and treatment challenges.

Grief

Grief reactions, particularly in connection with the death of a loved one, have much in common with depression, but it is only abnormal grief reactions, either in the form of delayed or distorted reactions, that require psychological intervention. Normal grief reactions include sadness, disturbed sleep, agitation, decreased ability to carry out normal responsibilities for a two- to four-month time period, and a gradual letting go of the loved one.

Abnormal grief reactions, in the form of pathological mourning, can be expected when there are overwhelming multiple losses or significant absence of social support during the bereavement period. Such reactions can be suspected when normal grief reactions are absent, when there is avoidance of commonly expected behaviors such as visiting the gravesite, when physical symptoms that mimic those of the deceased are reported, when reactions to the loss are pathologically prolonged or are precipitated too easily or frequently, when phobic behavior is displayed toward the cause of the death, when the environment of the loved one is scrupulously preserved, or when there is a radical change in the survivor's lifestyle.

The two general goals in the treatment of persons who are depressed following the loss of a loved one are to facilitate the normal mourning process and to help the survivor reestablish interests and social relationships that can substitute for those that have been lost, using such procedures as nonjudgmental exploration of feelings, reassurance, exploration of the patient's relationship with the deceased, and the development of increased awareness about that relationship, and the encouragement of appropriate subsequent behavior change.

Interpersonal Role Disputes

Role disputes, in the form of conflicts with important people in one's life, are an inevitable consequence of social interaction and are not often associated with depression. But when such disputes seem to be chronic or insoluble, they can lead to a sense of demoralization and a loss of the sense of self-efficacy that can result in significant depression. Thus, in working with depressed persons it is important to look for evidence of conflicts with the spouse, children, parents, colleagues or superiors in the work setting, neighbors, or other significant figures and to evaluate the extent to which these conflicts may be responsible for feelings of worthlessness, failure, or apathy.

Goals in the treatment of interpersonal conflict are to help the patient become more aware of the dispute and its characteristics, develop a plan for resolving the dispute, and make whatever changes in communication patterns are necessary, if maladaptive behaviors can be identified.

Role Transitions

Life changes often bring with them the need to develop new roles — for example, from that of wife to that of widow, or from husband to divorced person, or from employed person to job-seeker. To some extent we all are our roles. Thus, role transitions are not easy for anyone to make, and in some cases role transitions may be so difficult that they threaten the psychological equilibrium of the person. In treating depressed persons the therapist needs to be alert to the possibility that the patient is not coping well with the changes in roles that must be undertaken.

Two general goals in the treatment of depression associated with role transitions have been identified: enabling the patient to regard the challenge of establishing a new role or set of roles as an opportunity for growth; and restoring the sense of self-esteem by helping the patient master the demands of the process of role transition.

Interpersonal Deficits

Some patients have never developed the social skills necessary to maintain satisfying interpersonal relationships. This failure is often the result of long-standing interpersonal deprivations or difficulties and may be associated with chronic social isolation. When a patient is found who does not appear to have any close or intimate interpersonal relationships, it is likely that this deficit may be causally related to the depressive symptoms. In this case, dealing with the interpersonal deficit is critical for the successful management of the depression.

The goals of treatment must include efforts to reduce social isolation through the therapeutic review of past social relationships, analysis of the relationship with the therapist, and encouragement of the formation of new relationships.

Specific Therapeutic Techniques

While downplaying the uniqueness of the techniques that are particularly important in interpersonal psychotherapy, Klerman and colleagues (1984) devote considerable attention to a discussion of those techniques that seem to be most helpful to patients. They organize their discussion of these techniques in the order in which they are most often used as the therapeutic relationship develops.

Exploratory Techniques

Gathering information about presenting symptoms and problems is part of the beginning work of the therapy. Information is gathered with the use of nondirective exploration, supportive acknowledgment, and continuing discussion of topics already brought up. Direct inquiry can include the use of formal questionnaires and, of course, stresses the elicitation of information about important relationships the patient has with others. Questions generally proceed from the general ("Tell me about your husband") to the specific ("How did you feel when your husband said that?").

Encouragement of Affect

Deliberate encouragement of the expression of affect is a special attribute of most dynamic psychotherapies, including interpersonal psychotherapy, and is pursued by: (1) helping patients acknowledge the existence of painful but appropriate feelings, (2) helping patients identify emotional experiences that are associated with difficult interpersonal relationships, and (3) encouraging the development of new emotions that may facilitate growth and change in interpersonal relationships.

Among the techniques that Klerman and his colleagues identify as particularly important in the encouragement of affect are: (1) acceptance of painful affects, (2) using affects in interpersonal relationships, and (3) helping the patient generate suppressed affects. Klerman and colleagues caution, however, that when patients show signs of being overwhelmed by diffuse and intense emotional experiences, it may be prudent to suppress the expression of such affects until the patient is strong enough to tolerate their expression constructively.

Clarification

Clarifying remarks by the therapist serve to reformulate and feed back material previously presented by the patient. The purposes of clarification are to increase the patient's awareness of what has been communicated, in order to facilitate the continued exploration of previously suppressed material.

Among the clarifying techniques that Klerman and colleagues have identified are: (1) asking patients to repeat or rephrase what they have said, (2) rephrasing patient's statements, (3) calling attention to the logical implications of patient's statements, (4) identifying contrasts or contradictions in patient's statements, and (5) pointing out extremes in patient's beliefs when more modulated points of view seem more appropriate.

Communication Analysis

The interpersonal therapist can examine and identify communication failures in order to help the patient communicate more effectively. Such an analysis is central to the objectives of a therapist who is interested in increasing the interpersonal skills of patients. By exploring the details of an interpersonal interaction, it should be possible to identify how faulty communication may be responsible for disputes or other interpersonal difficulties. Among the most common communication difficulties are: (1) using ambiguous indirect nonverbal messages instead of direct verbal messages, (2) assuming that one has communicated to another person when in fact no such communication has taken place, (3) assuming that a communication has been understood when no such understanding has occurred, (4) being unnecessarily ambiguous in verbal communications, and (5) remaining silent when communication is needed.

The fundamental purpose for communication analysis is to guide patients to develop increased awareness of the nature and consequences of their methods of interpersonal communication. Successful communication analysis will increase patients' awareness of how their communications are received by others, particularly when disputes arise as a consequence.

Facilitating Behavior Change

According to Klerman and colleagues, lasting improvement from depression depends on helping patients make changes in their interpersonal behavior. Major therapeutic techniques available to the interpersonal therapist to help patients change their interpersonal behavior include directive techniques, such as educating, advising, modeling, limit setting, and direct suggestion; decision analysis by expanding the array of available choices open to the patient and helping the patient decide on a course of action from among those choices; and role playing—that is, the therapist's taking the role of some other person with whom the patient is in some interpersonal difficulty.

Klerman and colleagues believe that directive techniques should be used sparingly and only in the context of expanding options available to the patient, as in the phrase "One thing you might consider is . . . ." Suggestions should not be too specific or direct and should not undermine the patient's sense of autonomy and self-esteem. When the therapist is engaged in decision analysis, premture closure should be avoided. The therapist should make sure that choices are not too narrow and that the consequences of choices are fully explored. The principle seems to be that when in doubt, continue exploring decision alternatives. Role-playing techniques should also be used sparingly, but they can be helpful in providing an opportunity for patients to practice a course of action and to learn more about their feelings in specific interpersonal situations.

Becoming and Being an Interpersonal Psychotherapist

Klerman and his colleagues see interpersonal psychotherapy as a set of skills built upon prior completed traditional training and experience in any one of the mental health clinical disciplines—clinical psychology, psychiatry, social work, or psychiatric nursing. Training in interpersonal psychotherapy requires mastery of the Klerman and colleagues' training manual (1984), participation in a week-long didactic seminar, and careful supervision of a small number of cases. The central focus of the training is to help clinicians determine what aspects of their previous clinical experience and orientation are functional for undertaking interpersonal psychotherapy and what aspects need to be modified. The principal emphasis in interpersonal psychotherapy is on symptoms and present behavior. Thus, clinicians whose previous training has been in psychodynamic therapy tend to focus on historical, childhood phenomena without connecting these issues with the here and now and tend to spend too much time in overly long exploration of past history determinants of current behavior. Clinicians with previous training in behavior or cognitive therapy may find interpersonal psychotherapy difficult to master because of its commitment to understanding current behavior in a historical context.

The interpersonal psychotherapist takes a therapeutic stance that is both similar to and different from the general psychotherapist role. In interpersonal psychotherapy the therapist is not neutral; rather, he or she functions as an advocate of the patient. The therapist, according to Klerman and colleagues, is a "benign and helpful ally" (1984, p. 214). By not taking a neutral, withdrawn stance, the therapist discourages regression and excessive dependence on the part of the patient. Rather, the therapist remains non-judgmental, warm, supportive, gentle, accepting, and optimistic in the sense that the message is conveyed that a patient's problems are resolvable and not necessarily permanent.

In interpersonal psychotherapy the relationship between the therapist and patient is realistic rather than based on previous relationships with others. Transference issues are dealt with only when they appear to be impeding therapeutic progress.

In interpersonal psychotherapy the therapeutic relationship is not a friendship. If a patient wants the therapist to be more self-disclosing, this is permitted, provided that the therapist explores the patient's reasons for requesting such self-disclosure. While the therapist might appropriately become involved in helping a patient deal with life problems, or might testify on the behalf of the patient in a court action, or might make arrangements for other medical or mental health professionals to play a role in the treatment of the patient, the therapist would not become involved with the patient in social or business relationships.

The interpersonal therapist is active. At the start of therapy that activity might reflect itself in helping the patient focus on the presenting interpersonal problem, in eliciting the salient aspects of the patient's history, and in setting therapeutic goals. In intermediate sessions the therapist actively guides the patient using appropriate therapeutic techniques as previously discussed above. Yet, the therapist leaves in the patient's hands the decisions that must be made if interpersonal change is to take place.

Efficacy of Interpersonal Psychotherapy

Klerman and his colleagues have made a major commitment to evaluation of their therapy. In one of their early studies, eighty-one depressed patients were randomly assigned to one of four groups—(1) interpersonal psychotherapy, (2) antidepressant medication (amitriptyline), (3) a combination of interpersonal psychotherapy and amitriptyline, and (4) treatment on demand. All treatment programs lasted sixteen weeks, and outcome was assessed by the patients and treating clinicians and by a clinician who was blind to the treatment the patients were being provided.

Interpersonal psychotherapy, with or without medication, was found to be superior to nonscheduled treatment. Improvement in the treated groups continued to increase after the treatment was concluded, and at the one-year follow-up, patients who had received interpersonal psychotherapy were functioning at a less impaired level in social activities and with their spouses, children, and other relatives. The *rate* of improvement was similar in the groups who had received interpersonal psychotherapy and medication alone, but the *specific nature* of improvement differed. Patients in the interpersonal psychotherapy group demonstrated greatest consistent improvement in mood, work performance and interest, and in reductions in suicidal ideation and guilt. Amitriptyline had its most notable effect on reducing sleep and appetite disturbances and somatic complaints. Patients who were in the group that received interpersonal psychotherapy and medication showed the highest level of improvement, specifically including reduced symptoms and lower attrition rate (Weissman, 1979).

The use of interpersonal psychotherapy for maintenance treatment was also evaluated (see Klerman et al., 1984). A sample of 150 women who were recovering from depressive episodes after having been treated for six to eight weeks with medication were then randomly assigned to either interpersonal psychotherapy or to low-contact control employing either amitriptyline, placebo, or no medication. Maintenance interpersonal psychotherapy significantly improved social and interpersonal functioning, but, at the same time, the medication was more efficacious than the interpersonal psychotherapy in preventing symptomatic relapse. The effects of the interpersonal psychotherapy and the medication were additive; that is, patients who received both interpersonal psychotherapy and medication showed the lowest rate of relapse and highest rate of social improvement.

The maintenance experiment was concluded after eight months, but patients were followed for up to four years. At the one-year follow-up 30 percent were totally symptom-free, 60 percent had mild symptoms at some time during the year, and 10 percent remained chronically depressed. Additional studies of the efficacy of interpersonal psychotherapy are being conducted (see, for example, Elkin et al., 1985; Foley et al., 1987; Rounsaville et al., 1987; Rounsaville et al., 1988).

Concluding Comments

The single greatest contribution of Klerman's interpersonal therapy to the field of planned short-term psychotherapy is its emphasis on interpersonal relationships and on how disturbances in those relationships can help set the stage for significant psychopathology, particularly nonpsychotic depression. Based on this point of view, Klerman and his colleagues have set about working with patients for the purpose of analyzing and improving their interpersonal relationships.

In some ways, interpersonal psychotherapy holds a middle ground between psychodynamic therapy, with its focus on intrapsychic phenomena, and cognitive and behavior therapy, with their focus on external behavior that so often concerns itself with behavior in interpersonal settings.

Perhaps the most interesting question regarding Klerman's work is its applicability to disorders other than neurotic depression. The strategies employed by Klerman seem quite broad in nature, in no sense specific only to depression, and thus quite applicable to the treatment of patients with other conditions.

SECTION THREE

Cognitive and Behavioral Planned Short-Term Therapy

Behavioral and cognitive approaches to planned short-term psychotherapy have shown enough evidence of a productive union so that it seems appropriate to discuss them together. The radical behaviorist approach (see Wilson, 1978, 1981), identified with the work of Skinner, essentially held that all behavior is under the control of environmental factors external to the person. More contemporary views of behavior therapy include the social learning perspective, with its emphasis on cognitive mediational processes and self-regulatory capacities (see, for example, Lewinsohn, Sullivan, and Grosscup, 1982; Marks, 1986; McLean, 1982; Rush, 1982, 1984). Thus, how external events determine behavior is mediated by internal cognitive processes and capacities that are, in turn, based on prior experience.

Cognitive and behavioral therapies have grown rapidly in the past two decades, in part because of their successes with such a wide variety of patients, many of whom have presented problems that have been difficult to treat from a psychodynamic orientation (Phillips, 1985a). All the theories analyzed in this section share a central interest in contemporary behavior and its modification and share a set of values that dramatically distinguish cognitive and behavioral theories from psychodynamic viewpoints.

Among the ways that cognitive and behavior theory and therapy differ from psychodynamic theory and therapy, the most important are its central interest in the present, on the one hand, and its relative disinterest in the patient's past in helping the patient achieve insight, in determining causes, or in exploring transference relationships on the other hand. Indeed, the principal domain of inquiry of some psychotherapists seems to have moved from an initial preoccupation with the past to a later preoccupation with the present, and now to an emphasis in the future—that is, to solutions. This emphasis manifests itself by a conspicuous lack of interest in "how problems arose or even how they are maintained, but instead is concerned with how they will be solved" (O'Hanlon and Weiner-Davis, 1989, p. 12).

Strategic psychotherapy (see Chapter 16) shares this same general orientation toward the present and future. Goldsmith (1986) characterizes this orientation in the following statement: "Strategic psychotherapeutic practice is concerned, after all, with getting patients to change rather than getting them to be more aware of themselves" (p. 20).

O'Hanlon and Weiner-Davis (1989, ch. 2) contrast the assumptions of past-oriented psychotherapeutic theories with present- and future-oriented theories by noting that past-oriented theories tend to subscribe to the belief that: (1) There are deep underlying causes for symptoms; (2) symptoms are functional; (3) insight into the causes of symptoms is necessary for symptom resolution; (4) symptom removal in the absence of insight is useless and may even be dangerous; (5) patients are resistant to psychotherapy and ambivalent about changing; (6) change takes time and brief interventions do not last; and (7) the fundamental task of psychotherapy is to identify and correct psychopathology.

In contrast, present- and future-oriented psychotherapeutic theory is based on a quite different set of beliefs: (1) Patients bring with them into therapy the resources that are necessary to resolve their complaints; (2) personal change goes on continuously, with or without therapy; (3) the task of the psychotherapist is to identify and amplify change; (4) resolving symptoms does not require knowing the causes or the functions of the symptoms; (5) small changes are all that is necessary—these changes reverberate throughout the personality and can bring about changes in many areas of functioning; (6) patients define the goals for their own therapy; (7) rapid changes in behavior and problem resolution are possible; (8) there is no single right way to view symptoms; and (9) therapists should focus on what is possible and changeable rather than on what is impossible and intractable.

In more specific terms, cognitive and behavioral theories have a number of important common elements, including a careful and active assessment of current problems, the establishment of attainable and contracted therapeutic goals, obtaining prompt relief from the most pressing problems, and use of a wide variety of empirically based interventions that increase the patient's sense of self-efficacy (Peake, Borduin, and Archer, 1988). As will become evident in the following chapters, cognitive behavior therapy differs from psychodynamic therapy as much in terms of its specific intervention strategies as it does in terms of its underlying theories.

The five approaches to cognitively oriented short-term psychotherapy presented in this section are in no sense carbon copies of each other. Phillips and Wiener's approach exemplifies the resolute application of reinforcement theory in the clinical setting. Ellis insistently points out self-defeating beliefs and forcefully encourages changes in these beliefs and in their associated behaviors in a remarkably hortatory yet supportive manner. Farrelly is Machiavellian, using a kind of psychic ju-jitsu to disarm patients and to help them get well if only to spite their therapist. Beck combines rationality with empathy in his efforts to help patients change their cognitions. Erickson has rightly gained fame by skillfully assessing what change is possible for a patient and building a remarkably subtle therapeutic program around those possibilities.

CHAPTER TWELVE

Phillips and Wiener's Structured Behavior Change Therapy

Overview

Therapeutic Approach and Plan

Time-Lapse Protocols

Alternative Behavior Change Therapy Approaches

Concluding Comments

E. Lakin Phillips and Daniel Wiener's (1966) approach to short-term therapy proceeds from their basic premise that the goal of all therapists is the efficient production of significant behavior change. With this emphasis on prompt behavior change, they asert that

> long-term therapy is not, in fact, the most desirable, not even for those who can afford it or who prefer it. It is not a matter of efficiency alone that makes us favor short- over long-term therapy. Instead, our belief is that structured therapy (which tends to be short-term) is better than long-term, conventional therapy for this reason: structured therapy is purposely *as short-term as possible.* By "purposely," we mean structured to solve specific problems — *regardless of whether they are chronic and serious or only mildly disabling. (1966, p. 2)*

Phillips and Wiener believe that short-term therapies are particularly appropriate for dealing with current problems in living. With an emphasis on current functioning, psychotherapy can become more effective and more efficient. Time-limited psychotherapy, they believe, should have little, if any, concern with the past or with the inner life of the patient or with a "broad philosophical search for hidden meaning" (1966, p. 11).

To Phillips and Wiener it is not simply that short-term therapy can be supportive, provide guidance or the opportunity to discharge pent-up emotions, or fulfill dependency needs. They believe that short-term therapy can produce substantial and long-lasting behavior change, and they contend that the help most people need to develop more satisfying lives may be far more modest than therapists have been led to believe. In contrast to psychodynamic therapies that tend to emphasize person characteristics in understanding and modifying behavior, Phillips and Wiener's approach emphasizes characteristics of the external world and of the responses a person makes to it.

Therapeutic Approach and Plan

Many consequences follow this emphasis on externals and response patterns. First, since the focus of interest is on behavior change, there is relatively little concern with the origins of a person's difficulties—that is, with the original stimuli for the problem. Second, after the therapist and the patient have agreed upon the objectives of the therapy, patients can be taught to develop new responses to troublesome situations by changing their behavior, their environment, or both. Third, other people can be involved in the therapeutic process whenever they might be able to function as change agents.

Fourth, with the emphasis on behavior change procedures, there is relatively less need for traditional verbal, insight-oriented practices. Fifth, any and all problem-solving procedures should be encouraged. Sixth, rather than allowing undesired behavior to occur so that it might be studied and extinguished, it should be prevented from occurring whenever possible. Seventh, the general therapeutic task is to find, institute, and reinforce new desired behavior to substitute for the problem behavior.

Eighth, behavior change, like all learning, can be expected to take place step by step rather than by sudden bursts of insight. Ninth, corrective measures should be forward-looking and specific. The technical skills of the therapist should come into play in the process of identifying and promoting newly sought behavior patterns, with the use of such procedures as desensitization, operant conditioning, and aversive stimulation. Finally, there should be no need for a language that is not tied directly to behavior—that is, there should be no need for such concepts as diagnosis, anxiety, complexes, or the unconscious.

Phillips and Wiener take the position that since it is behavior change that the patient is seeking, the most direct approach to that goal is not only the most efficient, but it might very well also be the best. Their ideas and approaches would have less applicability in the case when behavior change is not the primary goal or not even a goal at all. Some therapists argue, for example, that the goal of psychotherapy is to increase a patient's self-understanding, and that changes a patient might make as a consequence of that increased understanding are of only secondary importance. But to the extent that behavior change is one of the major goals of psychotherapy, Phillips and Wiener's work provides an impressive justification for therapists to become skilled in the techniques of behavior analysis and behavior modification.

The principal purpose of the initial meeting with the patient is to develop a *therapeutic plan*. Such a plan ordinarily has three components: the change object, the change agent, and the change plan. The *change object* is the identified patient — it can be a specific individual or couple or family, for example, or a classroom of disturbed children. The *change agent* is the person or persons through whom changes can be attempted in the change object. In many cases the agent and the object are the same. But creating the concept of the change agent calls attention to the fact that there may be a potentially more effective but indirect way of bringing about change in the change object. Thus, a teacher or parent may be the change agent for an identified child who is the change object. In some situations several change agents may be identified and may work collaboratively to bring about change in a specific change object. Any person, condition, or situation can serve as a change agent, depending on the specific situation. The *change plan* identifies the behavior that has to change and develops the strategy and tactics for bringing the desired change about, including who, besides the therapist, should be involved in the process.

Behavior change is brought about through invoking the most appropriate learning theories. Certain behaviors can be modified through the use of classical conditioning theory, using such procedures as extinction, differential reinforcement, or desensitization. Other behaviors can employ operant learning theories, by concentrating on modifying the consequences of behavior as a way of modifying the behavior. It is the task of the therapist to develop a plan that makes the most intelligent use of learning theories and that has the best chance of success in changing behavior in the desired direction.

In Box 12-1 is a brief case history that exemplifies the process of developing a treatment plan.

Time-Lapse Protocols

Phillips and Wiener are, of course, interested in showing the special potential advantages of structured behavior change in affecting current behavior.

BOX 12-1 • *Developing a Treatment Plan*

Mrs. T sought help for her 9-year-old daughter who was a soiler (encopresis). The problem had existed for several years, but had worsened over the months just prior to referral. The child was scholastically able . . . was accepted socially by her peers except when the odor was strong, and she had good relations with adults. . . . Laxatives and suppositories did not help. . . . The parents alternately scolded, cajoled, and ignored the child, without success. The child responded by being alternately contrite, impervious, or angry. . . . She soiled only at home, during play inside or out, and never at school. . . . The mother revealed that she had tried, without success, to get the child to sit on the toilet a few minutes after breakfast; but since the mother was easily discouraged, she had soon abandoned this tactic when it was unsuccessful.

The hypothesis derived by the therapist . . . was that the child was too busy playing to heed the cues related to defecation. . . . The child "let go" to a small extent, thus allowing herself to continue to play uninterruptedly and to reduce somewhat the internal pressure at the same time. . . . The parents were told that they should not mention the habit, but that the mother should tell the child that she was to sit on the toilet a few minutes after each meal. If, after ten minutes, there was no bowel movement, the parent was advised by the therapist to say nothing, but to have the child come back after about one hour of play and sit on the toilet again. The child was to do this each hour until there was a movement. Then the child was to be free to play without another "sitting" that day unless continued observation showed that a second or third movement appeared to be necessary or likely.

In the second interview, three weeks later, the mother reported that the child had become symptom-free after two days of this regimen. In the next follow-up conversation, one year later, she reported that the child had had only one relapse, that otherwise the problem had disappeared, and that the child was continuing in a normal fashion with school and other activities. The mother said, "Well, I guess you trained me first and the child second, but it certainly worked!"

From Phillips and Wiener, 1966, pp. 72–73.

They select key moments in the therapeutic experience (similar to time-lapse photography) and examine four different prototypical approaches to dealing with these moments—psychodynamic, nondirective, eclectic (more or less directive), and structured behavior change. The statements made by the patients are accurate, in that they were actually made in the course of therapy.

Statements attributed to the therapists are not made in the form displayed. Rather, they are examples of statements that could be made by therapists from each of the four therapeutic orientations in response to the patient's statement. In Box 12-2, Box 12-3, and Box 12-4 are examples that illustrate their position about the potential usefulness of structured behavior change therapy.

BOX 12-2 · *Four Approaches to Psychotherapy: Protocol I*

Patient: I've got this problem, you see, being homosexual and all that. I'm afraid about it. I go to church and I feel guilty and I can't confess. And I'm nervous all the time. Can you help me get over this nervousness? I'm afraid I'll lose my job and all.

Therapist Responses:

Psychodynamic Orientation: Tell me about your home and family. What were they like? How did you feel toward your father? And mother? What dreams have you had lately? Do you see how this fear of getting too close to your mother, with her seductive ways, can make you fear women? And fear what your father would do if you loved your mother too much?

Nondirective Orientation: You feel very nervous about your homosexuality and don't know what to do about it. I wonder whether this feeling can be clarified. If I catch it correctly, you seem to be saying that you're worried more about being caught and about your guilt, than of the sex act itself.

Eclectic Orientation: Don't worry about homosexual thoughts. Everyone has them some time. And almost everyone has at least one homosexual experience. But try to control it or forget it. You should go out with girls. Keep busy. And try going to church, where you can get a grasp of good principles of living. If you feel too nervous to control the impulse, you can take a tranquilizer I'll give you a prescription for.

Structured Behavior Change Orientation: Can we decide, even tentatively, what your problem is and what you want to do about it? As a beginning, do you want to get over being a homosexual, or do you want only to get over your nervousness connected with it? You have this choice, and you must make it sooner or later if you want to get over your nervousness. You may not like the consequences of being homosexual, but you have to accept and suffer the consequences in terms of social dangers and penalties, if you practice it.

From Phillips and Wiener, 1966, pp. 143–144.

BOX 12-3 • *Four Approaches to Psychotherapy: Protocol II*

Patient: I can't stand it when my husband orders me around. He never really hits me or anything like that, but he's just terrible the way he raves and rants. And I can't ever please him. Nothing does, by me or the kids. I just can't do anything about it. It makes me feel terrible all the time.

Therapist Responses:

Psychodynamic Orientation: Apparently there's a great deal of hostility between you and your husband, and you can't stand it, so you develop symptoms and get sick. Now, why shouldn't you get angry when he treats you badly? Why shouldn't you even hate him at times? But tell me also, is this the way you felt toward your father?

Nondirective Orientation: You can't stand to be ordered around. And you feel pushed around and unappreciated no matter what you do. So you end up feeling bad, and getting sick, is that it?

Eclectic Orientation: Your husband probably doesn't mean anything by it. He's good to you otherwise, isn't he? Maybe he really loves you, but doesn't know how to show it. You'll have to try to pull yourself together. Have you tried this new drug yet?

Structured Behavior Change Orientation: Your husband orders you around and acts unreasonable, and you feel terrible because of the way he is. But if that's the way he is, and he's not about to act differently just because you want him to, then you have to look at yourself to change, to learn what you can do differently so that you don't end up feeling so terrible. Can you sometimes handle him in a way that brings him around?

From Phillips and Wiener, 1966, p. 151.

Alternative Behavior Change Therapy Approaches

Phillips and Wiener (1966) carry their concepts of structured behavior change therapy to the logical limit of envisioning therapy without the immediate presence of the therapist. Two examples that they examine are using principles from pedagogy to develop teaching approaches to therapy and conducting therapy by having the patient write rather than talk. Both approaches can result in the more efficient use of the therapist and in the development of useful adjuncts to the more traditional verbal interactional psychotherapies.

BOX 12-4 · *Four Approaches to Psychotherapy: Protocol III*

Patient: Well, I've been trying to think along the lines we talked about last time, and it just doesn't make sense to me. I admit that you've done me some good but my life still seems like such a mess and so hopeless that I can't see any use to going on with these interviews. So I've decided that this will be my last session.

Therapist Responses:

Psychodynamic Orientation: You seem to have reached a point where you're anxious about going on. I wonder why this is, what it is that's too threatening for you to face. And you have some positive feelings toward me, but also apparently some negative ones, and you have some resistance about going on with me. But wouldn't it be better to analyze these feelings? You don't have to be afraid of them. You can talk freely to me about them.

Nondirective Orientation: You have been trying to follow through on what we've been talking about, but you just can't figure it out. And you feel so hopeless that you've decided to give up at this point, and quit, is that right?

Eclectic Orientation: You're feeling pretty depressed, aren't you! Many patients have periods like this. But why quit now, when you've begun to get out of the woods? Of course, you could quit for awhile and see how it goes. Maybe your life isn't really such a mess as it seems right now. Perhaps you could go off on a vacation for awhile, and then come back and reconsider.

Structured Behavior Change Orientation: You're having trouble moving ahead along the lines we've been setting up, and you want to fall back on your old habits. But isn't that what got you into trouble in the first place and made you decide to see me? It is hard work to change long-time habits, of course. And you will always have periods of being discouraged. But if we go over your program again, and perhaps try to improve on it, you can get back to work on it. Then if you can continue to succeed with it as you began to do—instead of falling back on the old ways—you know that in a week or a month you'll be much more likely to feel good about yourself than if you follow your impulse of this moment.

From Phillips and Wiener, 1966, pp. 155–156.

Programmed Therapy

The nature of structured behavior change therapy lends itself to thinking about therapy as teaching and to considering the use of teaching techniques for carrying out therapeutic objectives. One example of this possibility is the use of step-by-step programmed instruction as a therapeutic adjunct. These programmed instructional steps could be presented to the patient in pamphlet form, or even on a computer screen, and, if the patient can read and follow directions and is willing to cooperate in this type of learning process, significant behavior change can take place.

For example, if a patient's presenting problem is that he loses his temper too often and too easily, it should be possible to develop a programmed instructional experience that could result in desired behavior change. Initial steps in such a program might look like those shown in Box 12-5.

Occasional meetings with the therapist would be very desirable in order to reinforce progress that has been made and in order to deal with issues that are not included in the programmed instruction.

Writing Therapy

Another example of an alternative approach to structured behavior change therapy is a procedure that Phillips and Wiener call writing therapy (see Phillips, Gershenson, and Lyons, 1977; Phillips and Wiener, 1966, ch. 9). Such a procedure could be particularly appropriate for patients who are

---

BOX 12-5 · *Initial Steps in a Programmed Therapeutic Process*

1. *Loss of temper is better described as "loss of self-control." One may notice this tendency when tired, ill, or highly irritated by another person's behavior. Whatever the reason, one has to develop ways of showing better s_____-c_____. (Write in correct answer) Answer: self-control.*

2. *People experience "loss of temper or self-control" in more than one type of situation. I tend to lose self-control of temper most commonly in the following ways: (write in replies)*

3. *Given knowledge of a situation in which loss of self-control is common, one can then attempt to foresee such situations and develop means to counteract this tendency. One does not need an "explanation" of the temper loss, only ways and means of c_____ the temper. Answer: controlling or counteracting.*

4. *To prepare in advance for a troublesome situation is the best way to offset a tendency to lose one's temper. One can use humor or delay his external action to someone when he is provoked. If one thinks ahead about his probable reaction, he can often_____ a tendency to react with anger or temper loss. Answer: change.*

From Phillips and Wiener, 1966, p. 120

articulate and who can write clearly; it has been used for some years in college settings. It should be noted that there is evidence that some patients prefer writing to being in a face-to-face situation and that they can be more open and more direct when they write than when they speak (see Phillips and Wiener, 1966, pp. 160–162).

Writing therapy is intended to help people with their personal, social, or academic problems. Patients have regular weekly appointments just as would be the case with traditional psychotherapy, but during the hour they are expected to write in a special notebook that is kept under lock and key and is available only to them and to their therapist. Patients are instructed to be as frank, complete, and cooperative as possible and to write as clearly as they can about themselves, their observations, their problems, and about how they have tried to cope with their difficulties in the past. The therapist reads and replies in writing to what the patient has written, and thus an exchange between therapist and patient takes place.

Phillips and Wiener report that dealing with written communication is about twice as efficient as dealing with oral communication, that the technique is unusually helpful for beginning therapists, that there is remarkably little wasted time in the interaction, and that the written protocols are always available for reconsideration as well as for evaluation of change in the patient. Both therapist and patient have access at any time to everything they have previously written.

In an evaluation of time-limited writing therapy, Phillips, Gershenson, and Lyons (1977) employed the technique with seventeen undergraduates who had not had previous therapy and who volunteered to try writing therapy instead of face-to-face therapy for ten sessions. Personality inventories were administered to the patients both immediately before and after the writing therapy process. In addition, experienced therapists rated the patients' writings in terms of the degree of successful problem resolution that was reported and the extent to which the patients' reactions to the therapy were favorable.

Patients wrote on average about 1200 words at the initial session. The number of words decreased fairly regularly, until at the final session an average of about 600 words were written. Therapist written comments averaged about 300 words for each session. Significant improvements in a number of personality dimensions were found when the pretherapy and posttherapy personality test results were compared. The personality dimensions that exhibited the greatest improvement were in psychasthenia, hypomania, social introversion, and becoming more assertive, outgoing, independent, and self-directed. Most patients had favorable reactions to the writing therapy, and when asked if they would continue writing therapy if given the opportunity, nine said that they would, seven said they would not, and one had no opinion. Of the seven who said they would not, four said that that they had already solved their problems and needed no further help.

Concluding Comments

Phillips and Wiener have proposed a highly rational behavioral cognitive therapy that is derived directly from data-based and theory-based learning approaches to the understanding of behavior. Their uncompromising focus is on examining and changing behavior, and their belief is that most people who enter into psychotherapy do so because there is some aspect of their internal or external behavior that they wish to modify.

Structured behavior change therapy incorporates the essence of planned short-term psychotherapy—it is structured to solve specific problems as quickly as possible and to make use of every available therapeutic resource in order to accomplish that goal. Structured behavior change therapy is upbeat in its orientation and democratic in its view of the legitimate actors in the therapeutic process. It carries with it the light baggage of learning theory, but none of what it considers the excess baggage of intrapsychic approaches. It professes no interest in the remote past, in developing insight, in making diagnoses, in establishing causes, or in such concepts as defenses, conflicts, or the unconscious.

Finally, Phillips and Wiener have courageously gone where their theories have led them—to the initial development of pedagogical approaches to psychotherapy that can be automated so as to give therapists an even less exclusive role than behavioral cognitive psychotherapists normally assign to them.

CHAPTER THIRTEEN

Ellis's Rational-Emotive Psychotherapy

Overview

Rational-Emotive Theory

Rational and Irrational Beliefs

A Case Example

The Belief System Between Stimulus and Response

Concluding Comments

Rational-emotive therapy (RET) is a relatively brief form of psychological treatment that, according to its proponents, is appropriate to consider for treating the vast majority of emotional disorders. Developed originally by Albert Ellis (1962; see also Ellis, 1989; Ellis and Abrahms, 1978; Ellis and Bernard, 1983; Ellis and Grieger, 1977; Ellis and Harper, 1961), RET is advocated as a treatment of choice for anxiety, depression, inadequacy, hostility, and low frustration tolerance. RET is a comprehensive and multimodal cognitive behavioral approach that is based on the theory that people's disturbance-creating beliefs underlie their self-defeating actions. It is designed for efficiency by stressing "directness, a high degree of activity by the therapist, bibliotherapy, and specific homework assignments for patients to perform in between the RET sessions" (Ellis and Abrahms, 1978, p. 4).

Rational-Emotive Theory

The goal of RET is to help a patient achieve full self-acceptance—the acceptance of one's self, one's aliveness, one's existence—without requirements and unconditionally. Self-acceptance is achieved, according to RET theory, by pure choice; no special reasons are required. Full self-acceptance implies that one's characteristics or personal traits can be evaluated, but not one's self. In the case of a person with severe hypochondriasis, for example, full self-acceptance would mean that the person: (1) believes that having the disorder is undesirable, perhaps unfortunate, but that it is not horrible; (2) can tolerate the symptoms of the disorder without extreme anxiety, depression, or rumination; (3) can cope with a medical examination or medical treatment; and (4) can apply the behavioral methods learned in the psychotherapy sessions to prevent or overcome similar symptoms in the future.

From this point of view, every person ought to be able to say:

> *First, I am alive. That is fairly evident and observable. Second, I choose to stay alive. Why? Simply because I choose to do so. Third, I desire, while alive, to live fairly happily, with relatively little pain and much pleasure. Because that seems conducive to my staying alive—and because I simply like being happy rather than miserable. Fourth, let me see how I can manage to decrease my pain and increase my short-range and long-range pleasure. (Ellis and Abrahms, 1978, p. 7)*

Self-acceptance is achieved to the extent that people can give up their inordinate needs to do well and to win the approval of others. The vignette in Box 13-1 illustrates how RET assists in achieving unconditional self-acceptance.

BOX 13-1 · *Working Toward Unconditional Self-Acceptance: A Case Vignette*

Patient: Why do I have to take those crummy pills? I can see that the doctors are right. I know that the drugs stop me from hearing voices. And I'm sure I'd be back in the hospital if I stopped taking my medicine. So I take the pills. But I think *it's terrible* to take them!

Therapist: Why is it terrible to take medication?

P: Because I have to remember to take it, and I have to take time to see you for appointments—and sometimes I get side effects from the medicine.

T: And that's why it's *inconvenient* for you to take the pills. That's a rational Belief—"I don't like to take the pills because I find some of their effects unpleasant." If you stayed only with that rational Belief—that taking medication is *inconvenient* or *unfortunate*—how would you feel?

P: I'd feel less depressed.

BOX 13-1 *Continued*

T: Yes. You'd probably, if you only stressed the inconvenience or unfortunateness of taking the pills, feel sorry, or sad, or regretful about taking them. And that would be okay, or what we call, "appropriate" in RET. For if you find something inconvenient, you certainly don't want to feel *good* about it! So when you feel depressed, you really have *two* feelings: first the appropriate feeling of sorrow or regret, because you don't *like* to take the pills and yet you know that you'd better take them; and second, the inappropriate feeling of depression. And this second feeling, your inappropriate feeling, doesn't come from that rational Belief, "I don't like to take the pills because I find some of their effects unpleasant." It comes, instead, from a second belief, or what we call an irrational Belief in RET. What do you think your irrational Belief is?

P: (30 second pause) The irrational Belief that causes me to be depressed? I guess, "It's *terrible* to take the pills!

T: That's exactly right. When you say to yourself irrationally, "It's *awful, horrible, or terrible"* to do anything, such as take pills, you're really creating your own depression.

P: Then what do I do to feel better about myself?

T: First, understand exactly what you are telling yourself irrationally, in the manner that we're now going over it; and then give up these irrational ideas.

From Ellis and Abrahms, 1978, pp. 9–10.

Rational and Irrational Beliefs

The distinction between rational and irrational beliefs is central to RET theory. The principal goal of RET is to help patients discover their irrational beliefs about themselves and others and abandon them if these beliefs are having negative consequences. According to RET theory psychological problems arise from irrational beliefs—that is, from misperceptions and misconceptions, from emotional underreactions or overreactions, and from dysfunctional behavior patterns. Rational thoughts, appropriate feelings, and effective behaviors are defined as those that aid human survival and happiness. RET actively and vigorously confronts cognitive, emotional, and behavioral pathology, principally by focusing on the rational and irrational intervening beliefs that lie between the activating experiences and the emotional consequences.

Ellis (1962) identified ten common irrational beliefs that, in his judgment, are ubiquitous in Western civilization and would seem inevitably to lead to widespread neurosis. These dysfunctional beliefs are listed in Box 13-2.

A Case Example

The best way to exemplify RET is to examine a representative interview. The excerpt in Box 13-3 comes from the second interview with a 27-year-old man whose symptoms included shyness and social inhibition, particularly around women; rapid ejaculation in intercourse; and hostility to authority figures, including his parents and his supervisor at work. The therapist is Albert Ellis.

BOX 13-2 • *Ellis's List of Common Irrational Beliefs*

1. It is a dire necessity for an adult human being to be loved or approved by virtually every significant other person in his community.
2. One should be thoroughly competent, adequate, and achieving in all possible respects if one is to consider oneself worthwhile.
3. Certain people are bad, wicked, or villainous, and they should be severely blamed and punished for their villainy.
4. It is awful and catastrophic when things are not the way one would very much like them to be.
5. Human unhappiness is externally caused, and people have little or no ability to control their sorrows and disturbances.
6. If something is or may be dangerous or fearsome one should be terribly concerned about it and should keep dwelling on the possibility of its occurring.
7. It is easier to avoid than to face certain life difficulties and self-responsibilities.
8. One should be dependent on others and need someone stronger than oneself on whom to rely.
9. One's past history is an all-important determiner of one's present behavior, and because something once strongly affected one's life, it should indefinitely have a similar effect.
10. One should become quite upset over other people's problems and disturbances.

Excerpted from Ellis, 1962, pp. 61–85.

BOX 13-3 · *Rational-Emotive Therapy in Action*

Therapist: You seem to be terribly afraid that you will fail to make good initial contacts with a woman and also succeed sexually.

Patient: Hell, yes! To say the least, I'm scared stiff on both counts.

T: Because if you fail in either area . . .

P: If I fail, I'll be an utter slob!

T: Prove it!

P: Isn't it obvious?

T: Not for me! It's fairly obvious that if a woman rejects you, socially or sexually, it'll hardly be a great thing. But how will that prove *you,* a total person, will be no good?

P: I still think it's obvious. Would this same woman reject *anyone?*

T: No, probably not. Let's suppose that she accepts many men, but not you. Let's also suppose that she rejects you because she finds that, first, you're not terribly good at conversation and second, you come quickly in intercourse. So she finds you doubly deficient. Now, how does that still prove that you're no good?

P: It certainly proves that I'm no good for *her.*

T: Yes, in a way. You're no good for her conversationally and sexually. You have two rotten *traits.*

P: And she doesn't want *me,* for having those traits.

T: Right. In the case we're assuming, she rejects *you* for having those two traits. But all we've proved is that one woman despises two of your characteristics; and that this woman therefore rejects you as a lover or a husband. Even she, mind you, might well accept you as a nonsexual friend. For you have, don't forget, many other traits — such as intelligence, artistic talent, reliability, etc.

P: But not the traits she *most* wants!

T: Maybe. But how does this prove that *all* women, like her, would find you equally wanting? Some, actually, might like you *because* you are shy and *because* you come quickly sexually — when they don't happen to like intercourse, and therefore want to get it over rapidly!

P: Fat chance!

Continued

BOX 13-3   *Continued*

T: Yes, statistically. For *most* women, presumably, will tend to reject you if you're shy or sexually inadequate, in their eyes. But a few, at least, will accept you for the very reasons that most refuse you, and many more, normally, will accept you in spite of your deficiencies, because they nonetheless become attached to you.

P: Who the devil wants *that!*

T: Most of us do, actually, if we're sane. For, since we're all highly imperfect, we're happy that some people accept us *with* those imperfections. But let's even suppose the worst — just to show how crooked your thinking is. Let's suppose that, because of your shyness and fast ejaculation, *all* women reject you for *all* time. Would you still be a worthless slob?

P: I wouldn't exactly be a great guy!

T: No, you wouldn't be Casanova! But many women, remember, wouldn't want you if you were. Most women, at least today, wouldn't want Casanova just *because* he was so sexy and promiscuous. Anyway, we're evading the question; *would* you be a total slob?

P: Well, uh, I — no, I guess not.

T: Because?

P: Well, because I'd still have other, uh, good traits. Is that what you're getting at?

T: Yes, partly. You'd still have other good traits. And *you,* if you were to rate yourself at all, would equal *all* of your traits, not merely two of them.

From Ellis and Abrahms, 1978, pp. 41–42.

The Belief System Between Stimulus and Response

In this patient's case, seeing an attractive woman and wanting to approach her produced shyness and inhibition. But between the stimulus and the response was a complex belief system consisting of both rational and irrational components. The rational component was the belief that he might be rejected if he approached the woman and that the rejection would be unfortunate and annoying and would make him feel sorry, regretful, and frustrated. The irrational component was the belief that the rejection would be awful, that he could not bear it, and that it would prove him to be an utter slob!

This irrational component earned that description because it treated the possible rejection as unbearable, because it signified that the patient was worthless, and because the patient viewed these self-descriptions as permanent. That is, the patient was evaluating himself as an entirety rather than evaluating his traits or his social performance. In a subsequent therapeutic session, after Ellis had pointed out the philosophic foundation of the patient's inhibitions and anxiety, the patient asked how he could get rid of his irrational beliefs. The excerpt in Box 13-4 demonstrates how this fundamental question was dealt with.

BOX 13-4 · *Rational-Emotive Therapy: Prescribing Homework*

Therapist: For ten minutes every day, take *any* irrational or nutty belief that you have, such as the one that it's terrible for you to be rejected by a woman you find attractive, and practice giving it up, even when you are not being rejected.

Patient: How?

T: By using the logical and empirical method of seeing whether your hypothesis is consistent with your other goals and hypotheses, and by asking for factual evidence to sustain or invalidate it.

P: Can you be more specific?

T: Yes, in my group therapy sessions, recently, I have been giving most of the members of the group disputing assignments . . . to help them carry out these ten-minute-a-day disputations. . . . the point is for you to decide exactly what hypothesis or nutty idea you want to work on for at least ten minutes a day. And, in your case, it would be the idea, again, that it's terrible for you to get rejected by a woman you find attractive. You would take this idea, and ask yourself several basic questions, in order to challenge and dispute it.

P: What kind of questions?

T: Usually, four basic questions — though they have all kinds of variations. The first one is, "What am I telling myself?" or "What silly idea do I want to challenge?" And the answer, in your case, is, "It's terrible if a woman whom I find attractive rejects me." The second question is, "Is this, my hypothesis, true?" And the answer is . . .

P: Uh, well, no, it isn't.

T: Fine. If you had said this was true, the third question would have been, "Where is the evidence for its being true?" But since you said it isn't true, the third question is, "Where is the evidence that it's not true?" Well . . . ?

Continued

BOX 13-4 *Continued*

P: Well, uh, it's not true because, as we said before, it may be *inconvenient* if an attractive woman rejects me, but it's not *more* than that, it's *only* damned inconvenient!

T: Right. And there's other logical and empirical evidence that it isn't terrible. For one thing, because *this* woman rejects you hardly means that *all* will. For another, you obviously have survived even though you have been rejected. For still another, lots of other people in the world have been rejected by the woman they most love, and it has hardly been terrible for all of them, has it?

P: I see. There are several evidences that my being rejected isn't awful. And there is no reason, as we again noted before, why I *should* not get rejected. The world simply isn't a totally nonrejecting place!

T: Yes, I think you're getting that well. Now, the fourth question is, "What is the worst thing that could happen to me, if an attractive woman rejects me?"

P: Very little, I guess. I was at first going to say that the worst thing that could happen to me was that I would be very depressed for a long time. But I now see that such a thing would not happen from any rejection but from my *view* of the horror of being rejected.

T: Really, then, not so much could happen to you, if you got rejected. Is that right?

P: Yes. As a matter of fact, I would learn something about approaching an attractive female. And I might learn something valuable about myself.

T: Right. Now, this method of asking yourself these four questions, and persisting until you get sensible answers to them, is something you can do at least ten minutes every single day, even when there is not much going on in your life and you are in no danger of being rejected.

From Ellis and Abrahms, 1978, pp. 43–45.

As can be seen from this case vignette, RET stresses the cognitive, philosophic, value-oriented aspects of human personality. RET holds that people largely manufacture their own psychological symptoms and have the ability to eliminate or minimize these symptoms and make themselves much less easily disturbed. It does not strive for symptom removal so much as for a profound philosophic solution to people's fundamental emotional problems. As such, RET is a significant example of the rapidly developing field of cognitive behavior therapy.

Concluding Comments

The singular contribution of Ellis to the world of time-limited psychotherapy is his insistence on the cognitive control that patients have over their own thoughts and feelings and, ultimately, over their own symptoms. According to Ellis, patients think themselves into psychological disorder and can think themselves out of it. While this approach may seem low on empathy and compassion, and perhaps somewhat strident, it communicates a message that is exceedingly affirming and supportive.

CHAPTER FOURTEEN

Farrelly's Provocative Therapy

Overview

Origins of Provocative Therapy

Assumptions, Hypotheses, and Goals

Therapeutic Techniques

The Therapeutic Process

Becoming a Provocative Therapist

Concluding Comments

Provocative therapy (Farrelly and Brandsma, 1974) is an aptly named form of relatively short-term individual, group, and family therapy (average number of interviews is twenty to twenty-five, with a range of two to one hundred) that has been practiced by its originator, Frank Farrelly, since 1963. Jeff Brandsma served to provide structure for Farrelly's thinking and to organize, monitor, and criticize, as well as to contribute to the process of putting these ideas down in written form.

Farrelly, a psychiatric social worker, expresses his indebtedness to Carl Rogers, with whom he worked at Mendota State Hospital in Wisconsin in the study of client-centered therapy with chronic schizophrenics, for helping him appreciate the importance of developing an empathic understanding of patients. But Farrelly moved past the role of a client-centered therapist as he slowly discovered that "the more passive, receptive, traditional role of the therapist" (1974, p. 20) was not for him.

Farrelly discovered that when he "threw therapy out the window" (1974,

p. 19) and began telling patients how he found himself reacting to them, they began to improve. That is, Farrelly had come to the conclusion that empathic understanding, warm caring, and genuine congruence were rarely enough and even when effective as a therapeutic strategy were far too slow. Furthermore, Farrelly found that these conclusions were as valid for private- as for public-sector patients and as appropriate for neurotics as for psychotics. Thus, Farrelly starts with the assumption that there are no patients for whom his approach is clearly unsuitable.

Origins of Provocative Therapy

Farrelly found that another strategy worked well with his patients — he could assist patients to develop stronger egos if he sided with their superegos. Farrelly wrote:

> *While in the 91st interview with the patient whom I'll call "Bill," I "stumbled" onto what felt like a crystallization of these previous experiences. Because I had not yet integrated my learning experiences and was a member of the project, I felt somewhat constrained to use a client centered approach with this patient. I had been essentially communicating three basic ideas to him: 1) You are worthwhile and of value; 2) You can change; and 3) Your whole life can be different. He, in turn, had been persistently communicating back to me three complementary responses: 1) I am worthless; 2) I'm hopeless and can never change; and 3) My life will always be one long psychotic episode and hospitalization. It was becoming increasingly clear that empathic understanding, feedback, warm caring, and genuine congruence were simply not enough and were getting us nowhere. At this point I "gave up" and said to him, "Okay, I agree. You're hopeless. Now let's try this for 91 interviews. Let's try agreeing with you about yourself from here on out."*
>
> *Almost immediately (within a matter of seconds and minutes, not weeks and months), he began to protest that he was not that bad, nor that hopeless. Easily observable and measurable characteristics of his in-therapy behavior started changing. For example, his rate of speech markedly increased, his voice quality changed from a dull, slow motion, soporific monotone to a more normal tone of voice with inflections and easily noticeable affect. He became less over-controlled and showed humor, embarrassment, irritation, and far more spontaneity. (1974, p. 26)*

Assumptions, Hypotheses, and Goals

In examining provocative therapy retrospectively, Farrelly and Brandsma have been able to identify ten assumptions that govern their behavior as therapists. These assumptions are shown in summary form in Box 14-1.

Two central hypotheses govern the behavior of a therapist practicing provocative therapy. First, "if provoked by the therapist (humorously, perceptively, and within the client's own internal frame of reference), the client will tend to move in the opposite direction from the therapist's definition of the client as a person" (1974, p. 52). Second, "if urged provocatively (humorously and perceptively) by the therapist to continue his self-defeating, deviant behaviors, the client will tend to engage in self- and other-enhancing behaviors which more closely approximate the societal norm" (1974, p. 52). As can be seen, the use of humor is an important therapeutic technique in provocative therapy (see also Furman and Ahola, 1988).

The assumptions and hypotheses invoked by Farrelly are crucial for the achievement of the major goals of provocative therapy—to help the patient: (1) affirm self-worth; (2) be appropriately assertive; (3) defend himself

---

BOX 14-1 • *Assumptions of Provocative Therapy*

1. People change and grow in response to challenge. ·
2. Clients can change if they choose to do so.
3. Clients have far more potential for achieving adaptive, productive, and socialized modes of living than they or most clinicians assume.
4. The psychological fragility of clients is vastly overrated both by themselves and others.
5. Clients' maladaptive, unproductive, antisocial attitudes and behaviors can be drastically altered whatever the degree of severity or chronicity.
6. Adult or current experiences are at least, if not more, significant than childhood or previous experiences in shaping client values, attitudes, and behaviors.
7. The client's behavior with the therapist is a relatively accurate reflection of his habitual patterns of social and interpersonal relationships.
8. People make sense; the human animal is exquisitely logical and understandable.
9. The more important messages between people are nonverbal.
10. The expression of therapeutic hate and joyful sadism toward clients can markedly benefit them.

From Farrelly and Brandsma, 1974, pp. 36–52.

or herself realistically; (4) respond to reality adaptively; and (5) communicate his or her own feelings in personal relationships freely and authentically.

Therapeutic Techniques

To accomplish the goals of provocative therapy, Farrelly and Brandsma believe in employing virtually any tactic—"obvious lying, denial, rationalization, invention (e.g., of 'instant research'), crying and zany thinking" (1974, p. 57). Farrelly and Brandsma write: "Figuratively therapists are often bound by Marquis of Queensbury type roles while patients use the psychological equivalent of knee to the groin and thumb in the eye. The outcome of such a contest is not often in doubt—to the ultimate detriment of the patient" (1974, p. 57). Box 14-2 gives an example of provocative therapy in action.

The therapist plays devil's advocate; sides with the negative half of the patient's ambivalent conflicts; urges the patient to continue deviant and pathological behavior (for plausible reasons); verbalizes the patient's worst self-doubts, thoughts, and fears; absurdly and ludicrously encourages the patient's symptoms; and lampoons, ridicules, and burlesques the patient's attitudes, always attempting to provoke the patient to give at least equal time to the positive, joyful, and growth-producing experiences in life. This orientation is reminiscent of Watzlawick's assertion that "jokes have a disrespectful ability to make light of seemingly monolithic world orders and world images. This may help to explain why it is that people who suffer from emotional problems are half over them once they manage to laugh at their predicament" (1978, pp. 55–56).

BOX 14-2 • *Provocative Therapy in Action*

Patient: (Loudly and furiously): Goddamn you! If you don't stop talking in that snotty, sarcastic way of yours, I'm going to quit therapy and not pay your bill!

Therapist: (With an alarmed, anxious, pleading expression): Please, *don't!* I need the money! (Slumps dejectedly in chair, holding forehead in hand, in a depressed, choked tone of voice.) Oh well, I'll just have to tell June and the kids no Christmas again *this* year.

P: (A kaleidoscope of emotions crossing his face—anger, laughter, suddenly placating): O.K., O.K., damn you, I know I need you more than you need me, but damn it, Frank, won't you please just . . .

From Farrelly and Brandsma, 1974, p. 69.

The Therapeutic Process

Stage One: Provocation

In conceptualizing the process of provocative therapy, Farrelly and Brandsma have identified four stages through which patients typically pass. First, "the client is precipitously provoked into a series of experiences that tend to leave him astonished, incredulous, uncertain and even at times outraged. He experiences a marked clash of expectational systems; his expectations of the therapist's role are not only disconfirmed but are almost reversed" (1974, pp. 131–132). Provocation is designed to help patients affirm their own worth, assert themselves appropriately, defend themselves realistically, and engage in risk-taking relationships. The excerpts in Box 14-3 illustrate this first stage; the italicized annotations are Farrelly's.

BOX 14-3 · *Examples of Provocative Therapy Stage One: Provocation*

[A female client was referred to me, her thirteenth therapist.]

Therapist: What's your name again?

Patient: Rachel Levin. (a pseudonym)

T: That's Jewish.

P: Yeah.

T: Where are you from?

P: New Yawk. *[She didn't even have her coat off, nor was she seated yet.]*

T: Oh, my God! . . .

P: I can't believe my ears, do you actually help people this way? I am just continually angry at you.

T: Help? Who's talking about help? Talking you can get, but help is harder to come by. Now you haven't been helped by those twelve other therapists whom you wore out, why demand the impossible of me?

* * *

P: I don't like what you're saying, but I'll say this for you. I don't have to sit around wondering what you're thinking of me like I did with my other therapist.

* * *

P: I found out I could twist other therapists around my little finger, easily embarrass them and make them blush. I can't bully you—and that's good.

BOX 14-3 *Continued*

And when I come in here and try to embarrass you with all that I've done sexually, you don't get embarrassed; you make *me* blush at *your* responses! And you know, that's good—you and Hank (her boy-friend) are the only persons I've found that I can't make jump through hoops.

From Farrelly and Brandsma, 1974, pp. 132–134.

Stage Two: Reorganization and Change

Farrelly and Brandsma describe the dynamics of the second stage:

The client typically decreases his protestations regarding the therapist's behaviors, begins to recognize that he and not the therapist must change, and starts reorganizing his expectational system toward the therapist. . . . There may emerge the feeble beginnings of the five types of desired behaviors that constitute the goals of provocative therapy [see above]. And finally this stage is characterized by a marked diminishing if not total extinction of psychotic defenses if these were initially present" (1974, p. 135)

Box 14-4 provides an example of provocative therapy in stage two.

BOX 14-4 · *Example of Provocative Therapy Stage Two: Reorganization and Change*

[A deeply religious young man entered my private practice with his staunchly Catholic parents. He had a history of a psychotic break, several hospitalizations and no jobs following a homosexual episode. Convinced that he was immortal, his behavior in traffic was bordering on suicidal. In the first interview it quickly became apparent that his "immortality" was connected in his mind to his homosexual episode. He further averred to the consternation of his appalled parents that anyone who engaged in fellatio with him would also become immortal.]

Therapist: (seriously) I also think it only fair and just that your mother and father here (gesturing toward parents), who are well into middle age and who gave you the gift of Life should, uh, in turn, uh—

Mother: (holding hand up to her mouth as though gagging) I think I'm going to be ill—do we have to talk about these things?

Continued

BOX 14-4 *Continued*

Father: (glaring at his son) God, you have sick patterns of thinking!

T: (trying and failing to keep a straight face but forging ahead) Uh, it's only fitting that Mom and Dad should be the first, uh, I don't quite know how to put this tactfully —

Patient: Dammit, will you quit talking on and on about this crazy shit? I never really believed this stuff for the past year anyhow, even when I was telling people it. It's just crazy, that's all.

T: ("surprised") What? What did you say?

P: (forcefully) I said I never really believed all that crazy crap anyway, so why don't you just shut up about it?

T: (with a Pollyanna-like smile, coaxingly) Would you repeat that?

P: (laughing) You heard me.

T: (still smiling) I know, but my favorite number is three and some things I like to hear three times. Just once more.

P: (noticing his parents are laughing with relief; laughing and smiling himself) Go to hell.

T: (with eyes toward ceiling, hands folded as though in prayer) Don't listen to him, God. You haven't for years. (to client, coaxingly) Aw, come on, just once more for your friendly therapist.

P: (smiling, nodding, in a serious tone) OK, OK, I never really believed all that crazy stuff I said about being immortal even when I said it. There. Satisfied?

From Farrelly and Brandsma, 1974, p. 136.

Stage Three: Clarification and Protest

In the third stage there is considerable clarification and movement. "The hallmark of this state is the client's congruent and increasingly firm protestations that the therapist's definition of him is a skewed, inaccurate one based on a distorted reading of inadequate samplings" (1974, p. 137). An example of stage three clarification and protest is given in Box 14-5.

BOX 14-5 · *Example of Provocative Therapy Stage Three: Clarification and Protest*

Patient: (persuadingly) But it's because I *don't* like myself that I *do* these things.

Therapist: (remonstrating) No, *no, no!* It's because you *do* these things, that's why you—

P: (interjecting) No—

T: (finishing) don't like yourself.

P: (louder) No—

T: (overriding her) Oh, you got it all back-asswards.

P: (even more loudly and firmly) You're *wrong!*

T: (matching her tone) What do you mean, I'm wrong?

P: (attempting to explain) It's 'cause—

T: (pompously, not waiting for her reply) Hell, you're just a patient and I'm a therapist. Now how the hell do you know, where do you get off telling me I'm wrong?

P: (evenly, with assurance) Well you're not infallible Mr. Frank Farrelly.

T: (laughs) Oh I'm not? And I could be wrong, is that what you mean?

P: (with assured firmness) Yes, you're wrong. You're wrong about me. I'm not as, as evil, and not as wicked, and not as—damnable, and not as, as hopeless—(phone rings, therapist ignoring it) and not as—(phone rings again, therapist puts hand on receiver but doesn't lift it, waits for patient to finish)—inadequate as you contend. (patient laughs, nods head abruptly) There!

From Farrelly and Brandsma, 1974, p. 137.

Stage Four: Consolidation and Integration

The fourth and final stage is one of consolidation and integration. "The client is now protesting significantly less if at all about the therapist's definition of him as a person. If he does protest, he does it impatiently or humorously and is increasingly confident in his present self's adaptive and coping capacities" (1974, p. 137). Box 14-6 provides an example of stage four consolidation and integration.

BOX 14-6 • *Example of Provocative Therapy Stage Four: Consolidation and Integration*

Patient: (thoughtfully, slowly, as though speaking with himself) You know, I have been getting so much warmth and real love from people lately. I can see that now, now that I'm different. But they really haven't changed that much, they were pretty much like that toward me all along. And yet, I just couldn't see it, or I would explain it away. But it was there all along and I was blind.

Therapist: (pauses, quietly sarcastic) Same old distorted perceptions huh?

P: (smiling, assuredly) No, no distorted perceptions this time, Frank. This time it's real, and it's been real for weeks. (pause, thoughtfully) You'd have to travel around with me for a couple of weeks to see the intensity of the warmth that people have toward me. I guess I never really, really noticed it before. But now that I'm more open to them, I can see it.

T: (disgustedly) Aw shit, you're getting grandiose.

P: (shakes head, chuckles and grins)

From Farrelly and Brandsma, 1974, p. 138.

Becoming a Provocative Therapist

Being a successful provocative therapist requires a good deal of personal learning. Practicing the techniques must involve far more than mechanical imitation. Farrelly and Brandsma have observed others in the process of being provocative therapists, and they have identified—somewhat impressionistically, they admit—seven stages that seem to appear fairly regularly (Box 14-7).

Concluding Comments

Farrelly and Brandsma's techniques tend to force their patients to prove how healthy they are, if only to prove how wrong their therapist is. It is clear that there is a strong underlying sense of good will that accompanies the provocations in this therapy and that the strategy of helping patients get well by pointing out, tongue in cheek, how wonderful it is to be sick can be effective if undertaken judiciously.

Farrelly stands out dramatically from other cognitive behavioral theorists. He believes that inside many traditional psychotherapists is a provocative therapist "screaming to be let out" (p. 171). Only each individual reader will know whether that hypothesis is true for him or her. But the

---

BOX 14-7 • *Stages in the Development of a Provocative Therapist*

Stage 1. *Cringing* — "My God! That's no way to talk to these poor people in pain."

Stage 2. *Intrigued fascination* — requests to observe interviews, watch videotapes, or listen to audiotapes.

Stage 3. *Initial attempts at trying provocative therapy* — accompanied by anxiety, considerable tentativeness. Careful supervision is particularly important in this stage.

Stage 4. *Release from traditionally constricted role behaviors* — accompanied by enthusiasm but much questioning.

Stage 5. *Use of whole self as a therapeutic instrument* — increasing ability to catch the nuances, flavors, and sounds of the patient's and the therapist's own experiencing.

Stage 6. *Increasing confidence* — usually combined by two new but easily corrected errors: (1) abrasive and unhelpful confrontations, and (2) the use of humor and provocation to meet the therapist's own needs. In supervision it is important to remind the student that the purpose of the therapy is to help the patient.

Stage 7. *Continued learning, growth, and development* — as a consequence of internalization of the supervisory process, and increasing self-monitoring and decreasing need for continuing supervision.

From Farrelly and Brandsma, 1974, pp. 139–142.

---

choice is not one of either "yes" or "no" to provocative therapy; there is much room along that continuum.

Some therapists report that after being exposed to the ideas of provocative therapy they feel differently about their patients — they no longer believe that their patients are as fragile or weak or incapable as they previously thought. They are able to use humor in their psychotherapy more easily than before. Some therapists report that they are more honest and open with patients, that they can work effectively with a wider variety of patients, or that they are far less uneasy about their own reactions to their patients, being now able to use those reactions therapeutically.

This book is designed to provide practicing clinicians with new ways of thinking about their patients and about what they are trying to do to be helpful to them. The ideas expressed in provocative therapy are exactly such a set of new ways of thinking. The ideas add one more arrow to the therapist's technical quiver. How this arrow is used will be an individual matter, of course, but the ideas, as well as the therapeutic techniques, are certainly provocative in more than one sense of the word.

CHAPTER FIFTEEN

Beck's Cognitive Restructuring Therapy

Overview

The Cognitive Theory of Depression

Cognitive Therapy

Concluding Comments

Aaron Beck's cognitive therapy, just like Klerman's interpersonal therapy, is identified primarily with the treatment of depression. But, in contrast to Klerman's psychodynamic/interpersonal approach, Beck and his colleagues (Beck, 1967, 1976; Beck et al., 1979; Young and Beck, 1982; see also Phillips 1985a, pp. 60–63)) believe that depression, regardless of its severity, is the result of cognitive distortions. These distortions are based on errors in thinking, derived from early learning experiences, particularly in drawing inferences about the self, the world, and the future. These inferences result in external events being inaccurately construed to represent loss or deprivation. These chronic logical errors form the basis for a world view or set of assumptions, referred to as *schemas,* that predispose vulnerable persons to repeated bouts of depression. Beck's therapy is designed to modify these cognitive distortions.

Beck (1976) suggests that there are some important similarities of his cognitive approach and traditional psychodynamic psychotherapy, in that both types of therapy require that patients engage in introspection, develop increased appreciation of the meanings they attach to people and events in the world around them, and modify the organization of their cognitions that results in distortions and unrealistic thinking. That is, Beck emphasizes that psychodynamic psychotherapy has important cognitive components. On the other hand, there are important differences between his cognitive approach and traditional psychodynamic psychotherapy. Beck focuses on conscious experience, while psychodynamic psychotherapy tends to be more interested in what is unconscious. Cognitive therapy may be more economical in time than psychodynamic psychotherapy and may be more easily researched and taught. Cognitive therapy rests on far fewer and far less complex assumptions than does psychodynamic therapy. Finally, while acknowledging the role of history in determining current behavior, cognitive therapy is less interested in causes than is psychodynamic therapy — it focuses on *how* the patient misinterprets reality, rather than on *why*.

The Cognitive Theory of Depression

While acknowledging that depression involves more than a cognitive disturbance, the cognitions are considered primary, in that they influence motivation, emotion, behavior, and vegetative functions. Cognitions influence feelings that, in turn, influence cognitions, resulting in the downward spiral of affect called depression. Depression is characterized in part by distorted schemas, or views of the self, the world, and the future.

Depressive Schemas

The view of the self is distorted in depression in that people see themselves as inadequate, unworthy, and defective, with the result that they underestimate themselves and are overly self-critical. People who are depressed tend to minimize successes and emphasize failures. Depressed persons tend to attribute socially undesirable traits to themselves and to rate themselves low on socially desirable traits such as self-esteem and optimism.

The view of the world is distorted in that depressives see it as overly demanding, obstructive, rejecting, depriving, defeating, and dependency-producing. In comparison with nondepressed persons, depressed individuals dream of frustration, desertion, injury, and deprivation, recall more negative events in their past, have fewer pleasant memories, and tend to believe that control of their fate is not in their hands.

The view of the future is thought of as negative, without worth, and doomed. Depressives are pessimistic and have a constricted view of the future. As a consequence of these views, all of which suggest that there is little if any hope in trying to overcome inevitable failure, psychomotor inhibition, apathy, and fatigue are produced (Rush and Giles, 1982).

Depression-Inducing Attitudes

Beck (1976) has identified a number of attitudes commonly held by persons who have become depressed. He believes that these attitudes predispose people to excessive sadness. One major aspect of his cognitive therapy is to make these attitudes more explicit, so that they can be reconsidered and modified as seems appropriate. The most common of these depression-inducing attitudes are summarized in Box 15-1. Note that about half of these attitudes are "shoulds."

BOX 15-1 • *Depression-Inducing Attitudes*

1. In order to be happy, I have to be successful in whatever I undertake.
2. To be happy, I must be accepted, liked, and admired by all people at all times.
3. If I'm not on top, I'm a flop.
4. It's wonderful to be popular, famous, wealthy; it's terrible to be unpopular, mediocre.
5. If I make a mistake, it means that I'm inept.
6. My value as a person depends on what others think of me.
7. I can't live without love. If my spouse or sweetheart or parent or child doesn't love me, I'm worthless.
8. If somebody disagrees with me, it means he doesn't like me.
9. If I don't take advantage of every opportunity to advance myself, I will regret it later.
10. I should be the utmost of generosity, considerateness, dignity, courage, and unselfishness.
11. I should be the perfect lover, friend, parent, teacher, student, spouse.
12. I should be able to endure any hardship with equanimity.
13. I should be able to find a quick solution to every problem.
14. I should never feel hurt.
15. I should always be happy and serene.
16. I should know, understand, and foresee everything.
17. I should always be spontaneous.
18. I should always control my feelings.
19. I should assert myself.
20. I should never hurt anybody else.
21. I should never be tired or get sick.
22. I should always be at peak efficiency.

Adapted from Beck, 1976, pp. 255–257.

Cognitive Therapy

Based on their theory of depression, Beck and his colleagues have developed a treatment plan that focuses on detecting, examining, and testing automatic thought processes; developing alternative understandings of day-to-day events; recording dysfunctional thoughts; developing more flexible assumptions about the world; and rehearsing cognitive and behavioral responses based on these new assumptions. Beck's cognitive therapy has been evaluated as well or better than most other forms of brief psychotherapy, and the evaluations have generally been quite positive (Rush and Giles, 1982, pp. 165–169). In general, cognitive therapy has been found to be as effective as or more effective than antidepressant medication or other types of psychotherapy such as behavior therapy, nondirective therapy, insight therapy, relaxation training, or supportive therapy.

Cognitive therapy is a comprehensive approach that involves therapeutic style as well as therapeutic technique; it requires a new way of viewing patients and their problems. Young and Beck (1982) refer to the therapeutic technique as *collaborative empiricism,* although the approach very much attends to the expression and investigation of maladaptive emotion and to the therapeutic relationship.

Collaborative Empiricism

The formation of a therapeutic alliance is as important in Beck's cognitive therapy as in any other short-term therapy. Collaboration is important to ensure that therapist and patient have similar goals, to minimize resistance, and to prevent misunderstandings. The development of such a collaborative relationship requires that the therapist be trustworthy, that communication be open and sincere, and at the same time that the therapist display a degree of confidence that can serve as an antidote to the patient's sense of despair.

Patient and therapist need to agree on a target problem, on the development of an agenda and an overall therapeutic plan, and on the importance of feedback both to the patient as well as to the therapist. In the process of cognitive therapy itself, the therapist and patient need to function as an investigative team, working together to collect information, to develop hypotheses about the patient, and to evaluate these hypotheses by a process of logical examination of the evidence. Establishing a productive collaborative relationship is illustrated in the vignette in Box 15-2.

The Process of Cognitive Therapy

Six goals characterize the early sessions of cognitive therapy: (1) defining the focal problems, (2) setting priorities for problem solution, (3) reduction

---

BOX 15-2 · *Establishing a Collaborative Relationship*

Therapist: Now that you've heard my formulation of the problem, what do you think of it?

Patient: It sounds O.K. to me.

T: While I was talking, did you have any feeling that there might be some parts that you disagree with?

P: I'm not sure.

T: You would tell me if you were uncertain about some of the things I said, wouldn't you? You know, some patients are reluctant to disagree with their doctor.

P: Well, I could see that what you said was logical, but I'm not really sure I believe it.

From Beck, 1976, pp. 223–224.

---

of the feeling of hopelessness, (4) demonstrating the relationships of cognition and emotion as they appear in the therapeutic sessions, (5) socializing the patient into the world of cognitive therapy, and (6) underlining the importance of self-help homework assignments.

Most sessions begin with agenda setting that, in turn, depends on the patient's experiences and homework since the last session. After the agenda for the session has been established, the therapist proceeds to explore the patient's most salient problem with a view toward identifying thoughts or behaviors to modify. Then the therapist selects and employs the most appropriate techniques to use and explains their rationale. Most sessions end with a request for the patient to summarize (sometimes in writing) the major conclusions that have been derived during the session, evaluate the session, and plan an appropriate homework assignment.

Cognitive Therapy Techniques

Cognitive therapy techniques can be divided into two major categories: (1) locating and investigating automatic thoughts and (2) identifying and analyzing the validity of maladaptive underlying assumptions (Young and Beck, 1982). Automatic thoughts occur, often without awareness, between the time an external event takes place and the person reacts to the event. These thoughts tend not only to be automatic, but also to be repetitive, plausible, and idiosyncratic, and it is crucial to identify them if cognitive therapy is to be successful. The techniques that have been developed for discovering such automatic thoughts include inductive questioning, imagery, role playing, examination of mood shifts during the therapy session, keeping a daily record, and ascertaining the meaning of an event.

The use of imagery is illustrated by the vignette in Box 15-3.

Once an automatic thought has been identified, its validity needs to be investigated — a process that requires the patient to be willing to consider the possibility that the thought may be inaccurate. The procedures that can be used to examine the validity of an identified automatic thought include examining available evidence, setting up an experiment, inductive questioning, operationalizing a negative construct, reattribution, and generating alternatives. Box 15-4 provides an example of setting up an experiment.

Behind automatic thoughts are, as we have seen, self-imposed rules, or assumptions, that help determine how people respond to life events. Many

---

BOX 15-3 · *Use of Imagery in Beck's Cognitive Therapy*

Patient: I can't go bowling. Every time I go in there, I want to run away.

Therapist: Do you remember any of the thoughts you had when you went there?

P: Not really. Maybe it just brings back bad memories, I don't know.

T: Let's try an experiment to see if we can discover what you were thinking. Okay?

P: I guess so.

T: I'd like you to relax and close your eyes. Now imagine you are entering the bowling alley. Describe for me what is happening.

P: (describes entering the alley, getting a score sheet, etc.) I feel like I want to get out, just get away.

T: What are you thinking now?

P: I'm thinking, "Everyone is going to laugh at me when they see how bad I play."

T: Do you think that thought might have led to your wish to run away?

P: I know it did.

From Young and Beck, 1982, p. 193.

BOX 15-4 • *Setting Up an Experiment in Beck's Cognitive Therapy*

Patient: I can't concentrate on anything any more.

Therapist: How could you test that out?

P: I guess I could try reading something.

T: Here's a newspaper. What section do you usually read?

P: I used to enjoy the sports section.

T: Here's an article on the Penn basketball game last night. How long do you think you'll be able to concentrate on it?

P: I doubt I could get past the first paragraph.

T: Let's write down the prediction (Patient writes, "one paragraph.") Now, let's test it out. Keep reading until you can't concentrate any more. This will give us valuable information.

P: (reads the entire article) I'm finished.

T: How far did you get?

P: I finished it.

T: Let's write down the results of the experiment. (Patient writes, "eight paragraphs.") You said before that you couldn't concentrate on anything. Do you still believe that?

P: Well, my concentration's not as good as it used to be.

T: That's right. However, you have retained some ability. The next step is to improve your concentration.

From Young and Beck, 1982, pp. 197–198.

---

of these assumptions are maladaptive, in that they are overly rigid, unrealistic, or absolutist. In addition, maladaptive assumptions are often more difficult to overcome than are automatic thoughts. Young and Beck (1982) tend to think of these maladaptive assumptions as life-guiding aphorisms, such as "In order to be happy, I have to be successful in everything I try to do," or "I should always work up to my potential," or "I can't live without love." The task of the therapist is to help the patient develop evidence against the assumption. In Box 15-5 are two examples of the skillful analysis of the validity of a maladaptive assumption.

BOX 15-5 · *Analyzing the Validity of a Maladaptive Assumption*

Patient: I guess I believe that I should always work up to my potential.

Therapist: What is that?

P: Otherwise I'd be wasting time.

T: But what is the *long-range* goal in working up to your potential?

P: (long pause) I've never really thought about that. I've just assumed that I should.

T: Are there any positive things you give up by always having to work up to your potential?

P: I suppose it makes it hard to relax or take a vacation.

T: What about "living up to your potential" to enjoy yourself and relax? Is that important at all?

P: I've never really thought of it that way.

T: Maybe we can work on giving yourself permission *not* to work up to your potential at all times.

* * *

Patient: I have to give a talk before my class tomorrow and I'm scared stiff.

Therapist: What are you afraid of?

P: I think I'll make a fool of myself.

T: Suppose you do make a fool of yourself—why is that so bad?

P: I'll never live it down.

T: "Never" is a long time. Now look here, suppose they ridicule you. Can you die from it?

P: Of course not.

T: Suppose they decide you're the worst public speaker that ever lived. Will this ruin your future career?

P: No, but it would be nice if I could be a good speaker.

T: Sure it would be nice. But if you flubbed it, would your parents or your wife disown you?

P: No. They're very sympathetic.

T: Well, what would be so awful about it?

Continued

BOX 15-5 *Continued*

P: I would feel pretty bad.

T: For how long?

P: For about a day or two.

T: And then what?

P: Then I'd be O.K.

T: So you're scaring yourself just as though your fate hangs in the balance.

P: That's right. It does feel as though my whole future is at stake.

T: Now somewhere along the line, your thinking got fouled up, and you tend to regard any failure as though it's the end of the world. What you have to do is get your failures labeled correctly—as failure to reach a goal, not as disaster. You have to start to challenge your wrong premises.

From Young and Beck, 1982, p. 201 and Beck, 1976, pp. 250-251.

Behavioral Therapy Techniques

While cognitive therapy techniques such as those just described are essentially intrapsychic in nature, a parallel in external behavior exists, in which patients are helped to cope more successfully with situational or interpersonal problems. Behavioral techniques, usually designed to modify dysfunctional cognitions, occur early in the therapy. Thus, a depressed person who believes that "I can't enjoy anything any more" (a dysfunctional cognition), for example, is asked to complete a series of behavioral assignments designed to increase the number and variety of activities that bring pleasure. The behavioral change can then be used to help bring about a cognitive change. Six behavioral techniques that have been specifically identified by Young and Beck (1982) are summarized in Box 15-6.

Use of Questions

According to Beck, most of the comments by the therapist should be in the form of questions. Questions can help make a patient aware of a particular problem area and the significance or meaning of that problem; can provide data to help the therapist assess the patient's reactions to this new awareness, for example, information about coping styles, tolerance for stress, or general level of functioning; can generate possible solutions or alternative

---

BOX 15-6 • *Behavioral Techniques Used in Cognitive Therapy*

Scheduling Activities: The therapist uses an activity schedule to help the patient plan activities hour by hour during the day. The patient then keeps a record of the activities that were actually engaged in, hour by hour.

Mastery and Pleasure: The patient rates each completed activity for both mastery and pleasure on a scale from 0 to 10. These ratings generally serve to contradict directly patients' beliefs that they cannot enjoy anything and cannot obtain a sense of accomplishment any more.

Graded Task and Assignment: The therapist breaks down an activity into sub-tasks, ranging from the simplest part of the task to the most complex and taxing. This step-by-step approach permits depressed patients eventually to tackle tasks that originally seemed impossible or overwhelming to them, and provides immediate and unambiguous proof to patients that they can succeed.

Self-Reliance Training: The therapist may have to teach some patients to take increasing responsibility for their day-to-day activities. Patients may begin by showering, then may go on to making their own beds, cleaning the house, cooking their own meals, shopping, and so forth. This responsibility also includes gaining control over their emotional reactions.

Role Playing: Role playing may be used to elicit automatic thoughts in specific interpersonal situations, to practice new cognitive responses in social encounters that had previously been problematic for a patient, and to rehearse new behaviors in order for the patient to function more effectively with other people.

Diversion Techniques: Patients can use various forms of diversion of attention to reduce temporarily most forms of painful affect, including dysphoria, anxiety, and anger. Diversion may be accomplished through physical activity, social contact, work, play, or visual imagery.

From Young and Beck, 1982, pp. 203–204.

---

approaches to troublesome dilemmas; can elicit automatic thoughts that seem to be generated by the problem; and can raise doubts in the patient's mind about current opinions or actions. Box 15-7 presents some excerpts that demonstrate the use of questioning in cognitive therapy.

BOX 15-7 • *Use of Questions in Cognitive Therapy*

Patient: I don't have any self-control at all.

Therapist: On what basis do you say that?

P: Somebody offered me candy and I couldn't refuse it.

T: Were you eating candy every day?

P: No, I just ate it this once.

T: Did you do anything constructive during the past week to adhere to your diet?

P: Well, I didn't give in to the temptation to buy candy every time I saw it at the store. : . . Also, I did not eat any candy except that one time when it was offered to me and I felt I couldn't refuse it.

T: If you counted up the number of times you controlled yourself versus the number of times you gave in, what ratio would you get?

P: About 100 to 1.

T: So if you controlled yourself 100 times and did not control yourself just once, would that be a sign that you are weak through and through?

P: I guess not—not *through* and *through*. (smiles)

* * *

Patient: I really haven't made any progress in therapy.

Therapist: Didn't you have to improve in order to leave the hospital and go back to college?

P: What's the big deal about going to college every day?

T: Why did you say that?

P: It's easy to attend these classes because all the people are healthy.

T: How about when you were in group therapy in the hospital. What did you feel then?

P: I guess I thought then that it was easy to be with the other people because they were all as crazy as I was.

T: Is it possible that whatever you accomplish you tend to discredit?

* * *

Therapist: Why do you want to end your life?

Patient: Without Raymond, I am nothing. I can't be happy without Raymond. But I can't save our marriage.

BOX 15-7 *Continued*

T: What has your marriage been like?

P: It has been miserable from the very beginning. Raymond has always been unfaithful. I have hardly seen him in the past five years.

T: You say that you can't be happy without Raymond. Have you found yourself happy when you are with Raymond?

P: No, we fight all the time and I feel worse.

T: You say you are nothing without Raymond. Before you met Raymond, did you feel you were nothing?

P: No, I felt I was somebody.

T: If you were somebody before you knew Raymond, why do you need him to be somebody now?

P: (puzzled) Hmmm.

T: Did you have male friends before you knew Raymond?

P: I was pretty popular then.

T: Why do you think you will be unpopular without Raymond now?

P: Because I will not be able to attract any other man.

T: Have any men shown an interest in you since you have been married?

P: A lot of men have made passes at me, but I ignore them.

T: If you were free of the marriage, do you think that men might be interested in you, knowing that you were available?

P: I guess that maybe they would be.

T: Is it possible that you might find a man who would be more constant than Raymond?

P: I don't know. I guess it's possible.

T: You say that you can't stand the idea of losing the marriage. Is it correct that you have hardly seen your husband in the past five years?

P: That's right. I only see him a couple of times a year.

T: Is there any chance of your getting back together with him?

P: No. He has another woman. He doesn't want me.

T: Then what have you actually lost if you break up the marriage?

Continued

BOX 15-7 *Continued*

P: I don't know.

T: Is it possible that you'll get along better if you end the marriage?

P: There is no guarantee of that.

T: Do you have a *real marriage?*

P: I guess not.

T: If you don't have a real marriage, what do you actually lose if you decide to end the marriage?

P: (long pause) Nothing, I guess.

From Young and Beck, 1982, pp. 206, 207 and Beck, 1976, pp. 289–291.

Homework Assignments

Homework assignments provide an opportunity for patients to try out ideas and concepts in their real lives that they have been exposed to in therapy sessions. Thus, successful completion of these assignments is considered to be extremely important in cognitive therapy. If homework assignments are skillfully selected, they should provide the patient with an opportunity to modify maladaptive behavior without relying on the therapist, by collecting necessary data, testing hypotheses, and, where such hypotheses seem incorrect, generating and testing new, optimally more appropriate, hypotheses.

To enhance the success of homework assignments, therapists need to provide a persuasive rationale for the specific assignment and should present the task clearly, ideally in written form so that the results of the assignment can be reviewed at the next therapeutic session. Early in therapy the patient plays a relatively small role in designing such assignments but, of course, plays an important role in reacting to and evaluating them. Later, patients can take an active role in helping create homework assignments.

Because the successful completion of homework assignments is so important in cognitive therapy, difficulties in complying with the assignments need to be discussed promptly. It is possible, for example, that the patient does not fully understand the assignment, or does not believe he or she can successfully complete the assignment, or does not really believe that completing the assignment can be helpful, or resents being given homework tasks, or is afraid that the task cannot be completed perfectly.

Concluding Comments

While Beck's cognitive therapy has been designed specifically for treating neurotic depressions, it has far broader implications for the treatment of psychological disorders. His cognitive approach serves as an antidote to the psychodynamic position that psychological difficulties are primarily to be understood as disorders of affect.

Beck has been singleminded in his examination of cognitive factors in the development and the treatment of psychological disorders. He insists that human beings are first and foremost cognitive animals and that cognitive problems demand cognitive solutions. There seems little doubt that cognitive approaches to treatment can be very efficient and effective when cognitive distortions can be implicated in a presenting problem. From this point of view psychological disorders are thought of as problems of the intellect, for which the optimal solution is a treatment that can be mastered by the intellect.

CHAPTER SIXTEEN

Erickson's Brief Strategic Psychotherapy

Overview

Psychopathology as an Interpersonal Phenomenon

Therapeutic Techniques

A Case Example

Concluding Comments

Milton Erickson, trained in psychology and psychiatry, was for many years known primarily for his contributions to the field of clinical hypnosis. In addition, however, he developed a unique and original style of brief psychotherapy based in large measure on concepts derived from his understanding of hypnosis. Erickson practiced and consulted in Phoenix, Arizona for a number of years before his death in 1980. Because Erickson's work is based on an interpersonal theory of psychopathology and psychotherapy, it is as pertinent and is employed as often for couples or families as it is for individuals.

Jay Haley, who first met Erickson in 1953, described Erickson's work and underlying theories in a volume (1973) that is primarily a casebook. Haley's book, read and approved by Erickson, is based on a two-decade–long collaboration, and details come from many hours of recorded conversations between Haley and Erickson. It is perhaps unnecessary to add that Haley is a great admirer of Erickson. He has tried Erickson's methods with success and believes that many psychotherapists can adapt these methods to their own styles.

Erickson has left an extraordinary intellectual and clinical legacy. His ideas spread through Haley to Watzlawick and his associates (Evans, 1989;

Haley, 1963, 1973, 1984, 1987; Watzlawick, 1978; Watzlawick, Weakland, and Fisch, 1974) and to Rabkin (1977), among others (see also Zeig, 1982). In addition to his contributions to psychotherapy in general, Erickson made important specific contributions to the field of brief therapy. Fisch (1982) describes those contributions in the following way:

> *In his work, Erickson opened the door for change and in that way had a major impact on brief therapy, as well as on therapy itself. . . . First and, I think, foremost was what he persistently did not do. . . . Erickson did not ask for lengthy histories before he intervened in the problem. Concomitantly, he did not attempt to elicit "interpretable" information or try to get his patients to gradually achieve insight. . . . Erickson did not emphasize "the session" as much as events outside his office. . . . He did not measure the session by the clock, but rather by the task to be performed in that contact. He did not "support" in the usual sense; he did not urge; he did not "confront with reality." . . . He did not place importance on getting people to "express their feelings." . . . In this manner of speaking, he cut out a lot of the work of conventional treatment, long-term or "brief."*
>
> *However, in addition to not doing things, Erickson did some intriguing things. While he did not spend time getting a psychological history, he did spend considerable effort in obtaining a rather detailed picture of the symptom, problem, or complaint. . . . He would not interpret resistance to the patient, but would use it to expedite client performance of therapeutic tasks. He simply did not waste time arguing with patients, focusing instead on the task the patient was to perform to resolve his or her problem. . . . In all of these above tactics, important messages are conveyed: that he and the patient are to get down to business, that change is expected, that there are some simple things to consider and understand and tasks to be undertaken, which, however arduous, can and are to be accomplished. (pp. 158–159)*

Psychopathology as an Interpersonal Phenomenon

A rather direct relationship exists between one's theory of psychopathology and one's approach to psychotherapy. If psychopathology is viewed as learned behavior, therapy is designed to extinguish or unlearn the behavior. If psychopathology is thought of as the consequence of repressed feelings, therapy is designed to help the patient become aware of those feelings. To the extent that Erickson thought of psychopathology, he thought of it in uncompromisingly interpersonal terms — as a way of gaining control of a relationship. As such, his therapy was designed to help the patient develop better ways of dealing with relationships.

Haley (1963) provides an illustration of the relationship of theory to therapy in the case of a woman who sought psychotherapy because of her compulsion to wash her hands and take showers several times each day. From an intrapsychic point of view, the symptom could be viewed as a defense against unacceptable impulses against her husband or her children. The problem would be hers, and there would be no particular need to see her husband in therapy. In this case, however, her husband was seen, and the struggle between the husband and wife regarding the wife's compulsive behavior was quickly evident. The husband was quite tyrannical, and although his wife objected to his behavior, she was unable to oppose him except by her handwashing—a strategy that allowed her to refuse almost any request he made.

A psychodynamic approach toward treating this woman might very well view the principal therapeutic task as helping the patient discover the causes of her compulsions in her own intrapsychic history. Such an approach would view the behavior of wife toward the husband as secondary gain. An interpersonal approach toward treating this woman would begin by noting the advantage the symptom gives the patient in gaining control of the relationship with her husband, even though the cost of this advantage in terms of personal distress is considerable. The pathology is not in attempting to gain control of a relationship, but rather in denying that that is what is occurring. Thus, one person's secondary gain can be another person's principal symptom (see also Watzlawick, Weakland, and Fisch, 1974, p. 26).

Erickson's interpersonal approach to brief psychotherapy was to be solely concerned with the patient's present predicament. He was not interested in helping the patient make connections between that predicament and the past, that is, with helping the patient gain insight, and ordinarily would spend no time exploring the patient's childhood or youth. Indeed, the most radical aspect of Erickson's approach was his apparent complete disinterest in helping a client discover the causes of the problem. Erickson did not help people understand their interpersonal difficulties, he did not attend to transference phenomena, he was not concerned with motivation, and he did not attempt to extinguish previously reinforced responses. Watzlawick, Weakland, and Fisch write: "Everyday, not just clinical, experience shows not only that there can be change without insight, but that very few behavioral or social changes are accompanied, let alone preceded, by insight into the vicissitudes of their genesis" (1974, p. 86; see also Duncan and Solovey, 1989). Erickson's theory of change was based on the interpersonal impact of the therapist outside the patient's awareness. It included providing directives that caused changes of behavior, and it emphasized communicating in metaphor.

Erickson did not actually find concepts associated with the fundamental notion of psychopathology to be particularly useful. Fisch (1982) has noted that Erickson's ideas in fact made the very concept of pathology largely irrelevant. He did not view patients' problems as exceptional or unusual. Rather, Erickson dealt with patients as if they were perfectly normal and resilient, simply struggling, as we all are, with the human condition. From this point of view, concepts such as symptoms, defenses, or mental illness made no sense. Not only did he deal with patients as if they were perfectly competent, but he did so with all of his patients, rather than with only some of them.

Therapeutic Techniques

Haley has used the word *strategic* to describe Erickson's therapeutic style. He writes:

> *Therapy can be called strategic if the clinician initiates what happens during therapy and designs a particular approach for each problem. When a therapist and a person with a problem encounter each other, the action that takes place is determined by both of them, but in strategic therapy the initiative is largely taken by the therapist. He must identify solvable problems, set goals, design interventions to achieve those goals, examine the responses he receives to correct his approach, and ultimately examine the outcome of his therapy to see if it has been effective. . . . Strategic therapy is not a particular approach or theory but a name for those types of therapy where the therapist takes responsibility for directly influencing people. (Haley, 1973, p. 17; see also Rabkin, 1977, pp. 5 ff.)*

Strategic therapy is thus directive and active in character and stands as a logical extension of hypnotherapy, where the therapist generally initiates all that is to happen. But Erickson thought of hypnosis far more broadly than as a procedure in which a person is "put to sleep" and given suggestions. For Erickson, hypnosis referred to a type of communication between people. Hypnosis shares goals and procedures with other forms of therapy, and in particular includes two types of directives. First, clients are asked to do something they can voluntarily do, for example, sit or lie down, look at a certain spot, or concentrate on a certain image or idea. Second, clients are asked to behave in ways that are not under their voluntary control; that is, certain behaviors are suggested, for example, feel better, free associate, see something that isn't there, or turn off a physiological process. Like all other forms of therapy, hypnosis is based on a relationship that is voluntary, yet tinged with hesitancy and resistance. In this sense, hypnotists, just like other therapists, must deal with resistance, motivate clients to cooperate, and use a certain amount of persuasion (Mathews, 1988).

Many of Erickson's specific techniques were unusual, and Haley has singled out several of them for special comment. Erickson was often able to deal with resistance by labeling it as cooperation, that is, by working with rather than against it. If a couple fought continually, in spite of good advice to the contrary, he was likely to direct them to have a fight, but he would specify the place or the time, thus causing a change in their behavior. If Erickson sensed that a patient could not help but withhold information, he might have directed the patient not to tell him everything.

Erickson would often direct a client to engage in one of a large class of behaviors, knowing that the specific suggestion would not be readily accepted. In that case the client would choose to engage in another behavior, but still in the desired class. For example, Erickson might have wanted clients to exercise and would instruct them to engage in a specific exercise that they would not find acceptable. As a consequence, clients would choose another more congenial exercise for themselves. Erickson would sometimes encourage a client to relapse, when the client had been improving "too rapidly." He might say, for example, "I want you to go back and feel as badly as you did when you first came in with the problem, because I want you to see if there is anything from that time that you wish to recover and salvage" (Haley, 1973, p. 31). Such instructions almost always prevented a relapse. Erickson would often encourage a response by inhibiting it, for example, encouraging a silent family member to speak by interrupting him for a period of time whenever he looked like he was about to say something. Erickson frequently communicated in metaphor and by analogy. Haley writes:

> If Erickson is dealing with a married couple who have a conflict over sexual relations and would rather not discuss it directly, he will approach the problem metaphorically. He will choose some aspect of their lives that is analogous to sexual relations and change that as a way of changing the sexual behavior. He might, for example, talk to them about having dinner together and draw them out on their preferences. He will discuss with them how the wife likes appetizers before dinner, while the husband prefers to dive right into the meat and potatoes. Or the wife might prefer a quiet and leisurely dinner, while the husband, who is quick and direct, just wants the meal over with. If the couple begin to connect what they are saying with sexual relations, Erickson will "drift rapidly" away to other topics, and then he will return to the analogy. He might end such a conversation with a directive that the couple arrange a pleasant dinner on a particular evening that is satisfactory to both of them. When successful, this approach shifts the couple from a more pleasant dinner to more pleasant sexual relations without their being aware that he has deliberately set this goal. (1973, p. 27)

Watzlawick (1978) recalls that Erickson might treat a case of frigidity by instructing his patient to

> *imagine in the greatest possible detail how she would go about defrosting her refrigerator . . . how she will approach this task, whether she will begin with the top shelf, or the bottom shelf, or perhaps in the middle. What she will take out first, what next? . . . How will she go about the actual thawing, and while she is doing this, what forgotten memories or completely unrelated thoughts might perhaps come to her mind? (p. 62)*

Erickson's willingness to accept working within metaphors applied not only to verbal interchange but even to persons who live a metaphoric life. Such a style of life is typical of schizophrenics, and Erickson assumed that with a schizophrenic the important message is the metaphor. For example, notes Haley,

> *when Erickson was on the staff of Worcester State Hospital, there was a young patient who called himself Jesus. He paraded about as the Messiah, wore a sheet draped around him, and attempted to impose Christianity on people. Erickson approached him on the hospital grounds and said, "I understand you have had experience as a carpenter?" The patient could only reply that he had. Erickson involved the young man in a special project of building a bookcase and shifted him to productive labor. (Haley, 1973, pp. 27–28)*

Rabkin (1977) has written about Erickson's therapeutic techniques using the phrase *reverse psychology*. More recently, Watzlawick, impressed with both the recent research and conceptualization regarding the two-brain theory (our left brains being concerned with speed, writing, counting, and reasoning; our right brains being concerned with concepts, totalities, configurations, abstractions, and emotions), has written about Erickson's therapeutic techniques as "blocking the left hemisphere" (see Watzlawick, 1978, pp. 91–126).

Directing the Patient

Brief psychotherapy is inevitably somewhat directive. Patients must be told to do something related to their problems. Haley provides an example of a woman who complained to Erickson of incapacitating headaches that lasted for hours. Erickson accepted the headache pain as real and as necessary, but he was able to direct the patient to change the time of occurrence and its duration, so that she then had the headache every Monday morning for ninety seconds. One technique for helping the patient change is to ask the patient when he would prefer to have his pain — daytime, evening, weekends, severe pain for a short time or mild pain for a long time, and so on (Haley 1963, pp. 44–45).

A patient complained to Erickson that he was lonely and had no contact with other people, spending most of his time in his room in idle work. Erickson directed him to go to the public library where he would have to be silent and not have contact with others, and where he could waste his time just as he was doing in his room. But the patient was curious and began reading magazines and then reading about cave exploration. One day someone at the library asked him if he was interested in exploring caves, and soon thereafter the patient became a member of a cave exploration group that led him into a more active social life.

A 17-year-old enuretic was instructed to go for a two-mile walk whenever he awoke during the night after wetting his bed and then get back into the wet bed. If he slept through an enuretic episode, he was to set the alarm for 2:00 AM the next morning and go for the two-mile walk and then get back into bed.

A 65-year-old recently widowed man who suffered from insomnia, and who had not slept more than two hours a night since his wife died, was told that he could be helped if he was willing to give up about eight hours of sleep and if he was willing to do some work. He agreed. He had informed Erickson that he lived with his son in a large house that had hardwood floors. He did most of the cooking and his son polished the floors, because the patient hated the smell of floor wax. Erickson directed the patient to polish the floors all night, quitting at 7:00 AM in order to get ready for work. He was to go to work and resume polishing the floors that evening. He was to do this for four nights in a row. The patient polished the floor for three nights after losing six hours of sleep, but on the fourth night he lay down to rest before starting the floor polishing and slept until 7:00 in the morning. A year later he informed Erickson that he had been sleeping every night. He would do anything to get out of polishing floors — even sleep (Haley, 1984, pp. 3–5).

Another example of this directive strategy can be found in the work of Bergman (1985). Bergman describes his efforts to be of help to a professor getting ready to go to Paris for several months whose aging mother was telling him that if he went abroad she would probably not be around when he returned, and might even commit suicide. Bergman continues:

I gave the professor the following homework: He was to take his mother out to dinner and at the appropriate moment tell her all the loving thoughts and feelings he has had for her, both presently and in the past. He was also to tell her in what ways she was a good mother to him.

If mother asked why he was telling her all these loving, positive things, he was to say something like, "Well, Mother, it sounds like you are probably not going to be around when I return from Paris and if that is the case, I wanted you to know how much I loved you, and I wanted to say these things to you before I no longer had the opportunity." Upon hearing this the professor's mother told him that he was talking nonsense and that there would be lots of opportunities for him to say these things when he returned from Paris. The professor left for Paris with a clear conscience and found his mother alive and well in New York six months later when he returned. (1985, p. 117)

Ordeal Therapy

Many of the demands made by Erickson in the cases just described create some sort of ordeal for the patient but at the same time keep the control of the problem in the patient's hands. Haley (1984) described the ordeal as a task that is imposed on a patient, which is appropriate to the problem but more severe than the problem (see also Goldsmith, 1986, pp. 69 ff). Furthermore, the ordeal should cause distress that is equal to or greater than the distress caused by the problem; should be good for the patient, such as doing exercise, eating a healthy diet, or making a sacrifice for others; should be something the person can do; should be something that the person cannot object to doing on moral or ethical grounds; and should not cause harm to the person or to anyone else. Usually, successful ordeals have significant effects not only on the patient but on the social contexts within which the patient functions.

Ordeals can be straightforward, as, for example, doing fairly strenuous exercises in the middle of the night if the symptom occurred during the previous day, or reading in the middle of the night from books that the patient should have read long ago but put off reading; or can be paradoxical, as, for example, scheduling a depression at a certain time in the day for a person who came for psychotherapy because of a depression, or scheduling a quarrel among a quarreling couple, or overeating or avoiding eating if those are the symptoms. What is important about these ordeals is that they put the symptoms under the control of the patient (see also Watzlawick, 1978, pp. 101 ff.).

In order for ordeal therapy to be effective, five steps must be followed: (1) the problem must be clearly defined, (2) the person must want to overcome the problem, (3) an ordeal must be selected, (4) the ordeal must have an explicit rationale, and (5) the ordeal must continue until the problem is resolved (see also Watzlawick, Weakland, and Fisch, 1974, pp. 110 ff.).

A Case Example

While there are numerous Ericksonian case histories in the literature (see, for example, Watzlawick, Weakland, and Fisch, 1974, ch. 10; Zeig, 1982), there are relatively few verbatim transcripts of the strategic therapist at work. The case in Box 16-1 is excerpted from Haley (1987) and is a good example of an active initial interview with a married couple who were considering separation and who had three children aged 14 to 22. Bracketed remarks are summaries of a number of exchanges between the therapist and the couple. Bracketed remarks in italics are Haley's comments about the therapeutic process. The therapist is Richard Belson, D.S.W., Professor of Social Work at Adelphi University. The interview was conducted in a one-way mirror room with Haley supervising it from behind the mirror. This initial interview is conducted with enormous skill, good humor, and a light hand. Only the first few minutes of the interview are excerpted here. The entire transcript is well worth examining in detail.

BOX 16-1 • *Ericksonian Marital Therapy: Initial Session Excerpts*

Therapist: Could you tell me a little bit about who you are and what you do? Let me begin with your wife. What kind of work do you do?

Wife: I work as a secretary in the university, and also attend class.

T: Why the class? Are you trying to form a new career, or is it just your own interest in an education?

W: Just my own interest.

T: What class are you taking?

W: Calculus.

T: (laughing) So you're an advanced mathematician.

W: No, only second semester.

T: I was taking some math in my college career, but when I came to calculus, I knew I was in the wrong field.

[The therapist then learned more about where the wife was working and then turned to the husband, who told him he was an electrical engineer and worked for a utility company.]

T: So both of you have this mathematical thing in common. I don't think it's the basis for a happy marriage, but it's rather remarkable. I don't know

BOX 16-1 *Continued*

many people in math, and least of all do I know a couple that both knew anything about math except to fight over the checks.

Husband: Well, she possibly knows more about math than I do.

T: No kidding. So you're being very gracious as a husband that is about to get divorced. Which I want to ask you about. Are you interested in changing your marriage, or what is the change you would like from your wife that we can help you with?

[In this casual way the therapist slides from a social discussion into the issue of why they are there.]

H: Well, my wife has, evidently, a great deal of difficulty talking to me. I detect that she doesn't tell me some things. She won't talk to me about some things. She is acting like she's afraid to talk to me, or she's hostile, or something. There's some hostility there. It is uncomfortable and she would like me to move out.

T: Why is she here today? What is it she wants from you?

[When beginning therapy with a couple, one usually finds that they have a list of complaints about each other. Sometimes they have rehearsed in their minds what they will say before they arrive. If a therapist asks each of them to say what the problem is, they can go on at length attacking the other. When that is done, the situation looks hopeless. It is sometimes best not to allow these speeches. One way to do that is to ask the husband, "If I asked your wife what the problem is, what would she say?" Then one does the same with the wife. Each then has to say what the other's complaints are. In this case, the therapist used a modified version of this approach by asking the husband what it is that the wife wants.]

H: Well, she said she would like me to come in for a couple of sessions, and I agreed to do this. I personally would like to see the marriage continue, but I think that she's getting very uncomfortable over the past few weeks, and I've become uncomfortable too.

T: Well, when things start to get bad, it's hardly enjoyable. What is it your wife wants you to do that you're not doing? Could you be just a little more specific?

H: Well, I have a temper.

T: You, an electrician engineer, have a temper?

H: I get mad at the kids sometimes.

Continued

BOX 16-1 *Continued*

T: I see. So she would like you to control your temper with the children. What is it she would like for herself from you?

H: Well, other than not yelling at the kids, I don't know exactly what she wants from me. She won't tell me.

T: Well, let's just guess and then we'll ask her. What do you think she would say if I asked her what it is that she wants?

H: Well, I think she would want me to control my temper, but other than that, I don't know. I think there are probably other things, but I don't know what they are.

T: Well, we'll find out very soon. Do you hit her?

H: I haven't for quite a few years.

T: I see. Did you used to hit her badly?

H: Well, I hit her a couple of times.

T: How long ago was that?

H: About twelve or fifteen years ago.

T: So it was a long time ago. Has she hit you recently?

H: No.

[The therapist has easily and quickly learned whether there is abuse in this family. In this approach there is no history taking to begin with, since that biases the therapy in a historical and information-gathering direction rather than one of change. Relevant aspects of the problem are sought and brought up as the first interview is conducted. The information gathered is then in context, not a sociological-historical review. The therapist asked more about what the wife wanted, and the husband said she would like him to read less and get involved in more hobbies.]

T: What are these hobbies that you used to do that she wants you to do? Make love to her?

[Again, in a casual way, the therapist slides in an important issue.]

H: Well, that is something she definitely does not want me to do now. She used to not feel that way.

T: Was there a time that was a hobby she liked?

H: I would say yes.

BOX 16-1 *Continued*

[When discussing the cost of hobbies, the therapist asks—]

T: Is money an issue between you?

H: I think it probably is.

T: She thinks you make too much?

H: She thinks I don't make enough.

T: How much money do you make?

[A brief discussion of income takes place.]

T: Is it enough to cover your costs? I notice you have three children.

[The therapist has straightforwardly asked about the couple's income, just as he did about sex, as a therapist should with a couple. In the discussion of the children, it turned out that one daughter had just graduated from college at the early age of nineteen. They had a son who was, as the father put it, "moving along toward getting a degree. Slowly." They agreed he could be doing better, but it turned out the father never saw his grades. The therapist asked why not.]

H: Because he doesn't choose to show me.

T: You're the father. Where does he get the nerve to talk that way to you?

H: I'm encouraged not to inquire (indicating his wife).

T: Really. So there is some issue going on there too. Who is paying for your son's education?

H: My wife is.

T: How did you make this arrangement between the two of you that the wife pays for the tuition? I mean it's an interesting idea. It's a new idea.

[The husband explained that when he had said he didn't have the money to send the son to college, the wife had gone to work to earn the money to pay his tuition. Apparently this couple quarreled over the years about this particular son. When the wife went to work to help the son, she benefited herself by becoming a more independent woman. Previously the husband had controlled all the money; when she went to work, she had money of her own. A problem for the couple was that the son was about to graduate from college, and they did not have his problems to communicate with each other about. That was when they began to have more trouble in the marriage. *This couple could be thought of as at the stage where a child who was an issue between them leaves home; then they must communicate with each other more*

Continued

BOX 16-1   *Continued*

directly. That situation can cause difficulties or even a separation, which was threatened here. The therapist turned to the wife and said—]

T: What if I asked your husband what he wants from you, what would he say?

W: Someone to wash the clothes and buy the food and prepare it and clean the house and run the errands and quit running up high bills.

T: What about the bills?

W: It seems that whenever a bill comes in, there is a confrontation over it. (mockingly) You've overspent the clothing category again. You are not to spend any more money for clothing.

T: So what you're saying is that you work together well around the money.

W: It's just easier not to say anything to him. We fight less if we don't say anything at all.

T: So you're like passing ships. You wave to each other occasionally that you still exist.

W: Nope. Don't even wave.

T: How long has this been going on?

W: Years and years.

T: This trouble about money is one of the major issues. Is that it?

W: The struggle about money is a power struggle, not a money struggle.

T: Sometimes in marriage people struggle about power. Are there any happy years you had together?

[Often with a couple in severe difficulty it is good to go to a time in the past when they got along well. That marks that period as a baseline and establishes the possibility that they can get along well again. In this case, the wife did not imply that they had ever got along better.]

W: There were years when we fought less.

[The wife described how they had been to several counselors over a period of years, sometimes in relation to their son and sometimes in relation to each other. She found it helpful. Her husband did not.]

T: (to the husband) What didn't you like about them? I don't want to make the same mistakes.

BOX 16-1 *Continued*

H: I didn't see any change in the marriage.

T: So that must make you a little bit cautious about whether or not this therapy is going to be helpful.

H: Well, I have serious doubts that it will be helpful. I think her mind is made up and she wants a separation. If that's true, this counseling is not going to prevent that.

T: Do you think your wife has the slightest interest in seeing what could still be done? You know, a lot of things turn around even when they've reached a very bad point.

H: Well, that's the reason I agreed to come in at all.

T: Yes. You've had a lot of experience in your life that sometimes when things look very black, they start to get better.

[The therapist emphasizes that a positive change is possible in their marriage, and he also begins to explore their plans for separation. Sometimes one can take a couple through a hypothetical separation and get rid of it. That is, they may find they will still be financially entangled, they will still be parents of the children together, and so on. The husband in this case says he would live nearby if they separated, and he would have to support the wife and children. He would also visit the children.]

H: I think it would be a financial hardship on both of us, but I don't contribute much to the house.

T: You mean emotionally, spiritually, sexually, or financially?

H: Oh, the tasks I do aren't much — dishes, a little work around the house. My wife would probably find the four-bedroom house too big for the one child left at home.

T: (to the wife) What is your view about the possible future separation?

W: The house is too big.

T: Would you stay in touch and speak with your husband?

W: Arguing on a false premise, I honestly don't know.

T: A false premise?

W: That he is not at home.

[This comment was the first suggestion by the wife that she was not assuming, and perhaps did not want, a separation.]

From Haley, 1987, pp. 179–185.

Concluding Comments

The literature on planned short-term therapy demonstrates dramatically the extraordinary influence that Erickson has had on both individual and family therapists. Like other therapists who have a cognitive behavioral orientation, Erickson and those he has influenced have remarkably little interest in causes, in the past, in insight, in motivation, or in transference. Their interest is exclusively in the here and now. It is hard to imagine an approach to therapy that shares so little with the psychodynamic orientation (Fisch, 1982).

Erickson believed that all brief psychotherapy must be directive. His own approach, called *strategic,* was in fact extremely directive. It is in that sense that its relationship to hypnosis was emphasized. In hypnosis, patients are instructed to do exactly what the therapist asks of them, even if they think that the therapist's instructions make no sense or cannot be carried out.

Perhaps the most original aspect of Erickson's work has been his use of metaphor and symbol in therapy. Many of the therapeutic techniques he developed have been adopted by brief therapists who subscribe to a wide variety of approaches to psychotherapy. Erickson's creative maneuvers that result in rapid control over symptoms or improvement in previously pathological relationships have become a legitimate part of much brief psychotherapy.

SECTION FOUR

Clinical Settings for Planned Short-Term Psychotherapy

In the past ten years or so, original contributions by clinicians to planned short-term psychotherapy theory and technique have decreased in number. In their place have appeared a very large number of contributions that deal with special approaches to short-term therapy that are associated with clinical settings and clinical tasks.

The most important of these varied settings are: (1) planned short-term group and family psychotherapy, (2) planned short-term psychotherapy in inpatient psychiatric wards or units, (3) planned short-term psychotherapy with patients who are medically ill, and (4) brief contact therapy.

In this section we shall examine these four areas of conceptualization and practice with specific reference to planned short-term psychotherapy. In many cases the chapters will identify contributors whose names have not appeared earlier in the book—such is the current nature of specialization within the already specialized field of planned short-term psychotherapy.

CHAPTER SEVENTEEN

Time-Limited Group and Family Psychotherapy

Overview

Historical Roots of Short-Term Group Psychotherapy

Budman's Short-Term Experiential Group Psychotherapy

The Crisis Group

Group Treatment of Children and Adolescents

Bergman's Systemic Family Psychotherapy

de Shazer's Ecosystemic Family Therapy

Weiss and Jacobson's Brief Behavioral Marital Therapy

Concluding Comments

While the majority of the literature on planned short-term psychotherapy concerns itself with individual therapy, there is a substantial and important body of work dealing with the clinical aspects of time-limited group, marital, and family psychotherapy (see for example, Aiello, 1979; Budman, Bennett, and Wisneski, 1980, 1981; Brown, 1980; Budman and Clifford, 1979; Budman et al., 1984; Budman, Demby, and Randall, 1980; Budman et al., 1988; Daley and Koppenaal, 1981; de Carufel and Piper, 1988; Donner and Gamson, 1968; Klein, 1985; Lewin, 1970, pp. 164–197; MacKenzie and Livesley, 1986; Marcovitz and Smith, 1986; Poey, 1985; Rabkin, 1977, pp. 181–207; Sabin, 1981; Sadock, Newman, and Normand, 1968; Schwartz, 1975; Small, 1979, pp. 140–147; 157–165; Sundel and Lawrence, 1977; Toseland and Siporin, 1986; and Wolf, 1965). The principles that appear to be useful in time-limited group psychotherapy bear a significant relationship both to those of time-unlimited group psychotherapy and to time-limited individual therapy.

Since group therapy tends in general to be longer than individual therapy, brief group therapy tends to be longer than brief individual therapy (Sabin, 1981). According to Budman and Gurman (1988), time-limited group psychotherapy is usually conducted in weekly ninety-minute sessions and lasts anywhere from eight to sixty weeks. Groups that focus on a specific circumscribed issue, such as the loss of a relationship or a recent geographic move or illness, may last as little as eight weeks (see also Goldberg et al., 1983; Oppenheimer, 1984). Groups that deal with a significant developmental issue or life transition typically last from fifteen to twenty sessions. Groups that aspire to make significant characterological changes may last a year or even longer. Membership in time-limited therapy groups may be open, that is, may admit new members from time to time, or closed, that is, may not admit new members once the group has begun, and the time limit may be predetermined for the group as a whole or for each individual group member.

A special form of group therapy that has attracted the attention of a number of short-term psychotherapists has been clinical work with couples and families (Baron, 1988; Dinkmeyer and Sherman, 1989; Dublin, 1983; Dulcan, 1984; Dulcan and Piercy, 1985; Farrelly and Brandsma, 1974, pp. 145–157; Fisher, 1984; Fox, 1987; Freeman, 1982; Friedman and Pettus, 1985; Gurman, 1981; Kinston and Bentovim, 1981; Parmenter, Smith, and Cecic, 1987; Perls and Perls, 1983; Pew, 1989; Rosenbaum, 1983; Weiss and Jacobson, 1981). Paralleling the variety of approaches to short-term individual therapy, short-term marital therapy approaches have been developed from both psychodynamic and cognitive behavioral perspectives (Gurman, 1981). As was indicated when the work of Milton Erickson was discussed in Chapter 16, strategic and structural approaches associated with his work with individuals have been carried over to marital and family therapy, where they are playing an unusually important role in influencing marital and family therapists. Gurman (1981) writes:

> In the structural-strategic view, the symptoms of individual family members are both system maintained and system maintaining, and all individual problems are seen as manifestations of marital-familial disturbance. Marital conflict is viewed as the result of interaction, largely unaffected by intrapsychic (especially unconscious) forces. The psychological symptoms of a husband or wife are assumed always to have interpersonal meaning and, in fact, to function as communicative acts, so that a symptomatic individual cannot be expected to change unless his or her family system changes. (p. 427)

In this chapter we shall examine a number of quite different approaches to short-term group and family psychotherapy. Each approach seems to have its special virtues and special possibilities.

Historical Roots of Short-Term Group Psychotherapy

According to Sabin (1981), present-day short-term group psychotherapy can be traced directly to the early work of Kurt Lewin. Lewin, a social psychologist, left Nazi Germany and came to the United States prior to World War II, bringing with him an abiding interest in how groups have an impact on individual behavior, feelings, and perceptions. Lewin believed that groups have enormous power to affect individuals, for better or worse, and that decisions made in a group setting have far more viability and power than do individual decisions, regardless of the nature of the decisions. Lewin's early action research included helping factory workers work together more productively and helping train community leaders to combat racial and religious prejudice.

Lewin and his colleagues chanced upon a strategy that transformed the working groups into training groups, or T-groups, as they were later called—a strategy that included having observers in attendance at the meetings who later presented and discussed their observations with the group members. This discussion, now called *feedback,* turned out to have an enormous impact on the group members and became the basis of training in group dynamics.

These T-groups subsequently became the basis for an entire strategy for organizational consultation, on the one hand, and for a newly developing type of sensitivity training that had a frankly personal therapeutic objective. It is these sensitivity training groups, or, as they were later called, *encounter groups,* that served as the direct predecessor of short-term group therapy.

Budman's Short-Term Experiential Group Psychotherapy

We shall first examine the seminal work of Budman and his colleagues (Budman, Bennett, and Wisneski, 1980; Budman, Bennett, and Wisneski, 1981; Budman and Clifford, 1979; Budman, Demby, and Randall, 1980; Budman and Gurman, 1988), who have for a number of years been thoughtfully describing their work at the Harvard Community Health Plan, a health maintenance organization located in Boston and Cambridge.

Budman uses the term *experiential* to describe his general approach to group psychotherapy because the model is "more than simply an economical way to treat several unrelated individual patients or couples simultaneously. Rather, the emphasis is upon those interpersonal factors (e.g., cohesion, group development, feedback, self-disclosure, etc.) that are believed to be pivotal elements of any experiential group treatment" (Budman and Gurman, 1988, p. 247).

Four principles govern Budman's approach to time-limited group psychotherapy: (1) pregroup preparation and screening, (2) establishing and maintaining a focus in the group, (3) developing group cohesion, and (4) establishing a time limit and coping therapeutically with its reality. Individual pregroup screening and preparation in both individual and workshop formats are taken very seriously. Individual sessions are designed to help prospective patients determine if their problems can be conceptualized in the context of what is likely to be the focus of the group.

Pregroup workshop sessions are used to develop skills in desirable group behaviors, to improve patient selection, to provide an opportunity for prospective patients to make an informed decision about the appropriateness of their participation in the envisioned group, and to help reduce subsequent dropout rate. The workshop takes place in a single ninety-minute session with eight to twelve prospective members and includes an opportunity for small-group and large-group experiences that are analogs of what is likely to take place in the therapy group. Following the pregroup individual meetings and workshop, prospective patients are in a position to decide whether they would like to become part of the time-limited therapy group.

Once the group itself begins, the fundamental initial task of the therapist is to establish a thematic focus. Budman distinguishes between what he calls the working focus and the emergent focus. The working focus represents the therapist's preliminary idea of what the group is to be all about—a definition that can help, for example, in recruiting members, in planning time limits, and in deciding whether the group is to be open or closed. A working focus might be to deal with difficulties young adults have in establishing intimate relationships or to help a number of married men and women deal with the breakdown of their marriages. Once the therapy group begins, a refined, more specific emergent focus develops—one that takes into account the unique pattern of needs and characteristics of the group members.

Much of the therapeutic value of groups comes from the sense of cohesion that develops among its members—the psychosocial forces that cause members to choose to remain part of the group. Budman and his colleagues have developed a broad concept of cohesion, one that includes six dimensions: (1) withdrawal and self-absorption versus interest and involvement, (2) mistrust versus trust, (3) disruption versus cooperation, (4) being unfocused versus being focused, (5) abusiveness versus expressed caring, and

(6) global fragmentation versus global cohesiveness. Cohesive groups are those in which members express interest and involvement, trust, cooperation, focus, and caring. These are the attributes that help create a setting in which individual group members can learn and profit from each other's experiences and struggles to cope with the stresses in their lives.

Budman and his colleagues believe that each short-term therapy group must have a clear and definite time limit. Their concept is reminiscent of Mann (see Chapter 6) and can be illustrated by the following statement:

> *When group members are able to explore the issues raised by the time limit, the fact that is often brought into focus is that the time available in one's life is also limited. Often, this realization helps to "get members moving" who have previously been too fearful or too stuck to attempt even minimal changes. (Budman and Gurman, 1988, p. 268)*

Budman also includes a follow-up group meeting in his planning. A group reunion takes place six to twelve months after the group has terminated. It provides an opportunity for group members to learn what has happened in each of their lives and for the therapist to develop a useful appreciation of the outcome of the group psychotherapy. Budman and Gurman (1988) conclude their description of time-limited group psychotherapy by noting:

> *Time-limited groups are an important therapeutic modality for the brief therapist. Such groups can, for some patients, be at least as effective as individual treatment. . . . For the therapist who is concerned about issues of time, efficiency, and organizational or financial constraints, time-limited groups may offer a significant opportunity for treating homogeneous populations of patients. Although it still remains unclear who will profit the most from group as opposed to individual therapy, we believe that with many people this "either-or" choice does not need to be made. Since a patient's group therapy, in our model, can be perceived of as part of an overall course of treatment, it is only one element in the broad array of tools available to the brief therapist. (p. 282)*

The Crisis Group

Donovan, Bennett, and McElroy (1981) describe the rationale for a special type of group treatment also developed at the Harvard Community Health Plan, designed to be of help to patients troubled by real life crises. They hypothesize that a timely but brief intervention could ameliorate symptoms of the crisis (see Prazoff, Joyce, and Azim, 1986), and that such a group would fit naturally into their organization, given its general belief in rapid access, rapid assessment, and rapid treatment.

Patients are referred via the medical triage department where patients in acute distress are first seen. Referrals to the crisis group are made when a patient reports acute onset of significant symptoms following an identifiable precipitating stressful life event, provided that the patient does not seem psychotic, homicidal, or suicidal and that he or she is interested in participating in a group along with six or seven other patients that meets twice a week for one and one-half hours for four weeks. The group is led by two co-therapists, a triage nurse and a mental health professional.

The crisis group focuses on the present, particularly on the problem that precipitated the crisis. Patients take turns telling their stories; the other group members listen and sometimes comment. When the story has been completed, the therapists and other patients raise questions, try to clarify issues, and provide advice. The general tone of the group is supportive, friendly, and task-oriented. Members of the group see its purpose as to help each member with a specific problem. The therapists are active and confrontive about both group and individual issues as seems appropriate—"What does this long silence in the group mean when this woman tells us she will be terminating the group early?" or "You're hanging onto this man who has been continually unfaithful. How come?" As group members learn how to be of help to each other, the therapists tend to become less active in promoting problem-solving behavior. There is a general effort to help patients help themselves, although supportive behavior by other group members is encouraged.

The crisis group is not optimal for everyone, since nearly half of patients who start the crisis group participate in fewer than four sessions. Social relationships among group members often continue after the group has terminated. About half of the patients seek additional therapy after the crisis group is over. Donovan and colleagues report that patients who remain with the group virtually always report that they benefitted from the experience. More formal evaluation conducted with a sample of forty-three patients who completed the crisis group yielded highly favorable results both at the conclusion of the group and one year later in terms of reduction of both anxiety and depression and increase in ego strength. The most common reasons given by these former patients for the helpfulness of the crisis group were: (1) the support from other group members, (2) knowing that other people had similar problems, and (3) the opportunity the group gave them to talk about their difficulties.

Group Treatment of Children and Adolescents

This book makes virtually no mention of planned short-term psychotherapy with children and adolescents, except, as will occur shortly, in the context of children being treated along with their families. When one considers the amount of individual short-term psychotherapy that goes on with children and adolescents just within the public school system alone, it is astonishing that so little has been written about short-term individual psychotherapy with young people (see, for example, Shapiro, 1984). Virtually all therapeutic contact with school-age children is short-term, and it is unfortunate that school personnel who have such rich experiences working with young people do not often share their experiences with others through the written word. Perhaps school counselors and special education teachers are uneasy about describing their contacts with school children as "therapy."

There is, however, something of a literature on brief group treatment of children and adolescents that is worthy of review and assessment. Scheidlinger (1984) has prepared an overview of approaches to short-term group therapy with children and finds it useful to distinguish between those groups that are conducted by professional, specially trained group practitioners and those that are not. The professional therapeutic groups are designed to help repair pathology; the nonprofessional groups have, according to Scheidlinger, goals that involve preventive intervention, remediation, or enhancement of optimum functioning. Scheidlinger insists that the two types of groups are not to be differentiated in terms of actual or alleged superiority, although the distinction he makes may help explain why school personnel may be reluctant to write about their experiences working with school-age children.

Examples of nonprofessionally-organized groups include discussion groups for children who share a common experience, for example, divorcing parents, summer therapeutic camping groups, groups of children of mentally ill parents, or groups of children facing a common transitional crisis, such as moving from an elementary school into a junior high school. Such groups are often located in school settings. Professional short-term therapy groups for children tend, on the other hand, to be located in traditional mental health settings, either inpatient or outpatient, and include play therapy, activity therapy, and, among older children, groups that focus on verbal interaction as their principal therapeutic modality and deal directly with a variety of developmental issues.

According to Scheidlinger, short-term group psychotherapy with children and adolescents should focus on current issues rather than on the resolution of unconscious conflicts. Its emphasis should be on encouraging corrective emotional experiences and on active participation in the change effort. Since children's character structure is more flexible than adults' and since children appear to be more resilient than had previously been assumed, Scheidlinger believes that short-term group treatment should be increasingly accepted as a treatment of choice for children.

Bornstein, Bornstein, and Walters (1984) have described a six-session group experience designed for children ages 7 to 12 whose parents have recently undergone a divorce. The primary objective of the sessions was to enhance communication between parents and children. The group met for one and one-half hours on six consecutive weeks with male and female co-therapists. While rules were kept to a minimum, the therapists provided a carefully thought-out structure to each of the sessions. Thus, at the first session, after a snack and general introductions, group members were asked to discuss a number of relatively safe topics, including why people get married, what makes a good marriage, how their parents met, why their parents got married, why some marriages fail, and why there are more divorces now. After this discussion the therapists helped the group members discuss why divorce is hard on children, what are the benefits of divorce, how the members found out that their parents were divorcing, and what happened when they talked with their parents about the impending divorce.

The second session was given over to a review of the previous session and a discussion of communication problems in a divorced family. Exercises were provided by the co-therapists that allowed group members to try out communicating with their parents under a variety of circumstances. Group discussion followed the exercises. The third session was devoted to a discussion of feelings, again with the use of a number of exercises. The fourth session was devoted to problem-solving techniques, and the fifth session to the control of anger. Parents were invited to take part in the final session, and with the use of videotapes children and parents were provided an opportunity to discuss a number of issues pertinent to being part of a divorced family.

Another short-term group program, this time with behaviorally disturbed young adolescents, was described by Rauch, Brack, and Orr (1987). This program, consisting of five one-hour meetings held after school, was offered as an alternative to suspension for boys in grades six through eight (ages 11 to 14) whose behavior would under normal circumstances have resulted in their being suspended from school.

A behavior management system using both group rewards and group consequences was used. A point system was negotiated, and at the end of the five sessions, group members could pool their remaining points for rewards—food from a neighboring fast food restaurant or free time use of the school gymnasium.

Rauch, Brack, and Orr (1987) describe their therapeutic orientation as follows:

The group leader used an approach in group sessions which stressed here and now, responsibility for and consequences of behavior, and exploration of feelings. The sessions allowed participants to examine their behavior and how it affected themselves and others. They were encouraged to consider the consequences of their actions as well as to identify alternate ways to obtain the response their negative behavior sought. Role playing the alternatives was used to help the participants use the alternative. (pp. 20–21)

During the five weeks of the group therapy, referrals to school officials for disciplinary action dropped dramatically, but the improvement was short-lived. Three months after the treatment program ended, referrals for disciplinary problems had returned to pretreatment levels. The authors suggest that lengthening the period of group treatment might extend its effectiveness. If so, the group treatment would be an inexpensive and useful alternative to school suspension.

One other finding deserves mention: In comparison with boys matched for age and school grade who did not present behavior problems, the boys in this group treatment program were significantly more sexually mature. If this observation is replicated in other studies, it would suggest that the group program might be modified by attention to the issues raised by this accelerated pubertal maturation.

As for professionally directed group therapy, clinical studies of short-term groups with sexually abused boys and girls have appeared in the literature (see, for example, Damon, Todd, and MacFarlane, 1987; Friedrich et al., 1988), and a review of short-term group therapy with depressed adolescent outpatients has recently been prepared by Fine and colleagues (1989). Their review suggests that brief group therapy has been found to be remarkably helpful with emotionally disordered adolescents in general.

Fine and colleagues (1989) examined two different twelve-session approaches to the brief group treatment of depressed adolescents — a social skills training program and a therapeutic discussion group. The social skills program made use of a previously prepared manual that dealt with seven specific social skills: (1) recognizing feelings in oneself and others, (2) assertiveness, (3) conversational skills, (4) giving and receiving positive feedback, (5) giving and and receiving negative feedback, (6) social problem solving, and (7) social conflict negotiation. The therapeutic discussion group provided an opportunity for group members to share ideas and gain an improved understanding of common concerns, as well as to provide mutual support. The therapist provided an atmosphere in which these opportunities could be maximized. As time went on, group leaders became less active as group members began taking greater responsibility for what was discussed in the sessions. Fine and his colleagues concluded that if therapists are skillful, particularly in recruiting new members for the group experience, the treatment can be unusually rewarding and successful, since adolescents seem to respond so much to their peers.

Bergman's Systemic Family Psychotherapy

Bergman (1985) thinks of his brief systemic psychotherapy with and about families as emergency road service, designed to get families who are stuck somewhere back on the road as quickly as possible. While Bergman works with a wide variety of individuals and families, always about family issues, he has a special interest in resistant families, those who have previously been unable to profit from contacts with mental health professionals. Bergman acknowledges his indebtedness to Bowen (1978), Palazzoli and colleagues (1978), Erickson (Haley, 1967, 1973), and Watzlawick, Weakland, and Fisch (1974; Watzlawick, 1978) and provides a very informative description of his therapeutic interventions and their rationale, and of his particular use of homework assignments and what he calls *rituals*.

Bergman is careful in selecting families for his therapy to make sure that their motivation for help is genuine and that their level of resistance is not so high as to preclude their being helped. After concluding that the family is suitable for therapy, Bergman's task is to "capture" them—that is, to create a truly therapeutic relationship as quickly as possible. His task is to join with the family in word (by being appropriately self-disclosing) and manner, while remaining sufficiently uninvolved so as not to become entangled in it. With such a therapeutic relationship in place, Bergman next formulates clinical hypotheses regarding the family, if only tentatively, and sets out to help them change the nature of their interrelationships.

Three assumptions guide the process of hypothesis formulation: "(1) all children's symptoms reflect some marital dysfunction; (2) the more serious the child's symptoms, the more intense and resistant the marital conflict; and (3) the more covert the marital conflict, the more resistant the family system will be to change" (pp. 64–65). Critical questions that Bergman raises in the process of hypothesis formulation may include: "Who has the problem?" "Why is the symptom a problem?" "Does anyone in the family not consider the symptom a problem?" "Who in the family is most upset about the problem?" Another set of questions deals with the symptom itself: "How often does it occur? When? Where? Who reacts to it? In what way?" "When did the symptom begin?" "How does the family account for the problem?" "Why has the family come into treatment now?"

As for attempted solutions, Bergman asks, "What has been tried, by whom, and for how long?" "Is there anything the family tried that they feel could have been done more?" "Do the parents agree or disagree about the solutions?" "How do family members react to each other's solutions?" "What would happen if the symptom got better or worse?" Finally, questions can be framed to deal with treatment goals: "What do the family members hope will happen from coming here?" "What is their ideal goal?" "What will they settle for?" "How optimistic are they about improvement?"

Bergman sees identified patients as taking the position of "victims," people who place other people's needs before their own; who are vulnerable, overly sensitive, and in need of approval from others; who feel angry, impotent, afraid, frustrated, helpless, and deprived; and who are usually unable to express their feelings directly. Other family members may be "killers," who are equally vulnerable but who hide this vulnerability behind a cold, tough, aggressive, snobbish, omniscient, inexpressive, selfish exterior; or they may be "snipers," who lash out against vulnerable family members when they themselves become frustrated or angry. Family members of all three types are in fact victims, but killers and snipers have the ability to cause victims considerable pain. Bergman's principal task in therapy is to help victims change, by helping them handle killers or snipers.

Victims can profit by being told that they are acting as victims. According to Bergman, victims are sufficiently reactive so that they start being mobilized out of the victim position when one points out to them that they are acting the part of a victim. In addition, asserting that the patient is assuming the role of victim and demonstrating how that role assumption manifests itself is fundamentally a hopeful stance, since it implies that the patient can assume a different role.

Depending on the specific situation, Bergman might point out to victims that they are spending much more time avoiding what they do not want than trying to obtain what they do want. Bergman might point out how a patient's adherence to the role of victim demonstrates protective loyalty to parents, by making them feel needed or by showing they are more unhappy than their parents. Deliberately demanding that the patient continue this practice can sometimes be therapeutic. For example,

> *I sometimes give a resistant victim a powerful ritual to perform. I tell him to find photographs (preferably enlargements) of his mother and father and each night to "tell" these photos what he did (or did not do) that particular day to insure that he remained unhappy or less happy than his parents. Then he is to say that he did these things for his parents and that he wanted them to know this. (Bergman, 1985, p. 105)*

Bergman's strategies for helping victims deal with killers are designed to reverse or reframe their typical ways of dealing with them.

> *If, for example, a victim becomes anxious because the killer is perceived as cold, I would encourage the victim to be affectionate, warm, or embracing. . . . The reversal . . . transfers the anxiety from the victim to the killer. After the reversal, the coldness no longer produces anxiety, and the victim no longer feels in a one-down position. At this point, the killer might become anxious because the level of affection (closeness)*

is now being controlled by the former victim. . . . Another reversal I find effective is used for victims who see their killers as aggressive, angry, attacking, or blaming. I encourage the victim, after he receives a shot from an attacker, to convert the killer into a mental patient with earnest sympathetic questions such as: "Are you all right?" "Is everything OK?" "Is something wrong?" When the killer responds with, "Of course everything is OK. Why do you ask?" the victim gently and sympathetically says "You seem so upset, unhappy, and I thought that maybe something was wrong." (1985, pp. 109–110, 111–112)

Since snipers strike irregularly, they are harder to identify in a family context and thus are harder for the victim to deal with. The first task, therefore, is for the victim to identify the possible sniper. The next step is to help the victim respond to the sniper with shorter periods of delay and in ways that neutralize the snipes. For example, Bergman writes:

My personal preference for responding to snipers is to use confusion and humor. . . . What I do after being sniped, and what my patients have done with considerable success, is to kiss the sniper on the nose, giving no explanation. People know immediately when they are being sniped, and although they cannot react fast enough to think, they can react fast enough to kiss a sniper on the nose. The kiss does several things. First, it provides an immediate (and therefore powerful) reaction to the sniper. Second, it probably confuses the sniper, since the last reaction to the snipe he expects is affection. Third, responding to a snipe with affection has a "forgiving" . . . quality about it. Thus, both the confusion induced in the sniper and the forgiving posture move the victim from a potential one-down position to an almost double one-up position. (1985, pp. 112–113)

Bergman concludes by discussing the difficulties family therapists face—for example, in dealing with a family where there is a clearly suicidal member, or dealing with the need to keep maximum leverage on the family in therapy while safeguarding their own psychological integrity. Among the techniques that Bergman mentions are working with co-therapists or with therapeutic teams and using such techniques as varying time intervals between sessions, humor, confrontation, provocation, and distraction.

de Shazer's Ecosystemic Family Therapy

de Shazer (1982, 1988; de Shazer and Molnar, 1984), who is affiliated with the Brief Family Therapy Center in Milwaukee, Wisconsin, describes his therapeutic lineage as deriving from Erickson (1977; Haley, 1967, 1973) and Bateson and others at the Mental Research Institute in Palo Alto, California (Bateson, 1979; de Shazer, 1979; Watzlawick, Weakland, and Fisch, 1974), and to a lesser extent from the work of the Milan Group (Palazzoli et al., 1978). de Shazer defines brief family therapy as an attempt to help people change their *frames,* that is, their viewpoints or customs that cause trouble in the family. The therapy is intended to change, that is, to *reframe* the ways in which family customs develop, so that the meaning of the same concrete situation is modified and viewed and reacted to differently. de Shazer writes:

> *The effects of reframing are confirmed by the appearance of a new set of beliefs, or perceptions,* and *behavior modifications that can be described as a logical consequence of the shift in perception. . . . The result is that the family can look at things from a different angle. Once they "see things differently," they can behave differently. (1982, p. 25)*

Each brief family therapy session is divided into six sections: (1) presession planning, (2) the prelude, (3) data collection, (4) the consulting break, (5) intervention, and (6) postsession assessment. The therapy is conducted by a team, one of whom (called the *conductor*) interacts with the family while the others observe the process through a one-way mirror and provide advice and consultation to the therapist during the consulting break. Because there is both a family group and a therapist group involved in the family therapy, de Shazer has called attention to the complex ecosystem that makes up the therapeutic environment—hence the adjective *ecosystemic* in the description of his family therapy.

Prior to the arrival of the family, during the presession planning, the team members briefly discuss the family situation as they understand it and work out a lighthanded temporary guide for the benefit of the conductor. The guide is not thought of as a rigid formula to be followed, but rather as a number of different provisional ideas about the family, derived from a number of different points of view.

The prelude usually takes up the first ten minutes of each hour-long session, during which the conductor focuses on the social context of the family in a manner that might seem like small talk. The conductor avoids discussion of the complaints that brought the family into therapy, trying rather to develop a helpful relationship with the whole family and to learn something about the specific world of this family.

The next half hour or so makes up the main part of the session, in which the family as a whole is asked to consider with which specific problem they hope the therapeutic group will be able to be most helpful, or what they hope to accomplish in their work in therapy. The conductor is accepting and noncritical and helps the family be as specific as possible about their complaints.

One particular approach is to ask family members about their observations of other family members. According to de Shazer, it seems easier for a person to describe the interactions between two other people than between himself or herself and another person. The conductor helps the family formulate therapeutic goals. In this process the conductor may ask how the family will know that progress has been made toward their goal or how one family member will know that another family member thinks that a start has been made in solving the problem. Meanwhile, the team is observing the family and the interactions between the conductor and the family, seeking to identify and outline frequently observed family interaction patterns.

At the conclusion of the data-collection period, the meeting with the family is adjourned briefly while the conductor meets with the other team members. The purpose of this meeting is to design an intervention. The intervention always involves two components, the "compliment" and the "clue." The purpose of the compliment is to provide positive statements with which the family can agree so that they will be more likely to accept suggestions or tasks (the clue) that follow. For example,

> *First of all, we are impressed with all the fine details you've given us about your situation. Most families we've met are nowhere near as observant of these details. Your descriptions have been very helpful to us. It's clear to us that you are both loving and dedicated parents who've been resourceful in trying to find ways to solve the problem. Another unusual thing struck us: You each seem to care a lot about how the other parent treats the boy. Many parents would be only interested in the boy's difficulties. . . . Between now and next time we meet, the team would like you each to observe what happens when you are alone with Jimmie and he misbehaves like this. And we would like to know some other details: When during the week — which days and what time — does Jim most frequently misbehave while both of you are there. (pp. 44–45)*

The team notes how the family reacts to the compliment and clue. The conductor gives the family a little time to clarify the suggestions and to react to the entire message and then moves to conclude the session quickly. Finally, after the family has left, the team meets to make its assessment of the entire session and to make its best guesses as to what is likely to take place with this family before the next session.

A Case Example

Box 17-1 provides an excerpt from the first session of a de Shazer case example that illustrates some of the principles of ecosystemic family therapy in working with a married couple. The annotations are de Shazer's.

BOX 17-1 • *de Shazer's Ecosystemic Family Therapy: A Case Example*

Therapist: What would you like to see change?

Wife [Barbara]: Get rid of a lot of shame that I seem to be carrying around with me. Get more self-confidence developed and become more, have more spontaneity and less tension. Get the tension out of me. *[Peter—Husband—is watching closely, nodding.]* And, in our relationship, I'd like to get more freed up in my sexual expression with you *[Peter]*, ah, my mind's gone blank.

T: Ah, OK.

W: I've got a lot thought up I'd really like to work on.

T: Obviously, we won't get it all in tonight anyway. So, when it comes back, that's the time to bring it up.

W: Sexual expression. I have a thing: I try to parent everybody, and I would like to be less of a parent to Peter . . . be more communicative than we have been. We've had some training, and that's improved everything, but I need to work on it more than I have been. And I really want to get out of this to be a better listener, particularly of Peter. That just goes across the board I think.

T: Ah, that's a pretty good picture. How about you Peter?

Husband [Peter]: Well, for me it's increasingly my confidence level to kind of develop or heighten my ability to accept responsibility for myself and behaviors. I tend to pass the buck, or blame situations on other people for my inactivity, or my lack of response. I think that is one of the real big hang-ups. I think—what Barbara said, sexual expression—freeing myself up to allow myself the pleasures, or to be in the here and now versus thinking about situations before they occur, or setting things up in rigid analytical thinking. Kind of putting aside my ego. Just accepting myself.

T: OK.

W: (overlapping) Are you done? A very big one for me is accepting self-responsibility.

T: Well, what prompted you to call last week? Why then and not, say, six weeks ago?

W: Well, it's been put off. Procrastination. I keep thinking—each of us thinking—well, if we just work at it, use our communication skills, we should be able to handle it. I don't know what happened last week. I really got down in the pits again.

Continued

BOX 17-1 *Continued*

H: I think it was, for me, increased irritability. Just kind of heightening to the point of being fed up with the way things were going. Our conversation being irritable to each other. My losing patience and kind of pulling out. And, Barb getting down in the pits and depressed. To me, that was kind of the height, and I said, "Maybe we should."

W: I just kind of got pretty scared of, ah, just how I feel? Which feels pretty hopeless. (Tears)

T: What's so hopeless? (Scratching his head)

W: Just me, and that I'm a worthwhile human being?

H: When Barb's like that, I find myself backing out of the relationship.

T: (looking puzzled) After you back out, how do you get back in?

H: At times like that, I get a hold of myself, realize what I'm doing. Or, sometimes when Barb breaks down and cries, or says she needs some closeness, or whatever. . . .

The only concrete material to come out . . . was that Peter was rebuilding a valuable antique. Through very careful questions, it was discovered that Peter had been working on this project for years. Lately, he did very little work on it. This "gnawed" at Barbara because it was their plan to sell the antique to finance a move to another part of the country. So, periodically, she would nag about it, but he still would not do anything. Barbara saw this as a big worry since she really did want to move. In fact, she was afraid Peter would never finish it and, therefore, they would never move. Peter said he did not work on it because he was afraid the move would not live up to their expectations, even though he saw the move as probably helping him reach his real "potential." Therefore, it was safe for him not to work on the project and face the possibility of losing this dream.

At this point in the first session, the team took its consulting break. The data around the antique were the only specific material developed in the first 40 minutes of the session. This type of systemic confusion paralyzed Barbara and Peter and left both of them to wonder about what it is that is going on. But finishing the antique was the only concrete item they both agreed about that the team could think of as a goal. However, the team decided not to pursue the matter actively because it wished to avoid seeming to be on "her side" by picking this as a formal goal. Although Barbara and Peter both said they wanted to move, when and where was very vague. Again, this seemed more "her goal" than his. The team decided to make further attempts at goal definition.

BOX 17-1 Continued

When the conductor returned to the session, he asked the couple to think about how they would know for sure that therapy had been successful. They thought this a good idea, and the session ended. The team predicted Barbara and Peter would return for the subsequent session.

From de Shazer, 1982, pp. 73–75.

The Solution-Focused Model

Continued clinical and theoretical work by de Shazer and his colleagues has resulted in the development of an additional component to their family therapy theory and practice—what they call the *solution-focused* model of family therapy (de Shazer, 1988; de Shazer et al., 1986; O'Hanlon and Weiner-Davis, 1989). This model can be illustrated by the modal question posed to families during their first session of brief family therapy: "Suppose that one night, while you were asleep, there was a miracle and this problem was solved. How would you know? What would be different?" (1988, p. 5).

According to de Shazer, family therapists need to pay as much attention to solutions as to problems, since solutions involve someone doing something different, and therapists are in the business of helping family members do something different. Most initial therapy sessions devote a large proportion of time to describing the problem that led the patient to seek help. de Shazer suggests that with growing interest in solutions, less and less time is now spent in exploring the presenting problem. Rather, more time is spent in looking for exceptions to the problem—that is, to times when the problem does not occur.

Exceptions can often be identified by asking the patients (usually at the first session) to observe and describe at the next session what happens in their family that they want to continue to have happen (de Shazer and Molnar, 1984). Successful completion of this task does not require the prior description of a presenting complaint. In the subsequent description the client will often report having done something different or having had something different happen—the observational basis for solution-focused therapy. de Shazer writes, "Solutions to problems are frequently missed because they often look like mere preliminaries; we end up searching for explanations believing that without explanation a solution is irrational, not recognizing that the solution itself is its own best explanation" (1988, p. 10).

Weiss and Jacobson's Brief Behavioral Marital Therapy

Behavioral marital therapy is, as its name suggests, essentially cognitive in character. Weiss and Jacobson (1981; see also Jacobson and Margolin, 1979) have developed such a form of marital therapy based on the assumption that problem behaviors represent current forms of maladaptation, although they may have adaptive qualities as well. It is particularly appropriate in the case of couples who are still involved enough with each other to work actively toward problem resolution.

Behavioral marital therapy seeks to make changes in four target areas — responses, skills, competencies, and contexts. By *responses,* Weiss and Jacobson refer to behaviors that one or both marital partners make that are seen as destructive to the relationship. Thus, in this form of crisis intervention, couples can be admonished not to engage in certain behaviors, for example, discuss whether or not to move or whether or not to separate, for a specified period of time, such as until after the next meeting with the therapist. By *skills,* Weiss and Jacobson mean specific proficiencies such as good listening or encouraging elaboration of something just said by the partner, that is, behaviors that can enhance communication and generalize to settings outside the therapeutic relationship.

Weiss and Jacobson use the term *competencies* to refer to more generic skills that apply to any content area. Examples of competencies include the ability to discriminate among and within different environments as opposed to thinking that all environments are the same, the ability to be supportive and understanding in interactions with the partner, the ability to problem solve in order to achieve mutually shared objectives, and the ability to effect change in oneself and one's partner. Finally, by *contexts,* Weiss and Jacobson refer to specific areas of marital interaction, such as child care or communication processes, and to how responses, skills, and competencies can be targeted to especially identified aspects of the marital relationship.

According to its proponents, behavioral marital therapy has the potential to help couples exercise better control over their context-specific behavior, their patterns of mutual reinforcement, their generation of alternatives when in conflict situations, their problem-solving skills, and their abilities to step back from their immediate conflicts in order to discern patterns to their own behavioral histories.

Marital therapy, say Weiss and Jacobson, requires a master plan that comprises a number of specific techniques designed to accomplish a specific set of objectives — objectives that are established on the basis of a careful pretreatment assessment followed by the development of a treatment contract. This contract is focused on the purposes of the sessions and their likely duration (usually eight to ten sessions). Behavioral marital therapy is far more concerned with the future than with the past and is far more concerned with problem solving than with rehashing old problems.

Behavioral marital therapy is brief by design — that is, brief because it is believed that shorter is better. The therapist has the specific responsibility of moving the therapy along, making sure that time is used wisely and is not wasted. This built-in brevity represents a special difficulty in marital therapy because it often requires that the couple temporarily sacrifice the little positive that they have in the present for the promise of increased rewards in the future. For example, Weiss and Jacobson comment:

> *Consider the directive that each spouse increase the frequency of pleasing behaviors during the ensuing week. The assignment requires effort; each spouse must concentrate on pinpointing behaviors in his or her repertoire that the other spouse finds pleasing and then generate these behaviors at a higher frequency. Neither spouse can be sure that the other will reciprocate; in other words, the overall consequences of compliance with the assignment are uncertain. Therefore, one would expect spouses to be ambivalent and behavioral resistance to be a rather common occurrence. (p. 411)*

The very brevity of the treatment creates a compelling focus on compliance with therapist directives, on overt verifiable behavior, and on attention to change. Thus, Weiss and Jacobson's position is that brief behavioral marital therapy can accomplish certain objectives that cannot be achieved in longer, time-unlimited therapy.

Weiss and Jacobson (1981) have undertaken a number of controlled experiments designed to evaluate their work; in fact, they indicate that their emphasis on empirical validation of their concepts and practices may be the "greatest strength" (p. 400) of behavioral marital therapy. They report that their treatment techniques, when applied conscientiously, appear to be very effective.

Concluding Comments

The variety of approaches to group and family therapy is well exemplified in this chapter. Strategic-systemic theories come into their own in group and family therapy, while psychodynamic approaches seem somewhat less important.

Two potential virtues of group and family therapy seem particularly evident in the writings just reviewed. First, group treatment seems especially suitable for dealing with a number of patients who share some life experience or life issue, for example, a crisis, a stressful life event, or a developmental transition. That is, a theme of some kind can serve as an organizing principle for group treatment. Second, treatment of more than one patient at a time allows for the possibility that the therapist may not be the only person in the room who is therapeutic. Patients can and do help each other, often in ways that are not easy for the therapist to emulate, such as by providing and receiving mutual support. Third, writings in the field suggest very strongly that therapeutic work with couples concerned with relationship issues may present unusual promise—perhaps far more than working with them one at a time.

There is probably far less planned short-term group and family therapy going on in the mental health field than individual therapy, and this may account for the fact that planned short-term group and family therapy theory is not as well elaborated as are the theories of planned short-term individual therapy. Because there is more than one patient in the room at the same time, an additional level of complexity is introduced into the clinical setting, one that is not welcome to all clinicians. Many clinicians find planned short-term individual therapy sufficiently challenging.

But some practitioners seem to be drawn to working with couples, families, or other groups, and it will only be a matter of time before short-term group therapy theory will have the same richness and variety as does short-term individual therapy. The critical issue may well be to determine whether the group setting will allow certain necessary therapeutic processes to take place that cannot take place in individual therapy. In addition, there is reason to believe that group or family therapy may be only one of what may be more general strategies for being of help to groups or families. Such strategies would include serving as a family consultant or even larger systems consultant (see Kreilkamp, 1989; Wynne, McDaniel, and Weber, 1987). These activities, in a sense alternatives to family or group therapy, under certain circumstances may offer a better way of being helpful to families and other groups. Family consultation, for example, may provide a family the opportunity to examine a variety of alternatives that might be open to them in dealing with a family issue, to identify poorly used family competencies, or to take stock when a complex family situation arises.

CHAPTER EIGHTEEN

Inpatient Settings for Planned Short-Term Psychotherapy

Overview

Characterizing Time-Limited Inpatient Psychiatric Treatment Programs

Evaluation of Time-Limited Inpatient Programs

General Principles of Time-Limited Inpatient Care

Time-Limited Inpatient Programs in Action

Concluding Comments

There was a time when virtually all psychiatric hospitalizations took place in publicly funded state and county mental hospitals and when treatment was routinely thought of as requiring years if not a lifetime. But that has not been true for many decades, certainly not since the advent of the community mental health movement in the early 1960s. In the last twenty years private psychiatric hospitals and psychiatric units in community general hospitals have flourished, and with their emergence came a complex change in the ways in which mental health professionals make use of these facilities.

Between the 1960s and 1980 the number of admissions into inpatient psychiatric facilities of all types increased considerably. Length of hospitalization decreased considerably in state and county mental hospitals but remained stable in private psychiatric hospitals and general hospitals with psychiatric inpatient units. Since 1980, however, while the number of inpatient facilities and number of admissions have continued to increase, length of hospitalization has also increased, particularly in nonpublic facilities, that is, general hospitals with psychiatric inpatient units and private psychiatric hospitals.

Between 1970 and 1980 the average length of hospitalization in public mental hospitals decreased from forty-one to twenty-three days (Taube and Barrett, 1985; see also Meyer and Taube, 1973; Faden and Taube, 1977), but between 1980 and 1986 average length of hospitalization increased to twenty-eight days (unpublished 1986 sample survey data, National Institute of Mental Health).

In the case of private psychiatric hospitals, average length of hospitalization was about twenty days from 1970 through 1980, but by 1986 average length of hospitalization had increased to twenty-four days. Only in the case of general hospitals, where psychiatric patients are most commonly admitted into psychiatric units or wards, has the average length of hospitalization remained steady, averaging about ten days during this entire time period (Graves and Lovato, 1981; National Center for Health Statistics, 1989).

The reasons for these changes in admission rates and length of hospitalization in public and private psychiatric facilities are complex. In the case of public mental hospitals, the increase in number of admissions and the recent increase in length of hospitalization is likely due to the fact that community facilities are not keeping up with the increasing demand for services for the chronically mentally ill. In the case of private psychiatric hospitals, the recent increase in number of facilities and in length of hospitalization is likely due to the nature of third-party health insurance. If a locally available insurance program will reimburse mental health care providers for a thirty-day inpatient alcoholism treatment program or a thirty-day inpatient treatment program for disturbed adolescents, you can be sure that such programs will quickly become available.

The initial reduction in duration of inpatient stay in public mental hospitals came about not only because of expanded services in the community, but also because of a conviction that outpatient care should always be the treatment of choice. In the early days of the community mental health movement (in the late 1960s and early 1970s), there was a growing belief that hospitalization could and should be avoided at all costs, and directors of public mental hospitals found themselves in a friendly competition to see who could empty out public mental hospitals most quickly. Program planners at the federal and state levels envisioned a time when state mental hospitals would be converted into community mental health facilities, chronic care hospitals, or perhaps vocational training schools (see Bloom, 1984).

But a few authors cautioned against excessively rapid abandonment of the psychiatric inpatient facility. Mendel (1967), for example, noted that hospitalization might be the treatment of choice under certain conditions, for persons: (1) who are so disturbed that they cannot maintain useful relationships with therapists as outpatients, (2) whose impulse control is so poor that they frighten members of their families who must care for them, (3) whose psychopathology has alienated them from family and friends who now refuse to care for them, (4) who are malnourished or who make excessive use of drugs, (5) who need to be protected against self-destructive impulses, (6) from whom regularly available supportive resources in the community need a brief vacation, and (7) who must be removed from a pathological environment (also see Gruenberg, 1974).

Needless to say, the psychiatric inpatient unit has not disappeared. In fact, there are more of them than was the case twenty years ago, again, in part, because of third-party insurance reimbursement practices that appeared until quite recently to be far more willing to reimburse inpatient care, seemingly regardless of its programmatic emphasis, duration, or effectiveness, than outpatient services. Once again, just as was the case twenty-five years ago, there is a growing interest in shortening the duration of psychiatric inpatient care.

Characterizing Time-Limited Inpatient Psychiatric Treatment Programs

To some extent the interest in shorter inpatient psychiatric care is part of the same phenomenon that is characterizing outpatient care. It is attributable, first, to a growing concern about reducing the cost of psychiatric care and, second, to the accumulating evidence that shortening the duration of inpatient care does not appear to reduce its effectiveness.

At the same time remarkable changes in the nature of psychiatric inpatient care undoubtedly have had an impact on its increasing efficiency as well as its efficacy. Among these changes has been the recognition that social processes in the inpatient environment, or, as it is frequently called, the *milieu,* can have a significant impact on the therapeutic experiences of hospitalized patients.

While many psychiatric inpatient units now provide treatment programs that take advantage of the therapeutic potential of the milieu, it is well to consider them in comparison with the older, more traditional medical model inpatient programs. These medical model programs, according to Oldham and Russakoff (1987), are characterized by: (1) little or no selection of patients for admission; (2) a hierarchical system of administration and decision making with the physician as the most expert, the other staff next, and the patient least; (3) a high degree of confidentiality among staff, with no general sharing of information with patients; (4) no patient government; (5) little use of group therapy or of patients in therapeutic roles for other patients; (6) medical uniforms; (7) emphasis on disease and its diagnosis, on individual psychotherapy, and on biological treatments such as psychopharmacology and electroconvulsive therapy; and (8) security precautions such as locked doors, restraints, and use of seclusion rooms.

In contrast, the therapeutic community model of inpatient psychiatric treatment emphasizes: (1) general exclusion of certain patients, such as involuntary admissions in order to maintain the therapeutic potential of the milieu; (2) shared responsibility among staff and patients for administration and clinical decision making; (3) frequent and open information sharing among all patients and staff; (4) creation of patient government with specific but broad responsibilities; (5) emphasis on groups for therapeutic purposes; (6) no uniforms for staff; (7) deemphasis of diagnosis and of medication or other forms of biological treatment; and (8) unlocked doors, no seclusion, and little use of restraints.

Because of the importance of group treatment in contemporary inpatient programs that emphasize the therapeutic community model of treatment, there has been a growing literature on the use of short-term group therapy within the inptient setting (see, for example, Beeber, 1988; Brabender, 1985, 1988; Dacey, 1989; Lefkovitz, 1988; Lettieri-Marks, 1987; McGuire, 1988; Rosegrant, 1988; and Starr and Weisz, 1989). Leibenluft and Goldberg (1987) have provided useful guidelines for conceptualizing the group therapy process in inpatient settings. They suggest that short-term inpatient groups go through three phases. In the first phase, when the patient is usually the most distressed, a therapeutic alliance must be established, goals of treatment must be set, a treatment contract must be developed and agreed to, and limits must be set on unacceptable acting-out behaviors. In the second phase, when the patient has begun to see the hospital environment as supportive and therapeutic and has begun to improve, the therapist must stay focused on the goals defined during the first phase while also keeping the issue of discharge from the hospital consistently near the top of the day-to-day agenda. In the third and final phase, issues of separation from the hospital are addressed, and the therapist has to help the patient disengage from the environment that has been found to be so helpful. Leibenluft and Goldberg (1987) write: "An unfortunate reality of inpatient treatment is that the therapist spends half his time engaging the patient in inpatient treatment and the other half disengaging him" (p. 42).

As can be noted, patients have far more active roles to play in the therapeutic community model than in the more traditional medical model. But duration of treatment has traditionally been longer in the therapeutic community model than in the medical model of ward organization and programming. Thus, efforts to shorten inpatient treatment programs while still making use of the milieu are all the more remarkable.

Evaluation of Time-Limited Inpatient Programs

A number of research evaluations of time-limited inpatient psychiatric treatment programs have been reported. In general, these reports indicate that such planned short-term hospitalizations have significant treatment effects. The larger context for viewing these studies is the startling general observation that inpatient care of seriously ill psychiatric patients is, in general, no more effective than any of a variety of alternative outpatient treatment programs. Kiesler (1982) has reviewed all ten published experimental studies he was able to locate that randomly assigned patients to either inpatient care or to some outpatient alternative. These studies included an impressive array of outcome measures, including psychiatric status, subsequent employment, school performance, and independent living arrangements.

Kiesler's conclusions are worthy of quotation:

> *For the vast majority of patients now being assigned to inpatient units in mental institutions, care of at least equal impact could be otherwise provided. There is not an instance in this array of studies in which hospitalization had any positive impact on the average patient which exceeded that of the alternative care investigated in the study. In almost every case, the alternative care had more positive outcomes. (1982, pp. 357–358)*

We shall return to this larger context in this book's final chapter. Meanwhile, it will be useful to examine briefly a number of published studies that have evaluated short-term inpatient care. Caffey, Galbrecht, and Klett (1971) contrasted three inpatient programs in fourteen different Veterans Administration hospitals to which 201 schizophrenic men were randomly assigned: (1) standard hospital care, (2) standard hospital care followed by a one-year outpatient aftercare program, and (3) an accelerated twenty-one-day hospital program followed by one year of outpatient aftercare.

In spite of the fact that length of hospitalization in the standard care groups was three times as long as in the accelerated care group, there were remarkably few differences among the groups during the one-year follow-up period. All three groups improved during their hospitalizations. While the patients in the longer hospitalization groups were less symptomatic at the time of discharge than were the patients in the short hospitalization group, these differences were no longer in evidence either six months or twelve months after discharge. Rehospitalization rates did not differ significantly among the three groups during the year following discharge, nor did the level and nature of community adjustment.

Glick, Hargreaves, and Goldfield (1974) have reported findings from a study in which outcomes were compared for two groups of schizophrenics hospitalized at Langley Porter Neuropsychiatric Institute in San Francisco. A total of 141 patients were randomly assigned to one of two treatment conditions: short-term (21 to 28 day) treatment oriented around crisis resolution and symptom relief, and long-term (90 to 120 day) treatment that emphasized psychotherapy and major rehabilitative measures.

The patients' level of functioning was repeatedly assessed through interviews and a variety of scales completed by the patients, their relatives, and members of the hospital staff. Assessments were made in terms of global outcome, course of posthospital treatment, reduction of symptomatology, family functioning, use of leisure time, and work functioning.

At the time of their preliminary one-year follow-up evaluation, based on about half of the sample, the long-term patients appeared to be functioning better, although they had had significantly more outpatient psychotherapy and more antipsychotic medication following discharge than the short-term group. In a second evaluation (Glick et al., 1975) detailed information on the inpatient phase of treatment was examined for the total group. In this evaluation short-term patients generally were found to have improved more quickly, but long-term patients functioned more adequately at the time of discharge than did short-term patients at the time of discharge.

Two years after the study began, Hargreaves and colleagues (1977) found that differences in their dependent measures were no longer significant between short-term and long-term patients, although there was consistent evidence that long-term hospitalization was particularly effective for patients with good prehospital functioning but not for patients with poor prehospital functioning. Long-term patients were continuing to receive more antipsychotic medication, regardless of level of prehospital functioning, but were no longer receiving more outpatient psychotherapy than short-term patients.

These researchers undertook this evaluation in part to examine the hypothesis that long-term hospitalization may be harmful. Although their long-term group was hospitalized a maximum of only four months, they concluded that "long-term subjects do not function worse in the community than do the short-term subjects" (Hargreaves et al., 1977, p. 310). Since the objection to long-term hospitalization tends to be raised in the case of persons who are hospitalized for years rather than for months, examination of the potentially negative consequences of long-term hospitalization will undoubtedly have to be continued. More important for our purposes is the fact that long-term patients, according to these studies, do not function any better in the community than do short-term patients.

Herz, Endicott, and Spitzer (1975, 1976; Endicott, Herz, and Gibbon, 1978) compared three treatment approaches to which a total of 175 newly admitted inpatients were randomly assigned into one of three different treatment programs: (1) brief hospitalization (often less than one week, and averaging 11 days) followed by transitional day care as needed ($N = 61$), (2) brief hospitalization followed by outpatient care as needed ($N = 51$), and (3) standard hospitalization (averaging 60 days) with discharge to outpatient care at the therapist's discretion ($N = 63$). The patients all had families who were willing to care for them following hospitalization.

The three groups were initially comparable on all measures of past and present psychopathology, role functioning, family burden, and most demographic characteristics. Patients and their families were evaluated at three weeks and at three, six, twelve, eighteen, and twenty-four months after admission.

All three groups of patients improved on almost all dependent measures of adjustment, and there were no significant differences among the three groups in amount of improvement at any of the observation points of the study or in readmission rates. Briefly hospitalized patients were able to resume their vocational roles sooner and were less of a financial burden to their families. The authors found that "there were few differences in psychopathology, role functioning, or effects on the family between groups. When differences did occur, they tended to favor the brief groups" (Herz, Endicott, and Spitzer, 1978, p. 708).

In terms of use of inpatient and day care services over the two-year period, the standard group had a significantly greater average number of inpatient days than did either of the brief groups, even when day care was included. From the beginning, brief hospitalization patients consistently received less antipsychotic or other medication (reducing both direct cost and long-term side effects). Costs to the family (e.g., percent of eligible patients not working at the six-month evaluation) and to the community (e.g., percent of families on welfare at the two-year evaluation) were both substantially greater for the standard hospitalization group.

Swartzburg and Schwartz (1976) contrasted therapeutic outcome over four years on a brief treatment (three to five days) inpatient unit with experiences during the fifth year when the unit was moved, converted to a more traditional long-term locked ward, and staffed by personnel who were unfamiliar with the concepts that had led to the initial development of the brief treatment unit. Nearly 1900 patients had been admitted to these programs during the five-year period.

Demographic characteristics of the patients did not change with the change in treatment approach, nor did distribution by diagnosis. Using rehospitalization or transfer rate as a primary dependent measure, the authors did not find any change as a function of the change in treatment program; that is, the brief treatment inpatient program was just as successful as the more traditional program in getting patients out of the hospital and keeping them out.

In a series of studies a group at the Hillside Medical Center in New York (Mattes, Rosen, and Klein, 1977; Mattes, Rosen, Klein, and Millan, 1977; Rosen et al., 1976) contrasted short-term hospitalization (less than 90 days) with unlimited stay hospitalization (averaging 179 days) by randomly assigning 173 patients to these two conditions and following them for three to four years.

At the time of discharge short-term patients were significantly more improved in both cognitive and affective symptoms. At the time of the three- to four-year follow-up, both groups were doing equally well, although long-term patients had been rehospitalized significantly more often than short-term patients during the follow-up period. The authors concluded that long-term hospitalization "should be avoided whenever possible since compared with shorter hospitalization, it does not lead to greater benefit in any of the evaluated areas of adjustment and, in fact, with some patients it appears to predispose to more and longer rehospitalization" (Mattes, Rosen, and Klein, 1977, p. 387).

In summary, no evidence has been reported that indicates the superiority of long-term over short-term hospitalization. Riessman, Rabkin, and Struening (1977) reviewed a group of studies that had similarly contrasted brief and standard psychiatric hospitalizations. They concluded:

> *Evidence from the studies that we have reviewed provides support for the null hypothesis that the effects of brief hospitalization are essentially equivalent to those of standard hospitalization. . . . These investigations cumulatively indicate that groups of patients hospitalized for an average of 3 to 60 days do not significantly differ from those with longer average hospitalizations with respect to symptoms, social functioning, global adjustment, or the risk of rehospitalization either at discharge or within the next 2 years. These findings appear to be consistent across diagnostic groups and across hospitals characterized by marked differences in treatment philosophy, patient-staff ratio, and other factors. (1977, pp. 8–9)*

General Principles of Time-Limited Inpatient Care

Peake, Borduin, and Archer (1988) provide a useful set of recommendations for planning effective brief inpatient psychiatric treatment. These proposals come from their own clinical experiences in inpatient settings, comparison with other psychiatric inpatient programs, and an examination of the recent inpatient treatment literature. Their recommendations are as follows (pp. 158–167):

1. Employ therapeutic goals and treatment objectives that are realistic within a time-limited environment.
2. Strengthen and improve discharge planning and aftercare services.
3. Reduce or eliminate the amount of "dead time" in inpatient services.
4. Form utilization review or efficiency groups at the unit level.
5. Provide unit leadership with individuals who have experience with short-term treatment modalities.

6. Modify the view of the role of the hospital to include the concept of intermittent or episodic care.
7. Base treatment intervention on a rapid operational assessment of what is needed to return the patient to the community.
8. Reduce the discrepancy between patient and staff treatment goals by mutually derived treatment contracts.
9. Don't be afraid to try something different, and do it early in the treatment process.

Closer examination of these recommendations reveals that they can be grouped into four categories. First are proposals that can result in setting more realistic treatment goals – keeping in mind the special role of the inpatient facility in the entire treatment spectrum and developing treatment goals through a process that involves the patient as well as the staff. Second are proposals that increase the efficiency of the treatment – reducing down time, forming utilization review groups, and rapid assessment and inauguration of treatment. Third are proposals that have the specific potential for improving treatment effectiveness – inaugurating discharge and outpatient follow-up planning virtually from the beginning of inpatient treatment, including the possibility of intermittent care in treatment planning, and trying new and different treatment approaches. Finally, Peake, Borduin, and Archer recognize the necessity of identifying clinical program directors who have a high level of competence and a strong commitment to time-limited inpatient care. This set of recommendations is unusually important not only because it may apply across a broad spectrum of inpatient treatment facilities, but also because it is very likely that similar recommendations will improve the efficacy of time-limited outpatient care.

Time-Limited Inpatient Programs in Action

A number of comprehensive time-limited psychiatric inpatient programs have been described in the literature. Oldham and Russakoff's (1987) unusually thoughtful description of their time-limited inpatient psychiatric treatment program places it as nearer to older medical model inpatient programs than to newer therapeutic community programs. Their program does, however, contain several modifications of the medical model program. Information is shared with staff and patients based on each patient's estimated needs. A patient government is created, but its functions are limited to a liaison and advisory role. Group therapy is available for selected patients. Community meetings are held, but they have a carefully structured agenda and are always chaired by a staff member. Staff personnel wear name tags but do not wear uniforms. Aside from these exceptions, the Oldham and Russakoff program follows the medical model.

Their program is located in a twenty-five-bed unit in a university-based training hospital. Median length of stay is about twenty-six days. Each patient is assigned to one of three multidisciplinary teams and, within each team, to a primary therapist as well as to a social worker, a nursing staff member, and a medical student. Each day begins either with team-based group therapy or with a ward-based community meeting. Following this meeting, patients participate in a variety of supervised therapeutic activities while team staff members meet to discuss patient progress, medical and psychiatric evaluations, and treatment planning. Each patient is seen in individual therapy by his or her primary therapist and meets regularly with the nursing staff member assigned to the case. The theoretical orientation of the ward is based on an object relations framework, one that is unusually applicable to severely disturbed patients, whose problems usually predate the oedipal period (Oldham and Russakoff, 1987, pp. 35 ff.).

Individual psychotherapy provides a critically important experience to the patient, one that helps counter the sense of failure and anger occasioned by the hospitalization itself. Individual psychotherapy can thus help build or maintain self-esteem at the same time that it enhances self-understanding (Oldham and Russakoff, 1987, pp. 51–68). Group psychotherapy provides an opportunity for patients to examine interpersonal aspects of their psychopathology through experiencing their effects upon other people, to increase their social skills, and to learn to behave interdependently (Oldham and Russakoff, 1987, pp. 69–84).

The community meeting, designed to provide a formal opportunity for interaction among the entire patient and staff membership of the ward, provides a vehicle for input into important ward- and patient-related decision making. On a twenty-five-bed unit there may be as many as forty or forty-five people present at the community meeting. Oldham and Russakoff (1987), noting that relatively little information about such meetings is available in the literature, provide a clear rationale and much insight as to how their community meetings are organized and conducted. They have found that forty-five minutes provides adequate time for significant work to be done without taxing the tolerance of the most severely disturbed patients. Staff members and patients sit together, with staff members deliberately assigned to sit alongside particularly disturbed patients (see Oldham and Russakoff, 1987, pp. 197–212 for a verbatim transcript of one such meeting).

Six techniques have been found useful by Oldham and Russakoff in conducting community meetings:

1. At the beginning of each meeting, roll call of patients and staff is taken with careful explanation given to account for any missing

      patient or staff member, and new members of the community, whether patients or staff, are introduced.

2. The agenda for the meeting is created by open discussion.

3. Information pertinent to carrying out the agenda is gathered openly, without recourse to knowledge not available to the entire community.

4. Each agenda issue is brought to a close before the next item on the agenda is introduced.

5. Impending departures from the community, whether of patients or staff, are formally noted.

6. Every effort is made to ensure that meetings begin and end on a positive and supportive note.

Concluding Comments

Evaluation studies of planned short-term inpatient psychotherapy have come to the same conclusion with the same degree of regularity as have evaluation studies of planned short-term outpatient psychotherapy: Short-term treatment is indistinguishable from time-unlimited treatment in its effects.

As we have seen, hospitalization is believed to be the treatment of choice under a number of circumstances. But in order to ensure that health insurance programs will be able to provide that inpatient care when it is needed, it is increasingly evident that hospitalization should be avoided when it is not necessary. The reasons for this avoidance are clinical as well as fiscal, for hospitalization inevitably induces a form of regression that may feed on itself. Thus, in the case of a psychiatric emergency, particularly when mental health personnel are not readily available, it is easy to decide to hospitalize the patient until morning, at which time the patient's condition can be reevaluated. But even by the next morning many patients have already come to the conclusion that they can only be treated successfully if their hospitalization is continued.

There is thus a kind of tension between administrators responsible for maintaining the viability of psychiatric hospitals, by making sure that all beds are filled, and those responsible for maintaining the viability of health insurance programs—a tension between clinicians and fiscal agents that parallels that found in general medical hospitals. In the case of medical disorders, the results of that tension are increasingly evident. Many medical procedures that used to be performed in hospitals are now routinely done in outpatient surgical and diagnostic facilities, with an attendant reduction in cost and sense of disability to the patient. Health insurance companies are well aware of evaluation studies such as those described in this chapter, and policies encouraging the reduced use of psychiatric inpatient units are likely to follow those regarding reduced use of general medical inpatient facilities. These developments are creating high levels of tension for medical administrators, particularly in communities where there may already be a surplus of medical or psychiatric beds.

Because reducing the duration of inpatient care plays such a significant role in reducing the cost of mental health services, alternatives to traditional psychiatric inpatient care should be sought with greater vigor. Many health care providers institute round-the-clock crisis intervention services so that patients being considered for hospitalization can be seen before being admitted. Fiscal agents typically require prior authorization for inpatient admission, a policy that helps reduce the unnecessary use of inpatient facilities. Another alternative to traditional hospitalization worthy of exploration is the use of hotel-type facilities in lieu of traditional inpatient settings. Such facilities are substantially less expensive than general hospital beds and may in fact be more therapeutic than being admitted into a general hospital psychiatric unit or a traditional private psychiatric hospital.

At the same time that issues of cost need to be considered, there is evidence that clinicians are increasingly interested in organizing inpatient treatment programs that take advantage of everything that is healthy in both patients and staff. Contemporary inpatient treatment programs are a far cry from the programs of a generation ago, in large measure because psychosocial approaches are being included in the treatment program alongside improved pharmacological approaches. Thus, inpatient psychiatric programs may shortly begin to diminish in number and in duration, while increasing in quality and effectiveness.

CHAPTER NINETEEN

Planned Short-Term Therapy in Medical Settings

Overview

Medical Cost-Offset Studies

Psychodynamic Psychotherapy in Medical Settings

Rational-Emotive Psychotherapy in Medical Settings

Strategic Psychotherapy in Medical Settings

Concluding Comments

The planned short-term psychotherapy literature of the past decade includes a substantial body of work demonstrating the use of time-limited therapy in working with patients who are medically ill. In this and the next chapter we shall examine the clinical approaches that have been suggested for providing time-limited psychotherapy to medically ill patients whose illnesses are complicated by the presence of some form of psychological disorder. In many cases the psychological disorder can be thought of as part of the causal complex related to the medical illness. In perhaps more cases the disorder can be the consequence of the stress induced by the illness.

The scope of such approaches is remarkably broad and includes efforts to be of help to patients with such disorders as chronic pain, migraine and tension headaches, tics, myocardial infarctions, cancer, diabetes, and herpes (Bassett and Pilowsky, 1985; Bell et al., 1983; Block, 1985; Croake and Myers, 1989; Drob and Bernard, 1985; Friedman and Taub, 1985; Klerman et al., 1987; Mumford, Schlesinger, and Glass, 1982; Nielsen et al., 1988; Rinsley, 1986; Stern, 1987; Teitelbaum and Kettl, 1988).

Reports of the use of planned short-term psychotherapy in working with the physically ill are remarkably uniform in their findings that brief psychotherapy has significantly reduced the negative consequences of these disorders. Mumford, Schlesinger, and Glass (1982), for example, reported that a brief psychological intervention with patients hospitalized following heart attacks reduced the average duration of hospitalization by approximately two days when contrasted with control groups for whom no psychological intervention was provided.

Two chapters will deal with planned short-term psychotherapy with medically ill patients because the literature is divided into two very discrete domains. This chapter will deal with time-limited psychotherapy provided by mental health professionals to patients who are medically ill. Such patients are generally referred to mental health professionals by primary care physicians, who continue to manage their patient's medical problems.

The next chapter will examine the literature concerned with psychotherapy provided to medically ill patients by their own primary care physicians. Since most primary care physicians are scheduled to see three or four patients every hour, often thirty or forty patients in a single day, a type of time-limited psychotherapy called brief contact therapy has been developed. Brief contact therapy limits the duration of individual treatment sessions to fifteen to twenty minutes, and the works that have been published on this topic are designed to train primary care physicians in how to help their medically ill patients cope with the emotional components and emotional consequences of their illnesses, working in blocks of time that match the physicians' typical busy working schedule.

Medical Cost-Offset Studies

One aspect of planned short-term psychotherapy evaluation studies has been the search for evidence of what has come to be called *medical offset*. These studies take place in medical settings and seek to determine whether time-limited psychotherapy can significantly reduce the use of medical care — that is, whether the cost of psychotherapy can be more than offset by savings in the cost of other aspects of medical care (Budman, Demby, and Feldstein, 1984). As the cost of medical care rises, the possibility that time-limited psychotherapy may save more than it costs has become increasingly attractive to persons interested in economic aspects of health care.

An example of this kind of study is the work of Mumford and colleagues (1984; see also Mumford and Schlesinger, 1987), who examined a number of published studies, including their own study of health insurance claims, in order to determine whether outpatient mental health services could be shown to reduce subsequent use of other medical services. These investigators found significant cost offset in the form of reduced inpatient care, particularly among patients over age 55. These authors suggest that the commonly observed underutilization of outpatient mental health services among the older population may not only result in needless suffering but also in unnecessary expenditures for inpatient care in this group.

Perhaps the most provocative findings reported in the literature are those linking a single therapeutic interview with subsequent reductions in the use of medical care. There is already a substantial body of literature showing that brief psychotherapy can have this effect (see, for example, Goldberg, Krantz, and Locke, 1970; Jameson, Shuman, and Young, 1978; Jones and Vischi, 1979; Rosen and Wiens, 1979), but to demonstrate it following a single interview is startling indeed.

Cummings and Follette (Cummings, 1977a, 1977b; Cummings and Follette, 1968, 1976; Cummings and Vandenbos, 1979; Follette and Cummings, 1967) undertook a series of studies investigating the role of psychotherapy in reducing medical care utilization in a prepaid health plan setting. In such settings they found that patients could easily somatize emotional problems and thus overutilize medical facilities. They estimated that "60% or more of the physician visits are made by patients who demonstrate an emotional, rather than an organic, etiology for their physical symptoms" (Cummings, 1977a, p. 711).

Among the groups they studied was a sample of eighty emotionally distressed patients who were assigned to receive a single psychotherapeutic interview. They found, totally unexpectedly, that one therapeutic interview, with no repeat psychological visits, reduced medical utilization by 60 percent over the following five years, and that the reduction was the consequence of resolving the emotional distress that was being reflected in physical symptoms.

The results of two other studies provide additional, equally startling findings. Goldberg and colleagues (1970) studied the effects of short-term outpatient therapy on utilization of medical services. Their sample consisted of 256 people who were enrolled in the Group Health Association prepaid medical program in Washington, DC and who had been referred for and found eligible and in need of outpatient psychiatric care. In the year following referral for psychiatric care, this group showed an average reduction of 31 percent in physician visits and 30 percent in laboratory and X-ray visits compared to the previous year. But this reduction was independent of whether those referred for care actually received it. In fact, while the reduction in physician visits was 23 percent among those who had had ten or more sessions of psychotherapy and 30 percent among those who had had between one and nine sessions, it was 39 percent among those who had had no psychotherapy at all.

In another study, Rosen and Wiens (1979) examined the same issue at the University of Oregon Health Sciences Center. Comparisons were made between four groups of patients: (1) those who received medical services but were not referred for psychological services, (2) those who were referred for services in the Medical Psychology Outpatient Clinic but never kept their scheduled appointments, (3) those who were referred for psychological services but received only an evaluation, and (4) those who were referred and who received both an evaluation and subsequent brief psychotherapy. Groups 1 and 2—that is, those who were either not referred or who were referred but did not keep their appointments—showed no subsequent reduction in the utilization of medical care including number of outpatient visits, emergency room visits, days of hospitalization, diagnostic procedures, and pharmaceutical prescriptions. Groups 3 and 4, those receiving only an evaluation or an evaluation and brief psychotherapy (averaging seven interviews), showed significant subsequent reduction in the utilization of medical care, but the group receiving only the evaluation demonstrated the most consistent reduction in, among other things, medical outpatient visits, pharmaceutical prescriptions, emergency room visits, and diagnostic services (see also Brown, 1984; Gask, 1986).

The one fact that links the findings of all these studies is that a single contact, virtually regardless of the purpose of that contact, appears to have salutary consequences for medically ill patients. That is, it appears to make no demonstrable difference whether the contact is designed to serve a primarily evaluative function or whether its purpose is primarily therapeutic in intent. With this consistent evidence of the usefulness of psychological help in the context of medical illness, it is appropriate to examine a number of approaches to such treatment. Three very different approaches to working with medically ill patients will be described—psychodynamic, rational-emotive, and strategic.

Psychodynamic Psychotherapy in Medical Settings

Bellak and Siegel (1983) suggest that brief psychotherapy may be necessary at the point where a physical illness or reaction to its proposed or past treatment becomes a psychiatrically incapacitating disorder. Such an event can occur, for example, when a patient is informed about the gravity of a disorder or the necessity for treatment procedures that are risky or painful, or postoperatively when the patient is in the midst of reacting to the procedures already completed.

Bellak and Siegel (1983) believe that in order for the mental health professional to be helpful to the physically ill patient, it is essential to understand the nature of patients' reactions to their illnesses in terms of their prior general life history. That is, the illness or surgery, for example, likely has specific meanings for the patient, and these meanings can be explored and clarified with considerable benefit.

Frightening experiences, such as having to confront a serious physical illness, can result in denial, depression, anxiety, or severe changes in the image of the self. In the event of impending surgery, for example, the mental health professional should carefully explore both the general and the specific fears associated with the impending event and how these fears can be understood in the context of the patient's life.

Bellak and Siegel suggest a number of specific techniques that can be useful in the therapeutic management of patients with severe physical illnesses. These include: (1) exploring the patient's concept of the illness or impending treatment, as well as the personal meaning and role of the illness; (2) educating the patient (see Bloom, 1988); (3) establishing contact with the treating physician or surgeon in order to enhance the mental health professional's effectiveness and to avoid being at cross-purposes with the medical treatment plan; (4) exploring the meaning of anesthesia to the patient, and the patient's attitudes and specific fears of death; and (5) exploring the patient's fantasies and attitudes about the specific illness and specific proposed treatment, paying particular attention to illnesses associated with organs of sexual significance, to malignancies, and to diseases of the heart.

Bellak and Siegel (1983) suggest that "specific kinds of surgery to sexual organs stimulate rather standard reactions. A prostate operation will usually arouse fears of impotence and reawaken old castration anxieties. Breast operations, on the other hand, are often perceived as threats to a patient's femininity" (p. 100). Regarding malignancies, Bellak and Siegel write: "For some cancer patients, the oral aggressive features of the patient's personality may find exaggeration in the disease so that they perceive the cancer as an eating, boring, destroying phenomenon. With others in whom the sadomasochistic features are predominant, the cancer may be perceived as a brutal, sadistic, attacking introject" (p. 101).

The heart has not only a vital physical significance but a special symbolic one. In the case of heart disease, postdischarge issues are often the most important. Bellak and Siegel note that "the therapist must anticipate the patient's feeling of depression following discharge from the hospital, and be prepared to take a supportive role in the follow-up treatment" (p. 101). The mental health professional can help the patient cope with excessive fear and passivity and thus avoid becoming a chronic and fearful invalid. Since the cardiovascular system reacts so quickly to stress of any kind, the mental health professional has the opportunity to help cardiac patients cope with their increased sensitivity to their illness and to their reactions to stress.

Patients who have had heart attacks often are afraid that any exertion may shorten their lives, and as a consequence they may view work as far more of a hazard to their health than is actually the case. Bellak and Siegel also suggest that physicians may be themselves uneasy about heart disease (in part because heart disease is so common among physicians) and may transmit some of that anxiety to their patients.

Rational-Emotive Psychotherapy in Medical Settings

Ellis and Abrahms (1978) have coined a number of terms to describe neurotic reactions of medically ill patients to their illnesses. Among them is "awfulizing," "musturbation," "self-downing," and "I-can't-stand-it-itis." All these terms describe a kind of whining that chronically characterizes the behavior of medically ill people who are not dealing with their illnesses in a healthy manner. *Awfulizing,* as its name suggests, is the term used to label the person who says, "It's *awful* that I have such a horrible ailment, and it would be absolutely *terrible* if I suffered greatly or died of it." *I-can't-stand-it-itis* describes the patient who says, "I *can't stand* this utterly abominable condition and the uncertainty that I have about it." *Self-downing* is the term used to describe the person who says, "Since I could have watched myself more carefully and gone for regular medical examinations, and I did not do this well enough, that is rotten behavior and I am an exceptionally stupid, rotten person for behaving in this manner."

These three forms of inadequate coping are all derivatives of thinking in *musts* rather than in preferences or desires. Thinking in musts is represented by the belief that patients *absolutely* have to do the right thing by themselves or by others. Such people nearly always conclude that they absolutely should have done everything they could have to ward off the disease, that they absolutely must not have the disease, and that since they have it, it absolutely must be their fault. Ellis would like medically ill patients to think, "Tough luck"—that is, the philosophy that makes it possible for a patient to say, "Tough luck—it is truly unfortunate that I have this ovarian problem. But that's the way it is. I damned well *can* stand the inconvenience, though I'll never like it. The problem likely won't mean the end of my life, and I can still live happily in spite of it."

Ellis and Abrahms (1978) recommend a kind of positive thinking that can be represented by "I can succeed and am therefore a pretty good individual." Contrast this with the negative thinking implicit in the statement "I can't succeed and am therefore a crummy person." They also recommend helping medically ill patients develop an unconditional self-acceptance by accepting the proposition that they haven't done everything they could have done to prevent becoming ill, but that doesn't mean that they are contemptible people. Primary care physicians should help their patients think of their illnesses as representing problems to be solved and medical regimens to be followed and should communicate their support and affection for their patients with all their failings, and the sense that they can do more to help themselves than they realize.

Specific techniques of rational-emotive therapy can help patients dissipate their sense of shame that is often associated with physical illness, talk about and disclose things about themselves in ways they have never previously dared to, and become appropriately emotional, rather than under- or overemotional.

Strategic Psychotherapy in Medical Settings

Goldsmith (1986) predicates his strategic approach to psychotherapy with medically ill patients on his assessment of their likely responses to psychotherapeutic intervention. Response tendencies to therapeutic interventions are grouped into three categories — straightforward compliance, defensive compliance, and opposition.

This assessment is particularly important in the case of medically ill patients because many such patients are opposed to psychological approaches to their difficulties. For these patients the only pertinent reality is their physical symptoms, and their only interest is in ameliorating those symptoms. For these patients, according to Goldsmith, a paradoxical intervention is required in which therapists ally themselves with the symptomatic side of the patient's ambivalence, allowing the patient to concentrate on the other side of the ambivalence, the side that wants to get rid of the symptom. Goldsmith calls this paradoxical intervention the position of the devil's advocate, and often it manifests itself in the therapist suggesting that the patient continue symptomatic behavior (see Boettcher and Dowd, 1988; Kovacs, 1982).

Goldsmith uses the patient's response to a restatement of the problem or to an empathic statement during the initial interview or to a homework assignment as part of the assessment procedure. For example, if the therapist repeats a remark that the patient has previously made and the patient rejects the comment as being inaccurate, or if a patient denies the validity of a carefully crafted empathic remark, or if a patient does not correctly or fully complete a homework assignment, these are all indications that paradoxical interventions may be the most effective in helping the patient.

Many medically ill patients resent being referred to a mental health professional for a consultation. They resent what they think of as not being taken seriously by the primary care physician, or the implication that their symptoms are thought of as imaginary or as malingering. Goldsmith (1986) writes:

> *A patient suffering from a physical symptom interrelated with life stresses, who is unaware of the influence of these stresses, will*

experience the physical symptom as the only valid subjective reality. An investigation or explanation of non-physical causes of these symptoms will indicate to such patients, consciously and unconsciously, a lack of understanding and empathy on the part of the clinician. . . . Even patients who . . . are aware . . . of such . . . influences on their symptoms will always be ambivalent about fully accepting the fact of an "emotional" causation. If this were not the case, they would probably no longer have their physical symptoms. (pp. 18–19)

Typically, mental health professionals cope with this resentment by some combination of empathy, reassurance, the promise that mental health assistance will help them cope with their symptoms, and education about the role of stress in precipitating physical illness. These mental health consultations often fail to accomplish their objectives because consultants often underappreciate why patients express their distress through physical symptoms and try to force the patient into thinking of the problem as *either* physical *or* psychological.

Goldsmith identifies two specific therapeutic techniques — the use of the therapeutic metaphor and reframing — as particularly helpful in working with medically ill patients. The therapeutic metaphor is a form of story telling, and its advantages lie in the fact that it can bypass a patient's resistance, since the therapist talks about other people; its telling can induce a kind of hypnotic trance; and it can stimulate an individual's mental associative processes in order to help find a creative solution to the presenting problem. The case example provided by Goldsmith in Box 19-1 illustrates the use of the therapeutic metaphor.

BOX 19-1 • *Use of the Therapeutic Metaphor*

A 58-year-old electrician who had been promoted to a supervisory position three months earlier and who had been suffering with tension, nausea, and vomiting and "jumpiness" in his abdominal region since his wife had died eight years earlier, and whose symptoms had become more severe since his promotion, wanted to be free of vomiting and to have his nausea reduced to manageable proportions. He felt he could take care of the tension and the jumpiness himself. At the third session, Goldsmith induced a hypnotic trance and told him the story of another patient he had seen who had had a similar problem.

I said that I told the other patient that the stomach was a marvelous organ of complex capabilities. I described in great detail the stomach's

BOX 19-1 *Continued*

sensory and secretory abilities, as well as its ability to adjust its size, shape, and the dimensions of its openings to the esophagus and small intestine by means of adjustments in the degree of muscular contraction at these openings. I told him how the walls of the stomach were lined with secretory cells and with powerful slabs of muscle, which contracted in order to break down food and pass it through to the small intestine. These wall muscles very capably and strongly broke down food, but their contractions could also produce vomiting. Vomiting was brought about by the contractions of these and other muscle groups, which produced a reversed flow of food up through the esophagus. Vomiting was a sign of great muscle strength and capability. The wall muscles of his stomach had quite sufficiently demonstrated their capability in that regard already, and why not just let them show their power in ways that could produce greater comfort for him, by their pulverizing food fully and propelling it properly and comfortably on to the small intestine, where it could really be enjoyed by the rest of the body.

In that way, he could be pleased and proud of the activity of these muscles. In addition, I said that I told this other patient that the human nervous system was really a marvelous set of intertwining electrical circuits. Nerves could be seen as electrical wires and cables. Junctions between nerves could be seen as switches and electrical junction boxes. The junctions of nerves and various parts of the body could be seen as outlets and electrical fixtures of various types. The brain could be imagined as a wonderfully capable electric service panel or else as an electrical box with a variety of switches, rheostats, and other mechanisms attached. Electrical information would be transmitted along the wires to the box in the brain, and the brain would send information to the various parts and organs of the body to govern the functioning of these organs. I described how such a flow of information was as true of the stomach as of any other part of the body. I invited him to see and even feel how he could construct his own electrical circuits in his mind that would regulate the functioning of his stomach and would regulate the flow of information from his stomach to his brain.

He was to construct such circuits in detail. Such circuits could prevent the occurrence of vomiting in the stomach when such an occurrence was no longer necessary, and, I added, it no longer did appear necessary. Such circuits could also prevent the experience of any unnecessary degree of nausea. Such circuits could still allow the experience of tension and jumpiness in his stomach area, should the continuing experience of these sensations still be necessary. I was then silent for a

Continued

BOX 19-1 *Continued*

minute or two in order to allow this unconscious activity to take place. I proceeded to give the patient post-hypnotic instructions to the effect that these circuits could operate for his benefit any time he wished in the future. . . . Upon awakening, he was able to describe to me a series of electrical circuits he had designed in a detailed and sophisticated manner. He was clearly pleased with the degree of expertise and prowess that went into that design, which he subsequently used successfully.

Three months later, Goldsmith learned that the patient was free of vomiting, had only occasional nausea that was mild and tolerable, and that he continued to have tension and jumpiness. The patient had no idea why he still had these symptoms or why the vomiting had disappeared. He was fully satisfied with the results of the therapy.

From Goldsmith, 1986, pp. 22–24.

Reframing, the second of Goldsmith's special therapeutic techniques for working with medically ill patients, consists of changing the context of some behavior, event, or emotion so that its meaning changes. Vomiting is labeled as a sign of strength rather than weakness. A patient who derives pleasure from baffling physicians is told that if her symptoms disappear, that would really baffle her physicians because it would prevent them from ever discovering the cause of her symptoms. A patient's symptoms are redefined as a noble sacrifice for the sake of helping his parents become more comfortable with their own lives. Communication difficulties between a husband and his terminally ill wife are reframed as evidence of his great concern for her and as evidence of her own inner strength in keeping feelings to herself when she wanted to. Willingness of a woman to tolerate her boyfriend's behavior (even though it included giving her gonorrhea) is reframed as evidence of great loyalty to him and as a wish to protect him from being alone (see also Kovacs, 1982, pp. 152–153).

Goldsmith notes that reframing is as old as the human race, particularly in the context of illness and death. Sick people gain the ability to appreciate life more fully or are grateful that their illnesses give them an opportunity to learn about courage and compassion. Adversity is said to build character. Death is a blessing. Soldiers die for their country. Mourners find meaning in seemingly senseless deaths of loved ones. Such reframing, whether it occurs naturally or is stimulated by the work of the therapist, can help people gain new perspectives of their lives and can decrease personal distress.

Concluding Comments

Once again the evidence of effectiveness of planned short-term psychotherapy is virtually unequivocal, in this case when working with patients who are medically ill. Furthermore, the evidence seems persuasive that the cost of providing psychological treatment is more than offset by the savings in the cost of subsequent medical care. Thus, efforts to study the role of psychological intervention in the treatment of medical illness seem entirely justified, and we can expect increasing application of planned short-term psychotherapy in the medical setting.

The three approaches to brief psychological intervention could not be more different from each other, but, as has been mentioned from time to time in this book, there is no evidence of any superiority of one approach over another. Each of the three approaches is faithful to its fundamental theories. Accordingly, it is important to be aware of a variety of approaches, if only to make a better match between the patient's difficulties and the therapist's clinical treatment preferences.

The psychodynamic approach, exemplified by the work of Bellak and Siegel (see also Chapter 3), begins with the assumption that there are both rational and irrational aspects to patients' reactions to their illnesses and that attention to both aspects is necessary in order for the patient to receive optimal relief of distress. The rational-emotive approach, exemplified by the work of Ellis (see also Chapter 13), treats patients' distresses essentially as neurotic thinking disorders and seeks to help patients think more positively about themselves in relation to their illnesses. These approaches are designed to reduce the sense of shame and guilt so often associated with physical illness and at the same time to promote a greater sense of self-acceptance. The strategic approach attempts to reframe or reconceptualize the symptom or the discomfort rather than removing it, creating the opportunity for patients to think about their distresses using an entirely different metaphor from the one that characterized their pretreatment adaptation.

What is clear from these approaches and from the evaluation studies that confirm their effectiveness is that we should expect a significant increase in the reports of psychological intervention in the case of an even wider variety of physical disorders, especially in the case of the elderly, in the near future (see, for example, Kirshner, 1988; Lazarus, 1988).

CHAPTER TWENTY

Brief Contact Therapy

Overview

Brief Contact Therapy in Psychiatric Settings

Brief Contact Therapy in Medical Settings

Concluding Comments

Planned short-term psychotherapy can be brief not only in terms of the number of sessions, but also in that each contact may be brief. In brief contact therapy the length of the interview is never more than half an hour and frequently less. As was indicated at the start of the previous chapter, brief contact therapy is identified primarily with the psychological treatment of medically ill patients by their own primary care physicians who have received specialized training in that modality (see, for example, Mohl, 1988; Sperry, 1987; Williamson, 1987; Zabarenko, Merenstein, and Zabarenko, 1971).

Some years ago there was interest in exploring the shortening of traditional psychotherapeutic interviews as conducted by mental health professionals, and there is some limited evidence that that interest is continuing. Mann and Goldman (1982), for example, have commented:

> *The common pattern in psychotherapy of any kind is for patients to make gains early in treatment, only to have progress grind to a halt for long periods as the patient's resistance mounts as a result of conflicts over passive-dependent wishes, the wish not to grow up, the fear of losing the therapist if improvement ensues, and more. It has long been observed that many patients can use a "thirty-minute hour" as effectively as a sixty-minute hour. Constrictions of time, such as the*

use of "deadlines," tend to mobilize the patient's demands on himself to complete a piece of work. (p. 14; see also O'Connell and Stubblefield, 1989)

Brief Contact Therapy in Psychiatric Settings

More than two decades ago Koegler (1966) proposed the use of brief contact therapy by mental health professionals in outpatient treatment settings, since he considered the greatest benefit of a psychotherapeutic interview to occur in the first few minutes, certainly within the first thirty minutes.

In proposing brief contact therapy, Koegler noted that

psychiatry is the only medical specialty in which the patient sees the doctor for a fixed period of time, regardless of the patient's needs. The patient is stretched or shortened to fit the psychiatrist's procrustean time-couch. Psychiatric patients arrive and leave at fixed times; and a psychiatrist whose patients are permitted to overstay their allotted time is thought to have "guilt about money" by his colleagues. Patients soon become accustomed to the system, too, and woe be it to the therapist who stops the session two minutes short. (1966, pp. 141–142)

Koegler cited several potential advantages of shorter therapy sessions. Greater numbers of clients could be accommodated, and psychiatric service would thus be made more economical and therefore more accessible. In addition, Koegler felt that briefer interviews would be more appropriate for certain clients—those with low verbal ability or those who are psychotic or prepsychotic.

An example of the empirical justification for brief contact therapy can be found in the work of Dreiblatt and Weatherley (1965), who conducted two studies examining the effect of very brief contacts with hospitalized psychiatric patients. In their first study, a group of forty-four new patients in a Veterans Administration hospital was divided into three subgroups after an initial evaluation of their self-esteem and anxiety level. One group received regular ward care; the second group received three 5- to 10-minute contacts per week for two weeks in addition to normal ward care; the third group received six 5- to 10-minute contacts per week for two weeks in addition to normal ward care. Self-esteem and anxiety measures were repeated at the end of the two-week program. There were no significant differences among the three groups on initial test scores. Contacts were made at various times of day and were quite informal. They usually began with an open-ended question and were carried out in a friendly, chatty manner. Not only did the two brief contact groups show a significant increase in self-esteem, but they both had significantly shorter periods of hospitalization than the control group. In addition, the group receiving the six brief contacts per week demonstrated a significant reduction in anxiety.

In a second study these authors organized the brief contacts so that they were provided by four different staff members. In addition, they systematically examined the effect of the nature of the brief contact by arranging for one experimental group to talk about their symptoms, a second group to talk about social matters unrelated to symptomatology, and a third group to be contacted to help with a contrived ward task. All experimental groups received six contacts per week. Again, there was a normal ward routine control group. In total, seventy-four new patients were involved in the second study.

The general usefulness of the brief contacts was confirmed. Among the brief contacts those patients who discussed issues unrelated to their symptoms seemed to gain most, and those who were contacted to help with a ward task gained least. The authors concluded that

> *brief contact therapy can have a markedly beneficial effect upon hospitalized psychiatric patients. . . . The beneficial effects of brief contacts are best understood as a product of an implicit message which they convey to the patient. The message is an ego-enhancing, supportive one; it tells the patient that he is accepted as a person. (1965, p. 518)*

Brief Contact Therapy in Medical Settings

Most of the writing about brief contact therapy is directed toward primary care physicians, in an effort to persuade them to think about their fifteen- or twenty-minute appointments as representing opportunities to deal with emotional as well as physical symptoms. In addition, there is some interest in brief contact therapy as practiced by mental health professionals in working with medically ill patients (see, for example, Goldsmith, 1986, p. 66). The role of the primary care physician in the treatment of the mentally ill can hardly be overestimated. Regier, Goldberg, and Taube (1978) analyzed some major characteristics of the mental health service delivery system in the United States and found that primary care physicians provide about two-thirds of all mental health services delivered to the mentally ill. Thus, helping primary care physicians provide more effective services to their patients with significant emotional difficulties within the reality constraints imposed by their modes of practice is not a trivial enterprise.

We shall examine four examples of the brief contact literature. As will be seen, these examples share many similarities, but they are not identical to each other. Each approach emphasizes special possibilities of brief contact therapy, and together these approaches display the rich opportunities that primary care physicians have to be of help to their patients.

The Work of the Balints

The first systematic study of brief contact therapy with medically ill patients took place between 1966 and 1971 at University College Hospital in London under the direction of Michael and Enid Balint. Michael Balint, whose work has been mentioned earlier in this book (see chapters 4, 8, and 9), had been examining the doctor-patient relationship in general medicine for the preceding decade (see Balint, 1957) and had been struck by the enormous therapeutic potential of that relationship. After his unexpected death in 1970, the London study was continued by his widow, under whose direction the report of the project was published (Balint and Norell, 1973). The Balints and their colleagues spent six years studying the six-minute interview — the average length of time a patient was found to spend with a primary care physician. In fact, the majority of contacts between patients and primary care physicians lasted between five and fifteen minutes, with a few being somewhat longer.

The Balints found that a meaningful and therapeutic relationship — a "brief, intense and close contact" (1973, p. xi) — could develop between patients and their primary care physicians even when only a few minutes were available for the contact. What was necessary was that the physician choose, instead of trying to pinpoint the physical problem, to provide patients with an opportunity to talk about whatever they wanted to, and to focus on what their patients were trying to say. Under these circumstances a positive therapeutic moment often occurred — Enid Balint called it a "flash." That therapeutic moment, the research group believed, was intensity-dependent rather than time-dependent and thus could occur even in a contact that was very brief. It only required that the physician make one genuinely insightful comment during each treatment contact with the patient.

No one has competed with the Balints for the world's record for the shortest time required to conduct a meaningful therapeutic interview with a medically ill patient, but the general idea of brief contact therapy has resulted in one book called *The Twenty-Minute Hour* (Castelnuovo-Tedesco, 1965), and, more recently, another called *The Fifteen Minute Hour* (Stuart and Lieberman, 1986).

Castelnuovo-Tedesco's Twenty-Minute Hour

Castelnuovo-Tedesco (1967, 1970, 1971) has experimented with a maximum of ten 20-minute interviews, in the context of training primary care physicians who must learn how to incorporate a psychotherapeutic orientation into their relatively busy medical practices. In addition to the problem of time, Castelnuovo-Tedesco suggests that primary care physicians hesitate to enter into psychotherapeutic relationships with their patients because of their lack of familiarity and training in short-term therapeutic techniques and because of the complexity of their attitudes toward psychotherapy — attitudes that simultaneously consider psychotherapy to be virtually inert (since the psychotherapist does not really *do* anything) and magically powerful (since one false step can release dark forces that can engulf both patient and doctor).

Attitudes toward psychotherapy on the part of primary care physicians can also be complicated by some discomfort about being emotionally close to a patient, about thinking of a patient as a human being rather than as an object, and about the fear that patients will become too dependent on them. All this means that primary care physicians will consider undertaking brief contact psychotherapy only if convinced that they will not need to transform themselves into someone different, that they can practice psychotherapy within the usual constraints of their busy schedules, that the concepts and principles of psychotherapy are rooted in empirical investigation, and that by undertaking brief contact therapy they can in many cases enhance their ability to understand and to heal.

The twenty-minute hour is designed for the primary care physician who is not a specialist in psychiatry; its goals are circumscribed and essentially supportive. Thus, its use is probably limited to patients with relatively simple neurotic disorders. Brief contact therapy would be contraindicated for patients whose neurotic disorders are disabling, who have gross disturbances in their thought processes or behavior, whose ability to deal with ordinary realities of life is significantly impaired, who are severely depressed, whose disorders appear to include organic pathology of the central nervous system, who have not been able to establish a stable pattern of living, who are victims of alcohol or other forms of drug abuse, whose problems include sexual perversions, who suffer from severe "psychosomatic" disorders, or who are unmotivated for any form of self-exploration.

On the other hand, brief contact therapy is appropriate for patients who suffer from neurotic or psychosomatic disorders that are minor in nature, that is, that are annoying, uncomfortable, or limiting but not seriously incapacitating, or who are mildly depressed or anxious. Medical patients who are suitable for brief contact therapy generally have a stable life situation and the capacity for satisfying and long-lasting social relationships and can point to some stressful life event or other precipitating factor that helps them understand their symptoms. Suitable patients are motivated to deal verbally with their difficulties.

Castelnuovo-Tedesco describes the two major steps in brief contact therapy as: (1) identifying the patient's major difficulties and selecting the goals of treatment, and (2) engaging in therapeutic maneuvers to help patients label their current problems in a useful manner and come to some decisions about what can be done to alter their current situation so that it is more satisfying to them. Note the almost total focus on the present and future, a strategy that effectively limits what must be accomplished in brief contact therapy.

Helping patients identify their major problems starts with the initial history that is taken when the patient first appears, and it requires that patients focus on those aspects of their current predicament that are creating difficulties for them. This requirement is often difficult for some patients to meet because they have become accustomed to neglecting or ignoring their problems since they are often both painful and seemingly hopeless. Castelnuovo-Tedesco reports that many patients show dramatic improvement just from successfully identifying and talking about their current difficulties.

In describing the general stance of the primary care physician, Castelnuovo-Tedesco suggests that the physician is a catalyst, a guide, a friendly mentor who keeps the patient on track and helps the patient avoid useless digressions by being facilitative, reflective, and questioning. The principal therapeutic techniques that are appropriate in achieving these goals are, according to Castelnuovo-Tedesco, confrontation, clarification, interpretation, education, advice giving, and reassurance.

Dubovsky's Primary Care Psychotherapeutics

Dubovsky (1981) also believes that psychiatric components of medical problems that are not severe or pervasive are best treated by the primary care physician, although he seems to think of the physician as someone with significantly developed psychotherapeutic skills and a high level of self-awareness. The milder problems that are amenable to primary care psychotherapy generally can be traced to some specific precipitating event and generally leave the patient fairly intact in most areas of functioning. From Dubovsky's point of view psychotherapeutic sessions with medical patients can last from fifteen to fifty minutes, depending on the nature of the problem and of the physician's practice. As for the number of interviews, they too depend on the same variables—with acute problems, meetings may be scheduled once or twice a week; for supportive care, appointments may be scheduled as infrequently as twice a year.

Even with mildly distraught patients, however, they and their physicians need to make sure that they start out with shared common goals for the psychotherapy. But more often than not, according to Dubovsky, goals are not overtly discussed. The physician may believe that the patient needs to examine why he or she is unable to maintain a relationship, while all the patient wants is to get out of a terrible marriage. Another patient may want never again to be depressed, while the physician may think that helping the patient recover from this depression is all that can realistically be hoped for.

Dubvosky provides a number of informative case studies showing how primary care physicians can work with the emotional difficulties of their patients. In Box 20-1 are some excerpts from his description of the treatment of an acutely depressed patient. Only the first two interviews are excerpted. The entire case study is presented in Dubovsky (1981, pp. 85–109). This case is particularly pertinent because depression is probably the most common psychiatric problem brought to the attention of the primary care physician. More than 10 percent of depressed adults commit suicide, and suicidal patients far more often visit primary care physicians than they visit psychiatrists.

BOX 20-1 · *An Acutely Depressed Patient Treated by the Primary Care Physician*

Emmelia Eckhart, a 30-year-old business woman, has been a patient of Dr. Durant's for the past few years. Conflicts over her involvement in her work resulted in divorce four years ago. Since then she has had little time for dating, and most of her spare time has been devoted to furthering her career. Emmelia is an interesting person, and during routine office visits she usually involves Dr. Durant in brief but animated discussions about everything from politics to art. Although Dr. Durant likes his patient, he feels that he really knows little about her. She has never discussed personal problems, and it has seemed appropriate to respect her apparent wish for privacy. Today, however, Emmelia seems preoccupied and unhappy. She does not engage her physician in the usual banter and seems in no hurry to be on her way. She seems to be saying "something is bothering me" without stating it openly, and Dr. Durant decides to use the time he would ordinarily spend chatting with her to find out what is wrong. Dr. Durant's thoughts are shown in italics.

Doctor: Emmelia, you seem upset today.

Patient: No, not really. I just haven't been feeling well. *[She seems more upset than she says she is.]*

D: Care to tell me about it?

P: Oh, you're much too busy. I don't want to bother you. *[She's right. I am busy.]*

D: It's true that I'm busy, but I have about 15 minutes in my schedule right

BOX 20-1 *Continued*

now, and I can make more time later today or tomorrow if necessary. Now, tell me what's been bothering you.

P: I don't know whether to talk about it or not.

D: Go on.

P: Well, I have been feeling kind of bad lately. *[Something about the way she says this makes her feelings sound more than "kind of bad."]*

D: How bad have you been feeling?

P: I get sad from time to time.

D: You seem very sad.

P: I guess I do wonder from time to time if it's worth it.

D: If what's worth it?

P: You know . . . life.

D: Have you had thoughts of dying?

P: I guess sometimes. *[She can't be talking about killing herself.]*

D: Have you been having thoughts of killing yourself?

P: Yes . . . *[What do I do now?]* Lately I've been thinking about how easy it would be to take the rest of the sleeping pills I have left from the prescription you gave me last year. *[Kill herself with my pills? How could she do that! I don't think I could stop her.]* I don't know . . . sometimes I think I'd be better off dead. Nobody would miss me anyway. People are so busy in this world, no one really cares. *[What is she talking about? She's got everything to live for!]*

D: Emmelia, you must be feeling desperate to have thought about killing yourself. *[Although this seems obvious to me, it may help her to know that I see how bad she's been feeling.]*

P: I guess I have been. I just haven't seen any other solution. *[She sounds hopeless. I hope I can help her.]*

D: I'm sure that we can work together and find out why you've been feeling the way you have. *[I want to sound confident without making promises I can't keep.]*

P: You seem awfully sure. *[This is an invitation to say more.]*

D: Depression is a problem that usually gets better with treatment. I'm

Continued

BOX 20-1 *Continued*

reasonably certain that we can work together to understand what went wrong and find a better solution.

P: Well, if you really think it will help, I'm willing to try. *[She seems to be responding to my confidence.]*

D: I'd like us to meet regularly for a while. For starters, how would it be if we met once a week for about a half-hour?

P: Do you think that's often enough? *[She may be telling me that she wants to meet more often. How can I help her to say this a little more directly?]*

D: Do *you* think it's often enough?

P: Well, I wouldn't want to take up a lot of your time. *[I may feel like I'm giving up a lot of my time, but it's important that I respond to her need for more contact with me. For some reason, she seems unable to be more direct in stating her needs, at least at this time.]*

D: Nevertheless, why don't we start by meeting twice a week and see how it goes?

P: If you think that's best, it's okay with me. *[She got me to take responsibility for this decision. She seems to have trouble asking for what she wants.]*

D: Now, I'd like to talk about how we'll work together.

(A few days later)

P: I felt a little better after we talked. I don't know why. *[That's a relief.]* I don't know where to go from here. What do I talk about? *[I don't know either. What should I tell her?]*

D: Why don't we start with whatever seems most important to you.

P: OK . . . I haven't told you about Jack, have I?

(With some encouragement from the physician, the patient describes her relationship with Jack, a married co-worker. She did not mention him earlier because of her shame at dating a married man, something she thought she would never do. . . . Eventually Jack told the patient that he planned to leave his wife and marry her. Although she was happy at first, when a year went by without him taking any action she began to realize that the plan was just a dream. She finally demanded that he decide whom he wanted. When he remained reluctant to commit himself, she discontinued the relationship.)

D: It must have really hurt when you realized that Jack wouldn't marry you.

P: I was crushed. I didn't know what to do. He's such a wonderful person.

BOX 20-1 *Continued*

And his wife is so nice, I don't blame him for staying with her. *[How can she not blame him? He sounds awful!]*

D: You don't sound very angry at Jack.

P: How could I be angry at him? He treated me so well! I just wish him the best. It was wrong of me to get involved with him anyway. *[She must be putting me on. She must hate him!]*

D: We'll have to stop for now. Let's pick up again at our next visit.

P: OK. Is it Thursday?

From Dubovsky, 1981, pp. 86–96.

Stuart and Lieberman's Fifteen-Minute Hour

Stuart and Lieberman (1986) are concerned with the same issue that was of interest to Castelnuovo-Tedesco twenty years earlier—how to persuade primary care physicians that they can incorporate a psychotherapeutic orientation into their medical practice so that they can increase their effectiveness in dealing with the emotional components of the problems that their patients bring to them. Stuart and Lieberman propose a flexible, practical approach that consists of relatively simple techniques that are easily learned and that are effective without requiring lengthy therapy sessions—that is, without the necessity for them to modify their ordinary mode of practice.

The primary care physician has several advantages in working with patients that a psychiatrist does not have. First, to the extent that being diagnosed as having a psychological problem may be stigmatizing, the primary care physician can treat the emotional problems of patients without labeling them as mental patients. Second, treatment of the emotional component of a physical illness can be incorporated into the normal medical treatment of the patient. The primary care physician ordinarily sees the patient far earlier in the history of the problem than does the mental health professional, and small amounts of psychologically oriented treatment over a long period of time can sometimes be much more effective than a large amount of treatment concentrated in a short time period. Third, since referrals to a mental health professional may be viewed by the patient as rejecting, if primary care physicians are willing to incorporate psychotherapeutic techniques into their everyday work with their patients, they can come to be viewed as unusually accepting of patients regardless of the nature of their difficulties. Fourth, since the body and mind are totally interdependent, the primary care physician is in a unique position to understand and treat the whole patient.

Stuart and Lieberman are clearly interested in persuading the primary care physician that treating the whole patient can be the best way of practicing medicine. While they acknowledge that in some cases a referral to a mental health professional may be necessary, they note that a high proportion of patients can have their emotional issues dealt with quite effectively within their time constraints. They do not think of brief contact therapy as consisting of a certain number of short sessions devoted only to the consideration of the psychological elements of an illness, but, rather, that every contact between a physician and a patient should include attention to the emotional components of the problems that the patient presents. To be sure, emotional problems may be of sufficient severity so that additional appointments may be necessary to help patients cope with their difficulties. But even these additional twice-weekly, weekly, or bi-weekly appointments should deal with the whole patient.

Trying to be of help to a patient within the context of the fifteen-minute appointment requires much self-discipline on the part of the primary care physician. The physician must begin with the realization that the problem belongs to the patient, that the physician can help the patient identify and become fully aware of an emotional problem that is contributing to physical symptoms, and that the physician can encourage the patient to explore potential solutions for the problem. But the physician is not responsible for determining the etiology of the problem, or its full impact on others, or for solving the problem. Stuart and Lieberman write:

> When the physician communicates to the patient that there is the expectation that the patient, having identified the problem, is expected to find some constructive resolution, a positive message is conveyed. The physician agrees to be part of the process, to make suggestions for strategies that can be employed, but it is clear to both parties that the patient has the responsibility to deal with the problem — which by definition is expected to yield to resolution. (1986, p. 89)

In order to keep the objectives of the brief therapeutic contact within realistic limits, Stuart and Lieberman suggest that the focus should be on the here and now and on the patient's strengths and that, when possible, the patient's family should be involved in trying to help the patient. The therapeutic approach they advocate includes, first and foremost, empathic concern for the patient, and, secondarily, the use of a variety of therapeutic techniques such as exploring options, encouraging new behavior, and providing explanations and anticipatory guidance.

When there are only a few minutes available to examine the psychological components of a medical problem, and when the patient is fortunate enough to have a primary care physician who allocates those few minutes for that purpose, the patient quickly learns to put emotional difficulties in some priority order. And because so little time is available, it is necessary for the patient to do some therapeutic work as a form of homework, the results of which can be discussed at the next appointment. Patients may be asked to keep track of their periods of upset; sleep patterns; instances of successful or unsuccessful coping; lists of options, wishes, advantages or disadvantages of some particular potential course of action; arguments; or accomplishments.

Stuart and Lieberman conceptualize how the limited amount of time in a normal appointment with a patient can be put to best use by the acronym BATHE—Background, that is, what is the context of the difficulty; Affect, that is, how does the patient feel about the problem; Trouble, that is, what about the situation is most troubling; Handling, that is, how is the patient coping with the problem; and Empathy, that is, legitimizing the patient's feelings. Box 20-2 provides an example of the use of these five components of the brief contact therapy.

BOX 20-2 • *Stuart and Lieberman's BATHEing the Patient*

A 34-year-old woman, who had been a patient at the family practice center for about a year, presented in the office complaining about a vaginal discharge. She appeared to be quite agitated. The physician inquired about what was going on in her life. The patient started to cry.

Patient: I just found out that my husband has been having an affair with my oldest sister for the past year and a half.

Therapist: How do you feel about that? *[The physician felt a little foolish. It seemed like this was an inane question to ask under the circumstances, but he really didn't know what else to ask.]*

P: I feel angry. I have mood swings. I go up and down. I also feel depressed.

T: What about the situation troubles you the most?

P: I have two children. They are two and five, and I really don't want to be a single parent. *[The physician was surprised. He would have expected her to be most troubled because of the familial involvement or the time frame.]*

T: How are you handling it?

P: I feel I am handling things very badly. I am angry and do a lot of shouting at my husband. I am afraid that the children are starting to be affected, and I don't want that.

Continued

BOX 20-2   *Continued*

T: [taken aback] That sounds like a horrendous situation.

P: Yes it is. *[visibly relaxed]*

T: Why don't we examine you now, and find out what we can do about your vaginal discomfort, and then we'll talk some more.

From Stuart and Lieberman, 1986, p. 103.

Stuart and Lieberman are fully cognizant of the fact that undertaking the treatment of the emotional components of a physical illness adds significantly to the stress under which the primary care physician operates. Accordingly, they have proposed a set of a dozen rules for physician survival—that is, rules that help ensure personal psychological well-being for physicians who seek to engage in brief contact therapy with their patients. The rules are well worth excerpting (Box 20-3).

BOX 20-3 • *Stuart and Lieberman's Rules for Physician Survival*

Rule 1: Do not take responsibility for things you cannot control.

Rule 2: Take care of yourself or you can't take care of anyone else.

Rule 3: Trouble is easier to prevent than to fix.

Rule 4: When you get upset, tune into what is going on with you and go through the three-step process—1. What am I feeling? 2. What do I want? 3. What can I do about it?

Rule 5: If the answer to Step 3, Rule 4 is "Nothing," apply Rule 1.

Rule 6: Ask for support when you need it; give people permission to feel what they feel.

Rule 7: In a bad situation you have four options—1. Leave it; 2. Change it; 3. Accept it; 4. Reframe it.

Rule 8: If you never make mistakes, you're not learning anything.

Rule 9: When a situation turns out badly, look at where the choice points were, then decide what you would do differently next time.

Rule 10: At any given time you can only make decisions based on the information you have.

Rule 11: Life is not fair—or a contest.

Rule 12: You have to start where the patient is.

From Stuart and Lieberman, 1986, pp. 167–171.

Concluding Comments

The writings in the field of brief contact therapy have an important message for mental health professionals, quite apart from what they say about primary care medicine. That message is that every minute counts. If the mental health professional has fifteen minutes to spend with a patient, as is often the case when monitoring psychopharmacologic regimens, for example, or when doing so-called routine follow-up interviews, those minutes are golden. What can take place during that brief period of time has the potential for significant impact on the patient. Mental health professionals who start from the premise that since they have only a short appointment with a patient they can't realistically expect to get any therapeutic work done need to rethink that point of view.

We have examined four approaches to brief contact therapy in the primary care setting. All share a set of assumptions: that only mildly disturbed patients are suitable for this therapeutic modality; that goals must be sharply limited; that the focus must be on the present and on the future; that it is patients and not the physician who have the responsibility for making changes in their lives; that the principal contribution of the primary care physician is to provide an opportunity for the patient to talk, in a setting that is supportive, empathic, and affirmative; and, of course, that the time allotted to the therapeutic contact must conform to the normal working schedule of the physician. While these assumptions seem to create very constricting limits on who may be helped, in fact these limits are more apparent than real, and, as we have seen, there are some special advantages to patient and physician alike if the primary care physician offers to be helpful to the patient in dealing with psychological difficulties.

The writings on brief contact therapy illustrate two different approaches to the task. On the one hand, as in the work of the Balints and of Stuart and Lieberman, primary care physicians are urged to incorporate a consistent interest in the psychological components of physical symptoms during every appointment with every patient. The other approach, as in the work of Castelnuovo-Tedesco and of Dubovsky, is to teach primary care physicians the elements of psychotherapeutic interventions so that they can emulate mental health professionals. From this vantage point, primary care physicians can schedule one or a series of brief psychotherapeutic interviews in order to help patients cope with their emotional problems. Both approaches can be valid, depending on the nature of the situation, and the wise mental health professional may be able to ascertain which approach may be most appealing to each specific primary care physician — for it must be recognized that not all primary care physicians are interested in or temperamentally capable of dealing with the mental health needs of their patients. For those primary care physicians who are interested, however, the mental health professional has much to contribute to enhancing their skill and effectiveness.

SECTION FIVE

Integrative Clinical Summary

This final section discusses two topics that transcend the individualized views of either the theory or practice of short-term psychotherapy. The first is the issue of patient selection, a topic that has been of interest to virtually every writer in the field. Following that discussion, we shall try to step back from the detailed chapters and consider the overall implications of the field of planned short-term psychotherapy, both in terms of its present status and its future potential.

CHAPTER TWENTY-ONE

Patient Criteria for Planned Short-Term Psychotherapy

Overview

Approaches to Selection Criteria

Two-Dimensional Selection Criteria: Type of Therapy by Type of Patient

Two-Dimensional Selection Criteria: Type of Therapist by Type of Patient

Contraindications for Planned Short-Term Psychotherapy

Patient Selection Case Examples

Concluding Comments

The literature dealing with selection criteria for identifying patients suitable for planned short-term psychotherapy is an extraordinary hodgepodge, with opinions ranging completely across the logical spectrum. At one extreme are assertions that no specific selection criteria have been reliably identified for potential short-term therapy patients, or, to put it another way, that every patient is as suitable for time-limited psychotherapy as for time-unlimited psychotherapy. At the other extreme are writings that propose quite specific criteria for establishing appropriateness for time-limited psychotherapy.

There is some evidence that selection criteria have become less stringent in recent years, perhaps as a consequence of the growing confidence of clinicians in the general effectiveness of planned short-term psychotherapy with a wide variety of patients (Budman, 1983). Certainly, very few studies have evaluated selection criteria in a way that would give them real credibility.

Furthermore, there is a growing realization that as long as one begins with the belief that certain people are unsuitable for planned short-term psychotherapy, the full utility of time-limited therapy will never be explored. We are left with clinical impressions — not to be dismissed out of hand, to be sure, but subject to the problems of interpretation that characterize all anecdotal assertions. We shall try in this chapter to review and evaluate the assertions and evidence that bear on the issue of patient selection criteria and come to some kind of judgment as to the state of the knowledge base.

Approaches to Selection Criteria

As has just been suggested, statements about selection criteria for planned short-term psychotherapy range from those that are extremely broad and inclusive to those that are quite narrow and exclusive.

Broad Selection Criteria

Broad criteria are of two types. First, some writers take the position that there are no criteria whereby prospective patients can be confidently excluded from time-limited psychotherapy, and, therefore, the most appropriate clinical decision to make regarding selection is to start with every patient in a time-limited mode (see, for example, Curtis and Silberschatz, 1986; Gillman, 1985; Kreilkamp, 1989; Krupnick and Horowitz, 1985; Manaster, 1989). This is the *accept everyone* approach.

Thus, Wolberg (1965b) writes:

> *The best strategy, in my opinion, is to assume that every patient, irrespective of diagnosis, will respond to short-term treatment unless he proves himself to be refractory to it. If the therapist approaches each patient with the idea of doing as much as he can for him, within the span of say up to twenty treatment sessions, he will give the patient an opportunity to take advantage of short-term treatment to the limit of his potential. If this expediency fails, he can always then resort to prolonged therapy. (p. 140)*

Wolberg equivocates, however. He elaborates this last sentence by noting that short-term psychotherapy will turn out to be sufficient in the case of three categories of patients: patients who have a history of adequate adjustment prior to current difficulty; patients who display disturbing symptoms and maladaptive behavior patterns, such as phobias; and patients whose symptoms are related to deep-seated intrapsychic problems and who suffer from personality disturbances with a prior history of marginal functioning. In the first case the goal is to return the patient to that prior level of adjustment, typically by using a crisis intervention model, usually of not more than six sessions. In the second case the goal is symptom relief, modification of destructive habits, and help in the development of more adaptive behavioral practices — a goal that can generally be achieved in eight to twenty sessions using a supportive-educational model of psychotherapy. In the third case the goal is some form of personality reconstruction plus symptomatic and behavioral improvement, requiring a somewhat longer treatment that employs a dynamic short-term therapy model.

As for those patient characteristics that make the necessity for prolonged psychotherapy more likely, Wolberg (1980) identifies two categories of patients. First are chronic psychotics, patients whose psychoses are in remission, alcoholics, drug addicts, persons with acting-out tendencies, persons fixated at infantile and childish levels or with excessive dependency needs, intractable obsessive-compulsives, paranoid personalities, psychosomatic and hypochondriacal conditions, and depressives. For this group, Wolberg believes that prolonged management will be needed after an initial course of short-term psychotherapy. Finally, Wolberg includes in the group for whom prolonged psychotherapy might be needed persons who require extensive reconstructive personality changes who have the financial ability, time, forebearance, and ego strength to tolerate long-term psychoanalysis or psychoanalytically oriented psychotherapy; and highly disturbed children and adolescents. Wolberg estimates that more than three-quarters of the typical patient load carried by the average mental health professional comprises patients who may be adequately managed by short-term approaches.

This appealing elaboration, one that would certainly be congenial to Wolberg's psychoanalytic colleagues, assumes that dynamic short-term psychotherapy is more effective than supportive-educational psychotherapy, which is, in turn, more effective than crisis intervention. In addition, it espouses the position that long-term psychotherapy is unquestionably more helpful than short-term psychotherapy. In fact, however, none of these assertions has any empirical evidence to support it, and, thus, for the moment these elaborations constitute hypotheses in need of verification. Let us not lose sight, however, of Wolberg's initial, perhaps fundamental assertion, namely, that the wise clinician will begin psychotherapy by assuming that every patient will respond favorably to planned short-term psychotherapy, even if the prediction is that some patients will respond more favorably than others.

Cummings and Vandenbos (1979) describe their conclusions of twenty years of research on the effectiveness of psychotherapy of varying durations in the following assertions:

> *The treatment of choice for all persons presenting themselves with emotional complaints and problems in living is active short-term psychological intervention without preselection criteria. For 85% of these unselected persons, such treatment is more effective than long-term psychotherapy, and for another 5% of patients, intensive long-term psychotherapy may actually be deleterious. (p. 432)*

Budman and Stone (1983) have come to the same conclusion, based on their own clinical experience and review of the literature—namely, that "it is unwarranted to exclude patients from brief therapy on the basis of diagnosis, symptoms, or apparent motivation" (p. 941). Garfield (1989) asserts that "with the exception of the very seriously disturbed . . . brief therapy can be considered for most patients who are in touch with reality, are experiencing some discomfort, and have made the effort to seek help for their difficulties" (p. 13). Manaster (1989) writes: "Brief therapy should be the treatment, the approach, and the intent in all cases" (p. 247).

Bellak discusses his broad approach to patient selection in an interesting autobiographic account in which he contrasts his approach with that of Malan. He writes:

> *My method has some similarities to Malan's (1963), who published his first book shortly before Small and I, unaware of his, published our own. . . . We both had a psychoanalytic background, and eventually Malan came to share my willingness to take on virtually all comers. . . . Malan's technique, however, was developed in the relative tranquility of the Tavistock Clinic. Thus, not only could Malan offer more time to his patients than I had available in my original settings, but he was also probably dealing with patients who were not as sick as mine. (1984, p. 12)*

Curtis and Silberschatz (1986) hypothesize that patients who enter psychotherapy have an unconscious plan for how to get better, and improvement depends on the skill of the therapist to respond to that plan. No other criteria seem important—the patient should direct the course of brief psychotherapy; there are no universal themes or focal issues; no special therapeutic techniques are required.

The second type of broad selection criterion asserts that there are no differential characteristics that distinguish patients suitable for long-term psychotherapy from those that are suitable for time-limited psychotherapy. This is the *accept everyone you would accept for long-term psychotherapy* approach. Strupp (1980c; see also Binder, Henry, and Strupp, 1987) asserts, for example, that only patients whose "criteria are essentially identical to those traditionally considered crucial in assessing a patient's suitability for psychoanalysis" (p. 953) are also good candidates for short-term therapy.

Similarly, Migone (1985) suggests that "we cannot even argue that the two techniques [psychoanalysis and short-term dynamic psychotherapy] are to be used for different indications, because the patients that are not considered good candidates for STDP are the same ones that have always been considered not suitable for psychoanalysis and for whom psychopharmacological treatments or support therapies have been preferred" (p. 615).

Budman and Gurman (1988) make an equivalent point when they note that

> *many of the attributes recommended in the past for patient selection have excluded those individuals who are most difficult and problematic in* any *form of psychotherapy. The vast array of selection criteria for brief psychotherapy have developed over the years despite a lack of empirical data to support the contention that some types of patients are better suited to brief treatment than are others. (p. 22)*

Narrow Selection Criteria

Narrow and relatively exclusive selection criteria specify patient characteristics that are required in order to be confident that planned short-term psychotherapy will be significantly helpful. In spite of the fact that there are virtually no data substantiating these selection criteria, there is a cumulative weight to these assertions (Lambert, 1979). Individual clinicians, of course, can and do propose selection criteria for their form of short-term therapy. Accordingly, it might be most useful to examine specific criteria for patient selection more or less historically, starting with the earliest systematic statements in the literature. Early reports in this historical review tend to be based primarily on clinical experience. Later reports are also based on clinical experience but make ready reference to corroborative earlier reports, which in the meanwhile have developed a certain cachet largely as a function of their age.

Balint (Balint, Ornstein, and Balint, 1972) arrived at impressions about what factors to keep in mind in selecting patients for brief focal psychotherapy (see Chapter 20), impressions that he readily acknowledged were based on clinical rather than statistical evidence. First, Balint believed that prospective patients should give the impression that they can develop a workable alliance with their therapist—an alliance that can withstand the interpersonal strains that therapy inevitably will cause. Second, the therapist should have the impression that patients see their symptoms as ego-dystonic and that they have the motivation to try to change. Third, patients have to appear capable of accepting interpretations, however tentatively, and doing some constructive work with them. Fourth, two people who interview a prospective patient independently of each other should come to the same general conclusions as to the nature of the difficulties the patient is facing. Finally, it should be possible to identify a focus for the envisioned therapy around which the work can take place.

Malan (1976, 1978a) listed the three essential criteria that he employs in selecting patients who are likely suitable for his form of brief psychotherapy. These criteria include: (1) the presence of an identifiable circumscribed problem, (2) the demonstrated ability to respond constructively to tentative interpretations made during the initial interview, and (3) clear evidence of sufficient motivation to enter into psychotherapy. Specifically, Malan suggests that the therapist should be able to identify "some circumscribed aspect of psychopathology, formulated in terms of a basic interpretation, which it seems feasible to try and work through in a short time" (1976, p. 256). And, in addition, it should be clear in accepting particular clients that they have the capacity to think of their problems in psychological terms and that they are in accord with the therapist's formulation of a problem focus.

As might be presumed, Malan's process of selection may require more than one interview, since it is necessary to assess the psychodynamic history of the applicant, to see if a therapeutic focus can be found, to test out the applicant's ability to accept and use interpretations, and to judge the level of motivation.

Sifneos (1978, 1979, pp. 22–39, 1981a, 1981b, 1987) believes that in order to profit from his short-term anxiety-provoking psychotherapy, a patient should have: (1) the ability to circumscribe a chief complaint, (2) above average intelligence and psychological-mindedness, (3) a history of at least one meaningful give-and-take relationship during early childhood, (4) motivation for change and not simply for symptom relief (Sifneos, 1980), and (5) an ability to relate to the therapist and to express feelings freely.

Concerning motivation for change, Sifneos includes a number of subcriteria: evidence that the prospective client has the ability to recognize that the symptoms are psychological in origin; appears to be introspective and honest; seems willing to be an active participant in the therapeutic situation; is actively curious and willing to understand the self; is wiling to explore, experiment, and change; has realistic expectations regarding psychotherapeutic outcome; and is willing to make reasonable sacrifices in the service of psychotherapy. Sifneos's selection criteria appear to comprise two dimensions — personal resources and motivation. A recent study by Barth and colleagues (1988) reports some evidence that the variables Sifneos uses in assessing these two dimensions may have a somewhat more complex factorial structure, that is, that there may actually be a third, as yet not clearly identified criterion.

The demanding selection criteria for the client chosen for *anxiety-*

provoking short-term psychotherapy can be seen when the preceding set of characteristics is contrasted with the shorter list of criteria by which selection can be made for *anxiety-suppressive* short-term therapy. Sifneos suggests that suitability for this more supportive therapy might be judged simply by: (1) the ability to maintain a job, (2) a strong appeal for help to overcome an emotional difficulty, (3) the recognition that the symptoms are psychological in origin, and (4) willingness to cooperate with psychotherapy. Indeed, Goldberg and Green (1986) suggest that Sifneos's selection criteria for anxiety-provoking short-term psychotherapy are so rigid as to restrict treatment to the "almost psychologically healthy" (p. 79).

Davanloo's (1978c, 1980a, 1980b) criteria for selection of patients for time-limited psychotherapy include the ability of the prospective patient to enter into an emotional interaction with the therapist, evidence that such interactions have occurred in the past, the ability to tolerate affect, a high level of motivation and psychological-mindedness, the ability to tolerate and respond to interpretations, above-average intelligence, and adequate flexibility of ego defenses.

Davanloo has formulated his selection criteria as a set of questions to be posed at the conclusion of the initial interview. These questions are essentially as follows:

1. Is the patient's problem a circumscribed one?
2. Is a crisis present?
3. Has a psychotherapeutic focus been established?
4. Is the psychotherapeutic focus related to a disturbance in interpersonal relationships?
5. How adequate have prior human relationships been?
6. How accessible are feelings to this patient?
7. What is the motivation to change?
8. Is the patient of above-average intelligence?
9. Does the patient display high psychological mindedness?
10. How adequate is the patient's ability to respond to interpretation? (Davanloo, 1980a, 1980b; see also Ursano and Hales, 1986, p. 1511)

Marmor (1979) identified seven criteria that had repeatedly been suggested in the literature as necessary for selection into brief psychotherapy: (1) evidence of satisfactory ego strength, as measured by such variables as intelligence or level of educational or work achievement; (2) at least one meaningful interpersonal relationship, indicating a capacity for basic trust, or what West, Sheldon, and Reiffer (1989) call "permeable attachment relationships"; (3) ability to interact with the therapist in the first session, that is, the capacity to form a positive transference; (4) psychological-mindedness, as shown, for example, by the demonstrated capacity for insight; (5) ability to experience feelings, particularly evidence of being in touch with one's own feelings; (6) existence of a focal conflict around which most of the patient's difficulties revolve; and (7) motivation to change, combined with the willingness to modify one's characteristic adaptational patterns in order to do so.

Mann and Goldman (1982) describe their selection criteria as follows:

> *Our criteria for case selection are lower than the Malan-Sifneos criteria, in some respects very much lower. On the a priori assumption that the patient who comes to us for help is already sufficiently motivated to change, we do not regard a statement from the patient of his wish to change as necessary. Further, the patient's motivation for change will be enhanced or diminished to the extent that the therapist appreciates the intensity of the patient's initial anxiety and can contain that anxiety in the initial interviews. An investigative approach that seeks to uncover recurrent painful events that affected feelings about the self becomes, at the same time, an effective means for diminishing frightening fantasies about the nature of the encounter with a therapist. Ego strength is determined primarily by assessing the patient's capacity to tolerate loss (as revealed in his history) rather than by assessing a wider variety of ego assets. Locating a focal problem is the therapist's responsibility, but it requires a patient who can speak coherently about himself. (pp. 26–27)*

Rogawski (1982) suggests that patients who do well in short-term dynamic psychotherapy have the following characteristics: (1) reasonably satisfactory psychosocial functioning; (2) the ability to establish meaningful interpersonal relationships; (3) psychological-mindedness; (4) the ability to mobilize, exhibit, experience, and tolerate feelings; and (5) high motivation for change. In addition, the therapist should be able to identify a circumscribed core problem, or what is often called a *focal conflict.*

Gustafson (1984) identifies three major selection criteria, as illustrated in the following statement:

> *I believe that the selection for brief dynamic therapy can be simplified to three fundamental questions. Has the patient been able to navigate safely through the worst periods of disturbance of his life? Has the patient been able to have a deep give and take with another person? Does the trial therapy bring about an actual breakthrough to deep feeling and the recurrent focal problem in the patient's life? (p. 942)*

Gustafson suggests that most time-limited psychotherapists would likely agree with the first two selection criteria, but that not all would require evidence that a significant breakthrough can occur in a therapy trial before starting a brief therapy program.

Reich and Neenan (1986) suggest six general selection criteria based on their review of the selection literature: (1) ability to formulate a focused chief complaint; (2) having had at least one meaningful interpersonal experience; (3) having achieved success in at least one area of their lives; (4) ability to communicate effectively about their problems; (5) motivation to change the presenting focus problem; and (6) effective patient-therapist interaction, such as might be demonstrated by a therapy trial.

In their examination of twelve different approaches to planned time-limited psychotherapy, Burlingame and Fuhriman (1987) have found that the most commonly used inclusion criteria (specified by about 60 percent of the approaches) are evidence that the prospective patient has shown the ability to form interpersonal relationships in the past and can express feelings and describe problems in affective terms. Next most commonly mentioned, in about 40 percent of the approaches, are the presence of a circumscribed complaint, evidence of psychological-mindedness, and motivation to change.

Bauer and Kobos (1987, pp. 139–141) have provided an integration of selection criteria by identifying the following six patient characteristics that appear to be repeatedly identified as important in short-term psychodynamic psychotherapy assessment: (1) *motivation for change* — acceptance of the need to change maladaptive coping strategies and an inclination to become actively involved in the change process; (2) *psychological-mindedness* — the ability to attend to and verbally communicate thoughts, feelings, and fantasies; a willingness to reflect on the functioning of inner psychic processes and to introspect and think in psychological terms; (3) *ego strength* — adequate intelligence, academic and vocational achievements, stability of interpersonal relationships, persistent and successful goal-directed behavior, and ability to tolerate frustration and painful affects through the flexible use of a variety of ego defenses and coping strategies and to tolerate the stresses of therapy and to use this experience constructively toward further growth; (4) *ability to interact with the therapist* — to develop a sense of basic trust and to believe in the basic benevolence of others; (5) *response to trial interpretations* — evidence of being able to work with early interpretations, to collaborate with the therapist in examining thoughts, feelings, and reactions, even though such work elicits painful affect (e.g., guilt, anxiety, dysphoria), to accept and elaborate on therapist interpretation, to explore; and (6) *establishment of treatment focus* — ability to identify a central area of conflict to be focused on in treatment.

Finally, MacKenzie (1988), reviewing the most recent literature on the topic of patient selection, identifies: (1) capacity to relate, (2) psychological-mindedness, (3) motivation, (4) successful trial interpretations, and (5) adaptational strengths as the principal bases of the decision to accept a patient into planned short-term psychotherapy.

If one examines this large group of recommendations, the most commonly mentioned include high motivation for change, the ability to establish a productive working relationship with the therapist, a history of meaningful relationships with others in the past, psychological-mindedness, and an identifiable and compelling focal issue of concern. It is hard to argue with the position that these are also the most commonly mentioned criteria for selecting patients for long-term psychotherapy.

A few empirical studies have attempted to identify patient characteristics that are significantly associated with planned short-term therapy outcome, and their results tend to be consistent with some of these specific selection criteria, although patient characteristics do not account for a large amount of the variance in therapeutic outcome. In a recent study reported by Piper, de Carufel, and Szkrumelak (1985) support was found for at least two of the assertions in the previous paragraph. Both maturity of defenses and quality of relationships with important people in the patient's life were found to be significantly associated with degree of improvement in brief dynamically oriented psychotherapy. Marziali (1987) has also found that patients' judgment of the quality of their supportive relationships were significantly associated with outcome in brief psychodynamic psychotherapy.

Another empirical study (Gelso and Johnson, 1983) examined patient characteristics associated with good outcomes in time-limited psychotherapy (eight to fifteen sessions) in a university counseling center. The sample consisted of thirty-eight students who had completed time-limited psychotherapy an average of twelve months prior to the follow-up. The therapists included nine senior clinical or counseling psychologists, six predoctoral counseling psychology interns, and six advanced practicum students who had received at least one year of time-limited therapy supervision prior to the study. In their summary, Gelso and Johnson (1983) somewhat freely combined their empirical findings with their clinical impressions and with other literature already in the field and concluded that the effectiveness of time-limited psychotherapy was associated with a number of client characteristics— relatively mild disturbances of short duration, high motivation to change, and a good fit with the therapist. Their experiences are summarized in Box 21-1.

Two-Dimensional Selection Criteria: Type of Therapy by Type of Patient

As we have seen, different therapists have very different approaches to short-term psychotherapy. Accordingly, it should not be surprising that efforts have been made to identify patient characteristics that are thought to bode well for various approaches to brief therapy.

BOX 21-1 · *Initial Client Characteristics Associated with Successful Short-Term Therapy: Gelso and Johnson*

1. Client comes to the agency seeking help with troubling behaviors or feelings.
2. Client's difficulties are relatively recent in onset.
3. Client's difficulties are not ego-syntonic.
4. Client's behavior does not appear very disturbed to others.
5. Client believes that needed changes can be made.
6. Client sees the time as ripe for change.
7. Client has good self-concept.
8. Client's ideal self is not vastly different from real self.
9. Client can make good emotional contact with therapist.
10. Client and therapist hit it off well from the beginning.
11. Client willing and able to be active in the therapy sessions.
12. Client may have some unresolved dependency desires, but is not afraid of intimacy.
13. Client able to see the psychological aspects of presenting problems.
14. Client able to see necessity for a time limit on psychotherapy.
15. Client views therapy as having started some new ways of thinking.
16. Client believes improvement will continue after termination of therapy.

Adapted from Gelso and Johnson, 1983, pp. 205–206.

Reviewing the chapters in the earlier sections of this book, one can note that writers have taken one of two positions on selection criteria: – either that their approach is equally suitable for all patients or, alternatively, that it is suitable for specific types of patients. Writers in the first category, that is, those who are generalists regarding issues of patient selection, include Wolberg, Bloom, Phillips and Wiener, Ellis, Farrelly, and Erickson.

The other theoreticians believe that their techniques of planned short-term psychotherapy are particularly suitable for specific types of patients. As has already been mentioned (see Chapter 3), Bellak provides specific suggestions for a wide variety of diagnostic categories. Davanloo and Sifneos have developed an approach to short-term psychotherapy of particular pertinence to high-functioning patients with unresolved oedipal issues, although Davanloo also asserts that his approach can be used profitably with more regressed neurotic patients. Mann's approach seems unusually useful in helping patients cope with pre-oedipal issues. Gustafson and Horowitz see their approaches as specifically useful for treating relatively well-functioning patients who are having difficulties with a current stressful life event or circumstance. Lewin, Gustafson, and Horowitz all view their approaches as useful with character or personality disorders. Lewin suggests that his approach is particularly useful with masochistic personalities; Horowitz has commented on the use of his approach in the case of hysterical, compulsive, narcissistic, and borderline personalities. Klerman and Beck have developed short-term psychotherapies specifically to be of help to patients who are suffering from neurotic depressions. Horowitz suggests his approach to be specifically pertinent in working with patients who are coping with post-traumatic stress disorders.

Burke, White, and Havens (1979), while urging caution in the degree of specificity that therapists should employ in selecting patients, have contrasted a number of differing approaches to planned short-term psychotherapy in terms of the implications of these differences for optimal patient selection. They suggest, for example, that Sifneos, who deals primarily with oedipal patients (see Chapter 5), looks for patients who are relatively healthy—curious, highly motivated, and able to withstand high levels of anxiety and establish a rational alliance with the therapist. Mann, on the other hand (see Chapter 6), who works with patients at earlier developmental levels who are more passive and dependent on nurturant figures, looks for patients who are aware of and can express their chronic sense of suffering and who establish an irrational alliance with an imagined omnipotent therapist. For these patients the inevitable separation brings with it the opportunity for significant growth.

Clarkin and Frances (1982) have also carried the development of selection criteria one additional step by suggesting selection criteria for various forms of brief psychotherapy. They subdivide the brief psychotherapies into five categories—crisis intervention, psychodynamic therapy, behavioral therapy, problem-solving therapy, and family therapy—and derive their selection criteria from an analysis of the existing empirical literature and of opinions expressed by leaders in the field and from their own clinical experience. The selection criteria are presented tentatively and as an impetus for further research and revision.

As for selection criteria for crisis intervention, defined as an intense goal-directed treatment intended to resolve a major crisis of recent onset within less than a month, Clarkin and Frances suggest that the indications include the presence of: (1) severe symptoms, distress, or risk factors; (2) a major precipitating stress that may be accidental, interpersonal, or developmental; (3) relatively recent symptom onset; (4) an adequate social support system; and (5) a willingness on the part of the patient to participate in the treatment, to keep appointments, take medications, and so forth.

If intense crisis intervention is not warranted, the next question is whether any form of time-limited psychotherapy is appropriate. The selection criteria that Clarkin and Frances propose in coming to that decision include: (1) a clearly defined focus, precipitating event, or intervention target; (2) sufficient motivation and sufficiently limited goals to ensure a reasonably successful treatment outcome; (3) sufficient ego strength so that there will be no significant difficulty at the time of termination; and (4) a generally adequate level of interpersonal functioning outside of the immediate area of difficulty.

In terms of selection criteria for different types of time-limited psychotherapy, indications for brief psychodynamic therapy include: (1) at least one reported significant interpersonal relationship during childhood, (2) evidence that the patient can relate to the therapist and can freely express feelings, (3) agreement regarding the focus of the therapy, (4) motivation to obtain greater self-awareness and to change behavior, (5) the recognition that the problems are of psychological origin and the willingness to undertake the examination of the self, (6) ability to experience and to tolerate painful feelings, and (7) adequate ego strength and intelligence.

As for problem-solving therapy, in which careful attention is paid to defining and resolving a specific presenting problem, the selection criteria are the most tolerant. All that is really required is that there is some problem that is disturbing to the patient and that the patient is willing to participate in the therapy, cooperate with suggestions, and make behavioral changes as appropriate.

Brief marital or family therapy is indicated when there is an identifiable focal marital or family conflict, when there is evidence that family members are contributing to the conflict, when it is necessary to mobilize family cooperation to resolve the problem, or when a couple needs immediate help such as in deciding whether to separate or remain together. Selection criteria that seem important in deciding about the appropriateness of brief marital or family therapy include: (1) The family is willing to meet together with some degree of civility; (2) a focal problem can be identified and agreed upon by the therapist and the family; and (3) there is sufficient motivation in the family to change relationship patterns.

Time-limited behavior therapy is indicated when symptoms include anxiety disorders, agoraphobia with or without panic, simple or social phobias, mild to moderate depression, social skill deficit, sexual dysfunction, or compulsive rituals.

Two-Dimensional Selection Criteria: Type of Therapist by Type of Patient

There is a small literature on outcome of planned short-term psychotherapy in relation to the interaction of patient and therapist variables. In an especially useful study of treatment characteristics and their relationships to outcome,

Jones, Cumming, and Horowitz (1988) found that with severely troubled patients, outcome was most positive when therapists gave explicit advice and guidance, when physical symptoms and body functions were discussed, when dialogue had a specific focus, and when the therapist was reassuring. In the case of patients whose difficulties were milder and less disabling, outcome was best when therapists explained the nature of psychotherapy and the rationale of their particular approach, when interpersonal relationships were a major theme of the sessions, when the patient's feelings and behavior in the present were linked to past situations, and when the therapist drew attention to the connections between the therapeutic relationship and other relationships. Thus, a more traditional psychodynamic therapist appeared to warrant selection for patients who were only mildly disturbed, while for patients who were more seriously disturbed, a more supportive and directive therapist appeared to be justified.

Contraindications for Planned Short-Term Psychotherapy

Except for the finding that lower social class patients have higher dropout rates, no other demographic variables (age, sex, level of intelligence) have been shown to be significantly related to therapeutic outcome (MacKenzie, 1988), although Chinen (1986) has found that high levels of what he calls "self-contexting"—citing beliefs as opinions rather than as objective truths—are associated with improvement in brief psychotherapy among older patients but not among younger patients. Thus, contraindications to planned short-term psychotherapy are rarely found in demographic characteristics. Rather, the contraindications that have been suggested are mainly found in characterological and symptomatic domains.

Malan and his group (1976) have gone to considerable lengths to specify the criteria for rejection of applicants. First, a potential client with any of the following clinical characteristics is rejected because these conditions are often severe and disabling: (1) serious depression or gross destructive or self-destructive acting out, (2) drug addiction, (3) a history of long-term hospitalization or other signs of latent or actual psychosis, (4) more than one course of electroconvulsive therapy, (5) chronic alcoholism, (6) incapacitating chronic obsessional symptoms, and (7) incapacitating chronic phobic symptoms (see also Courtenay, 1968, chs. 7 and 8).

Second, clients are rejected if it is judged that any of the following events has a strong likelihood of taking place in therapy: (1) inability to make contact, (2) necessity for prolonged work in order to generate motivation for treatment, (3) necessity for prolonged work in order to penetrate rigid defenses, (4) inevitable involvement in complex or deep-seated issues that there seems no hope of working through in a short time, (5) severe dependence or other forms of unfavorable intense transference, and (6) intensification of depressive or psychotic disturbance. The first three of these predicted events would result in an inability to start effective therapeutic work within the limits of time imposed by the nature of the therapy; the next two events would result in an inability to terminate; and the last predicted event would result in a depressive or psychotic breakdown.

Mann (1973) has minimized selection as a central issue for brief psychotherapy, but he has proposed a number of exclusionary criteria— serious depression, acute psychosis, borderline personality organization, and the inability to identify a central issue. In their later publiction, Mann and Goldman (1982) expanded their list of contraindications. Patients who may have difficulty engaging and disengaging rapidly from treatment are excluded. This group includes schizoid patients, certain obsessional and narcissistic patients, patients with strong dependency needs, depressive patients who are not able to form a rapid therapeutic alliance, and patients with psychosomatic disorders who do not tolerate loss well (see Ursano and Hales, 1986). Davanloo (1978c) has indicated that prospective short-term therapy patients have tended to be rejected by his group if they place high reliance on projection, denial, or acting out.

Three relative contraindications for planned short-term psychotherapy have been proposed by Reich and Neenan (1986). These include (1) psychosis or major thought disorder; (2) multiple severe psychiatric problems; and (3) character disorder, if patients lack a specific focus for treatment. As for exclusion criteria, among those most commonly mentioned in the approaches examined by Burlingame and Fuhriman (1987) are the presence of psychosis and inadequate ego strength.

MacKenzie (1988), in his review of recent developments in brief psychotherapy, has identified the following commonly employed exclusion criteria: (1) patients who cannot attend to the process of active verbal interaction, (2) patients with diagnoses for which other treatment modalities take precedence, and (3) patients with a characterologic style that precludes the likelihood of enduring through the psychological work.

All of these patients are severely and chronically ill, and it would be naive to believe that short-term psychotherapy could accomplish any more than the modest achievements of time-unlimited psychotherapy. Wolberg (1965b) provides a poignant description of the general type of chronically ill patient who requires virtually perpetual therapy. He writes:

There are conditions that respond to no other instrumentality than continuous psychotherapy, no matter how assiduously the therapist applies himself toward releasing forces of assertiveness within the patient. The situation is akin to diabetes in which the patient survives solely because he receives life-giving insulin. In certain problems, dependency is so deep-rooted that the patient can exist only in the medium of a protective relationship in which he can receive his dosages of support. The patient appears to thrive in therapy and seemingly may be utilizing his insights toward a better integration. But this improvement is illusory; the patient constantly needs to maintain a life-line to the helping authority to whom he clings with a desperation that defies all efforts at treatment termination. Such patients obviously will not do well with short-term methods, although long-term approaches may be inadequate also. (p. 139)

Just as the criteria for acceptance into planned short-term psychotherapy seem remarkably similar to those for long-term psychotherapy, so do the criteria for rejection. These criteria—chronic severe psychopathology, history of previous failure of psychotherapy to be helpful, lack of adequate reality testing, or insufficient motivation—certainly describe patients who would be difficult to treat in any form of psychotherapy.

Patient Selection Case Examples

Sifneos (1987) has provided a number of interesting examples of patient selection at work in the initial clinical interview, examples that illustrate both success and failure in meeting one or another of his criteria for acceptance into planned short-term psychotherapy. Boxes 21-2 through 21-5 provide four examples of assessing the extent to which the patient meets three criteria: a circumscribed chief complaint, a meaningful relationship during childhood, and evidence of psychological-mindedness. The rationale for Sifneos's decisions regarding success or failure in meeting these criteria will become self-evident.

BOX 21-2 • *Success in Meeting the Circumscribed Chief Complaint Criterion*

Patient: (a 34-year-old secretary) I have had several problems which I would like to solve. In the last three years I had two unsuccessful relationships with men. I find that I have a tendency to be controlled, yet they complain that it is I who try to control them. This problem has led to the end of my relationships with them.

Therapist: Who ended it, you or they?

Box 21-2 *Continued*

P: They did. The first one actually had said that he was unhappy to terminate our relationship because he liked me very much. He said, "Look here, I cannot see any point in going on because I don't want to be involved with someone who leaves me no breathing space. Everything I do you want to control. I can't take it any longer."

T: And how did you feel?

P: I felt anxious and sad. These symptoms I also want to get rid of, but before I tell you about these symptoms, I want to add that what actually made me call and make an appointment to see you has to do with recognizing that I am developing this "controlling or being controlled" tendency with my current boyfriend, Mike, whom I like very much, and I would hate to lose him.

T: Any other difficulties?

P: Yes, I don't get along very well with women. Here is an example of what I mean. I had an opportunity to live with two other women in a nice apartment in Cambridge, but I turned them down because I don't like the idea of having roommates. So I now live in a rooming house all by myself and I pay a much higher rent.

T: Anything else?

P: Coming back to these symptoms, I think that my feeling anxious upsets my stomach. I haven't had much appetite, I lost some weight, and I don't sleep very well. I am restless at night. I wake up several times during the night and I keep on thinking about all these difficulties.

T: Have you seen a doctor about these physical symptoms, the stomach upset, the loss of weight, and so on?

P: No, I haven't.

T: Well, first things first. We must have a look at all these physical symptoms. Although you may be right that they are associated with your anxieties, nevertheless they may also be due to other causes. Thus I shall make an appointment for you to be examined in the medical clinic. Is this all right?

P: Oh, yes. That is OK.

T: But let us return to your complaints. You have symptoms psychological and physical, you have difficulties about control with your boyfriends, and you don't get along very well with women. Now, which is the most important problem?

P: They are all important. I want help in overcoming them all.

Continued

BOX 21-2 *Continued*

T: I understand that that is what you want, but if we were to help you only with *one* of these difficulties, which one would you choose? Which one would you give top priority for its resolution?

P: It is difficult to choose.

T: I know, but do try to answer my questions.

P: Maybe they are all interrelated.

T: Maybe they are, but maybe they are not. So which one would you choose?

P: OK. Come to think of it, I would say that the problem with my boyfriends is the most important. The anxiety and the sadness I can tolerate, even if they prevailed. The problems that I have with women in a sense I have avoided by living by myself, so if I have to choose I'd pick the issue with men.

From Sifneos, 1987, pp. 28–29.

BOX 21-3 • *Failure to Meet the Meaningful Relationship Criterion*

Patient: (a 24-year-old single female model who complained of asthmatic attacks) My grandmother loved me. She took care of me. She gave me everything I wanted. You will say as others do that she spoiled me, but this is not true, because I was also very good to her.

Therapist: What do you mean?

P: I did exactly what she wanted.

T: Can you give me an example?

P: Of course. You see, I was a good child. I never gave my grandmother cause for concern. I never spoke back to her. I never crossed her. I—

T: (interrupting) Did you enjoy doing all these things?

P: Oh, yes!

T: Well, if this is the case, did you do anything to please your grandmother which you did not enjoy doing?

P: Oh, no, no, no. I always enjoyed it.

T: Let me put it differently. Did you do anything that you disliked in order to make your grandmother happy, just to please her?

BOX 21-3 *Continued*

P: Of course not! You don't understand. My grandmother never wanted me to do anything that I disliked doing. She called me her "little princess." She used to say, "My little adorable child should never raise her little finger. She should never do anything for anyone else." It was good advice! I never did anything for someone else and I never felt such a need. Actually, on second thought, by modeling I give pleasure to a lot of people.

T: I see. Tell me, does that make you happy?

P: Yes, it does. I love to wear beautiful new clothes. I look good in them. My grandmother always admires me. I work hard but I like my work.

T: Well, that is not exactly what I had in mind. Let me ask you a question. Would you do anything to please someone else?

P: (reflecting) To be perfectly honest with you doctor — the answer is no.

T: Not even your grandmother?

P: Oh, I see. You don't seem to understand. My grandmother would not want me to sacrifice anything for her. It's against her teachings. She wants me to be happy, and I'm perfectly happy. These attacks of asthma, I'm sure, are due to allergies, although the doctor who referred me to your clinic thinks that they are due to an emotional upset. I am unaware of any such upset.

T: Let me ask you one last question. Do you have or have you ever had a steady boyfriend or a close girlfriend?

P: That's a funny question. Steady, of course not. Boyfriends? Yes, many. I'm going out with three fellows right now. I like them all. They amuse me, they entertain me, they take me out to nice places. They don't ask for anything in return. Oh, a little sex here and there, but I enjoy that too. I know that you'll say I'm spoiled. Everyone says that. Whatever you want to call it is your business. Any more questions?

T: No, thank you.

From Sifneos, 1987, pp. 33–34.

BOX 21-4 • *Success in Meeting the Meaningful Relationship Criterion*

Therapist: Did you have one good friend in your childhood?

Patient: (a 21-year-old male college student) Oh, yes. When I was seven years old John and I were inseparable. He lived very close by and many times he would come and spend the weekend with me. My mother was very fond of him and felt sorry for him.

Continued

BOX 21-4   *Continued*

T: Why?

P: You see, his father was an alcoholic or drank too much. He had a violent temper. They never invited me to their house because of his father. John was very apologetic about it. His mother, on the other hand, was very nice.

T: So, what was your friendship like?

P: Well, we used to play soccer. John was poor. He had no toys. When we played soccer it was always with my soccer ball or one of the other kids'. I remember how happy John was when he had received a soccer ball as a Christmas present from his uncle. He showed it to me with great pride and he was planning to use it the next time that we were planning to play the following week. But when the time came John came to my house early. He was crying. When I asked him what was the matter, he said that he had accidentally broken his father's favorite beer mug—one that his father had brought back from Germany after World War II. It seems that his father was furious. He had been drinking, so as a punishment he took a kitchen knife and tore John's soccer ball to ribbons. John was very upset about it and he felt humiliated when he was thinking of how to explain all this to the other kids that afternoon. He wanted me to tell them that he was sick just as an excuse. I said to him, "No, John, you are taking the easy way out if you don't show up. But I am going to help you." So I went up to my room, where I had two soccer balls—one was also brand-new and the other an old one. I said to myself, Well, I'll give John the old one, but I thought that the other kids would have expected John to have a new one, so I took my own new one and gave it to John. He didn't want to accept it but I convinced him. He was very happy. I was a bit sad to give it up but his happiness made me happy.

From Sifneos, 1987, pp. 35–36.

BOX 21-5 • *Success in Meeting the Psychological-Mindedness Criterion*

Patient: (a 37-year-old fruit vendor with a phobia) There's something else, doc. I don't know if it's important, but I thought that I should talk about it.

Therapist: Go on.

BOX 21-5 *Continued*

P: Well, it has to do with my mother (hesitating) — see, when I get close to Cambridge Street, you know the street which I'm afraid to cross, I start hearing my mother's voice calling me.

T: (startled) You hear voices?

P: Oh, no doc! I'm not crazy, you know. No, it's just like this. It's my mother's voice inside my head. It's my thinking, see! It's that I think that she's calling me.

T: And what does she say in your thoughts?

P: Well, she says, "Mario, come home," and then I ask, "Is father home?" "No," she says, "the house is all yours and I've cooked a good meal for you." So you see, doc, I can't cross the street because there's something pulling me back and making me go home.

T: So, you are not afraid of crossing the street; it is that something pulls you back.

P: Gee, doc! I never thought of it this way, but you're right.

T: Well, it is you who put it this way. But then you say that you ask her about your father. Why do you do that?

P: Well, I don't feel like rushing back to my house when he's around. He always has something to complain about. When my mother and I are alone (smiling) we have such a good time, doc!

T: So, your father has also something to do with your trouble?

P: Well, they both do. You see, I've been thinking about all this. My dad's pushing me to go away. He wants me to take over the other shop and leave the West End. My mother wants me to stay home. So, you see, doc, I'm having a problem, but this fear makes it impossible for me to leave.

T: Well, as we have seen, it's not the fear that stops you but rather the wish to be alone with your mother. When your father is around, he stops the good time you have with your mother.

P: (smiling) You're smart, doc. That's really it, I guess. So what do you think? Is there hope for me?

T: What do *you* think?

P: Yeah. I guess so. If it's all in my head I must be able to help myself.

From Sifneos, 1987, pp. 40–41.

Concluding Comments

As we take stock of the ideas and the empirical studies described in this chapter, two alternatives to selecting patients for planned short-term psychotherapy recommend themselves. First, if you use the same criteria as are used for time-unlimited therapy, you won't go far wrong. On the other hand, you won't learn very much about patient selection. Second, if you want to take a risk, don't use any selection criteria. Put everyone in time-limited psychotherapy and work on the assumption that if they don't do as well as you thought they should have done, it is your fault, not your patient's. The easiest hypotheses that suggest themselves if your patient doesn't show sufficient improvement are that either the patient simply isn't suitable for your therapy, or that the patient would have shown more improvement if the therapy had gone on longer. Harder to assert, but much more challenging, is the hypothesis that if you had only been wiser or more alert or had used a better approach, your patient would have shown more improvement. This second alternative is the more intellectually exciting and if used systematically can lead to a significant increase in knowledge about how different kinds of patients can profit from planned short-term psychotherapy.

As for the narrow selection criteria identified by a number of writers in the field, it seems likely that they are not independent of each other — that is, patients who meet one of those criteria likely meet others. Thus, for example, the presence of high motivation for change, the ability to establish a productive working relationship with the therapist, a history of meaningful relationships with others, psychological-mindedness, and an identifiable and compelling focal issue of concern are likely to be significantly correlated with each other; if one of these criteria is present, the others are likely to be present as well.

If one moves from selecting patients simply on the basis of patient characteristics to selecting them specifically for certain types of short-term therapy or for certain therapist characteristics, then the selection process becomes geometrically more complex without promising compensatory gains in knowledge. Since all forms of planned short-term psychotherapy have been found to be essentially equally effective, it is not likely that we will find that significant differences in outcome will occur simply on the basis of therapy or therapist type. Furthermore, it is not yet clear how one is to group short-term therapies so as to divide them into meaningfully different categories. For the moment, then, there is no appreciable downside to starting patients of all types in time-limited psychotherapy. We have the chance to be very surprised by our results.

CHAPTER TWENTY-TWO

The Status of Planned Short-Term Psychotherapy

Overview

General Principles of Planned Short-Term Psychotherapy

The Challenge to Traditional Psychotherapy

Increasing the Flexibility of Psychotherapy

Administrative and Organizational Aspects of Planned Short-Term Psychotherapy

Shaping the Future of Planned Short-Term Psychotherapy

Concluding Comments

We now have the opportunity and the challenge to step back from the detailed individualized views of planned short-term psychotherapy that have been presented. The focus of this book has been on how these various approaches to planned short-term psychotherapy differ from each other. There are, in fact, very few critiques of any of the specific approaches to planned short-term psychotherapy. At the moment, it is as if the field is encouraging, perhaps quite wisely, the unlimited development of different approaches to time-limited therapy.

What is clear in the literature is that planned short-term psychotherapy is thought of as being applicable to a very wide variety of psychiatric disorders and stressful life circumstances. Among these conditions are retirement (Salvendy, 1989), military service (Bleich et al., 1988), the stress of university life (May, 1988), sexual dysfunctions (Herman and Schatzow, 1987;

Morokoff and LoPiccolo, 1986; Rockwell, 1987; Schwartz and Masters, 1984), eating disorders (Connors, Johnson, and Stuckey, 1984; Frommer et al., 1987; Hall and Crisp, 1987; Moley, 1987), phobic and obsessive-compulsive disorders (Beckfield, 1987; Sifneos, 1985), posttraumatic stress disorders (Marmar and Freeman, 1988), bereavement (Horowitz et al., 1984; Leon, 1987; Marmar et al., 1988), mood disorders (Canter, 1984; Dreyfus, 1988; Gordon and Gordon, 1987), chemical dependence (Wallen et al., 1987; Weiner, 1987), schizophrenia (Kanas, Stewart, and Haney, 1988), hostility (Rokach, 1987), and personality disorders (Leibovich, 1981). It is almost impossible to identify a disorder that has not been found to be responsive to one or another form of time-limited psychotherapy.

Indeed, it should be noted that the field of planned short-term psychotherapy is quickly achieving all the hallmarks of an independent profession. Nearly a hundred English language books and edited collections of papers exclusively devoted to the topic have been published in the past twenty-five years; perhaps as many as a thousand journal articles on the topic have appeared in print; courses on short-term therapy are increasingly available in graduate and continuing education programs in the mental health professions; and the field now has its own journal, the *International Journal of Short-Term Psychotherapy,* founded in 1986.

This final chapter will be integrative in nature. Similarities that can be discerned in these different approaches to time-limited psychotherapy will be briefly examined. Then, we shall turn our attention to the future, to the implications of the extraordinary fervor of activity that has characterized the field of planned short-term psychotherapy during the past two decades for the entire psychotherapeutic enterprise.

General Principles of Short-Term Psychotherapy

A number of authors have attempted to identify the common characteristics of planned short-term psychotherapies (Brodaty, 1983; Butcher and Koss, 1978; Budman, 1981; Budman and Gurman, 1983; Donovan, 1987; Gustafson, 1984; Reich and Neenan, 1986). These common characteristics—the limitation on time, the limitation on goals, the establishment of a focal issue, and a more active and flexible therapeutic approach—have been repeatedly referred to in this book, and little new can be added here.

General principles of planned short-term psychotherapy can also be viewed as a subset of the identified general principles of all psychotherapies. Frank (1984), in his search for these general principles that help account for the fact that psychotherapies appear to be equally effective and for those components of all psychotherapies that transcend specific assertions regarding specific techniques or theories, has approached the task in the following way:

> *One way to identify some of these components would be to ask yourself what qualities you would seek in a guide if you were a tenderfoot about to embark on an exploration into unknown territory with various unknown dangers. Two qualities you would certainly want in a guide would be trustworthiness and competence. You would expect to be able to rely fully on the guide's concern about your welfare. . . . you would want the guide to be thoroughly familiar with the terrain and how to cope with the hardships and dangers you might meet. (p. 422)*

These attributes, according to Frank, form the cornerstones of the general psychotherapeutic effort. Regarding trustworthiness, Frank suggests that therapists must be able to convey the fact that they have the patient's interest at heart and that they care about and are concerned about the patient's welfare. In addition, they must be able to create a sense of personal security for the patient, a sense that the patient is accepted and the therapist can be counted on. As for competence, Frank believes that therapists must have mastered the therapeutic procedures they practice and that regardless of what these techniques are, they must be able to carry out the procedures common to them all—to listen, to understand their patients, and to convey that understanding in a useful way. Frank comments that "it is hard to overestimate the anxiety-allaying power of the therapist's ability simply to listen in an understanding way" (1984, p. 423).

Frank believes that trustworthiness, caring, and competence set the stage for effective psychotherapy—therapy that is emotionally arousing and that reinforces the sense of self-efficacy that has so often been lost or lowered. With emotional arousal comes increased motivation. With the increased sense of self-efficacy comes a greater willingness to explore issues formerly unexplored. From this perspective we can immediately see one therapeutic virtue to time-limited psychotherapy. For its fundamental message is very affirming—most patients need only a little help to get back on track and to manage their affairs on their own. Note that Frank's concepts are not specific to any particular theory of psychotherapy; they are extratheoretical, applying equally well to any theoretical approach.

Freud once said that the aim of psychoanalysis is to transform neurotic misery into ordinary misery. Kreilkamp (1989) suggests that "all too often this remark is not taken seriously, but rather is heard as a form of cynicism or jaded world-weariness" (p. 224). In fact, it is a realistic description of the psychotherapeutic task, and the research literature suggests that taking the neurosis out of misery may take far less time than was formerly thought.

Short-term psychotherapies may be equivalent in their effectiveness because everything inside the patient is connected to everything else. Whatever a caring, competent, and trustworthy therapist does, regardless of what specific techniques and theories are espoused, has the potential for being helpful. In fact, it may be that theories of psychopathology and of psychotherapy serve their primary purpose by keeping therapists alert during their interviews with patients.

If the therapist simply asks patients to think more deeply about themselves, as virtually all psychotherapists do, such requests may have significant therapeutic potential. The request provides an opportunity for patients that is rarely present in normal social interactions. Exploration of the self can lead to discoveries that can clarify and demystify. A single discovery about the self that can then be further explored can lead the way to significant change in how individuals think about themselves and others and in how they carry out their interpersonal interactions.

Freud made this point very clearly in his insistence that psychotherapy served the patient by helping make conscious the unconscious. Describing his view of the difference between the conscious and the unconscious, Freud noted that everything conscious is subject to a process of wearing away, while what is unconscious is relatively unchangeable. Freud (1909/1953) once reconstructed his comments to a patient to whom he was pointing out the antiques standing about in his office as follows: "They were, in fact, I said, only objects found in a tomb, and their burial had been their preservation: the destruction of Pompeii was only beginning now that it had been dug up" (p. 313; see also Malcolm, 1987; Straker, 1986). Wearing away might not be good for the unburied treasures of Pompeii, but it is exactly what mental health professionals hope will happen in psychotherapy.

The Challenge to Traditional Psychotherapy

While the move toward planned short-term psychotherapy is not universally greeted as a blessing (see, for example, Good, 1987; Shulman, 1988), the overwhelming research evidence regarding the effectiveness of short-term psychotherapy, the growing interest on the part of most consumers to be done with their therapy and get on with their lives, and the financial drain to society of long-term psychotherapy have combined to raise serious questions about the continued application of time-unlimited approaches (Cochrane, 1972; MacKenzie, 1988).

In addition, Goldin and Winston (1985) believe that short-term dynamic psychotherapy is having a significant impact on traditional psychoanalytic psychotherapy, particularly in the matter of assessment and the handling of resistance and transference reactions. Regarding assessment of patients, traditional psychoanalytic psychotherapists who observe the work of time-limited psychodynamic psychotherapists tend to "become more active, more courageous in pursuing feelings, appreciably more specific and concrete in delineating chief complaints, and generally more in control of the interview"

(Goldin and Winston, 1985, p. 69). In handling resistance traditional psychodynamic psychotherapists tend to become more active, ask more detailed questions, and are more assertive in thwarting regression on the part of the patient after becoming more familiar with the work of short-term dynamic psychotherapists. Finally, regarding dealing with transference reactions, after being exposed to the work of short-term therapists, traditional psychodynamic psychotherapists tend to decrease their encouragement of the development of the regressive transference neurosis and to interpret the transference relationship earlier.

Rogawski (1982), himself a psychoanalyst, has thoughtfully considered three crucial questions that have arisen as a consequence of the increasing evidence of the effectiveness of planned short-term psychotherapy. First, in view of the fact that planned short-term psychotherapy and long-term therapy appear to be equally effective, are there any specific indications for long-term therapy? Rogawski suggests that patients suffering from character disorders or borderline syndromes whose core problems cannot be identified need supportive long-term psychotherapy. In addition, Rogawski believes that the intensive psychoanalytic method remains a unique instrument for the study of human psychology as well as for the education of psychotherapists.

Second, Rogawski asks how the demonstrated effectiveness of planned short-term psychotherapy will affect clinical practice. He suggests that these demonstrations will put pressure on mental health professionals to treat patients more efficiently, if they are to survive economically, and will put pressure on professional training facilities to teach short-term therapeutic techniques. Finally, Rogawski asks why psychodynamic approaches to short-term psychotherapy should continue to be advocated, given the evidence that they have not been shown to be superior to other approaches. His reply is that the psychodynamic approach provides a unique conceptual framework for understanding human behavior and that it is reestablishing links with other scientific disciplines, such as neurophysiology, psychopharmacology, and information theory, and has the potential to become a basic element of a general scientific psychology. This loyal defense of psychodynamic theory and the long-term psychotherapy associated with it is sobering in its modesty.

While research studies certainly make it appropriate to conclude that psychotherapy is better than no psychotherapy, its lack of more firmly established effectiveness should make practitioners and educators somewhat uneasy (Gallagher, 1987). The most optimistic figures that have appeared in the literature regarding the general effectiveness of psychotherapy are that about 75 percent of treated patients are doing better after therapy than the average untreated patient. While this sounds on the surface as a rousing endorsement of psychotherapy, in fact it should give us pause. For these findings mean that while three treated patients out of four demonstrate substantial improvement when contrasted with untreated patients, one treated patient out of every four ends up worse off than the average untreated patient. And a further examination of the existing evaluation literature makes it clear that we cannot confidently identify in advance who that one patient out of four might be.

Increasing the Flexibility of Psychotherapy

The last two decades have witnessed a significant loosening of the rigid definitions of psychotherapeutic approaches. This increasing flexibility in attitudes regarding the conduct of psychotherapy may well be part of a generally growing liberalization of attitudes toward human service delivery. In the case of psychotherapy in particular, this increasing flexibility can be seen in attitudes toward the therapeutic approach, toward the concept of cure, and toward the length and frequency of appointments.

Flexibility in Therapeutic Approach

Increasing liberalization of approaches toward how to conduct psychotherapy can be seen in increasing eclecticism; increasing recognition, even by therapists who are themselves very doctrinaire, of the important and necessary contributions of therapists with different theoretical persuasions; and increasing attention to the literature regarding therapist characteristics, as opposed to therapy characteristics, that appear to be associated with therapy outcome.

The increasing eclecticism can be seen in the review of time-limited psychotherapy prepared by Budman and Stone (1983):

> It seems to us inevitable that brief therapy will increasingly become pragmatic eclectic therapy. As we have noted, the movement toward eclecticism is already affecting many therapists, regardless of whether they view themselves as doing brief treatment. Because psychotherapists heavily engaged in short-term treatment activities begin such endeavors with an interest in time, effectiveness, and innovation, they are individuals who will be (and already have been) open to creative intervention strategies. Such intervention strategies will undoubtedly draw widely from psychoanalytic, behavioral, and humanistic psychotherapy. (pp. 944–945)

Eclecticism in theoretical approach can be seen in the shift from intrapsychic to interpersonal approaches (Horowitz and Vitkus, 1986; MacKenzie,

1988) and in the growing integration of psychodynamic and cognitive behavioral psychotherapy. MacKenzie (1988), for example, has noted:

> *Brief psychotherapy has also incorporated a number of strategies from behavior modification, particularly the emphasis on establishing a contract to work on a restricted interpersonal focus. Application of principles learned in therapy to current outside relationships frequently takes the form of specific homework assignments. Patients' use of diaries to identify social reinforcers and to monitor application of tasks is not uncommon. Relaxation techniques may help the patient attain a sense of personal mastery, and assertiveness training techniques may complement psychodynamic approaches. (p. 750)*

The literature examining therapist characteristics that appear to be associated with positive therapeutic outcome has identified a number of variables that deserve further study. The first of these is expertise. Clinical consensus is that planned short-term psychotherapy requires a greater level of experience and sophistication than does time-unlimited psychotherapy. For example, Wolberg (1965b) has suggested that:

> *Short-term treatment requires a sophistication borne of the wisdom of experience. Only a therapist schooled in the widest varieties of technic and seasoned through treatment of the broadest spectrum of emotional problems, can move the patient beyond the comforts of support into areas that hold promise of personality change. The tolerances in short-term therapy are fine; there is place for only the barest margin of error. (p. 128)*

Mann and Goldman (1982) suggest that "time-limited psychotherapy is not for the beginning therapist; the best preparation for it is extensive experience in long-term psychotherapy so that one can gain a full appreciation for the unconscious functions of the mind, the ego defenses, transference, and resistance" (p. 17). They continue their commentary on the importance of clinical experience by noting that:

> *Even after a personal analysis . . . the therapist still requires the help of experienced supervisors to translate his personal experience into a therapeutic tool. Peer supervision with experienced therapists is most useful for learning how to arrive at a meaningful central issue from the patient's history and for following the course of treatment to a successful conclusion. From such cooperative peer groups, there will then emerge a cadre of supervisors who can help the less experienced in doing the rewarding work of time-limited psychotherapy. (p. 18)*

Malan's attitude toward the importance of clinical experience in conducting planned short-term psychotherapy can easily be discerned in the parenthetical phrase in the following review of his thinking provided by Gustafson (1981):

> *If the patient responds . . . with deeper material and increased motivation, the therapist will set up an agreement to see the patient for brief therapy, ending on a definite date—after 20 sessions if the therapist is experienced, or 30 if the therapist is a trainee or the therapy has some other special complication. (Gustafson, 1981, p. 97; see also Ursano and Hales, 1986)*

Turning to other therapist characteristics, Gelso and Johnson (1983) in their research studies in a university counseling center found a number of therapist characteristics significantly related to patient outcome. These characteristics are displayed in Box 22-1.

Other characteristics of the therapist and of the therapeutic relationship that appear to be significantly related to outcome have been identified. One example can be seen in the work of Free and colleagues (1985), who attempted to assess therapist empathy and to determine whether that measure was related to therapeutic outcome. Empathy was assessed by means of a sixteen-item questionnaire that included items such as "He tries to see things through my eyes," "He nearly always knows exactly what I mean," and "He can be deeply and fully aware of my most painful feelings without being distressed or burdened by them himself." They found that patients' ratings of therapist empathy were significantly positively correlated with a number of outcome measures.

BOX 22-1 · *Therapist Characteristics Associated with Successful Short-Term Therapy*

1. Therapist's behavior reflects confidence that short-term therapy can be effective.
2. Therapist establishes challenging but limited therapeutic goals.
3. Therapist works toward insight but not to the exclusion of behavior change.
4. Therapist's goal is to start a therapeutic process that can continue after termination.
5. Therapist follows up terminated patients to explore the consolidation of changes that has taken place.

Adapted from Gelso and Johnson, 1983, p. 206.

A related therapist variable that has been examined is what is referred to as the *therapeutic alliance,* but it is not clear from the existing research just how different this variable is from what has been called *therapist empathy.* An example of an item from the therapist alliance scale developed by Marziali (1984) is "To what extent did your therapist's comments help you to feel good about yourself?" — an item that could as easily be used to assess therapist empathy as the strength of the therapeutic alliance. Patients' ratings of the therapist alliance were found by Marziali (1984; see also Marmar, Weiss, and Gaston, 1989; Marziali, Marmar, and Krupnick, 1981) to be significantly associated with therapeutic outcome. Thus, the measure of the strength of the treatment alliance appears to be in part a characteristic of the patient while it is at the same time a measure of the therapeutic relationship.

Hill and colleagues (1988) examined verbatim transcripts of 127 sessions of eight cases of brief psychotherapy with anxious-depressed patients and found that experienced therapists had better immediate results when their behavior was characterized by relatively high levels of self-disclosure, interpretation, approval, paraphrasing, and asking open questions. Least helpful were confrontations, provision of information, and closed questions.

Silberschatz, Fretter, and Curtis (1986) found that validity of interpretations, as assessed by their relationship to the dynamic case formulation, was significantly associated with therapeutic outcome. In another study, Cox, Rutter, and Holbrook (1988) found that when the therapist employed a higher feeling-oriented therapeutic style, particularly when clients' spontaneous levels of expressed feelings were low, expressed feelings on the part of clients significantly increased.

As these studies indicate, certain therapist behaviors are associated with unusually high levels of improvement, sometimes in certain types of patients. These studies need to be replicated and extended, but what seems clear is that under potentially specifiable conditions certain varieties of therapist behavior can result in significant increases in the likelihood of patient improvement, regardless of the theoretical approach to the therapy.

Thus, there are a number of principles of psychotherapy that are not theory-specific; that is, they apply to all approaches to therapy, psychodynamic as well as cognitive behavioral. Cummings (1983) has identified the most important of these general principles, as the excerpts in Box 22-2 indicate.

Flexibility Regarding the Concept of Cure

Mental health professionals in sharply increasing numbers are beginning to reconsider their earlier views of the goals of psychotherapy. That

---

BOX 22-2 • *Cummings's General Psychotherapeutic Principles*

1. *Hit the ground running.* The first session must be therapeutic. The concept that you must devote the first session to taking a history . . . is nonsense.
2. *Perform an operational diagnosis.* . . . The operational diagnosis asks one thing, "Why is the patient here today instead of last week or last month, last year, or next year?" And when you answer that, you know what the patient is here for. The operational diagnosis is absolutely necessary for you to set about your treatment plan, and it is best that it be done in the first session.
3. *Create a therapeutic contract.* . . . Every patient makes a therapeutic contract with every therapist in the first session, every time. But in 99% of the cases, the therapist misses it. . . . If a patient comes into the office and says, "Doctor, I'm glad you have this comfortable chair because I'm going to be here awhile" and the therapist doesn't respond to that, the therapist has just made a contract for long-term therapy.
4. *Do something novel the first session.* . . . Find something novel, something unexpected, to do the first session. This will cut through the expectations of the "trained" patient and will create instead an expectation that problems are to be immediately addressed.
5. *Give homework in the first session and every therapy session thereafter.* It isn't possible to have some cookbook full of homework that you just arbitrarily assign. Tailor the homework to be meaningful for that patient's goals and the therapeutic contract. The patient will realize, "Hey, this guy isn't kidding. I'm responsible for my own therapy."

Adapted and excerpted from Cummings, 1983, p. 430.

---

traditional perspective on the therapeutic process, virtually unknown in the rest of the healing arts but still held by a number of mental health practitioners, is that first, getting better will take a long time, and, second, once you are better, you probably will never need to come back. Budman (1981, pp. 464–465) traces these beliefs to early Freudian thinking that Freud himself later repudiated, but not before the beliefs became firmly fixed as part of psychoanalytic folklore (see also Donovan, 1987).

Cummings and Vandenbos (1979) describe this belief system well:

Any recontact with a former mental health patient is labeled a "relapse" and is viewed as evidence that the earlier intervention was either unsuccessful or incomplete. We usually act as if contact with a professional psychologist is for a single, simple, unified problem, and that six sessions will solve everything forever. No other field of health care holds this conceptualization of treatment outcome. (p. 433)

Watzlawick (1978) describes this unrealistic fantasy in the following words:

In virtually no other, comparable realm of human endeavor is it postulated and accepted that changes must be final and complete. Everywhere, except in classical psychotherapy, it is considered a simple fact of life that there are no perfect solutions, to be reached once and for all, that problems can recur and that existence is a life-long process of perhaps optimal, but certainly never perfect adaptation . . . because the scenario of life constantly changes. In therapy, however, we talk about such wondrous states as full genital organization, individuation, and self-actualization, and we consider a treatment to have been successful only if the difficulty or the symptom never occurs again. (p. 159)

A number of other writers have commented on other aspects of this somewhat utopian view of psychotherapy. Budman and Gurman (1988) have noted that:

patients return to therapy at various points in their lives. Assuming that as a therapist one can (or should) provide a patient with a "definitive" treatment is like assuming that a teacher should provide the definitive class, that a physician should provide the definitive antibiotic, or that a travel agent should provide the definitive vacation. What one hopes is that the . . . therapy provided has had sufficient impact to alleviate some of the problems with which the patient presented upon entry into therapy, and that the patient takes with himself or herself some useful tools for dealing with similar problems in the future. (p. 248)

Wilson (1981), writing from the point of view of behavior therapy, also critiques the traditional concept of cure:

A common occurrence in behavior therapy is for the patient to consult the therapist on periodic occasions in the months or even years following termination of treatment. . . . Usually, patients seek "follow-up" consultations to obtain guidance or clarification about coping with new, emerging difficulties they begin to encounter following the therapeutic changes they made during treatment. In short, people continue to grow and change following a course of successful therapy, short-term or otherwise, and occasionally need brief therapeutic assistance during the course of this continuing evolvement of lifestyle changes. In most instances, these subsequent contacts are not to be taken as signs of failure or even incomplete treatment; neither can they be rationalized in terms of the now discredited notion of "symptom substitution." In clinical practice, these sporadic, posttreatment contacts with the therapist are usually unscheduled and initiated by the patient. Behavior therapists often deliberately schedule posttreatment maintenance or booster sessions, however, as an integral part of the overall treatment program. (p. 143; see also Phillips, 1985, p. ix)

Most general human service providers—and mental health professionals in increasing numbers—hold an alternative point of view, one that seems more persuasive in the context of planned short-term psychotherapy: First, let us try to help you as quickly as possible; and, second, something might very well go wrong in the future, in which case come back and we will try to help you once again. Many mental health professionals have yet to learn the lesson that most primary health care providers seem to understand instinctively: Patients have their own restitutive potential, and if the therapist can help the patient inaugurate that potential, the patient can do a great deal without additional help from the care giver.

With this orientation, commitment to the client can be seen from a very different point of view. Rabkin (1977) described the short-term therapy orientation to that commitment well when he wrote:

Under the best of conditions, relationships with professionals other than psychotherapists are not regarded as terminating at all. They are seen as intermittent. For example, the accountant, lawyer, family doctor, or barber may have permanent relationships with clients and perhaps their families, although the actual face-to-face contacts occur only for specific tasks or problems. Particularly in relationships of confidence, as in the case of the accountant and the physician, the tie may last a lifetime. (p. 211)

Flexibility in Length and Frequency of Appointments

Two aspects of the growing flexibility in how one determines the length and frequency of clinical appointments deserve special note. First, there is increasing evidence that therapists are moving away from routinely scheduling fifty-minute once-weekly interviews. And, second, attention is beginning to be directed to what may be the most profound aspect of the concept of short-term therapy, namely, how one is to know when enough psychotherapy has been provided.

Time-limited psychotherapy can be scheduled, as we have seen, in many different time frames — weekly one-hour sessions; half-hour sessions; meetings every two, three, or four weeks, or even twice a year; as well as longer sessions of one and one-half or two hours' duration.

MacKenzie (1988) has noted that

> *three recommendations for setting time limits are made in the literature. The first is the Procrustean alternative, or one size fits all: establish the number of sessions and the date of termination at the outset, perhaps as a program policy. Second is the sporting alternative, which marks the finishing line but varies the pace; set the date of termination but leave the number of sessions open, allowing for more frequent sessions earlier in therapy and less frequent sessions later. The third recommendation is the elastic alternative, expandable but always pressing to be shorter: set neither the number of sessions nor the duration, imply that therapy will be as brief as required and in any case not too long, and keep the pressure on for rapid work. (p. 744)*

Budman (1983) has suggested that it may be most effective to see patients initially on a weekly basis and then to move toward longer intervals as it becomes appropriate. In addition, he proposes planned follow-up and periodic return visits. Such proposals "may be more in line with reality than the now-prevalent therapeutic cure model, where no provision is made for follow-up and maintenance of change by the patient often is not considered" (p. 943). Similarly, Goldsmith (1986) has noted that

> *it is not unusual, either in my work or in the work of other strategic therapists, for intervals between sessions to be irregular, or to be every two to four weeks. The longer intervals provide more time for a consolidation of the therapeutic gains within the context of the patient's outside life. Longer intervals can also indicate to a patient that the most important problem-solving efforts will be going on outside the therapeutic sessions. The irregularity of intervals between sessions, the variability in the length of the actual sessions, and the relatively lengthy time that can occur between sessions are all consistent with the belief that change is discontinuous. That is, the rate of therapeutic change that individuals manifest cannot be represented by a single sloping line on a graph. (p. 60)*

As for when enough therapy has been provided, there is perhaps no question of greater current importance in the field of short-term psychotherapy. For, indeed, attention to this issue transforms the entire debate in psychotherapy from one in which time is the central concept to one in which sufficiency is the central concept.

In spite of the importance of the issue regarding the optimal duration of psychotherapy, comments are still rare. It is as if the issue has just recently been recognized. Mann and Goldman (1982), in the context of their own sharply time-limited psychotherapy, have written:

A common question is: How does the therapist know that enough work has been done? . . . If the therapist fails to end the treatment at the agreed-on time because of his own objections, the following conclusions can be drawn. The therapist has not done the work he should have, usually because he has not permitted himself to work directly and without fear on his own inhibitions with respect to the separation-termination issue during the final two or three sessions. Yielding to one's anxiety about separation-termination and prolonging the treatment become a vote of no confidence in the patient. The adult patient, with rare exceptions, has strengths and assets that should not be underestimated. Prolonging the treatment reinforces the old hostile-dependent attachment and humiliates the adult in the patient. (pp. 15–16)

In a more general context, Kreilkamp (1989) has commented:

But there still remains the question of how much therapy is enough for a particular problem or a particular patient. All . . . therapists must struggle with the difficult question of whether more meetings or more effort expended on a patient or family will make a difference. . . . But the best defense of our position—that brief, intermittent therapy will suffice for many people, is in the first place to admit that there are some people who are not going to improve just because the therapist tries to help them; second, to argue that some people need more than any system of care is going to be able to offer them (more resources, more money, more housekeeping help, etc.); and finally, to keep in mind always that a different approach, or a different provider applying a similar approach, may help the patient more than we are able to do. So we make an explicit part of our system the idea that not every therapist can necessarily provide therapy to every patient who comes his way. (pp. 222–223)

Neither of these quotations is, however, exactly on the mark. The greatest objection raised by traditional psychotherapists to the ideas promulgated by short-term therapists is usually what they see as an arbitrary, inflexible, and often capricious ceiling set on the total number of psychotherapy sessions that will be permitted for every patient in their agency. If a mental health service delivery system functions on the basis of sufficiency instead of time, then it is possible to circumvent completely the issue of what constitutes the upper limit of short-term therapy, thus circumventing a profoundly refractory clinical objection to short-term psychotherapy. In place of an ongoing debate regarding how many interviews the agency should permit as its maximum, the issue becomes how to know when the therapy that has already been provided is sufficient to meet the patient's needs — a far more interesting and challenging topic of discussion that we shall return to at the end of this chapter.

Administrative and Organizational Aspects of Planned Short-Term Psychotherapy

Because traditional fee-for-service mental health care and planned short-term psychotherapy are based on two entirely different sets of economic assumptions and incentives, they do not make a good fit. Thus, it should not be surprising that the growing interest in time-limited psychotherapy and in alternatives to fee-for-service health care are occurring at the same time (Cummings, 1988; Cummings and Vandenbos, 1979; Duhl and Cummings, 1987; Kovacs, 1982; Langsley, 1988; MacKenzie, 1988; Peake and Ball, 1987; Scheffler, 1987).

Before commenting on the principal alternatives to traditional fee-for-service mental health care, it is worth noting that the findings regarding the effectiveness of planned short-term psychotherapy argue for a major change in policy within the traditional third-party reimbursement system. Insurance coverage should be limited to reimbursement for most if not all of the cost of psychotherapeutic appointments (up to some dollar maximum, to be sure) for the first two or three interviews, concluding with perhaps 50 percent of the cost reimbursed for the next two or three interviews. The burden of proof for requesting reimbursement beyond this normal maximum could rest with the psychotherapist and an associated peer review procedure.

Two major alternatives to fee-for-service mental health care are now competing in the mental health service marketplace. These include the provision of mental health–related services within the context of the health maintenance organization (HMO) (Altman and Goldstein, 1988; Bonstedt and Baird, 1979; Chubb, Nauts, and Evans, 1984; Feldman and Goldman, 1987; La Court, 1988; Siddall, Haffey, and Feinman, 1987) and the provision of mental health–related services through a specialized and separate mental health maintenance organization (Cummings, 1986; Cummings and Duhl, 1987) that may or may not be affiliated with a traditional health maintenance organization.

These two approaches share three important fiscal similarities – the cost of care is fixed, entirely predictable to the patient, and unrelated to the amount or nature of services that are provided (Bloom, 1990). Thus, while the fee-for-service health care delivery system derives income from providing services, health maintenance organizations derive income from not providing services, or, to put it less starkly, from not providing services that are not necessary. It once was axiomatic that the effectiveness of psychotherapy was diminished when the patient did not directly pay for the service. Fortunately, this belief is fading, in the face of accumulating experimental evidence to the contrary (see, for example, Yoken and Berman, 1987).

Comprehensive health maintenance organizations and specialized mental health maintenance organizations each have their potential advantages and disadvantages. The potential of the comprehensive health maintenance organization to deliver high-quality mental health and substance abuse services is great. In addition, with the evidence of the strong connection between mental and physical well-being (Bloom, 1990) and the evidence that brief psychotherapy can result in significant reductions in medical care utilization and expenditures (see Chapter 19), the idea of embedding mental health and substance abuse services in the same service delivery system that provides general health care has special appeal. Goldman (1988) has described this appeal eloquently:

> Comprehensive mental health and substance abuse services in a prepaid, managed health care system offers one of the few opportunities available today to serve most, if not all, members of a community. HMOs hold the potential for both excellence and comprehensiveness of services. For the vast majority of its members HMOs can reduce barriers to care for both physical and psychological needs. At their best and most innovative, these plans can provide rational, individual treatment plans that manifest commitment to professional ideals, to improved patient care and to cost consciousness. (p. 200)

The mental health maintenance organization typically provides comprehensive outpatient and inpatient mental health and substance abuse services. Such organizations can contract with employers, insurers, or HMOs to provide a specified set of mental health and substance abuse services, usually through a fixed, prepaid fee. Its primary advantage is that it is an organization of mental health professionals and, running its own house, it can provide the best mental health-related services available. Its disadvantage is that it has no necessary interdependence with general health services.

Perhaps the best-known mental health maintenance organization is American Biodyne (Cummings, 1986, 1988). The term *biodyne* was coined from two Greek words that mean *life change,* and, as can be inferred, the organization views its function as helping patients resolve emotional distress and avoid physical and emotional disorders in the future by altering their lifestyles.

American Biodyne practices what is called "brief, intermittent psychotherapy throughout the life cycle" (Cummings, 1988, p. 314)—an orientation to mental health and substance abuse services that is entirely consistent with contemporary views regarding the appropriate goals of psychotherapy previously discussed in this chapter. As the term suggests, the medical concept of cure is abandoned, and the treatment relationship is interrupted when presenting problems are resolved, but is never terminated. The concept of intermittent psychotherapy can, of course, be applied in comprehensive health maintenance organizations as well (see, for example, Siddall, Haffey, and Feinman, 1988).

Shaping the Future of Planned Short-Term Psychotherapy

How then can a mental health service delivery system successfully build a psychotherapy program that is responsive to the incontrovertible evidence of the effectiveness of planned short-term therapy in the context of the changes that are taking place in how the psychotherapeutic enterprise is viewed? Success in developing such a program will depend on wise recruitment and ongoing supervision and continuing education, on thoughtful program planning and implementation, and on a reward system that is tied to evidence of increasing skill.

Recruitment and Continuing Education

A new generation of therapists is on the horizon—clinicians who are well trained in brief psychotherapy techniques and who have confidence in the effectiveness of these techniques and in their own clinical competencies. If a therapist does not believe that time-limited psychotherapy can be effective and functions as if saying, in one way or another, "We only have six interviews available to us, so I do not think we can accomplish very much," then you have a prescription for failure. Put together a therapist who believes that he or she can be helpful to a patient in a brief period of time with patients who want to and believe that they will be helped and you have the perfect package for a good therapeutic outcome.

Supervision and continuing education need to be provided by staff members — or, less preferably, outside consultants — who are well trained in and committed to short-term psychotherapy strategies and techniques. Training and supervision can be offered in a variety of modalities — preemployment comprehensive training programs, ongoing short-term therapy that is observed by trainees, regularly scheduled case consultation and case conferences, live observation and supervision of trainees engaged in time-limited psychotherapy, journal clubs, as well as more formal seminars.

Program Planning and Implementation

Under no conditions should an agency have a policy that sets an upper limit on the number of therapy sessions that can be made available to any patient during a time period (Cummings, 1983). Preoccupation with time limits has to be replaced with concern for how much treatment is necessary. When there is a specified upper limit on the number of psychotherapy sessions to which a patient is entitled, patients will often feel cheated if they do not get their full entitlement. It would be far better to have no explicit limit, simply offering patients all the psychotherapy that they need.

With this latter policy, clinicians can be allowed maximum flexibility in planning their own therapy schedules. Each clinician can be expected to meet an annual average number of sessions per therapeutic episode. The figure can be based on each clinician's years of experience and training, both prior to and after joining the staff, and on a measure of prior performance, with less experienced therapists being permitted a greater number of sessions per patient. Since it is an average number of sessions that constitutes the contracted standard, each therapist can then be allowed to deviate from that average depending on the nature of each patient's individual problem. Thus, some patients can be discharged after having fewer sessions than the anticipated average, while others may require more sessions than that expected average.

Flexibility should be encouraged not only in duration of therapy but also in the frequency of therapy sessions; duration of sessions; plans for follow-up interviews (Malan, 1980c) or return visits; and in the use of alternatives to face-to-face interviews, such as contact by telephone or by letter. Initial interviews can be set up for ninety minutes or two hours, for example, and later interviews, if needed, can be shortened or lengthened and scheduled more or less frequently, depending on the nature of the presenting problem.

Patients should be encouraged to keep in touch with the agency, and therapists should be encouraged to check in with former patients from time to time. It should be clear to patients that they can return for additional therapeutic interviews anytime they feel the need. Appointments should be negotiated interview by interview. At the end of each interview, patient and therapist can consider together whether an additional appointment seems indicated and, if so, when and for how long it should be scheduled, as well as what subject matter should be discussed and what work should be done before the session takes place. Therapists should avoid the routine ending statement, "See you next week at the same time." The question of whether an additional appointment is indicated lies at the heart of the issue of when enough therapy has been provided. That is, a beginning approach to the question of whether enough therapy has been done is to ask if patients can now manage on their own.

In addition to providing help to the patient, the therapist should be alert for opportunities to provide consultation to the patient regarding salient family-related or work-related issues. If the agency is part of a larger health maintenance organization or is embedded within a public general hospital, staff should be on the alert for other services that can be provided for the patient on the same occasion as the visit for mental health services. In the case of public general hospitals, for example, the prevalence of one-time visits is so high that staff members might profitably assume that they will have but a single opportunity to be of help to the patient and they should "work the waiting room," trying to identify whatever other clinical or educational services are needed and making those services available on the spot.

Flexible Reward Structure

Increasing clinical experience should bring with it increasing efficiency and effectiveness. This expectation provides the rationale for a flexible reward structure for mental health personnel that can be tied to an appropriately calculated expected work product. Annual salary increments and job performance ratings could be related to work productivity during the previous year, for example, and that productivity can be calculated on the basis of whatever variables are crucial to an agency's mandate. Thus, in some cases, salary increments can be tied to absolute average number of sessions per discharge. In other cases, increments can be tied to improvement compared to the previous year, or to total number of patients seen, or to recidivism rate, or to some combination of these or other variables. But clinical directors should be able to negotiate an annual plan for each clinician that sets agreed-upon standards for performance during the coming year and establishes salary increment levels that are associated with those standards.

Concluding Comments

If we step back from the chapter-by-chapter details in this book, the overall conclusions regarding time-limited interventions that one could appropriately come to are the following: (1) Psychotherapy of any variety appears to be generally superior to no psychotherapy, (2) short-term outpatient care appears to be equal in effectiveness to time-unlimited outpatient care, (3) outpatient care appears to be equal in effectiveness to inpatient care, and (4) short-term inpatient care appears to be equal in effectiveness to time-unlimited inpatient care. The implication for public policy is abundantly clear. In legal language, it is the policy of the *least restrictive alternative.*

Cummings (1988) has invoked the concept of the least restrictive alternative in the psychotherapy domain by encouraging the patient to retain the major responsibility for what decisions are made in the therapeutic encounter. He writes:

> *In making a therapeutic contract with the patient, we want to make clear that we are there to serve as a catalyst, but the patient is the one who will do the growing. This contrast is stated: "I will never abandon you as long as you need me, and I will never ask you to do something until you are ready. In return for this I ask you to join me in a partnership to make me obsolete as soon as possible." (pp. 312–313)*

Based on this general orientation to the therapist-patient relationship, Cummings has proposed a simple but yet profound Patient's Bill of Rights that has become a guiding principle in his clinical practice and research: "The patient is entitled to relief from pain, anxiety, and depression in the shortest time possible and with the least intrusive intervention" (1988, p. 312). This Patient's Bill of Rights may well hold the key to the psychotherapy of the future.

The observation that planned short-term psychotherapy is indistinguishable from time-unlimited psychotherapy in its effects is not only the most consistent finding in the psychotherapy literature; it is also the most affirmative. The repeatedly observed ability of mental health professionals to be helpful to their patients in remarkably short periods of time should bring an enormous sense of satisfaction to psychotherapists whose years of training have been designed to enhance their abilities to understand and be of help to troubled people. This book has been prepared in the hopes of making it easier for mental health professionals to find new and congenial ways of meeting those goals.

References

Aiello, T. J. (1979). Short-term group therapy of the hospitalized psychotic. In H. Grayson (Ed.), *Short-term approaches to psychotherapy* (pp. 101-123). New York: Human Sciences Press.

Aldrich, C. K. (1968). Brief psychotherapy: A reappraisal of some theoretical assumptions. *American Journal of Psychiatry, 125,* 585-592.

Altman, L., & Goldstein, J. M. (1988). Impact of HMO model type on mental health service delivery: Variation in treatment and approaches. *Administration in Mental Health, 15,* 246-261.

American Psychiatric Association. (1980). *Diagnostic and statistical manual of mental disorders: DSM-III* (3rd ed.). Washington, DC: American Psychiatric Association.

American Psychiatric Association. (1987). *Diagnostic and statistical manual of mental disorders: DSM-III-R* (3rd ed. revised). Washington, DC: American Psychiatric Association.

Applebaum, S. A. (1975). Parkinson's law in psychotherapy. *International Journal of Psychoanalytic Psychotherapy, 4,* 426-436.

Avnet, H. H. (1965a). Short-term treatment under auspices of a medical insurance plan. *American Journal of Psychiatry, 122,* 147-151.

Avnet, H. H. (1965b). How effective is short-term therapy? In L. R. Wolberg (Ed.), *Short-term psychotherapy* (pp. 7-22). New York: Grune & Stratton.

Balint, E., & Norell, J. S. (Eds.). (1973). *Six minutes for the patient: Interactions in general practice consultation.* London: Tavistock Publications.

Balint, M. (1957). *The doctor, his patient and the illness.* New York: International Universities Press.

Balint, M., Ornstein, P. H., & Balint, E. (1972). *Focal psychotherapy: An example of applied psychoanalysis.* London: Lippincott.

Barkham, M. (1989). Brief prescriptive therapy in two-plus-one sessions: Initial cases from the clinic. *Behavioural Psychotherapy, 17,* 161-175.

Baron, J. (1988). Use of family psychotherapy techniques on the college campus. *Journal of College Student Psychotherapy, 3,* 83-96.

Barten, H. H. (1971). The expanding spectrum of the brief therapies. In H. H. Barten (Ed.), *Brief therapies* (pp. 3-23). New York: Behavioral Publications.

Barth, K., Havik, O. E., Nielsen, G., Haver, B., Mølstad, E., Rogge, H., Skåtun, M., Heiberg, A. N., & Ursin, H. (1988). Factor analysis of the evaluation form for selecting patients for short-term anxiety-provoking psychotherapy: The Bergen Project on brief dynamic psychotherapy. *Psychotherapy and Psychosomatics, 49,* 47-52.

Barth, K., Nielsen, G., Havik, O. E., Haver, B., Mølstad, E., Rogge, H., Skåtun, M., Heiberg, A. N., & Ursin, H. (1988). Assessment for three different forms of short-term dynamic psychotherapy: Findings from the Bergen Project. *Psychotherapy and Psychosomatics, 49,* 153–159.

Bassett, D. L., & Pilowsky, I. (1985). A study of brief psychotherapy for chronic pain. *Journal of Psychosomatic Research, 29,* 259–264.

Bateson, G. (1979). *Mind and nature: A necessary unity.* New York: Dutton.

Bauer, G. P., & Kobos, J. C. (1984). Short-term psychodynamic psychotherapy: Reflections on the past and current practice. *Psychotherapy, 21,* 153–170.

Bauer, G. P., & Kobos, J. C. (1987). *Brief therapy: Short-term psychodynamic intervention.* Northvale, NJ: Jason Aronson.

Beck, A. T. (1967). *Depression: Clinical, experimental, and theoretical aspects.* New York: Hoeber.

Beck, A. T. (1976). *Cognitive therapy and the emotional disorders.* New York: International Universities Press.

Beck, A. T., Rush, A. J., Shaw, B. F., & Emery, G. (1979). *Cognitive therapy of depression.* New York: Guilford Press.

Beckfield, D. F. (1987). Importance of altering global response style in the treatment of agoraphobia. *Psychotherapy, 24, 752–758.*

Beeber, A. R. (1988). A systems model of short-term open-ended group therapy. *Hospital and Community Psychiatry, 39, 537–542.*

Bell, N. W., Abramowitz, S. I., Folkins, C. H., Spensley, J., & Hutchinson, G. L. (1983). Biofeedback, brief psychotherapy and tension headache. *Headache, 23,* 162–173.

Bellak, L. (1984). Intensive brief and emergency psychotherapy. In L. Grinspoon (Ed.), *Psychiatry update: The American Psychiatric Association Annual Review* Vol. III (pp. 11–24). Washington, DC: American Psychiatric Press.

Bellak, L. & Siegel, H. (1983). *Handbook of intensive brief and emergency psychotherapy (B.E.P.).* Larchmont, NY: C.P.S. Inc.

Bellak, L., & Small, L. (1965). *Emergency psychotherapy and brief psychotherapy.* New York: Grune & Stratton.

Bellak, L., & Small, L. (1978). *Emergency psychotherapy and brief psychotherapy* (2nd ed.). New York: Grune & Stratton.

Bergler, E. (1949). *The basic neurosis, oral regression and psychic masochism.* New York: Grune & Stratton.

Bergman, J. S. (1985). *Fishing for barracuda: Pragmatics of brief systemic therapy.* New York: Norton.

Berman, J. S., & Norton, N. C. (1985). Does professional training make a therapist more effective? *Psychological Bulletin, 98,* 401–407.

Binder, J. L., Henry, W. P., & Strupp, H. H. (1987). An appraisal of selection criteria for dynamic psychotherapies and implications for setting time limits. *Psychiatry, 50,* 154–166.

Binder, J. L., Strupp, H. H., & Schacht, T. E. (1983). Countertransference in time-limited dynamic psychotherapy. *Contemporary Psychoanalysis, 19,* 605–623.

Bleich, A., Garb, R., Kottler, M., & Neumann, M. (1988). Short-term psychotherapy with Israeli youth during military service. *Israeli Journal of Psychiatry and Related Sciences, 25,* 88–101.

Bloch, S., Bond, G., Qualls, B., Yalom, I., & Zimmerman, E. (1977). Outcome in psychotherapy evaluated by independent judges. *British Journal of Psychiatry, 131,* 410–414.

Block, L. R. (1985). On the potentiality and limits of time: The single-session group and the cancer patient. *Social Work with Groups, 8,* 81–99.

Bloom, B. L. (1975). *Changing patterns of psychiatric care.* New York: Human

Sciences Press.

Bloom, B. L. (1981). Focused single-session therapy: Initial development and evaluation. In S. Budman (Ed.), *Forms of brief therapy* (pp. 167–216). New York: Guilford Press.

Bloom, B. L. (1984). *Community mental health: A general introduction* (2nd ed.). Monterey, CA: Brooks/Cole.

Bloom, B. L. (1988). *Health psychology: A psychosocial perspective.* Englewood Cliffs, NJ: Prentice-Hall.

Bloom, B. L. (1990). Managing mental health services: Some comments for the overdue debate in psychology. *Community Mental Health Journal, 26,* 107–124.

Blowers, C., Cobb, J., & Mathews, A. (1987). Generalized anxiety: A controlled treatment study. *Behavior Research and Therapy, 25,* 493–502.

Bochner, R., Carruthers, G., Kampmann, J., Steiner, J., & Azarnoff, D. L. (1978). *Handbook of clinical pharmacology.* Boston: Little, Brown.

Boettcher, L. L., & Dowd, E. T. (1988). Comparison of rationales in symptom prescription. *Journal of Cognitive Psychotherapy, 2,* 179–195.

Bonstedt, T., & Baird, S. H. (1979). Providing cost-effective psychotherapy in a health maintenance organization. *Hospital & Community Psychiatry, 30,* 129–132.

Bornstein, M. T., Bornstein, P. H., & Walters, H. A. (1984). Children of divorce: A group treatment manual for research and application. *Journal of Child and Adolescent Psychotherapy, 2,* 267–273.

Bouchard, M-A., Lecomte, C., Carbonneau, H., & Lalonde, F. (1987). Inferential communications of expert psychoanalytically oriented, gestalt and behaviour therapists. *Canadian Journal of Behavioral Science, 19,* 275–286.

Bowen, M. (1978). *Family therapy in clinical practice.* New York: Aronson.

Bowers, T. G., & Clum, G. A. (1988). Relative contribution of specific and nonspecific treatment effects: Meta-analysis of placebo-controlled behavior therapy research. *Psychological Bulletin, 103,* 315–323.

Brabender, V. M. (1985). Time-limited inpatient group therapy: A developmental model. *International Journal of Group Psychotherapy, 35,* 373–390.

Brabender, V. (1988). A closed model of short-term inpatient group psychotherapy. *Hospital and Community Psychiatry, 39,* 542–545.

Breuer, J., & Freud, S. (1895/1957). *Studies on hysteria.* New York: Basic Books.

Brockman, B., Poynton, A., Ryle, A., & Watson, J. P. (1987). Effectiveness of time-limited therapy carried out by trainees: Comparison of two methods. *British Journal of Psychiatry, 151,* 602–610.

Brodaty, H. (1983). Techniques in brief psychotherapy. *Australian and New Zealand Journal of Psychiatry, 17,* 109–115.

Brodaty, H., & Andrews, G. (1983). Brief psychotherapy in family practice: A controlled prospective intervention trial. *British Journal of Psychiatry, 143,* 11–19.

Brown, J. S., & Kosterlitz, N. (1964). Selection and treatment of psychiatric outpatients. *Archives of General Psychiatry, 11,* 425–438.

Brown, L. M. (1984). A single consultation assessment clinic. *British Journal of Psychiatry, 145,* 558.

Brown, S. L. (1980). Dynamic family therapy. In H. Davanloo (Ed.), *Short-term dynamic psychotherapy* (pp. 193–206). Northvale, NJ: Aronson.

Budman, S. H. (1981). Looking toward the future. In S. H. Budman (Ed.), *Forms of brief therapy* (pp. 461–467). New York: Guilford Press.

Budman, S. H., Bennett, M. J., & Wisneski, M. J. (1980). Short-term group psychotherapy: An adult developmental model. *International Journal of Group Psychotherapy, 30,* 63–76.

Budman, S. H., Bennett, M. J., & Wisneski, M. J. (1981). An adult developmental model of short-term group psychotherapy. In S. H. Budman (Ed.), *Forms of brief therapy* (pp. 305–342). New York: Guilford Press.

Budman, S. H., & Clifford, M. (1979). Short-term group therapy for couples in a health maintenance organization. *Professional Psychology: Research and Practice, 10,* 419–429.

Budman, S., Demby, A., & Feldstein, M. L. (1984). Insight into reduced use of medical services after psychotherapy. *Professional Psychology: Research and Practice, 15,* 353–361.

Budman, S. H., Demby, A., Feldstein, M., & Gold, M. (1984). The effects of time-limited group psychotherapy: A controlled study. *International Journal of Group Psychotherapy, 34,* 587–603.

Budman, S., Demby, A., & Randall, M. (1980). Short-term group psychotherapy: Who succeeds, who fails? *Group, 4,* 3–16.

Budman, S. H., Demby, A., Redondo, J. P., Hannan, M., Feldstein, M., Ring, J., & Springer, T. (1988). Comparative outcome in time-limited individual and group psychotherapy. *International Journal of Group Psychotherapy, 38,* 63–86.

Budman, S. H., & Gurman, A. (1983). The practice of brief therapy. *Professional Psychology: Research and Practice, 14,* 277–292.

Budman, S. H., & Gurman, A. S. (1988). *Theory and practice of brief therapy.* New York: Guilford Press.

Budman, S. H., & Springer, T. (1987). Treatment delay, outcome, and satisfaction in time-limited group and individual psychotherapy. *Professional Psychology: Research and Practice, 18,* 647–649.

Budman, S. H., & Stone, J. (1983). Advances in brief psychotherapy: A review of recent literature. *Hospital and Community Psychiatry, 34,* 939–946.

Burke, J. D., White, H. S., & Havens, L. L. (1979). Which short-term therapy? *Archives of General Psychiatry, 36,* 177–186.

Burlingame, G. M., & Behrman, J. A. (1987). Clinician attitudes toward time-limited and time-unlimited therapy. *Professional Psychology: Research and Practice, 18,* 61–65.

Burlingame, G. M., & Fuhriman, A. (1987). Conceptualizing short-term treatment: A comparative review. *The Counseling Psychologist, 15,* 557–595.

Butcher, J. N., & Koss, M. P. (1978). Research on brief and crisis-oriented therapies. In S. L. Garfield & A. E. Bergin (Eds.), *Handbook of psychotherapy and behavior change: An empirical analysis* (2nd ed.) (pp. 725–767). New York: Wiley.

Butcher, J. N., Stelmachers, Z. T., & Maudal, G. R. (1983). Crisis intervention and emergency psychotherapy. In I. Wiener (Ed.), *Clinical methods in psychology* (2nd ed.) (pp. 572–633). New York: Wiley.

Caffey, E. M., Galbrecht, C. R., & Klett, C. J. (1971). Brief hospitalization and after-care in the treatment of schizophrenia. *Archives of General Psychiatry, 24,* 81–86.

Canter, A. (1984). Contemporary short-term psychotherapies. In R. Muñoz (Ed.), *New directions for mental health services,* No. 23 (pp. 13–31). San Francisco: Jossey-Bass.

Cappon, D. (1964). Results of psychotherapy. *British Journal of Psychiatry, 110,* 35–45.

Carmona, P. E. (1988). Changing traditions in psychotherapy: A study of therapists' attitudes. *Clinical Nurse Specialist, 2,* 185–190.

Casey, R. J., & Berman, J. S. (1985). The outcome of psychotherapy with children. *Psychological Bulletin, 98,* 388–400.

Castelnuovo-Tedesco, P. (1965). *The twenty-minute hour: A guide to brief psychotherapy for the physician.* Boston: Little, Brown.

Castelnuovo-Tedesco, P. (1967). The twenty-minute hour: An approach to the post-graduate teaching of psychiatry. *American Journal of Psychiatry, 123,* 786–791.

Castelnuovo-Tedesco, P. (1970). The "20-minute hour" revisited: A follow-up. *Comprehensive Psychiatry, 11,* 108–122.

Castelnuovo-Tedesco, P. (1971). Decreasing the length of psychotherapy: Theoretical and practical aspects of the problem. In S. Arieti (Ed.), *The world biennial of psychiatry and psychotherapy* Vol. 1 (pp. 55–71). New York: Basic Books.

Chapman, P. L. H., & Huygens, I. (1988). An evaluation of three treatment programmes for alcoholism: An experimental study with 6- and 18-month follow-ups. *British Journal of Addiction, 83,* 67–81.

Chick, J., Ritson, B., Connaughton, J., Stewart, A., & Chick, J. (1988). Advice versus extended treatment for alcoholism: A controlled study. *British Journal of Addiction, 83,* 159–170.

Chinen, A. B. (1986). Adult development, self-contexting, and psychotherapy with older adults. *Psychotherapy, 23,* 411–416.

Chubb, H., Nauts, P. L., & Evans, E. L. (1984). The practice of change: A working MRI/brief therapy clinic. *Australian Journal of Family Therapy, 5,* 181–184.

Ciarlo, J. A., Brown, T. R., Edwards, D. W., Kiresuk, T. J., & Newman, F. L. (1986). *Assessing mental health treatment outcome measurement techniques.* DHHS Pub. No. (ADM) 86-1301. Washington, DC: U.S. Government Printing Office.

Clarkin, J. F., & Frances, A. (1982). Selection criteria for the brief psychotherapies. *American Journal of Psychotherapy, 36,* 166–180.

Cochrane, A. L. *Effectiveness and efficiency: Random reflections on health services.* London: Nuffield Provincial Hospitals Trust, 1972.

Cogswell, J. F. (1983). Reflections of a grandfather. *Counseling Psychologist, 11(4),* 61–63.

Cole, N. J., Branch, C. H. H., & Allison, R. B. (1962). Some relationships between social class and the practice of dynamic psychotherapy. *American Journal of Psychiatry, 118,* 1004–1012.

Connors, M. E., Johnson, C. L., & Stuckey, M. K. (1984). Treatment of bulimia with brief psychoeducational group therapy. *American Journal of Psychiatry, 141,* 1512–1516.

Cook, N. R., & Ware, J. H. (1983). Design and analysis methods for longitudinal research. *Annual Review of Public Health, 4,* 1–23.

Courtenay, M. (1968). *Sexual discord in marriage: A field for brief psychotherapy.* Philadelphia: Lippincott.

Cox, A., Rutter, M., & Holbrook, D. (1988). Psychiatric interviewing techniques: A second experimental study: Eliciting feelings. *British Journal of Psychiatry, 152,* 64–72.

Croake, J. W., & Myers, K. M. (1989). Brief family therapy with childhood medical problems. *Individual Psychology, 45,* 159–177.

Cross, D. G., Sheehan, P. W., & Khan, J. A. (1982). Short- and long-term follow-up of clients receiving insight-oriented therapy and behavior therapy. *Journal of Consulting and Clinical Psychology, 50,* 103–112.

Cummings, N. A. (1977a). The anatomy of psychotherapy under national health insurance. *American Psychologist, 32,* 711–718.

Cummings, N. A. (1977b). Prolonged (ideal) versus short-term (realistic) psychotherapy. *Professional Psychology, 8,* 491–501.

Cummings, N. A. (1986). The dismantling of our health system: Strategies for the survival of psychological practice. *American Psychologist, 41,* 426–431.

Cummings, N. A. (1988). Emergence of the mental health complex: Adaptive and maladaptive responses. *Professional Psychology: Research and Practice, 19,* 308–315.

Cummings, N. A., & Duhl, L. J. (1987). The new delivery system. In L. J. Duhl & N. A. Cummings (Eds.), *The future of mental health services: Coping with crisis* (pp. 85–98). New York: Springer.

Cummings, N. A., & Follette, W. T. (1968). Psychiatric services and medical utilization in a prepaid health plan setting: Part II. *Medical Care, 6,* 31–41.

Cummings, N. A., & Follette, W. T. (1976). Brief psychotherapy and medical utilization. In H. Dorken & Associates (Eds.), *The professional psychologist today: New developments in law, health insurance and health practice* (pp. 165–174). San Francisco: Jossey-Bass.

Cummings, N. A., & VandenBos, G. R. (1979). The general practice of psychology. *Professional Psychology, 10,* 430–440.

Curtis, J. T., & Silberschatz, G. (1986). Clinical implications of research on brief dynamic psychotherapy: I. Formulating the patient's problems and goals. *Psychoanalytic Psychology, 3,* 13–25.

Dacey, C. M. (1989). Inpatient group psychotherapy: Cohesion facilitates separation. *Group, 13,* 23–30.

Daley, B. S., & Koppenaal, G. S. (1981). The treatment of women in short-term women's groups. In S. H. Budman (Ed.), *Forms of brief therapy* (pp. 343–357). New York: Guilford Press.

Damon, L., Todd, J., & MacFarlane, K. (1987). Treatment issues with sexually abused young children. *Child Welfare, 66,* 125–137.

Davanloo, H. (Ed.). (1978a). *Basic principles and techniques in short-term dynamic psychotherapy.* New York: Spectrum.

Davanloo, H. (1978b). Short-term dynamic psychotherapy of one to two sessions' duration. In H. Davanloo (Ed.), *Basic principles and techniques in short-term dynamic psychotherapy* (pp. 307–326). New York: Spectrum.

Davanloo, H. (1978c). Evaluation, criteria for selection of patients for short-term dynamic psychotherapy: A metapsychological approach. In H. Davanloo (Ed.), *Basic principles and techniques in short-term dynamic psychotherapy* (pp. 9–34). New York: Spectrum.

Davanloo, H. (1979). Techniques of short-term dynamic psychotherapy. *Psychiatric Clinics of North America, 2,* 11–22.

Davanloo, H. (1980a). Trial therapy. In H. Davanloo (Ed.), *Short-term dynamic psychotherapy* (pp. 99–128). Northvale, NJ: Aronson.

Davanloo, H. (1980b). Response to interpretation. In H. Davanloo (Ed.), *Short-term dynamic psychotherapy* (pp. 75–91). Northvale, NJ: Aronson.

Davanloo, H. (1980c). A method of short-term dynamic psychotherapy. In H. Davanloo (Ed.), *Short-term dynamic psychotherapy* (pp. 43–71). Northvale, NJ: Aronson.

Davanloo, H. (1980d). The technique of crisis evaluation and intervention. In H. Davanloo (Ed.), *Short-term dynamic psychotherapy* (pp. 245–281). Northvale, NJ: Aronson.

Davanloo, H. (1980e) (Ed.). *Short-term dynamic psychotherapy.* Northvale, NJ: Aronson.

de Carufel, F. L., & Piper, W. E. (1988). Group psychotherapy or individual psychotherapy: Patient characteristics as predictive factors. *International Journal of Group Psychotherapy, 38,* 169–188.

de Shazer, S. (1979). On transforming symptoms: An approach to an Erickson procedure. *American Journal of Clinical Hypnosis, 22,* 17–28.

de Shazer, S. (1982). *Patterns of brief family therapy: An ecosystemic approach.* New York: Guilford Press.

de Shazer, S. (1988). *Clues: Investigating solutions in brief therapy.* New York: Norton.

de Shazer, S., Berg, I. K., Lipchik, E., Nunnally, E., Gingerich, W., & Weiner-Davis, M. (1986). Brief therapy: Focused solution development. *Family Process, 25,* 207–222.

de Shazer, S., & Molnar, A. (1984). Four useful interventions in brief family therapy. *Journal of Marital and Family Therapy, 10,* 297–304.

Dinkmeyer, D., & Sherman, R. (1989). Brief Adlerian family therapy. *Individual Psychology, 45,* 148–158.

Donner, J., & Gamson, A. (1968). Experience with multifamily, time-limited, outpatient groups at a community psychiatric clinic. *Psychiatry, 31,* 126–137.

Donovan, J. M. (1987). Brief dynamic psychotherapy: Toward a more comprehensive model. *Psychiatry, 50,* 167–183.

Donovan, J. M., Bennett, M. J., & McElroy, C. M. (1981). The crisis group: Its rationale, format, and outcome. In S. Budman (Ed.), *Forms of brief therapy* (pp. 283–303). New York: Guilford Press.

Dorosin, D., Gibbs, J., & Kaplan, L. (1976). Very brief interventions: A pilot evaluation. *Journal of the American College Health Association, 24,* 191–194.

Dreiblatt, I. S., & Weatherley, D. (1965). An evaluation of the efficacy of brief-contact therapy with hospitalized psychiatric patients. *Journal of Consulting and Clinical Psychology, 29,* 513–519.

Dreyfus, J. K. (1988). The treatment of depression in an ambulatory care setting. *Nurse Practitioner, 13(7),* 14–15, 18, 25–26, 29, 32–33.

Drob, S., & Bernard, H. (1985). Two models of brief group psychotherapy for herpes sufferers. *Group, 9(3),* 14–20.

Dublin, H. S. (1983). A psychodynamic couples' group led by married co-therapists. In M. Rosenbaum (Ed.), *Handbook of short-term therapy groups* (pp. 197–215). New York: McGraw-Hill.

Dubovsky, S. L. (1981). *Psychotherapeutics in primary care.* New York: Grune & Stratton.

Duhl, L. J., & Cummings, N. A. (Eds.). (1987). *The future of mental health services: Coping with crisis.* New York: Springer.

Dulcan, M. K. (1984). Brief psychotherapy with children and their families: The state of the art. *Journal of the American Academy of Child Psychiatry, 23,* 544–551.

Dulcan, M. K., & Piercy, P. A. (1985). A model for teaching and evaluating brief psychotherapy with children and their families. *Professional Psychology: Research and Practice, 16,* 689–700.

Duncan, B. L., & Solovey, A. D. (1989). Strategic-brief therapy: An insight-oriented approach? *Journal of Marital and Family Therapy, 15,* 1–9.

Durlak, J. A. (1979). Comparative effectiveness of paraprofessional and professional helpers. *Psychological Bulletin, 86,* 80–92.

Edelstein, M. G. (1990) *Symptom analysis: A method of brief therapy.* New York: Norton.

Edwards, G., Orford, J., Egert, S., Guthrie, S., Hawker, A., Hensman, C., Mitcheson, M., Oppenheimer, E., & Taylor, C. (1977). Alcoholism: A controlled trial of "treatment" and "advice." *Journal of Studies on Alcohol, 38,* 1004–1031.

Elkin, I. E., Parloff, M. B., Hadley, S. W., & Autry, A. H. (1985). NIMH treatment of depression collaborative research program: Background and research plan. *Archives of General Psychiatry, 42,* 305–316.

Elkin, I. W. E., Weissberg, R. P., & Cowen, E. L. (1988). Evaluation of a planned short-term intervention for schoolchildren with focal adjustment problems. *Journal of Clinical Child Psychology, 17,* 106–115.

Ellis, A. (1962). *Reason and emotion in psychotherapy.* New York: Stuart.

Ellis, A. (1989). Using rational-emotive therapy (RET) as crisis intervention: A single session with a suicidal client. *Individual Psychology, 45,* 75–81.

Ellis, A., & Abrahms, E. (1978). *Brief psychotherapy in medical and health practice.* New York: Springer.

Ellis, A., & Bernard, M. E. (Eds.). (1983). *Rational-emotive approaches to the problems of childhood.* New York: Plenum.

Ellis, A., & Grieger, R. (Eds.). (1977). *Handbook of rational-emotive therapy.* New York: Springer.

Ellis, A., & Harper, R. A. (1961). *A guide to rational living.* Englewood Cliffs, NJ: Prentice-Hall.

Endicott, J., Herz, M. I., & Gibbon, M. (1978). Brief versus standard hospitalization: The differential costs. *American Journal of Psychiatry, 135,* 707–712.

Erickson, M. H. (1977). Hypnotic approaches to therapy. *American Journal of Clinical Hypnosis, 20,* 20–35.

Erstling, S. S., & Devlin, J. (1989). The single-session family interview. *Journal of Family Practice, 28,* 556–560.

Evans, T. D. (1989). Brief therapy: The tradition of individual psychology compared to MRI. *Individual Psychology, 45,* 48–56.

Ewalt, P. L. (1973). The crisis-treatment approach in a child guidance clinic. *Social Casework, 54,* 406–411.

Ewing, C. P. (1978). *Crisis intervention as psychotherapy.* New York: Oxford University Press.

Faden, V. B., & Taube, C. A. (1977). *Length of stay of discharges from non-federal general hospital psychiatric inpatient units, United States, 1975* (Statistical Note No. 133. National Institute of Mental Health). Washington, DC: U.S. Government Printing Office.

Fago, D. P. (1980). Time-unlimited brief and longer-term psychotherapy with rural clients. *Journal of Rural Community Psychology, 1,* 16–23.

Farrelly, F., & Brandsma, J. *Provocative therapy.* Cupertino, CA: Meta Publications, 1974.

Feldman, S., & Goldman, B. (1987). Mental health care in HMOs: Practice and potential. In L. J. Duhl & N. A. Cummings (Eds.), *The future of mental health services: Coping with crisis* (pp. 71–84). New York: Springer.

Fiester, A. R., & Rudestam, K. E. (1975). A multivariate analysis of the early dropout process. *Journal of Consulting and Clinical Psychology, 43,* 528–535.

Fine, S., Gilbert, M., Schmidt, L., Haley, G., Maxwell, A., & Forth, A. (1989). Short-term group therapy with depressed adolescent outpatients. *Canadian Journal of Psychiatry, 34,* 97–102.

Fisch, R. (1982). Erickson's impact on brief psychotherapy. In J. K. Zeig (Ed.). *Ericksonian approaches to hypnosis and psychotherapy* (pp. 155–162). New York: Brunner/Mazel.

Fisher, S. G. (1984). Time-limited brief therapy with families: A one-year follow-up study. *Family Process, 23,* 101–106.

Flegenheimer, W. V. (1982). *Techniques of brief psychotherapy.* New York: Aronson.

Flegenheimer, W. (1985). History of brief psychotherapy. In A. J. Horner (Ed.), *Treating the Oedipal patient in brief psychotherapy* (pp. 7-24). New York: Aronson.

Foley, S. H., O'Malley, S., Rounsaville, B. J., Prusoff, B. A., & Weissman, M. M. (1987). The relationship of patient difficulty to therapist performance in interpersonal psychotherapy of depression. *Journal of Affective Disorders, 12,* 207-217.

Follette, W., & Cummings, N. A. (1967). Psychiatric services and medical utilization in a prepaid health plan setting. *Medical Care, 5,* 25-35.

Fox, R. (1987). Short-term, goal-oriented family therapy. *Social Casework, 68,* 494-499.

Frances, A., & Clarkin, J. F. (1981). No treatment as the prescription of choice. *Archives of General Psychiatry, 38,* 542-545.

Frank, J. D. (1968). Methods of assessing the results of psychotherapy. In R. Porter (Ed.), *The role of learning in psychotherapy* (pp. 38-60). Boston: Little, Brown.

Frank, J. D. (1984). The psychotherapy of anxiety. In L. Grinspoon (Ed.), *Psychiatry update: The American Psychiatric Association Annual Review* Vol. III (pp. 418-426). Washington, DC: American Psychiatric Press.

Free, N. K., Green, B. L., Grace, M. C., Chernus, L. A., & Whitman, R. M. (1985). Empathy and outcome in brief focal dynamic therapy. *American Journal of Psychiatry, 142,* 917-921.

Freeman, D. R. (1982). *Marital crisis and short-term counseling.* New York: Free Press.

Freud, S. (1909/1953). Notes upon a case of obsessional neurosis. In A. Strachey & J. Strachey (Eds.), *Sigmund Freud, M.D., LL.D. Collected papers.* Vol. III (pp. 293-383). London: Hogarth Press.

Friedman, H., & Taub, H. A. (1985). Extended follow-up study of the effects of brief psychological procedures in migraine therapy. *American Journal of Clinical Hypnosis, 28,* 27-33.

Friedman, S., & Pettus, S. (1985). Brief strategic interventions with families of adolescents. *Family Therapy, 12,* 197-210.

Friedrich, W. N., Berliner, L., Urquiza, A. J., & Beilke, R. L. (1988). Brief diagnostic group treatment of sexually abused boys. *Journal of Interpersonal Violence, 3,* 331-343.

Frings, J. (1951). What about brief services? — A report of a study of short-term cases. *Social Casework, 32,* 236-241.

Frommer, M. S., Ames, J. R., Gibson, J. W., & Davis, W. N. (1987). Patterns of symptom change in the short-term group treatment of bulimia. *International Journal of Eating Disorders, 6,* 469-476.

Furman, B., & Ahola, T. (1988). The use of humour in brief therapy. *Journal of Strategic and Systemic Therapies, 7(2),* 3-20.

Gallagher, D. E., & Thompson, L. W. (1983). Effectiveness of psychotherapy for both endogenous and nonendogenous depression in older adult outpatients. *Journal of Gerontology, 38,* 707-712.

Gallagher, T. J. (1987). Accountability and implications for supervision and future training. In L. J. Duhl & N. A. Cummings (Eds.), *The future of mental health services: Coping with crisis* (pp. 117-131). New York: Springer.

Garfield, S. L. (1989). *The practice of brief psychotherapy.* New York: Pergamon Press.

Garfield, S. L., & Affleck, D. C. (1959). An appraisal of duration of stay in outpatient psychotherapy. *Journal of Nervous and Mental Disease, 129,* 492-498.

Gask, L. (1986). What happens when psychiatric out-patients are seen once only? *British Journal of Psychiatry, 148,* 663–666.

Gedo, J. E. (1981). Advances in clinical psychoanalysis. New York: International Universities Press.

Gelso, C. J., & Johnson, D. H. (1983). *Explorations in time-limited counseling and psychotherapy.* New York: Teachers College Press.

Gerald, M. C. (1981). *Pharmacology: An introduction to drugs* (2nd ed.). Englewood Cliffs, NJ: Prentice-Hall.

Getz, W. L., Fujita, B. N., & Allen, D. (1975). The use of paraprofessionals in crisis intervention: Evaluation of an innovative program. *American Journal of Community Psychology, 3,* 135–144.

Gillman, R. D. (1965). Brief psychotherapy: A psychoanalytic view. *American Journal of Psychiatry, 122,* 601–611.

Gilman, A. G., Goodman, L. S., Gilman, A., Mayer, S. E., & Melmon, K. L. (Eds.). (1980). *Goodman and Gilman's The pharmacological basis of therapeutics* (6th ed.). New York: Macmillan.

Glasscote, R., & Fishman, M. E. (1973). *Mental health on the campus: A field study.* Washington, DC: American Psychiatric Association.

Glick, I. D., Hargreaves, W. A., & Goldfield, M. D. (1974). Short vs. long hospitalization: A prospective controlled study: The preliminary results of a one-year follow-up of schizophrenics. *Archives of General Psychiatry, 30,* 363–369.

Glick, I. D., Hargreaves, W. A., Raskin, M., & Kutner, S. J. (1975). Short vs. long hospitalization: A prospective controlled study: II. Results for schizophrenic inpatients. *American Journal of Psychiatry, 132,* 385–390.

Goldberg, D. A., Schuyler, W. R., Bransfield, D., & Savino, P. (1983). Focal group psychotherapy: A dynamic approach. *International Journal of Group Psychotherapy, 33,* 413–431.

Goldberg, I. D., Krantz, G., & Locke, B. Z. (1970). Effect of a short-term outpatient psychiatric therapy benefit on the utilization of medical services in a prepaid group practice medical program. *Medical Care, 8,* 419–428.

Goldberg, R. L., & Green, S. A. (1986). A learning-theory perspective of brief psychodynamic psychotherapy. *American Journal of Psychotherapy, 40,* 70–82.

Goldin, V. (1985). Problems of technique. In A. J. Horner (Ed.), *Treating the Oedipal patient in brief psychotherapy* (pp. 55–74). New York: Aronson.

Goldin, V., & Winston, A. (1985). The impact of short-term dynamic psychotherapy on psychoanalytic psychotherapy. In A. Winston (Ed.), *Clinical and research issues in short-term dynamic psychotherapy* (pp. 62–79). Washington, DC: American Psychiatric Press.

Goldman, W. (1988). Mental health and substance abuse services in HMOs. *Administration in Mental Health, 15,* 189–200.

Goldsmith, S. (1986). *Psychotherapy of people with physical symptoms: Brief strategic approaches.* Lanham, MD: University Press of America.

Good, P. R. (1987). Brief therapy in the age of regapeutics. *American Journal of Orthopsychiatry, 57,* 6–11.

Gordon, V. C., & Gordon, E. M. (1987). Short-term group treatment of depressed women: A replication study in Great Britain. *Archives of Psychiatric Nursing, 1,* 111–124.

Gottschalk, L. A., Mayerson, P., & Gottlieb, A. A. (1967). Prediction and evaluation of outcome in an emergency brief psychotherapy clinic. *Journal of Nervous and Mental Disease, 144,* 77–96.

Grand, S., Rechetnick, J., Podrug, D., & Schwager, E. (1985). *Transference in brief psychotherapy: An approach to the study of psychoanalytic process.* Hillsdale, NJ: Analytic Press.

Graves, E., & Lovato, C. (1981). Utilization of short-stay hospitals in the treatment of mental disorders: 1974–1978. *Vital and Health Statistics of the National Center for Health Statistics.* No. 70. May 22, 1981. Washington DC: U.S. Government Printing Office.

Groddeck, G. (1951). *The unknown self.* New York: Funk & Wagnalls.

Gross, M. L. (1978). *The psychological society.* New York: Random House.

Gruenberg, E. M. (1974). Benefits of short-term hospitalization. In R. Cancro, N. Fox, & L. E. Shapiro (Eds.), *Strategic intervention in schizophrenia: Current developments in treatment* (pp. 251–259). New York: Behavioral Publications.

Gurman, A. S. (1981). Integrative marital therapy: Toward the development of an interpersonal approach. In S. Budman (Ed.), *Forms of brief therapy* (pp. 415–457). New York: Guilford Press.

Gustafson, J. P. (1981). The complex secret of brief psychotherapy in the works of Malan and Balint. In S. Budman (Ed.), *Forms of brief therapy* (pp. 83–128). New York: Guilford Press.

Gustafson, J. P. (1984). An integration of brief dynamic psychotherapy. *American Journal of Psychiatry, 141,* 935–944.

Gustafson, J. P. (1986). *The complex secret of brief psychotherapy.* New York: W. W. Norton.

Hadley, S. W., & Strupp, H. H. (1976). Contemporary views on negative effects: An integrated account. *Archives of General Psychiatry, 33,* 1291–1302.

Haley, J. (1963). *Strategies of psychotherapy.* New York: Grune & Stratton.

Haley, J. (1967). *Advanced techniques of hypnosis and therapy: Selected papers of Milton H. Erickson.* New York: Grune & Stratton.

Haley, J. (1973). *Uncommon therapy: The psychiatric techniques of Milton H. Erickson, M.D.* New York: Norton.

Haley, J. (1984). *Ordeal therapy.* San Francisco: Jossey-Bass.

Haley, J. (1987). *Problem-solving therapy* (2nd ed.). San Francisco: Jossey-Bass.

Hall, A., & Crisp, A. H. (1987). Brief psychotherapy in the treatment of anorexia nervosa: Outcome at one year. *British Journal of Psychiatry, 151,* 185–191.

Hargreaves, W. A., Glick, I. D., Drues, J., Shaustack, J. A., & Feigenbaum, E. (1977). Short vs. long hospitalization: A prospective controlled study: VI: Two-year follow-up results for schizophrenics. *Archives of General Psychiatry, 34,* 305–311.

Hattie, J. A., Sharpley, C. F., & Rogers, H. J. (1984). Comparative effectiveness of professional and paraprofessional helpers. *Psychological Bulletin, 95,* 534–541.

Havens, L. (1986). *Making contact: Uses of language in psychotherapy.* Cambridge, MA: Harvard University Press.

Hawton, K., McKeown, S., Day, A., Martin, P., O'Connor, M., & Yule, J. (1987). Evaluation of out-patient counselling compared with general practitioner care following overdoses. *Psychological Medicine, 17,* 751–761.

Hazelrigg, M. D., Cooper, H. M., & Borduin, C. M. (1987). Evaluating the effectiveness of family therapies: An integrative review and analysis. *Psychological Bulletin, 101,* 428–442.

Herman, J. L., & Schatzow, E. (1987). Recovery and verification of memories of childhood sexual trauma. *Psychoanalytic Psychology, 4,* 1–14.

Herz, M. I., Endicott, J., & Spitzer, R. L. (1975). Brief hospitalization of patients with families: Initial results. *American Journal of Psychiatry, 132,* 413–418.

Herz, M. I., Endicott, J., & Spitzer, R. L. (1976). Brief versus standard hospitalization: The families. *American Journal of Psychiatry, 133,* 795–801.

Hildebrand, H. P. (1986). Brief psychotherapy. *Psychoanalytic Psychology, 3,* 1–12.

Hill, C. E., Helms, J. E., Tichenor, V., Spiegel, S. B., O'Grady, K. E., & Perry, E. S. (1988). Effects of therapist response modes in brief psychotherapy. *Journal of Counseling Psychology, 35,* 222–233.

Hoch, P. H. (1965). Short-term versus long-term therapy. In L. W. Wolberg (Ed.), *Short-term psychotherapy* (pp. 51–66). New York: Grune & Stratton.

Hoffman, D. L., & Remmel, M. L. (1975). Uncovering the precipitant in crisis intervention. *Social Casework, 56,* 259–267.

Hoppe, E. W. (1977). Treatment dropouts in hindsight: A follow-up study. *Community Mental Health Journal, 13,* 307–313.

Horner, A. J. (1985). The Oedipus complex. In A. J. Horner (Ed.), *Treating the Oedipal patient in brief psychotherapy* (pp. 25–54). New York: Aronson.

Horowitz, L. M., & Vitkus, J. (1986). The interpersonal basis of psychiatric symptoms. *Clinical Psychological Review, 6,* 443–469.

Horowitz, M. (1976). *Stress response syndromes.* New York: Aronson.

Horowitz, M., & Kaltreider, N. (1978). Brief therapy of the stress response syndrome. *Psychiatric Clinics of North America, 2,* 365–378.

Horowitz, M., Marmar, C., Krupnick, J., Wilner, N., Kaltreider, N., & Wallerstein, R. (1984a). *Personality styles and brief psychotherapy.* New York: Basic Books.

Horowitz, M., Marmar, C. R., Weiss, D. S., Kaltreider, N. B., & Wilner, N. R. (1986). Comprehensive analysis of change after brief dynamic psychotherapy. *American Journal of Psychiatry, 143,* 582–589.

Horowitz, M., Wilner, N., & Alvarez, W. (1979). Impact of event scale: A measure of subjective stress. *Psychosomatic Medicine, 41,* 209–218.

Horowitz, M. J. (1987). *States of mind: Configurational analysis of individual psychology* (2nd ed.). New York: Plenum.

Horowitz, M. J., Marmar, C., Weiss, D. S., DeWitt, K., & Rosenbaum, R. (1984b). Brief psychotherapy of bereavement reactions: The relationship of process to outcome. *Archives of General Psychiatry, 41,* 438–448.

Howard, K. I., Kopta, S. M., Krause, M. S., & Orlinsky, D. E. (1986). The dose-effect relationship in psychotherapy. *American Psychologist, 41,* 159–164.

Hoyt, M. F. (1985). Therapist resistances to short-term dynamic psychotherapy. *Journal of the American Academy of Psychoanalysis, 13,* 93–112.

Hoyt, M. F., & Farrell, D. (1984–85). Countertransference difficulties in a time-limited psychotherapy. *International Journal of Psychoanalytic Psychotherapy, 10,* 191–203.

Husby, R., Dahl, A. A., Dahl, C-I., Heiberg, A. N., Olafsen, O. M., & Weisaeth, L. (1985). Short-term dynamic psychotherapy: II. Prognostic value of characteristics of patients studied by a 2-year follow-up of 39 neurotic patients. *Psychotherapy and Psychosomatics, 43,* 8–16.

Jacobson, G. F., Wilner, D. M., Morley, W. E., Schneider, S., Strickler, M., & Sommer, G. J. (1965). The scope and practice of an early-access brief treatment psychiatric center. *American Journal of Psychiatry, 121,* 1176–1182.

Jacobson, N. S., & Margolin, G. (1979). *Marital therapy: Strategies based on social learning and behavior exchange principles.* New York: Bruner/Mazel.

Jameson, J., Shuman, L. J., & Young, W. W. (1978). The effects of outpatient psychiatric utilization on the costs of providing third-party coverage. *Medical*

Care, 16, 383-399.

Johnson, D. H., & Gelso, C. J. (1980). The effectiveness of time limits in counseling and psychotherapy: A critical review. *Counseling Psychologist, 9,* 70-83.

Jones, E. (1955). *The life and work of Sigmund Freud.* New York: Basic Books.

Jones, E. E. (1980). Multidimensional change in psychotherapy. *Journal of Clinical Psychology, 36,* 544-547.

Jones, E. E., Cumming, J. D., & Horowitz, M. J. (1988). Another look at the nonspecific hypothesis of therapeutic effectiveness. *Journal of Consulting and Clinical Psychology, 56,* 48-55.

Jones, K. R., & Vischi, T. R. (1979). Impact of alcohol, drug abuse and mental health treatment on medical care utilization: A review of the research literature. *Medical Care, 17,* (Supp.), 1-82.

Kaffman, M. (1963). Short term family therapy. *Family Process, 2,* 216-234.

Kanas, N., Stewart, P., & Haney, K. (1988). Content and outcome in a short-term therapy group for schizophrenic outpatients. *Hospital and Community Psychiatry, 39,* 437-439.

Karasu, T. B. (1987). The psychotherapy of the future. *Psychosomatics, 28,* 380-381, 384.

Keilson, M. V., Dworkin, F. H., & Gelso, C. J. (1979). The effectiveness of time-limited psychotherapy in a university counseling center. *Journal of Clinical Psychology, 35,* 631-636.

Keller, A. (1984). Planned brief psychotherapy in clinical practice. *British Journal of Medical Psychology, 57,* 347-361.

Kiesler, C. A. (1982). Mental hospitals and alternative care: Noninstitutionalization as potential public policy for mental patients. *American Psychologist, 37,* 1051-1057.

Kinston, W., & Bentovim, A. (1981). Creating a focus for brief marital or family therapy. In S. Budman (Ed.), *Forms of brief therapy* (pp. 361-386). New York: Guilford Press.

Kirshner, L. A. (1988). A model of time-limited treatment for the older patient. *Journal of Geriatric Psychiatry, 21,* 155-168.

Kleber, R. J., & Brom, D. (1987). Psychotherapy and pathological grief controlled outcome study. *Israeli Journal of Psychiatry and Related Sciences, 24,* 99-109.

Klein, R. H. (1985). Some principles of short-term group therapy. *International Journal of Group Psychotherapy, 35,* 309-330.

Klerman, G. L. (1983). The efficacy of psychotherapy as the basis for public policy. *American Psychologist, 38,* 929-934.

Klerman, G. L., Budman, S., Berwick, D., Weissman, M. M., Damico-White, J., Demby, A., & Feldstein, M. (1987). Efficacy of a brief psychosocial intervention for symptoms of stress and distress among patients in primary care. *Medical Care, 25,* 1078-1088.

Klerman, G. L., & Weissman, M. M. (1982). Interpersonal psychotherapy theory and research. In A. J. Rush (Ed.), *Short-term psychotherapies for depression* (pp. 88-106). New York: Guilford Press.

Klerman, G. L., Weissman, M. M., Rounsaville, B. J., & Chevron, E. S. (1984a). *Interpersonal psychotherapy of depression.* New York: Basic Books.

Klerman, G. L., Weissman, M. M., Rounsaville, B. J., & Chevron, E. S. (1984b). Interpersonal psychotherapy for depression. In L. Grinspoon (Ed.), *Psychiatry update: The American Psychiatric Association Annual Review* Vol. III (pp. 56-67). Washington, DC: American Psychiatric Press.

Koegler, R. R. (1966). Brief therapy with children. In G. J. Wayne & R. R. Koegler (Eds.), *Emergency psychiatry and brief therapy* (pp. 155-175). Boston: Little, Brown.

Kogan, L. S. (1957a). The short-term case in a family agency Part I: The study plan. *Social Casework, 38,* 231-238.

Kogan, L. S. (1957b). The short-term case in a family agency Part II: Results of study. *Social Casework, 38,* 296-302.

Kogan, L. S. (1957c). The short-term case in a family agency Part III. Further results and conclusion. *Social Casework, 38,* 366-374.

Koss, M. P., & Butcher, J. N. (1986). Research on brief psychotherapy. In A. E. Bergin & S. L. Garfield (Eds.), *Handbook of psychotherapy and behavior change: An empirical analysis* (3rd ed.) (pp. 627-670). New York: Wiley.

Koss, M. P., Butcher, J. N., & Strupp, H. H. (1986). Brief psychotherapy methods in clinical research. *Journal of Clinical and Consulting Psychology, 54,* 60-67.

Koss, M. P., Butcher, J. N., & Strupp, H. H. (1986). Brief psychotherapy methods in clinical research. *Journal of Consulting and Clinical Psychology, 54,* 60-67.

Kovacs, A. L. (1982). Survival in the 1980s: On the theory and practice of brief psychotherapy. *Psychotherapy: Theory, Research and Practice, 19,* 142-159.

Kreilkamp, T. (1989). *Time-limited, intermittent therapy with children and families.* New York: Bruner/Mazel.

Krupnick, J. L., & Horowitz, M. J. (1985). Brief psychotherapy with vulnerable patients: An outcome assessment. *Psychiatry, 48,* 223-233.

La Court, M. (1988). The HMO crisis: Danger/opportunity. *Family Systems Medicine, 6,* 80-93.

Lambert, M. J. (1979). Characteristics of patients and their relationship to outcome in brief psychotherapy. *Psychiatric Clinics of North America, 2,* 111-123.

Lambert, M. J., Shapiro, D. A., & Bergin, A. E. (1986). The effectiveness of psychotherapy. In S. L. Garfield & A. E. Bergin (Eds.), *Handbook of psychotherapy and behavior change.* (3rd ed.) (pp. 157-211). New York: Wiley.

Landman, J. T., & Dawes, R. M. (1982). Psychotherapy outcome: Smith and Glass' conclusions stand up under scrutiny. *American Psychologist, 37,* 504-516.

Langsley, D. G. (1988). The definition of a psychiatrist: Eight years later. *American Journal of Psychiatry, 145,* 469-475.

Lazare, A., Cohen, F., Jacobson, A. M., Williams, M. W., Mignone, R. J., & Zisook, S. (1972). The walk-in patient as a "customer": A key dimension in evaluation and treatment. *American Journal of Orthopsychiatry, 42,* 872-883.

Lazarus, L. W. (1988). Self-psychology — Its application to brief psychotherapy with the elderly. *Journal of Geriatric Psychiatry, 21,* 109-125.

Lefkovitz, P. M. (1988). The short-term program. *New Directions in Mental Health Services.* No. 38, 31-49.

Leibenluft, E., & Goldberg, R. L. (1987). Guidelines for short-term inpatient psychotherapy. *Hospital and Community Psychiatry, 38,* 38-43.

Leibovich, M. A. (1981). Short-term psychotherapy for the borderline personality disorder. *Psychotherapy and Psychosomatics, 35,* 257-264.

Leon, I. G. (1987). Short-term psychotherapy for perinatal loss. *Psychotherapy, 24,* 186-195.

Lettieri-Marks, D. (1987). Research in short-term inpatient group psychotherapy: A critical review. *Archives of Psychiatric Nursing, 1,* 407-421.

Lewin, K. K. (1970). *Brief encounters: Brief psychotherapy.* St. Louis, MO: Green.

Lewinsohn, P. M., Sullivan, J. M., & Grosscup, S. J. (1982). Behavioral therapy:

Clinical applications. In A. J. Rush (Ed.), *Short-term psychotherapies for depression* (pp. 50–87). New York: Guilford Press.

Littlepage, G. E., Kosloski, K. D., Schnelle, J. F., McNees, M. P., & Gendrich, J. C. (1976). The problems of early outpatient terminations from community mental health centers: A problem for whom? *Journal of Community Psychology, 4*, 164–167.

Luborsky, L. (1984). *Principles of psychoanalytic psychotherapy: A manual for supportive-expressive treatment*. New York: Basic Books.

Luborsky, L., Singer, B., & Luborsky, L. (1975). Comparative studies of psychotherapies: Is it true that "everyone has won and all must have prizes"? *Archives of General Psychiatry, 32*, 995–1008.

MacKenzie, K. R. (1988). Recent developments in brief psychotherapy. *Hospital and Community Psychiatry, 39*, 742–752.

MacKenzie, K. R., & Livesley, W. J. (1986). Outcome and process measures in brief group psychotherapy. *Psychiatric Annals, 16*, 715–720.

MacMahon, B., & Pugh, T. F. (1970). *Epidemiology: Principles and methods*. Boston: Little, Brown.

Malan, D. H. (1963). *A study of brief psychotherapy,* London: Tavistock.

Malan, D. H. (1976). *The frontier of brief psychotherapy: An example of the convergence of research and clinical practice*. New York: Plenum.

Malan, D. H. (1978a). Evaluation, criteria for selection of patients. In H. Davanloo (Ed.), *Basic principles and techniques in short-term dynamic psychotherapy* (pp. 85–97). New York: Spectrum.

Malan, D. H. (1978b). Principles of technique in short-term dynamic psychotherapy. In H. Davanloo (Ed.), *Basic principles and techniques in short-term dynamic psychotherapy* (pp. 332–342). New York: Spectrum.

Malan, D. H. (1979). *Individual psychotherapy and the science of psychodynamics*. London: Butterworth.

Malan, D. H. (1980a). The most important development in psychotherapy since the discovery of the unconscious. In H. Davanloo (Ed.), *Short-term dynamic psychotherapy* (pp. 13–23). Northvale, NJ: Aronson.

Malan, D. H. (1980b). The nature of science and the validity of psychotherapy. In H. Davanloo (Ed.), *Short-term dynamic psychotherapy* (pp. 319–347). Northvale, NJ: Aronson.

Malan, D. H. (1980c). Basic principles and technique of the follow-up interview. In H. Davanloo (Ed.), *Short-term dynamic psychotherapy* (pp. 349–377). Northvale, NJ: Aronson.

Malan, D. H., Heath, E. S., Bacal, H. A., & Balfour, F. H. G. (1975). Psychodynamic changes in untreated neurotic patients. II. Apparently genuine improvements. *Archives of General Psychiatry, 32*, 110–126.

Malan, D. H., Rayner, E. H., Bacal, H. A., Heath, E. S., & Balfour, F. H. G. (1968). Psychodynamic assessment of the outcome of psychotherapy. In R. Porter (Ed.), *The role of learning in psychotherapy* (pp. 61–67). Boston: Little, Brown.

Malcolm, J. (1987). J'appelle un chat un chat. *The New Yorker, April 20, 1987,* 84–92, 95–102.

Manaster, G. J. (1989). Clinical issues in brief psychotherapy: A summary and conclusion. *Individual Psychology, 45*, 243–247.

Mann, J. (1973). *Time-limited psychotherapy*. Cambridge, MA: Harvard University Press.

Mann, J. (1981). The core of time-limited psychotherapy: Time and the central issue.

In S. Budman (Ed.), *Forms of brief therapy* (pp. 25–43). New York: Guilford Press.

Mann, J. (1984). Time limited psychotherapy. In L. Grinspoon (Ed.), *Psychiatry update: The American Psychiatric Association Annual Review* Vol. III (pp. 35–44). Washington, DC: American Psychiatric Press.

Mann, J., & Goldman, R. (1982). *A casebook in time-limited psychotherapy.* New York: McGraw-Hill.

Marcovitz, R. J., & Smith, J. E. (1986). Short-term group therapy: A review of the literature. *International Journal of Short-term Psychotherapy, 1,* 49–57.

Marks, I. (1986). Behavioural psychotherapy in general psychiatry: Helping patients to help themselves. *British Journal of Psychiatry, 150,* 593–597.

Marmar, C. R., & Freeman, M. (1988). Brief dynamic psychotherapy of post-traumatic stress disorders: Management of narcissistic regression. *Journal of Traumatic Stress, 1,* 323–337.

Marmar, C. R., Horowitz, M. J., Weiss, D. S., Wilner, N. R., & Kaltreider, N. B. (1988). A controlled trial of brief psychotherapy and mutual-help group treatment of conjugal bereavement. *American Journal of Psychiatry, 145,* 203–209.

Marmar, C. R., Weiss, D. S., & Gaston, L. (1989). Toward the validation of the California Therapeutic Alliance Rating System. *Psychological Assessment: A Journal of Consulting and Clinical Psychology, 1,* 46–52.

Marmor, J. (1968). New directions in psychoanalytic theory and therapy. In J. Marmor (Ed.), *Modern psychoanalysis: New directions and perspectives* (pp. 3–15). New York: Basic Books.

Marmor, J. (1979). Short-term dynamic psychotherapy. *American Journal of Psychiatry, 136,* 149–155.

Marziali, E. (1984). Three viewpoints on the therapeutic alliance: Similarities, differences, and associations with psychotherapy outcome. *Journal of Nervous and Mental Disease, 172,* 417–423.

Marziali, E., Marmar, C., & Krupnick, J. (1981). Therapeutic alliance scales: Development and relationship to psychotherapy outcome. *American Journal of Psychiatry, 138,* 361–364.

Marziali, E. A. (1987). People in your life: Development of a social support measure for predicting psychotherapy outcome. *Journal of Nervous and Mental Disease, 175,* 327–338.

Mathews, B. (1988). Planned short-term therapy utilizing the techniques of Jay Haley and Milton Erickson: A guide for the practitioner. *Psychotherapy in Private Practice, 6,* 103–118.

Mattes, J. A., Rosen, B., & Klein, D. F. (1977). Comparison of the clinical effectiveness of "short" *versus* "long" stay psychiatric hospitalization. II. Results of a 3-year posthospital follow-up. *Journal of Nervous and Mental Disease, 165,* 387–394.

Mattes, J. A., Rosen, B., Klein, D. F., & Millan, D. (1977). Comparison of the clinical effectiveness of "short" versus "long" stay psychiatric hospitalization. III. Further results of a 3-year posthospital follow-up. *Journal of Nervous and Mental Disease, 165,* 395–402.

Maturana, H. R., & Varela, F. J. (1980). *Autopoiesis and cognition: The realization of the living.* Boston: Reidel.

May, R. (1988). Brief psychotherapy with college students. *Journal of College Student Psychotherapy, 3,* 17–38.

McGuire, T. G., & Frisman, L. K. (1983). Reimbursement policy and cost-effective mental health care. *American Psychologist, 38,* 935–940.

McGuire, T. J. (1988). A time-limited dynamic approach to adolescent inpatient group psychotherapy. *Adolescence, 23(90)*, 373–382.

McLean, P. (1982). Behavior therapy: Theory and research. In A. J. Rush (Ed.), *Short-term psychotherapies for depression* (pp. 19–49). New York: Guilford Press.

Meltzoff, J., & Kornreich, M. (1970). *Research in psychotherapy*, New York: Atherton.

Mendel, W. M. (1967). Brief hospitalization techniques. In J. Masserman (Ed.), *Current psychiatric therapies: 1966* Vol. 6 (pp. 310–316). New York: Grune & Stratton.

Menninger, K. (1963). *The vital balance.* New York: Viking Press.

Meyer, A-E., Bolz, W., Stuhr, U., & Burzig, G. (1981). VI. Outcome results by clinical evaluation based on the blind group ratings. *Psychotherapy and Psychosomatics, 35*, 199–207.

Meyer, N. G., & Taube, C. A. (1973). *Length of stay of admissions to state and county mental hospitals, United States, 1971* (Statistical Note 74, National Institute of Mental Health). Washington, DC: U.S. Government Printing Office.

Migone, P. (1985). Short-term dynamic psychotherapy from a psychoanalytic viewpoint. *Psychoanalytic Review, 72*, 615–634.

Miller, W. R., & Hester, R. K. (1986). Inpatient alcoholism treatment: Who benefits? *American Psychologist, 41*, 794–805.

Mohl, P. C. (1988). Brief supportive psychotherapy by the primary care physician. *Texas Medicine, 84*, 28–32.

Moley, V. A. (1987). Brief therapy and eating disorders. *Family Therapy Collections, 20*, 40–54.

Morokoff, P. J., & LoPiccolo, J. (1986). A comparative evaluation of minimal therapist contact and 15-session treatment for female orgasmic dysfunction. *Journal of Consulting and Clinical Psychology, 54*, 294–300.

Mumford, E., & Schlesinger, H. J. (1987). Assessing consumer benefit: Cost offset as an incidental effect of psychotherapy. *General Hospital Psychiatry, 9*, 360–363.

Mumford, E., Schlesinger, H. J., & Glass, G. V. (1982). The effects of psychological intervention on recovery from surgery and heart attacks: An analysis of the literature. *American Journal of Public Health, 72*, 141–151.

Mumford, E., Schlesinger, H. J., Glass, G. V., Patrick, C., & Cuerdon, T. (1984). A new look at evidence about reduced cost of medical utilization following mental health treatment. *American Journal of Psychiatry, 141*, 1145–1158.

National Center for Health Statistics (1989). *Health, United States, 1988.* DHHS Pub. No. (PHS) 89-1232. Washington, DC: U.S. Government Printing Office.

Neu, C., Prusoff, B. A., & Klerman, G. L. (1978). Measuring the interventions used in the short-term interpersonal psychotherapy of depression. *American Journal of Orthopsychiatry, 48*, 629–636.

Nielsen, G., Barth, K., Haver, B., Havik, O. E., Mølstad, E., Rogge, H., & Skåtun, M. (1988). Brief dynamic psychotherapy for patients presenting physical symptoms. *Psychotherapy and Psychosomatics, 50*, 35–41.

O'Hanlon, W. H., & Weiner-Davis, M. (1989). *In search of solutions: A new direction in psychotherapy.* New York: Norton.

Oldham, J. M., & Russakoff, L. M. (1987). *Dynamic therapy in brief hospitalization.* Northvale, NJ: Aronson.

Oppenheimer, B. T. (1984). Short-term small group intervention for college freshmen. *Journal of Counseling Psychology, 31*, 45–53.

Oremland, J. D. (1976) A curious resolution of a hysterical symptom. *International Review of Psycho-Analysis, 3*, 437–477.

Palazzoli, M. S., Boscolo, L., Cecchin, G., & Prata, G. (1978). *Paradox and counter-paradox*. New York: Aronson.

Parad, H. J., & Parad, L. G. (1968). A study of crisis-oriented planned short-term treatment: Part I. *Social Casework, 49*, 346–355.

Parad, L. G. (1971). Short-term treatment: An overview of historical trends, issues, and potentials. *Smith College Studies in Social Work, 41*, 119–146.

Parad, L. G., & Parad, H. J. (1968). A study of crisis-oriented planned short-term treatment: Part II. *Social Casework, 49*, 418–426.

Parloff, M. B. (1982). Psychotherapy research evidence and reimbursement decisions: Bambi meets Godzilla. *American Journal of Psychiatry, 139*, 718–727.

Parmenter, G., Smith, J. C., & Cecic, N. A. (1987). Parallel and conjoint short-term group therapy for school-age children and their parents: A model. *International Journal of Group Psychotherapy, 37*, 239–254.

Peake, T. H., & Ball, J. D. (1987). Brief psychotherapy: Planned therapeutic change for changing times. *Psychotherapy in Private Practice, 5(4)*, 53–63.

Peake, T. H., Borduin, C. M., & Archer, R. P. (1988). *Brief psychotherapies: Changing frames of mind*. Beverly Hills, CA: Sage.

Pekarik, G. (1983). Follow-up adjustment of outpatient dropouts. *American Journal of Orthopsychiatry, 53*, 501–511.

Perls, R. D., & Perls, S. R. (1983). A workshop approach to couples' therapy. In M. Rosenbaum (Ed.), *Handbook of short-term therapy groups* (pp. 217–226). New York: McGraw-Hill.

Pew, M. L. (1989). Brief marriage therapy. *Individual Psychology, 45*, 191–200.

Phillips, E. L. (1985a). *A guide for therapists and patients to short-term psychotherapy*. Springfield, IL: Thomas.

Phillips, E. L. (1985b). *Psychotherapy revised: New frontiers in research and practice*. Hillsdale, NJ: Erlbaum.

Phillips, E. L., Gershenson, J., & Lyons, G. (1977). On time-limited writing therapy. *Psychological Reports, 41*, 707–712.

Phillips, E. L., & Wiener, D. N. (1966). *Short-term psychotherapy and structured behavior change*. New York: McGraw-Hill.

Piper, W. E., Debbane, E. G., Bienvenu, J. P., & Garant, J. (1984). A comparative study of four forms of psychotherapy. *Journal of Consulting and Clinical Psychology, 52*, 268–279.

Piper, W. E., de Carufel, F. L., & Szkrumelak, N. (1985). Patient predictors of process and outcome in short-term individual psychotherapy. *Journal of Nervous and Mental Disease, 173*, 726–733.

Poey, K. (1985). Guidelines for the practice of brief, dynamic group therapy. *International Journal of Group Psychotherapy, 35*, 331–354.

Powers, R. L., & Griffith, J. (1989). Single-session psychotherapy involving two therapists. *Individual Psychology, 45*, 99–125.

Prazoff, M., Joyce, A. S., & Azim, H. F. A. (1986). Brief crisis group psychotherapy: One therapist's model. *Group, 10*, 34–40.

Rabkin, R. (1977). *Strategic psychotherapy: Brief and symptomatic treatment*. New York: Basic Books.

Rasmussen, A., & Messer, S. B. (1986). A comparison and critique of Mann's time-limited psychotherapy and Davanloo's short-term dynamic psychotherapy. *Bulletin of the Menninger Clinic, 50*, 163–184.

Rauch, S. P., Brack, C. J., & Orr, D. P. (1987). School-based, short-term group treatment for behaviorally disturbed young adolescent males: A pilot intervention. *Journal of School Health, 57*, 19–22.

Reed, L. S., Myers, E. S., & Scheidemandel, P. L. (1972). *Health insurance and psychiatric care: Utilization and cost*. Washington, DC: American Psychiatric Association.

Regier, D. A., Goldberg, I. D., & Taube, C. A. (1978). The de facto U.S. mental health services system. *Archives of General Psychiatry, 35,* 685–693.

Reich, J., & Neenan, P. (1986). Principles common to different short-term psychotherapies. *American Journal of Psychotherapy, 40,* 62–69.

Reider, N. (1955). A type of psychotherapy based on psychoanalytic principles. *Bulletin of the Menninger Clinic, 19,* 111–128.

Riessman, C. K., Rabkin, J. G., & Struening, E. L. (1977). Brief versus standard psychiatric hospitalization: A critical review of the literature. *Community Mental Health Review, 2(2),* 1, 3–10.

Rinsley, D. B. (1986). Successful treatment of a case of ocular tic utilizing brief, intensive psychoanalytic psychotherapy. *Bulletin of the Menninger Clinic, 50,* 447–455.

Robinson, H. A., Redlich, F. C., & Myers, J. K. (1954). Social structure and psychiatric treatment. *American Journal of Orthopsychiatry, 24,* 307–316.

Rockwell, W. J. K. (1987). Brief psychotherapy of sexual impotence in college students. *Journal of College Student Psychotherapy, 1(4),* 119–131.

Rogawski, A. S. (1982). Current status of brief psychotherapy. *Bulletin of the Menninger Clinic, 46,* 331–351.

Rokach, A. (1987). Anger and aggression control training: Replacing attack with interaction. *Psychotherapy, 24,* 353–362.

Rosegrant, J. (1988). A dynamic/expressive approach to brief inpatient group psychotherapy. *Group, 12,* 103–112.

Rosen, B., Katzoff, A., Carrillo, C., & Klein, D. F. (1976). Clinical effectiveness of "short" vs "long" psychiatric hospitalization. I. Inpatient results. *Archives of General Psychiatry, 33,* 1316–1322.

Rosen, J. C., & Wiens, A. N. (1979). Changes in medical problems and use of medical services following psychological intervention. *American Psychologist, 34,* 420–431.

Rosenbaum, C. P. (1964). Events of early therapy and brief therapy. *Archives of General Psychiatry, 10,* 506–512.

Rosenbaum, C. P., & Beebe, J. E. (1975). *Psychiatric treatment: Crisis/clinic/consultation*. New York: McGraw-Hill.

Rosenbaum, M. (Ed.). (1983). *Handbook of short-term therapy groups*. New York: McGraw-Hill.

Rosenthal, A. J., & Levine, S. V. (1970). Brief psychotherapy with children: A preliminary report. *American Journal of Psychiatry, 127,* 646–651.

Rosenthal, A. J., & Levine, S. V. (1971). Brief psychotherapy with children: Process of therapy. *American Journal of Psychiatry, 128,* 141–146.

Rosenthal, D., & Frank, J. D. (1958). The fate of psychiatric clinic outpatients assigned to psychotherapy. *Journal of Nervous and Mental Disease, 127,* 330–343.

Rounsaville, B. J., & Chevron, E. S. (1982). Interpersonal psychotherapy: Clinical applications. In A. J. Rush (Ed.), *Short-term psychotherapies for depression* (pp. 107–142). New York: Guilford Press.

Rounsaville, B. J., Chevron, E. S., Prusoff, B. A., Elkin, I., Imber, S., Sotsky, S., & Watkins, J. (1987). The relation between specific and general dimensions of the psychotherapy process in interpersonal psychotherapy of depression. *Journal of Consulting and Clinical Psychology, 55,* 379–384.

Rounsaville, B. J., Gawin, F., & Kleber, H. (1985). Interpersonal psychotherapy adapted for ambulatory cocaine abusers. *American Journal of Drug and Alcohol Abuse, 11,* 171–191.

Rounsaville, B. J., O'Malley, S., Foley, S., & Weissman, M. M. (1988). Role of manual-guided training in the conduct and efficacy of interpersonal psychotherapy for depression. *Journal of Consulting and Clinical Psychology, 56,* 681–688.

Rubin, Z., & Mitchell, C. (1976). Couples research as couples counseling. *American Psychologist, 36,* 17–25.

Rush, A. J. (Ed.). (1982). *Short-term psychotherapies for depression.* New York: Guilford Press.

Rush, A. J. (1984). Cognitive therapy. In L. Grinspoon (Ed.), *Psychiatry update: The American Psychiatric Association Annual Review* Vol. III (pp. 44–56). Washington, DC: American Psychiatric Press.

Rush, A. J., & Giles, D. E. (1982). Cognitive therapy: Theory and research. In A. J. Giles (Ed.), *Short-term psychotherapies for depression* (pp. 143–181). New York: Guilford Press.

Ryder, D. (1988). Minimal intervention: A little quality for a lot of quantity? *Behaviour Change, 5,* 100–107.

Sabin, J. E. (1981). Short-term group psychotherapy: Historical antecedents. In S. H. Budman (Ed.), *Forms of brief therapy* (pp. 271–282). New York: Guilford Press.

Sachs, J. S. (1983). Negative factors in brief psychotherapy: An empirical assessment. *Journal of Consulting and Clinical Psychology, 51,* 557–564.

Sadock, B., Newman, L., & Normand, W. C. (1968). Short-term group psychotherapy in a psychiatric walk-in clinic. *American Journal of Orthopsychiatry, 38,* 724–732.

Salvendy, J. T. (1989). Brief group psychotherapy at retirement. *Group, 13,* 43–57.

Sarvis, M. A., Dewees, S., & Johnson, R. F. (1959). A concept of ego-oriented psychotherapy. *Psychiatry, 22,* 277–287.

Scheffler, R. M. (1987). The economics of mental health care in a changing economic and health care environment. In L. J. Duhl & N. A. Cummings (Eds.), *The future of mental health services: Coping with crisis* (pp. 47–53). New York: Springer.

Scheidlinger, S. (1984). Short-term group psychotherapy for children: An overview. *International Journal of Group Psychotherapy, 34,* 573–585.

Schlesinger, H. J. (1984). Research in dynamic psychotherapy. *Psychoanalytic Psychology, 1,* 83–84.

Schlesinger, H. J., Mumford, E., Glass, G. V., Patrick, C., & Sharfstein, S. (1983). Mental health treatment and medical care utilization in a fee-for-service system: Outpatient mental health treatment following the onset of a chronic disease. *American Journal of Public Health, 73,* 422–429.

Schwartz, M. D. (1975). Situation/transition groups: A conceptualization and review. *American Journal of Orthopsychiatry, 45,* 744–755.

Schwartz, M. F., & Masters, W. H. (1984). The Masters and Johnson treatment program for dissatisfied homosexual men. *American Journal of Psychiatry, 141,* 173–181.

Scrignar, C. B. (1979). One-session cure of a case of speech anxiety with a 10 year follow-up. *Journal of Nervous and Mental Disease, 167,* 315–316.

Seagull, A. A. (1966). Must the deeply disturbed have long-term treatment? *Psychotherapy: Theory, research, and practice, 3,* 36–42.

Shapiro, D. A., & Shapiro, D. (1982). Meta-analysis of comparative therapy outcome studies: A replication and refinement. *Psychological Bulletin, 92,* 581–604.

Shapiro, D. A., & Shapiro, D. (1983). Comparative therapy outcome research: Methodological implications of meta-analysis. *Journal of Consulting and Clinical Psychology, 51,* 42–53.

Shapiro, L. E. (1984). *The new short-term therapies for children: A guide for the helping professions and parents.* Englewood Cliffs, NJ: Prentice-Hall.

Shepherd, M., Lader, M., & Rodnight, R. (1968). *Clinical psychopharmacology.* Philadelphia: Lea & Febiger.

Shiffman, S. (1987). Clinical psychology training and psychotherapy interview performance. *Psychotherapy, 24,* 71–84.

Shulman, B. H. (1989). Single-session psychotherapy: A didactic demonstration. *Individual Psychology, 45,* 82–98.

Shulman, M. E. (1988). Cost containment in clinical psychology: Critique of Biodyne and the HMOs. *Professional Psychology: Research and Practice, 19,* 298–307.

Shyne, A. W. (1957). What research tells us about short-term cases in family agencies. *Social Casework, 38,* 223–231.

Siddall, L. B., Haffey, N. A., & Feinman, J. A. (1988). Intermittent brief psychotherapy in an HMO setting. *American Journal of Psychotherapy, 42,* 96–106.

Sifneos, P. E. (1967). Two different kinds of psychotherapy of short duration. *American Journal of Psychiatry, 123,* 1069–1074.

Sifneos, P. E. (1968). Learning to solve emotional problems: A controlled study of short-term anxiety-provoking psychotherapy. In R. Porter (Ed.), *The role of learning in psychotherapy* (pp. 87–99). Boston: Little, Brown.

Sifneos, P. E. (1972). *Short-term psychotherapy and emotional crisis.* Cambridge, MA: Harvard University Press.

Sifneos, P. E. (1978). Evaluation, criteria for selection of patients. In H. Davanloo (Ed.), *Basic principles and techniques in short-term dynamic psychotherapy* (pp. 81–85). New York: Spectrum.

Sifneos, P. E. (1979). *Short-term dynamic psychotherapy: Evaluation and technique.* New York: Plenum.

Sifneos, P. E. (1980). Motivation for change. In H. Davanloo (Ed.), *Short-term dynamic psychotherapy* (pp. 93–98). Northvale, NJ: Aronson.

Sifneos, P. E. (1981a). Short-term anxiety-provoking psychotherapy: Its history, technique, outcome, and instruction. In S. Budman (Ed.), *Forms of brief therapy* (pp. 45–81). New York: Guilford Press.

Sifneos, P. E. (1981b). Short-term dynamic psychotherapy: Its history, its impact and its future. *Psychotherapy and Psychosomatics, 35,* 224–229.

Sifneos, P. E. (1984). Short-term anxiety-provoking psychotherapy. In L. Grinspoon (Ed.), *Psychiatry update: The American Psychiatric Association Annual Review* Vol. III (pp. 24–35). Washington, DC: American Psychiatric Press.

Sifneos, P. E. (1985). Short-term dynamic psychotherapy of phobic and mildly obsessive-compulsive patients. *American Journal of Psychotherapy, 39,* 314–322.

Sifneos, P. E. (1987). *Short-term dynamic psychotherapy: Evaluation and technique* (2nd ed.). New York: Plenum.

Silberschatz, G., Fretter, P. B., & Curtis, J. T. (1986). How do interpretations influence the process of psychotherapy? *Journal of Consulting and Clinical Psychology, 54,* 646–652.

Silverman, W. H., & Beech, R. P. (1979). Are dropouts, dropouts? *Journal of Community Psychology, 7,* 236–242.

Sloane, R. B., Staples, F. R., Cristol, A. H., Yorkton, N. J., & Whipple, K. (1975).

Short-term analytically oriented psychotherapy versus behavior therapy. *American Journal of Psychiatry, 132,* 373–377.

Small, L. (1979). *The briefer psychotherapies* (rev. ed). New York: Brunner/Mazel.

Smith, M. L., & Glass, G. V. (1977). Meta-analysis of psychotherapy outcome studies. *American Psychologist, 32,* 752–760.

Smith, M. L., Glass, G. V., & Miller, T. I. (1980). *The benefits of psychotherapy.* Baltimore, MD: Johns Hopkins University Press.

Speers, R. W. (1962). Brief psychotherapy with college women: Technique and criteria for selection. *American Journal of Orthopsychiatry, 32,* 434–444.

Sperry, L. (1987). ERIC: A cognitive map for guiding brief therapy and health care counseling. *Individual Psychology, 43,* 237–241.

Spoerl, O. (1975). Single session-psychotherapy. *Diseases of the Nervous System, 36,* 283–285.

Springmann, R. R. (1982). Some remarks on psychotherapy by a single interpretation. *Journal of Psychiatric Treatment and Evaluation, 4,* 327–332.

Starr, A., & Weisz, H. S. (1989). Psychodramatic techniques in the brief treatment of inpatient groups. *Individual Psychology, 45,* 143–147.

Sterba, R. (1951). A case of brief psychotherapy by Sigmund Freud. *Psychoanalytic Review, 38,* 75–80.

Stern, T. A. (1987). Psychiatric management of acute myocardial infarction in the coronary care unit. *American Journal of Cardiology, 60,* 59J–67J.

Stiles, W. B., & Shapiro, D. A. (1989). Abuse of the drug metaphor in psychotherapy process-outcome research. *Clinical Psychology Review, 9,* 521–543.

Stiles, W. B., Shapiro, D. A., & Elliott, R. (1986). "Are all psychotherapies equivalent?" *American Psychologist, 41,* 165–180.

Straker, G. (1986). Brief-term psychodynamic psychotherapy: A contradiction in terms? *South African Journal of Psychology, 16,* 57–61.

Strassberg, D. S., Anchor, K. N., Cunningham, J., & Elkins, D. (1977). Successful outcome and number of sessions: When do counselors think enough is enough? *Journal of Counseling Psychology, 24,* 477–480.

Strupp, H. H. (1980a). Success and failure in time-limited psychotherapy. *Archives of General Psychiatry, 37,* 595–603.

Strupp, H. H. (1980b). Success and failure in time-limited psychotherapy: A systematic comparison of two cases, Comparison 2. *Archives of General Psychiatry, 37,* 708–716.

Strupp, H. H. (1980c). Success and failure in time-limited psychotherapy: Further evidence (Comparison 4). *Archives of General Psychiatry, 37,* 947–954.

Strupp, H. H. (1980d). Success and failure in time-limited psychotherapy with special reference to the performance of a lay counselor. *Archives of General Psychiatry, 37,* 831–841.

Strupp, H. H. (1980e). Problems of research. In H. Davanloo (Ed.), *Short-term dynamic psychotherapy* (pp. 379–392). Northvale, NJ: Aronson.

Strupp, H. H. (1981). Toward the refinement of time-limited dynamic psychotherapy. In S. H. Budman (Ed.), *Forms of brief therapy* (pp. 219–242). New York: Guilford Press.

Strupp, H. H. (1989). Psychotherapy: Can the practitioner learn from the researcher? *American Psychologist, 44,* 717–724.

Strupp, H. H., & Binder, J. L. (1984). *Psychotherapy in a new key: A guide to time-limited dynamic psychotherapy.* New York: Basic Books.

Stuart, M. R., & Lieberman, J. A. (1986). *The fifteen minute hour: Applied psychotherapy for the primary care physician.* New York: Praeger.

Stuhr, U., Meyer, A-E., & Bolz, W. (1981). V. Outcome results in psychological tests. *Psychotherapy and Psychosomatics, 35,* 138–198.

Sue, S., Allen, D. B., & Conway, L. (1978). The responsiveness and egality of mental health care to Chicanos and Native Americans. *American Journal of Community Psychology, 6,* 137–146.

Sundel, M., & Lawrence, H. (1977). A systematic approach to treatment planning in time-limited behavior groups. *Journal of Behavior Therapy and Experimental Psychiatry, 8,* 395–399.

Swartzburg, M., & Schwartz, A. (1976). A five-year study of brief hospitalization. *American Journal of Psychiatry, 133,* 922–924.

Talmon, M. (1990). *Single-session therapy: Maximizing the effect of the first (and often only) therapeutic encounter.* San Francisco: Jossey-Bass.

Tannenbaum, S. A. (1919). Three brief psychoanalyses. *American Journal of Urology and Sexology, 15,* 145–151.

Taube, C. A., & Barrett, S. A. (1985). *Mental health, United States, 1985.* DHHS Pub. No. (ADM) 85-1378. Washington, DC: U.S. Government Printing Office.

Tedeschi, D. H., & Tedeschi, R. E. (Eds.) (1968). *Importance of fundamental principles in drug evaluation.* New York: Raven.

Teitelbaum, M. L., & Kettl, P. (1988). Brief psychotherapy with a patient suffering from Guillain-Barré Syndrome. *Psychosomatics, 29,* 231–233.

Tennov, D. (1975). *Psychotherapy: The hazardous cure.* New York: Abelard-Schuman.

Thompson, L. W., Gallagher, D., & Breckenridge, J. S. (1987). Comparative effectiveness of psychotherapies for depressed elders. *Journal of Consulting and Clinical Psychology, 55,* 385–390.

Thorpe, S. A. (1987). An approach to treatment planning. *Psychotherapy, 24,* 729–735.

Toseland, R. W., & Siporin, M. (1986). When to recommend group treatment: A review of the clinical and research literature. *International Journal of Group Psychotherapy, 36,* 171–201.

Ursano, R. J., & Dressler, D. M. (1977). Brief versus long-term psychotherapy: Clinician attitudes and organizational design. *Comprehensive Psychiatry, 18,* 55–60.

Ursano, R. J., & Hales, R. E. (1986). A review of brief individual psychotherapies. *American Journal of Psychiatry, 143,* 1507–1517.

VandenBos, G. R., & Pino, C. D. (1980). Research on the outcome of psychotherapy. In G. R. VandenBos (Ed.), *Psychotherapy: Practice, research, policy* (pp. 23–69). Beverly Hills, CA: Sage.

Wallen, M. C., Weiner, H. D., Mansi, A., & Deal, D. (1987). Utilization of 12-step theme groups in a short-term chemical dependence treatment unit. *Journal of Psychoactive Drugs, 19,* 287–290.

Waring, E. M., Chamberlaine, C. H., McCrank, E. W., Stalker, C. A., Carver, C., Fry, R., & Barnes, S. (1988). Dysthymia: A randomized study of cognitive marital therapy and antidepressants. *Canadian Journal of Psychiatry, 33,* 96–99.

Watzlawick, P. (1978). *The language of change: Elements of therapeutic communication.* New York: Basic Books.

Watzlawick, P., Weakland, J., & Fisch, R. (1974). *Change: Principles of problem formation and problem resolution.* New York: Norton.

Weiner, H. D. (1987). An innovative short-term group therapy model for inpatient addiction treatment. *Employee Assistance Quarterly, 2(4),* 27–30.

Weiss, R. L., & Jacobson, N. S. (1981). Behavioral marital therapy as brief therapy. In S. Budman (Ed.), *Forms of brief therapy* (pp. 387–414). New York: Guilford Press.

Weissman, M. M. (1979). The psychological treatment of depression: Evidence for the efficacy of psychotherapy alone, in comparison with and in combination with pharmacotherapy. *Archives of General Psychiatry, 36,* 1261–1269.

West, M., Sheldon, A., & Reiffer, L. (1989). Attachment theory and brief psychotherapy: Applying current research to clinical interventions. *Canadian Journal of Psychiatry, 34,* 369–375.

White, H. S., Burke, J. D., & Havens, L. L. (1981). Choosing a method of short-term therapy: A developmental approach. In S. Budman (Ed.), *Forms of brief therapy* (pp. 243–267). New York: Guilford Press.

Williamson, P. S. (1987). Psychotherapy by family physicians. *Primary Care, 14,* 803–816.

Wilson, G. T. (1978). On the much discussed nature of the term "behavior therapy." *Behavior Therapy, 9,* 89–98.

Wilson, G. T. (1981). Behavior therapy as a short-term therapeutic approach. In S. H. Budman (Ed.), *Forms of brief therapy* (pp. 131–166). New York: Guilford Press.

Winnicott, D. W. (1971). *Consultations in child psychiatry.* New York: Basic Books.

Winnicott, D. W. (1975). *Through paediatrics to psycho-analysis.* New York: Basic Books.

Wolberg, L. R. (1965a). *Short-term psychotherapy.* New York: Grune & Stratton.

Wolberg, L. R. (1965b). The technic of short-term therapy. In L. R. Wolberg (Ed.), *Short-term psychotherapy* (pp. 127–200). New York: Grune & Stratton.

Wolberg, L. (1965c). Methodology in short-term therapy. *American Journal of Psychiatry, 122,* 135–140.

Wolberg, L. R. (1968). Short-term psychotherapy. In J. Marmor (Ed.), *Modern psychoanalysis* (pp. 343–354). New York: Basic Books.

Wolberg, L. R. (1980). *Handbook of short-term psychotherapy.* New York: Thieme-Stratton.

Wolf, A. (1965). Short-term group psychotherapy. In L. R. Wolberg (Ed.), *Short-term psychotherapy* (pp. 219–255). New York: Grune & Stratton.

Wortman, P. M. (1983). Evaluation research: A methodological perspective. *Annual Review of Psychology, 34,* 223–260.

Wynne, L. C., McDaniel, S. H., & Weber, T. T. (1987). Professional politics and the concepts of family therapy, family consultation, and systems consultation. *Family Process, 26,* 153–166.

Yapko, M. D. (1988). *When living hurts: Directives for treating depression.* New York: Brunner/Mazel.

Yoken, C., & Berman, J. S. (1987). Third-party payment and the outcome of psychotherapy. *Journal of Consulting and Clinical Psychology, 55,* 571–576.

Young, J. E., & Beck, A. T. (1982). Cognitive therapy: Clinical applications. In A. J. Giles (Ed.), *Short-term psychotherapies for depression* (pp. 182–214). New York: Guilford Press.

Zabarenko, R. N., Merenstein, J., & Zabarenko, L. (1971). Teaching psychological medicine in the family practice office. *Journal of the American Medical Association, 218,* 392–396.

Zeig, J. K. (Ed.) (1982). *Ericksonian approaches to hypnosis and psychotherapy.* New York: Brunner/Mazel.

Zilbergeld, B. (1983). *The shrinking of America: Myths of psychological change.* Boston: Little, Brown.

Zweben, A., Pearlman, S., & Li, S. (1988). A comparison of brief advice and conjoint therapy in the treatment of alcohol abuse: The results of the marital systems study. *British Journal of Addiction, 83,* 899–916.

Author Index

349

Subject Index